THE MINOR PROPHETS AND THE APOCRYPHA

THE SERIES

Volume I
The Pentateuch

Volume II
Old Testament History

Volume III
Wisdom Literature and Poetry

Volume IV
The Major Prophets

Volume V
The Minor Prophets and the Apocrypha

Volume VI
The Gospels

Volume VII
Acts and Paul's Letters

Volume VIII
Revelation and the General Epistles

INTERPRETER'S CONCISE COMMENTARY

THE
MINOR
PROPHETS
AND THE
APOCRYPHA

A COMMENTARY ON
HOSEA, JOEL, AMOS, OBADIAH, JONAH, MICAH, NAHUM,
HABAKKUK, ZEPHANIAH, HAGGAI, ZECHARIAH, MALACHI,
THE OLD TESTAMENT APOCRYPHA

By
Charles F. Kraft
Roland E. Murphy, O. Carm.
Bruce T. Dahlberg
Simon J. De Vries
Roger N. Carstensen
Charles T. Fritsch
Robert C. Dentan
H. Neil Richardson
Edward Lee Beavin
Stanley Brice Frost
George A. F. Knight

Edited by Charles M. Laymon

Abingdon Press
Nashville

Interpreter's Concise Commentary
Volume V: THE MINOR PROPHETS AND THE APOCRYPHA

Copyright © 1971 and 1983 by Abingdon Press

Library of Congress Cataloging in Publication Data

Main entry under title:
The Minor Prophets and the Apocrypha
    (Interpreter's concise commentary; v. 5)
    "Previously published . . . as part of The Interpreter's
one-volume commentary on the Bible." Verso t.p.
    Bibliography: p.
    1. Bible. O.T. Minor Prophets—Commentaries.
    2. Bible. O.T. Apocrypha—Commentaries. I. Kraft, Charles
Franklin, 1911– . II. Laymon, Charles M. III. Series.
BS491.2.I57   1983 vol. 5   220.7s   83-8826
[BS1560]   [224'.907]

ISBN 0-687-19236-6

(Previously published by Abingdon Press in cloth as part of
The Interpreter's One-Volume Commentary on the Bible, regular ed.
ISBN 0-687-19299-4, thumb-indexed ed. ISBN 0-687-19300-1.)

Scripture quotations unless otherwise noted are from the Revised
Standard Common Bible, copyright © 1973 by the Division of Christian
Education, National Council of Churches, and are used by permission.

MANUFACTURED BY THE PARTHENON PRESS AT
NASHVILLE, TENNESSEE, UNITED STATES OF AMERICA

EDITOR'S PREFACE

to the original edition

A significant commentary on the Bible is both timely and timeless. It is timely in that it takes into consideration newly discovered data from many sources that are pertinent in interpreting the Scriptures, new approaches and perspectives in discerning the meaning of biblical passages, and new insights into the relevancy of the Bible for the times in which we live. It is timeless since it deals with the eternal truths of God's revelation, truths of yesterday, today, and of all the tomorrows that shall be.

This commentary has been written within this perspective. Its authors were selected because of their scholarship, their religious insight, and their ability to communicate with others. Technical discussions do not protrude, yet the most valid and sensitive use of contemporary knowledge underlies the interpretations of the several writings. It has been written for ministers, lay and nonprofessional persons engaged in studying or teaching in the church school, college students and those who are unequipped to follow the more specialized discussions of biblical matters, but who desire a thoroughly valid and perceptive guide in interpreting the Bible.

The authorship of this volume is varied in that scholars were chosen from many groups to contribute to the task. In this sense it is an ecumenical writing. Protestants from numerous denominations, Jews, and also Roman Catholics are represented in the book. Truth cannot be categorized according to its ecclesiastical sources. It is above and beyond such distinctions.

It will be noted that the books of the Apocrypha have been included and interpreted in the same manner as the canonical writings. The value of a knowledge of this body of literature for understanding the historical background and character of the Judaic-Christian tradition has been widely recognized in our time, but commentary treatments of it have not been readily accessible. In addition, the existence of the Revised Standard Version and the New English Bible translations of these documents makes such a commentary upon them as is included here both necessary and significant.

The commentary as a whole avoids taking dogmatic positions or representing any one particular point of view. Its authors were chosen throughout the English-speaking field of informed and recognized biblical scholars. Each author was urged to present freely his own interpretation and, on questions where there was sometimes a diversity of conclusions, each was also asked to define objectively the viewpoints of others while he was offering and defending his own.

Many persons have contributed to the writing and production of this volume. One of the most rewarding of my personal experiences as editor was corresponding with the authors. On every hand there was enthusiasm for the project and warmth of spirit. The authors' commitment to the task and their scholarly sensitivity were evident in all of my relationships with them. The considerate judgments of the manuscript consultants, Morton S. Enslin, Dwight M. Beck, W. F. Stinespring, Virgil M. Rogers, and William L. Reed, were invaluable in the making of the character of the commentary. The copy editors who have worked under the careful and responsible guidance of Mr. Gordon Duncan of Abingdon Press have contributed greatly to the accuracy and readability of the commentary.

—Charles M. Laymon, Editor

PUBLISHER'S PREFACE

The intent of *The Interpreter's Concise Commentary* is to make available to a wider audience the commentary section of *The Interpreter's One-Volume Commentary on the Bible*. In order to do this, the Publisher is presenting the commentary section of the original hardback in this eight-volume paperback set. At the same time, and in conjunction with our wish to make *The Interpreter's One-Volume Commentary* more useful, we have edited the hardback text for the general reader: we have defined most of the technical terms used in the original hardback text; we have tried to divide some of the longer sentences and paragraphs into shorter ones; we have tried to make the sexually stereotyped language used in the original commentary inclusive where it referred to God or to both sexes; and we have explained abbreviations, all in an attempt to make the text more easily read.

The intention behind this paperback arrangement is to provide a handy and compact commentary on those individual sections of the Bible that are of interest to readers. In this paperback format we have not altered the substance of any of the text of the original hardback, which is still available. Rather, our intention is to smooth out some of the scholarly language in order to make the text easier to read. We hope this arrangement will make this widely accepted commentary on the Bible even more profitable for all students of God's Word.

WRITERS

Charles F. Kraft
Professor of Old Testament Interpretation, Garrett Theological Seminary, Evanston, Illinois

Roland E. Murphy, O. Carm.
Professor of Old Testament, Catholic University of America, Washington, D. C.

Bruce T. Dahlberg
Professor of Religion, Smith College, Northampton, Massachusetts

Simon J. DeVries
Professor of Old Testament, Methodist Theological School in Ohio, Delaware, Ohio

Roger N. Carstensen
Dean of the College, Christian College of Georgia, Athens, Georgia

Charles T. Fritsch
Professor of Hebrew and Old Testament Literature, Princeton Theological Seminary, Princeton, New Jersey

Robert C. Dentan
Trinity Church Professor of Old Testament Literature and Interpretation, General Theological Seminary, New York, New York

H. Neil Richardson
Professor of Old Testament, Boston University School of Theology, Boston, Massachusetts

Edward Lee Beavin
Professor of Religion, Kentucky Wesleyan College, Owensboro, Kentucky

Stanley Brice Frost
Professor of Old Testament Studies and Dean of the Faculty of Graduate Studies and Research, McGill University, Montreal, Canada

George A. F. Knight
Principal (President) of the Pacific Theological College, Suva, Fiji

CONTENTS

THE APOCRYPHA

THE BOOK OF HOSEA

Charles F. Kraft

INTRODUCTION

Hosea is the first in the Book of the Twelve Prophets in the Old Testament canon. It is the collection of writings of the second great prophet of the eighth century B.C., who was probably a younger contemporary of Amos. It is unique among the prophetic books in its clear division into two unequal parts: The first (chapters 1–3) is mostly biographical (chapter 1) or autobiographical (chapter 3). The second (chapters 4–14) is the collected sayings of the prophet and has no evident biographical information whatever.

Authenticity

Most of the book is regarded as the authentic experiences or words of the prophet, whether recorded by himself or by disciples. There is wide diversity of scholarly opinion on the meaning of the biographical and autobiographical sections and their relation to each other. The prevailing view is that they are accurate accounts of the prophet's personal family experiences.

Hosea's message consists primarily of warning, with only a hint of promise. Therefore some scholars doubt the authenticity of the apparently sudden switches from doom to hope— for example, 1:10–2:1; 2:14-23; and 14:1-9). The oracles complimentary to Judah are also thought to be later additions. The Hebrew text has in many places been so badly preserved that it scarcely makes sense (see Revised Standard Version footnotes). Therefore the reader who compares English versions will note many differences in translation.

Hosea's Life and Times

Surprisingly little is revealed in the book about the prophet himself. His primary concern with the northern kingdom of Israel indicates that his ministry took place there. Thirty-six times he uses Ephraim as a synonym for Israel. This suggests that he may have lived in the southern part of the kingdom, which was the territory of the tribe of Ephraim. The most obvious biographical fact is his marriage to Gomer and fathering of her children. Interpreters do not agree, however, on whether she was a priestess—that is, cult prostitute—from a Baal fertility shrine or simply a young wife who turned out to be unfaithful. Hosea's marriage to Gomer and his love for the unnamed woman of chapter 3, whether Gomer or not, were very important for his message. But it seems more likely that both experiences were demonstrations of his message which God commanded rather than that his message grew out of meditation on his family experiences.

According to 1:1 (see comment) Hosea's prophetic ministry took place during the reign of Jeroboam II (782/81-753). No doubt it began during the final years of that prosperous reign (see below on 1:4-5). But the background reflected in the oracles is the turbulent period of political and social upheaval in Israel which followed, when king after king gained the throne by assassinating his predecessor.

Jeroboam's son Zechariah reigned only six months (753-752). He was murdered by Shallum, who fell after one month to a second usurper, Menahem (752-742/41). Soon Tiglath-pileser III (Pul, 745-727) renewed the Assyrian expansion to the west and attacked Israel. Menahem found himself in danger from dissident elements in his kingdom, quickly came to terms with the invader and agreed to a huge tribute "that he might help him to confirm his hold of the royal power" (II Kings 15:19). With this help he was able to die in his bed.

His son Pekahiah, after ruling about two years (742/41-740/39), was killed and replaced by Pekah (740/39-732/31). Together with Rezin of Syria, Pekah engaged in the Syro-Ephraimitic War (735-734) in an effort to depose Ahaz of Judah and gain Judean aid in opposing Assyria. At the invitation of Ahaz Tiglath-pileser intervened. He seized most of Galilee and Transjordan, exiling many of the inhabitants. With his blessing, and perhaps connivance, Hoshea slew Pekah and became the last ruler of the northern kingdom (732/31-723/22).

The Syro-Ephraimitic War seems to provide the background for 5:8-14 (see comment). But no prediction of destruction and exile at the hands of Assyria shows specific knowledge of the final catastrophe in 722 or of the three-year siege of the capital by Tiglath-pileser's son Shalmaneser V. Therefore it appears that Hosea's career ended sometime between the Syro-Ephraimitic War and the beginning of the siege of Samaria. Thus his prophetic ministry should be dated around 755-730.

Hosea's Message

In such a time a prime concern of Hosea was the failure of leadership. Priests and cult prophets were worse than useless. The monarchy was an affront to the real kingship of Yahweh. But the basic problem was the cultural and religious sellout of the national life to Baalism. In addition to Baal worship the worship of Yahweh was paganized until the two were indistinguishable.

Hosea was profoundly concerned about the covenant history of God's people. He believed that the lack of basic faithfulness, covenant loyalty, and personal knowledge of God was leading the nation to imminent destruction at the hands of Assyria. He saw in the impending calamity Yahweh's intention to make the people start over again from a new Egyptian slavery. Baalism is shortly to be smashed, and the people are to be disciplined by exile.

Yet basically this act of wrath and judgment will result from Yahweh's suffering and redemptive love for God's people. They are the bride of the exodus period (cf. 2:15), the once elect but

3

now wayward son (cf. 11:1-4). God's father love calls to repentance, rebirth, and resurrection to new life. There is no record of the immediate response of Israel to Hosea's new and unique revelation of the nature of God the Father. But we know that it profoundly influenced later prophets (cf. Jeremiah 1–2) as well as all subsequent centuries.

I. SUPERSCRIPTION (1:1)

This prose title for the book was supplied by an editor to introduce the accounts of the prophet's experiences and his poetic messages. The heading marks Hosea as a true prophet, for it is **the word of the LORD that came** to him, not his own words, which he must proclaim.

In Hebrew, **Hosea** is the same as Hoshea. It is a shortened form of Jehoshua, anglicized in the Old Testament as Joshua and in the New Testament as Jesus, which means "Yahweh saves." Of Hosea's father, **Beeri** (meaning "well"), nothing further is known.

Possibly the editor was a Judean, since he dates Hosea's ministry first by the Judean kings **Uzziah, Jotham, Ahaz, and Hezekiah.** Of the kings of Israel, where Hosea's ministry was primarily directed, he mentions only **Jeroboam II.** Hosea probably began to prophesy during Jeroboam's reign (see below on verses 4-5). But the background of most of his message is not the prosperity of that reign, which is reflected in the oracles of Amos, but the following descent toward disaster (see Introduction).

II. GOD'S WORD THROUGH HOSEA'S FAMILY EXPERIENCE (1:2–3:5)

In this section the word of Yahweh is declared through dramatic accounts of the prophet's family life. One account is told in the third person (chapter 1), another in the first person (chapter 3). Interpreters' judgments vary widely on

(1) the meaning and relation of these accounts,
(2) the identity of the unnamed woman in the second,
(3) the chronological order of the incidents described,
(4) the legitimacy of the second and third children,
(5) whether the experiences are actual or allegorical, and
(6) the authenticity of the hopeful passages. Many of these problems are perhaps unsolvable.

The main theme is Israel's unfaithfulness to its God and what God proposes to do about it. This theme is presented in three successive family metaphors.

The first and third are doubtless parables acted out by the prophet in his family life at God's command.

The second may be an allegory based on the figure which seems to underlie all three—namely that idolatrous Israel has forsaken its true God to join in the sexual fertility rites of the nature god Baal. It has done so through appalling ignorance and must be punished, disciplined, reeducated, and redeemed. Thus there are 3 family analogies:

(1) God's people are children of harlotry (1:2–2:1);
(2) Israel is a mother of harlotry (2:2-23);
(3) despite all this God loves Israel and will reeducate it through discipline (3:1-5).

A. THE CHILDREN OF HARLOTRY (1:2–2:1)

When the Lord first spoke through Hosea may literally be translated "the beginning of the word of Yahweh through Hosea." This is apparently a title for the account of Hosea's wife and children in verses 2-9. **The LORD said** introduces each of the four stages in the narrative: God's command to Hosea to marry (verse 2) and God's naming of the three children (verses 4, 6, 9). Hosea obeys the command and the children are born. Presumably all this occupies around six to nine years, as ordinarily a child was **weaned** at the age of perhaps two or three.

1:2b. God's Command. Traditional interpretations of Hosea's experience have been strongly influenced by western marriage

customs and by the desire for an appropriate analogy between
the relation of Hosea to Gomer and that of Yahweh to Israel. A
minority view is that the account is only allegorical. But most
commentators have understood **wife of harlotry** to mean that
Gomer either had or developed harlotrous tendencies unsuspected by the young prophet when he fell in love with her. As a
result of his bitter experience and the discovery that he still
loved her (cf. 3:1), it has been supposed, Hosea came to realize
that his own human love was but dimly comparable to that of
God for the faithless bride Israel.

The love of God for the wayward people is an essential
message of Hosea. It is later expressed in such terms (3:1) and is
also exemplified by father-son love (11:1-9). But the clearly
stated point of this opening biographical narrative is to
demonstrate that **the land commits great harlotry by forsaking
the LORD.** It is to convey this meaning that God commands the
marriage and, even more important, the naming of the children.

The passage is not primarily an account of Hosea's family
experience. Rather it is God's speaking **through Hosea.** Hence
Hosea's marriage to Gomer is not a love marriage. In the custom
of the ancient Near East it is an arranged marriage, and God
does the arranging.

1:3. The Wife. The name **Gomer** may mean "complete" or
"perfection." **Diblaim** means "lumps" of figs or raisins. No
particular point is made of the meaning, as is done with the
names of the children. But the father's name may connect
Gomer with the raisin cakes which were part of the food in the
Baal fertility rites (cf. 3:1).

God's demand is that the prophet demonstrate Israel's
harlotry. Surely the analogy here is with the Canaanite theology
in which the dying-and-rising fertility god Baal was seen as the
husband of mother earth.

The god died and descended into the underworld at the onset
of the summer dry season. The god returned from the
underworld and married the earth goddess when vegetation
revived with the autumnal rains. The descent and return were
celebrated with popular rites. "Cult prostitutes," literally "holy

women" (cf. 4:14), were the celebrants. Presumably Gomer was one of these sacred persons who assisted in the rites, providing "the grain, the wine, and the oil" (2:8) for her people.

Hosea must proclaim that true fertility comes, not from the marriage of Baal with mother earth, but from the God of Israel. He therefore feels commanded, whether he likes it or not, to marry one of these supposedly holy cult women. In calling her a **wife of harlotry** he is saying that this popular holiness of Baalism is no more than common prostitution. By this act Hosea may be declaring that Gomer's marriage and motherhood is superior to the supposedly higher calling of a cult priestess.

1:4-9. *The Children.* The same idea is probably seen in the names of the three children. These seem to be parodies on names of Baal cult children. It has been suggested that the children were not simply walking prophetic messages. They may have appeared in some public drama at the sanctuary where their mother had been employed. Their names seem to refer in ascending order to the ruling dynasty, the nation, and finally the whole people.

1:4-5. The name **Jezreel** may have a double meaning. Historically it announces the end of the dynasty begun by the bloody purge of **Jehu.** In 841 this ruler toppled the Omri dynasty by murdering Israel's King Joram and Judah's King Ahaziah near Jezreel (II Kings 9:14-29). Jehu's subsequent massacre of the Baal prophets (II Kings 10:18-29), though done in the name of Yahweh, apparently increased his guilt in the eyes of Hosea.

God will punish this evil dynasty by breaking the **bow**—that is, the power—**of Israel.** In Hosea's day this power was evident in the reign of Jeroboam II, Jehu's great-grandson. The prediction was fulfilled in 752 when Jeroboam's son Zechariah was murdered by the usurper Shallum (II Kings 15:10). Thus Jehu's dynasty was ended.

Jezreel means "El sows." El was originally the name of the high god of the Canaanite pantheon. It became the Semitic word for "god," meaning "power." Thus a most appropriate name for a child of a Canaanite fertility-rite priestess would be Jezreel—suggesting that the god sows seed, fertility, and agricultural prosperity. But Hosea may mean that God sows destruction for an evil dynasty.

1:6. The name of the daughter, **Not pitied,** declares that God will no longer **forgive** the **house** of Israel—that is, the Israelite nation state. The "not" in this name and that of the third child (verse 9) may be a grim pun on cult children's names. The two letters of the Hebrew word "not" are the reverse of those in "El" or "God." Hence instead of the cult name "God pities" the daughter is called "Not pitied" or "Not loved." This also expresses the rejection of motherly compassion, for the Hebrew word "pitied" is from the same root as "womb." God's patience is at an end. The death of the nation is at hand.

1:7. Apparently some later Judean editor added this note concerning God's protection of the southern kingdom. Its point may be that Judah escaped the fate of Israel in 722. Or perhaps it alludes to the deliverance of Jerusalem from Sennacherib's siege in 701.

1:8-9. Again Hosea may be parodying a cult name (see above on verse 6). **Not my people** presumably would be "God with me" or "God of my people." The shocking announcement in this name means that the covenant bond between God and the people is broken. The sacred ties going back to the days of Abraham are severed.

1:10-2:1. *The Children Renamed.* Perhaps the shock of those awful words of divine repudiation (1:6, 9) brought forth these immediately following words of hope, as well as the later reversal of "Not my people" to "You are my people" (2:23). Scholarly opinion is divided on whether Hosea himself promised this restoration and renewal. It is predicted that **Judah** and **Israel** will be **gathered together** under **one head** and **go up from the land.** This sounds like a promise from the time of the Exile or afterward that the scattered Jews will be reunited and a messianic ruler will bring them to Jerusalem from the farthest corners of the earth.

This **day of Jezreel** will be a reversal of the previously predicted day of doom (1:4-5). God will sow, not seeds of destruction, but seeds of posterity. The promises of numberless descendants of Abraham and Jacob will be fulfilled (cf. Genesis

8

15:5; 22:17; 32:12). They will not be devotees of a dying-and-rising fertility deity but **sons of the living God.**

2:1. In the exuberance of the hour Not pitied will be commanded to call her brother **My people** instead of Not my people. He in turn will rename her **She has obtained pity.** The Hebrew text simply removes the negative signs to form the new names. Its reading, "brothers" and "sisters," if correct, probably recognizes the fact that the children are symbols of the whole people. Thus in God's infinite mercy God will reclaim as God's own beloved people those who, through unfaithfulness, have lost all claim to being God's own.

B. THE MOTHER OF HARLOTRY (2:2-23)

Using the language of the law court Hosea now summarizes the case against faithless Israel as Yahweh's ignorant wife, the mother of **children of harlotry.** The imaginary court hearing opens with Yahweh telling the children to **plead with your mother** and get her to reform before God carries out his threatened action. The action he will take is expressed in three subsequent announcements, each beginning **Therefore** (verses 6, 9, 14).

2:2-5. *The Indictment of Israel.* In the language of the formula for divorce Yahweh declares: **She is not my wife**—that is, the marriage bond is broken. Possibly the woman is even wearing the dress and ornaments of the cult prostitute (cf. verse 13).

Harlotry and **adultery** are Hosea's terms for false worship, the sexual rites of the Baal cult. According to the law codes the penalty for adultery was death (cf. Leviticus 20:10; Deuteronomy 22:22). Here the penalty is nakedness, being stripped of the clothing furnished by her former husband. Her crime is neither adultery nor harlotry in the ordinary sense but ritual prostitution. Hence Hosea ironically declares that these rites which should produce fertile fields will bring only the nakedness of a desert. The **children** must share the divine condemnation as the mother continues to run after her **lovers,** the local Baal gods who she believes provide her food and clothing.

2:6-8. *Separation.* Yahweh announces the action first. Yahweh will protect the mother from her own willful ways. God will fence her in behind a hedge of thorns and a **wall,** stopping her search for false gods. Then she may come to her senses and realize that life with her **first husband,** Yahweh, was preferable. The pathos of the situation is Israel's theological ignorance. She does not recognize that it is not the local Baals, but Yahweh, who provides both the blessings of the earth—**the grain, the wine, and the** olive **oil**—and the imported **silver and gold.**

2:9-13. *Deprivation.* Yahweh's second announced action will be to cause complete crop failure. The Baal gods will be proved impotent, for there will not even be enough produce to carry on the customary lavish Baal rituals and festivals. There will be no clothing (verse 9), no joyous Israelite festivals (verse 11), and no Baal orgies with **incense** and **jewelry** and sexual license (verse 13). The **vines** and **fig trees** were her wages, supposedly given her by her Baal **lovers.** Their vineyards and orchards will become a devastated jungle.

2:14-15. *A New Courtship.* Yahweh's third announced action will complete the reeducation of wayward mother Israel. Yahweh will return her to the place of their first honeymoon and woo her back to himself. As at the Exodus he will **allure her . . . into the wilderness** and **speak tenderly to her,** literally "speak to her heart." The **Valley of Achor,** literally "trouble," will no longer be a place of setback (cf. Joshua 7:24-26) but will become a **door of hope.**

2:16-23. *A New Betrothal.* The glorious renewal is now set forth in glowing terms beginning with **in that day** (verses 16, 21). Whether these words come from Hosea himself or from a disciple, they express a true new covenant relation between God and the people (cf. Jeremiah 31:31-34). Yahweh will truly be Israel's **husband,** not her **Baal**—her "owner" or "master." Indeed the very word "Baal" will no longer be **mentioned** because of its pagan associations.

2:18-20. There will be a universal **covenant** of peace with all creatures of the world, from wild animals to warring nations (cf. Isaiah 11:6-9; Ezekiel 34:25-31). The new covenant of betrothal will be eternal. God offers as bride-price or dowry: **righteous-ness,** right action in relation to God; **justice,** right action in relation to one's fellows; **steadfast love,** loyal covenant devotion; **mercy,** motherlike compassion; and **faithfulness,** steady permanence. Thus will God's people **know**—that is, intimately experience—their God.

2:21-23. This new covenant will be evident in the real **Jezreel** ("God sows"; see above on 1:4-5)—the true fertility cycle of God's rain, responding crops, and abounding harvest. The negative names will become affirmative. **My people** will in adoration declare: **My God.**

C. THE WIFE OF HARLOTRY LOVED AND REEDUCATED (3:1-5)

The theme of this autobiographical story of Hosea's marriage is God's love for the people, God's discipline of them, and its result. As in the opening account, the action is initiated by God. God commands Hosea to **love** a most unlovable woman, just as God loves the most unlovely people. Traditional interpretation has assumed that this woman is Gomer and that the story is a sequel to the previous narrative. She has left Hosea and become a cheap **adulteress.** He comes upon her being sold as a slave and buys her, but refuses marital relations. This may be the meaning. On the other hand the story may recount a second marriage. In either case the point is the same. Hosea's marriage is to demonstrate God's love and its disciplining and redeeming nature.

3:1-2. In the light of the possible identification of Gomer as a cult prostitute (see above on 1:3) and the allegory of Israel deludedly worshiping her Baal lovers instead of her first husband Yahweh (chapter 2) it may be that this woman is also a Baal cult priestess, described figuratively as **beloved of a paramour** and an **adulteress** (cf. 2:2; 4:14).

The **cakes of raisins** were the cult food of worshipers of Baal idols (see above on 1:3). The price for the woman (verse 2) is perhaps equal to the value of a slave specified in Exodus 21:32. If so, it is paid half in **silver,** half in **barley.** Hosea pays it either as a

11

bride-price or as the cost of releasing a sacred prostitute from her cult obligations.

3:3-5. The basic point of the story is the necessity and the cost of redemptive love. For discipline, God's prophet must love one whom his natural inclination might be to abhor. It has been suggested that **many days** refers to the time required to take away the taint of a woman's profession as cult priestess. By analogy Israel in exile will be deprived of political leadership and ceremonial objects. **Prince** refers, not to a king's son, but to any person with governmental authority.

A pillar was a large stone set upright as a memorial or as a Canaanite fertility symbol. The word **ephod** seems to have been used both for a priestly garment and an image of some kind. **Teraphim** were household gods.

Hosea vows to remain physically faithful to his wife during the **many days** of her discipline. Presumably this implies a promise of Yahweh that God will not forsake Israel and adopt another people during their discipline of exile. The outcome will be worth all the effort. Israel will return to God in **fear,** its trembling awe, before God's undeserved **goodness.**

III. GOD'S WORD THROUGH HOSEA'S ORACLES (4:1–14:8)

Most of the book is a series of oracles which were originally spoken. They were probably collected and written down by a disciple. Some scholars hold that they circulated orally for many years before being put into written form. There is little discernible organization. Perhaps the following grouping into sections—partly on the basis of form and partly on the basis of similarity of content—may be reasonable.

A. CORRUPT LEADERS, CORRUPT PEOPLE (4:1-19)

4:1-3. *Yahweh's Controversy with Israel.* The **word of the LORD** which Hosea speaks begins in the language of the law court. This is God's direct indictment, stating the case against all the people. The historical background is doubtless that turbulent period of political and social decline which followed the reign of Jeroboam II in Israel (see Introduction).

In Hosea's view the problem is primarily theological. The language is that of covenant relationship with God, even though the word "covenant" is used only twice in the oracles (6:7, 8:1). There is no **faithfulness**—no firm stability in keeping the covenant. There is no **kindness,** literally "loyal covenant love"—no response to God's outpouring love through the covenant. There is no **knowledge of God**—no real understanding of the divine. Perhaps this refers to the nature of deity in general, in a wider sense than "knowledge of Yahweh," Israel's historically experienced covenant deity.

4:2-3. This theological failure in relationship to God results in moral chaos, failure in the area of human relations. Verse 2*a* may be a specific allusion to the Ten Commandments as the summary of Israel's obligations under the covenant (cf. Exodus 20:13-16). Human moral failure even affects nature. Ironically **the land mourns** rather than revives under the sinful nature-cult practices. Though these are aimed at giving nature life, they actually produce death.

4:4-9 *Corrupt Religious Leaders.* The blame for Israel's corrupt state rests on the religious leaders. The **priest,** who **by day** should declare God's **law**—God's instruction handed down from Moses' day—has **forgotten.** The cult **prophet,** who should see visions **by night,** is evidently blind. So God will **destroy** the priestly line, if not the whole family of Israel. On **mother** and **children** cf. 2:2-4. The **glory** of being God's priests will become **shame** because they are **greedy** profiteers from the sacrificial system. Priesthood brings no divine favors, no rescue from punishment which the **people** face.

4:10-19. *The Absurdity of Baal Worship.* The whole system of Baal fertility rites is ineffectual as well as degrading. Its purpose is to provide fertility for human beings, flocks, and crops. But though the people **play the harlot**—that is, carry on the sexual fertility acts at the shrine—they do not **multiply.** The drunken revelry, the tree worship and divination by dead wooden rods, and the *sensual* sacrifices in the secrecy of shady groves—all are meaningless magical rites.

4:13e-14. Despite woman's usual secondary place in ancient society, there will be no double standard. The **men** are responsible for the shame of cult prostitution. It is they who require their **daughters** to become **cult prostitutes**, literally "holy women," at the shrines, to be used by male worshipers to provide fertility (see above on 1:3). This practice is not holiness but harlotry, and **a people without understanding shall come to ruin.**

4:15-16. Let **Judah** avoid the false swearing of Israel's sanctuaries at **Gilgal** (cf. 9:15; 12:11) and **Beth-aven**—"house of evil," a sarcastic substitute for Bethel, "house of God." God can hardly treat that **stubborn heifer** Israel as though she were a docile **lamb.**

4:17-19. Israel is here for the first time called **Ephraim**, Hosea's affectionate term for the people of the northern kingdom (see Introduction). Israel may as well be left undisturbed in its hopeless idolatry. But these harlotrous **drunkards** will be truly ashamed when God's **wind** of destruction blows.

B. ISRAEL'S ABSENT GOD (5:1-7)

5:1-2. *Summons to Officials.* God calls to task three groups of leaders—the **priests**, the **house of Israel**, (probably government officials), and the royal **house**. They have led the people astray, and God promises chastisement. Three widely separated cult centers are named as places where the leaders have trapped the people:

(1) **Mizpah,** the shrine in Gilead associated with Jacob and Jephthah (cf. Genesis 31:49; Judges 11:11), or possibly the Benjaminite town if it belonged to Israel at this time (cf. I Samuel 7:56);

(2) **Mt. Tabor** in southern Galilee (cf. Deuteronomy 33:19);

(3) **Shittim,** northeast of the Jordan mouth, where their fathers sinned with Baal of Peor (cf. Numbers 25:1-5).

5:3-7. *Israel's Harlotry.* Though God knows the people, their **spirit of harlotry** prevents their knowing God. Their **deeds** of Baal worship have so corrupted them that they have lost the power of repentance, the ability to **return to their God.** Their human **pride** is their own condemnation. When, as in the frenzied ritual searching for the dead Baal god, they come with sacrifices to **seek the LORD** they will find that the LORD is deliberately absent. In their Baal worship they give birth to **alien children,** the offspring of sexual cult rites, who do not know their sacred covenantal heritage. Therefore the expected joy of the **new moon** festival will become a day of destruction.

C. ISRAEL'S DEATHLY SICKNESS (5:8–7:16)

Israel's political, social, and spiritual disease is deplored in a seemingly unconnected series of oracles.

5:8-14. *War's Alarm.* The occasion for sounding the alarm is apparently the Syro-Ephraimitic War of 735-734, when Rezin of Syria and Pekah of Israel unsuccessfully attempted to force Judah into an alliance against Assyria (see Introduction). Verse 8 seems to allude to a counterattack by Judean forces, moving north from Jerusalem past the nearby strongholds of **Gibeah** and **Ramah** in their own territory of **Benjamin.** They entered the Israelite territory at Bethel, here again sarcastically called **Beth-aven** (see above on 4:15-16).

5:9-14. The **princes of Judah** (see above on 3:3-5) are violating the Israelite border by moving the stone which marked it. But, their call for the Assyrian Tiglath-pileser III to attack the northern kingdom and rescue them from the immediate crisis is folly. Ephraim and Judah alike will suffer crushing defeat by Assyria (verses 9, 11-12, 14). Indeed neither the sending of tribute to the **great king,** Tiglath-pileser, by Ahaz of Judah nor a renewal of the alliance with Assyria which Menahem of Israel made can be a **cure** (see Introduction). The sickness is much deeper than mere human warfare. It is God's judgment now

15

eating away the social fabric like **moth** and **dry rot.** It will soon bring sudden destruction **like a lion** (cf. 13:7-8).

5:15–6:6. *Complacency and Instability.* Yahweh now vows to return to the **place,** probably the heavenly temple, until people repent. The insertion here of **saying,** which is not in the Hebrew, gives the misleading impression that Yahweh goes on to quote the expression of repentance which God desires. Instead Hosea is portraying with subtle irony the people's presumptuous confessional liturgy (6:1-3). It may be based on figures of speech from the dying-and-rising-god cult (see above on 1:3). In some forms of the myth Baal was **torn** as by wild beasts when with the dry summer season he suffered death and went into the underworld. He was revived by the **showers** of November and December, and completely restored to life by the crop-maturing **spring rains** of April.

After two days . . . on the third day may be a way of saying "after only a short time"—meaning that the repentance need not be real, for God's punishment will soon be over. Or possibly it expresses a customary expectation that renewal will take place on the third day of a sacred occasion (cf. Exodus 3:18; 19:11; II Kings 20:5).

6:4-5. Yahweh's response to the people's confession sounds like utter exasperaton. Yahweh's people are as unstable as the mist driven away by the rising sun. The prophets' lethal word of **judgment,** as obvious as **light,** may hammer to pieces those who resist. As God's word it has a power all its own. Its purpose, however, is not to destroy but to redeem.

6:6. This is Hosea's keynote verse (cf. 2:19-20; 4:1, 6; Matthew 9:13; 12:7). God longs to find in the people **steadfast love,** constantly loyal devotion, and true **knowledge of God,** intimate experience of communion with God, not mere information about God. Whether Hosea believed the sacrificial system to be totally evil or simply irrelevant is debatable. But his emphasis on the importance of total inner commitment to God in understanding and obedience to God's will is clear.

6:7–7:7. *Examples of Israel's Sins.* The tragedy of Israel is that instead of steadfast love and the knowledge of God its record shows only a catalog of crimes. Perhaps with a deliberate play on words the list begins with the note that **at Adam,** the place where the waters of the Jordan were dammed up so that their forefathers could cross over (Joshua 3:9-17), they have **transgressed,** literally "crossed over" **the covenant** made at Mt. Sinai. This probably refers to a recent scandal otherwise unrecorded.

The allusion in 6:8 may be to Pekah's seizing the throne of Israel by his treacherous conspiracy with fifty Gileadites to assassinate King Pekahiah (II Kings 15:25). Shechem was famous for its ancient temple of Baal-berith but was also ironically a city of refuge. That bands of priests **murder on the way** may be figurative for religious murder in the Baal cult rites, or it may be an allusion to a contemporary incident.

6:10–7:2. The utter depravity of the **harlotry** of Baalism can result only in a **harvest** of evil. When God tries to **heal** Israel, the cancerous illness of its society becomes evident in open thievery and banditry—probably a reflection of the sad deterioration of social conditions in the last days of the northern kingdom. Past **evil works** cannot be wiped out. They are inevitably **before** God's **face.**

7:3-7. Comparable to evil social conditions are the debauchery and intrigue in the palace (on **princes** see above on 3:3-5). Inflamed by passion, conspirators **devour their rulers**—a reference to the series of assassinations and dynastic changes in Israel's last three decades (see Introduction). During the drunken revelries at each coronation festival plotters deceive the new ruler (verses 5-6) until **all their kings have fallen,** for **none of them calls upon** Yahweh. The **baker** banks the embers of the **oven** while preparing the **dough.** Then **in the morning** the **fire** is again built up red hot. There is no security in the palace, for **all** the plotters are **hot as an oven.**

7:8-12. *Foreign Intrigues.* Internal conditions in Israel are bad enough. But the attempts at international dealings prove Israel to be a half-baked **cake,** burned on one side and sticky dough on the other. Foreign alliances weaken the nation to senility by draining its resources—perhaps a reference to the heavy tribute paid to Assyria. Yet Israel does not recognize its sad condition. **Pride** prevents its **return** to its one source of strength. Torn internally by two parties—one pro-Egyptian, the other pro-Assyrian—Israel will continue to flit between the two foreign powers until Yahweh snares Israel in a **net.**

7:13-16. *Rebellion Against God.* Yahweh desires to redeem the people. But God cannot do so when they **cry** only in cult ritual, lacerating themselves in the wailing rites for the dead god of vegetation. They treacherously appear to be warriors for Yahweh, who **trained** them. But their unfaithfulness will bring them again into Egyptian slavery. Interpreters differ on whether **Egypt** in this and other passages (especially 8:13; 9:3; and 11:5) should be understood literally as a threat to Israel or figuratively as a symbol of foreign domination. In Hosea's day Egypt was militarily at low ebb. Yet before Tiglath-pileser's western campaigns (see Introduction) it may have seemed the major power on the horizon. Thereafter apparently some Israelites viewed it as the counterbalance to Assyrian might (cf. verse 11; II Kings 17:4).

D. National Death Ahead (8:1-14)

8:1-3. *A Call to Arms.* The **trumpet,** the ram's horn *shophar,* calling to battle is again sounded. The **vulture,** i.e. Assyria, is wheeling above Yahweh's **house**—referring perhaps to the Bethel sanctuary but more probably to Israel as Yahweh's earthly dwelling place. The people delude themselves by their ritual cries to God and claim intimate knowledge of God. But actually they have violated God's **covenant** and rebelled against his **law.** Hence the divine sentence is death (verse 3).

8:4-6. *Causes of National Death.* The nation is doomed for two reasons: the selection of rulers without divine approval and idolatry. The **calf** of **Samaria** refers to a bull image such as Jeroboam I set up at Bethel and Dan, to create religious centers for the new northern kingdom as rivals to the Jerusalem temple (I Kings 12:26-33). Doubtless the original intent was not apostasy. The image was probably understood to be a pedestal on which Yahweh was invisibly enthroned. But since the days of Jeroboam I the Canaanite Baal cult with its sexual fertility worship had baalized the original Yahwism. Hence Hosea's vehement attacks on these human constructions (cf. 10:5-6; 13:2).

8:7-10 *The Approaching Whirlwind.* A familiar proverb is quoted here. It underlines the disastrous result of sowing mere **wind**—that is, the nothingness of futile idolatry. Such seed brings forth sterile **grain** with no wheat in the **heads.** By its idolatry, which is foreign in origin and thus indicates no trust in its own God, Israel is already **swallowed up.** It is **among the nations as a useless vessel.** A **wild ass** is a pun on the name **Ephraim** in the Hebrew. **Wandering alone,** contrary to the natural herd instinct, Israel is forsaken by its **hired lovers,** both Baal consorts and international allies. The death of the nation will soon end the rapid succession of kings.

8:11-14. *Cult Without Obedience.* The people **love sacrifice.** They have **multiplied altars** in mistaken devotion. But they regard God's teaching as a **strange thing.** Hosea is a true colleague of his contemporary Amos, in language as well as in message. He pronounces judgment on both concentration on the sacrificial system and dependence on material **strongholds** (cf. Amos 1:4, 7, 10, 12, 14; 2:2, 5; 5:21-24). But, unlike Amos, he predicts at least figurative return to Egyptian slavery. This is to be Israel's penalty for forgetting **his Maker** (see above on 7:13-16).

E. FERTILITY'S FAILURE (9:1–10:15)

The appeal to **rejoice not . . . like the peoples** (9:1) perhaps marks the beginning of a new series of oracles delivered at the autumn harvest festival at Bethel. If so, this section of the book may picture most clearly Hosea's public encounter. He is defining the role and the plight of the prophet (9:7-8). He cries out to God to punish the faithless children (9:14).

9:1-7c. *The Food of Exile.* Israel is rejoicing in the ritual Baal marriage rites **upon all threshing floors.** The worshiper must pay the **harlot's hire** for these sexual ceremonies—that is, the fee to the cult prostitute for the privilege of baalized worship with her. The rites are expected to produce crop renewal for the new season, but they fail to provide grain and wine (verse 2).

God's punishment will be exile to **Egypt** or **Assyria** (see above on 7:13-16) to live on a starvation diet. The food will be **unclean** because it is devoted to a foreign god (verse 4; cf. Amos 7:17). With such food Israel cannot keep an **appointed festival** of Yahweh (cf. 2:11). Israel will be away in Assyria or in Egypt at the burial ground near **Memphis,** capital of Lower Egypt. Its own land, where once there were jewelry of **silver** and bedouin **tents,** will become a brier patch. Israel will **know** the terrible **days** of God's **recompense.**

9:7d-9. *The Prophet's Role.* Verse 7*de* may mean that other prophets are **mad** (cf. 4:5). More likely, however, Hosea is quoting the disparaging words of his hearers. They declare him to be crazed because their **iniquity**—their guilt—drives them to such **hatred.** The true prophet, however, filled with God's **spirit** is a **watchman** over the **people of . . . God.** But he is despised in the **house of God** when he declares his unpopular word—possibly an allusion to the banishment of Amos (Amos 7:10-13), though Hosea himself no doubt experienced similar rejection.

Sinful Israel is as corrupt as the depraved people of the Benjaminite city of **Gibeah,** who abused the Levite's concubine until she died (Judges 19:16-30). From the days of Saul's establishment of his capital there (I Samuel 10:17-26) Israel has rejected God's kingship by setting up its own kings one after another.

9:10-17. *Loss of Posterity.* This oracle is probably a continuation of Hosea's words at the harvest festival (see above on 9:1–10:15).

9:10. What more delightful sight to the weary traveler in the desert than an oasis with ripe **grapes,** or to a patient farmer than the **first fruit on the fig tree.** But God's delight at the discovery of Israel came to a disillusioned end. God discovered that the **fathers** who had covenanted to be God's alone had **consecrated**

themselves to Baal. The story of their yielding to the nature cult at Baal-peor (Numbers 25:1-5) was well known. It illustrated that one becomes what one loves.

9:11-14. The **glory** that will **fly away** is every Israelite's pride in an ongoing family. God will shut up the wombs (verse 11). Famine, pestilence, and war will destroy the nation's sons (verses 12-13). Like Jeremiah, Hosea starts to pray for his people (verse 14). But his prayer ends in the bitter plea that miscarriages will prove to them that their dependence on Baal is folly.

9:15-17. From the time of their entrance into the western Jordan territory at **Gilgal** (Joshua 4) the people's conduct has merited God's hatred. God will now **slay their beloved children**—perhaps a reference to the inevitable toll of war. Driven like a faithless wife out of God's house they will become **wanderers among the nations** (cf. Genesis 4:12-16).

10:1-8. *Loss of King and Image.* The prosperity of the **luxuriant vine** Israel, as in the days of Jeroboam II, meant many **altars** and **pillars.** Because the guilty people's **heart is false** God will destroy the equipment of this flourishing cult.

10:3-8. Hosea predicts that the petty king of Israel will prove to be helpless, **like a chip on the face of the waters.** The dwellers in the capital city will **tremble for the calf of Beth-aven** (see above on 4:15-16; 8:4-6), whose **glory** will be lost as it is carried off **as tribute to the great king** (see above on 5:9-14).

This may be a historical reference to inclusion of the image in the enormous tribute paid to Assyria in the reign of Menahem (cf. II Kings 15:19-20). More likely it is a prediction that the calf image will be carried off when the nation finally collapses.

In any case the problem is blasphemous lack of confidence in the divine king Yahweh or God's earthly representative (verse 3) and meaningless **oaths** of allegiance (verse 4). Therefore God's judgment will spring up like **weeds** over the abandoned cult centers. The people will wish to be hidden by the **mountains** from the day of judgment or be crushed by falling rocks in order to avoid a worse fate (verse 8).

10:9-15. *The Storm of War.* As Hosea has previously proclaimed (9:9), Israel's sin is of long standing. **Double iniquity**

may refer to two crimes of **Gibeah**—the rape and murder of the Levite's concubine (Judges 19:22-28) and the rebellion against God in setting up the kingship (I Samuel 10:17-26). Or it may simply mean the compounded guilt of the centuries.

10:11-12. Here Hosea uses a farming metaphor. The **trained heifer** Ephraim, perhaps in the earlier wilderness period, **loved to thresh.** It docilely and leisurely treaded out the grain, free to eat as it wished (cf. Deuteronomy 25:4). But because of its sin Israel will now be forced to bear a heavy **yoke** and to **plow** and **harrow.** Changing the figure, Hosea pleads for a changed national life. **Righteousness** should be sowed, so that the **fruit of steadfast love**—covenant loyalty—may be reaped. If the people **seek the LORD** instead of Baal, the Lord will **come and rain salvation** on them.

10:13-15. The hope is only momentary, however. The trust in **chariots** and **warriors** will bring final destruction, a **storm** in which Israel's **house** will be ended. The example of the destruction of **Beth-arbel** and its accompanying atrocities is not known. The city may have been located in Gilead. **Shalman** may be the Moabite king Salamanu mentioned in Tiglath-pileser's annals, or possibly Shalmaneser V of Assyria, who dealt the final blow to Israel.

F. GOD'S UNREQUITED LOVE (11:1–13:16)

The death blow to Israel as punishment for its unfaithfulness has occupied much of God's word to Israel thus far in the book. Attention now turns chiefly to divine reminiscence and appeal based on the lessons of covenant history.

11:1-11. *The Love of God the Father.* One of the greatest passages in the Bible now begins. Hosea portrays the depth and nature of God's love. It is notable that not husband-wife love but father-son love is described.

11:1-2. According to tradition God's choice of Israel as the chosen people when they left Egyptian slavery was figuratively the birth of God's "first-born son" (Exodus 4:22). Hosea spells out the meaning of that loving fatherhood. God **called** the son presumably to be the agent of the divine purpose for the world—though Hosea says nothing of fulfillment of the covenant with Abraham. Yet despite God's persistent call the son almost at once succumbed to the **Baals.**

11:3-4. The marvel of divine love is God's care and patience. God **taught Ehpraim to walk,** lovingly carried him in his **arms,** and **healed** him when ill, though the infant did not know it. In verse 4 the figure seems to change to what has been called "God's harness of love." By this God would impel rather than compel the people, as the farmer does a favorite donkey or yoke of oxen. God **led them with cords of compassion,** literally "cords of a man," perhaps meaning "human cords." God made their **yoke** light and tenderly **fed them.** On the other hand some scholars believe the shift in the figure is due to textual error. Various emendations of verse 4*cd* have been suggested—for example, "And I was to them as one who lifts a baby to his cheek."

11:5-7. The nation has grown through childhood to adolescence and still has **refused to return** to its father. God must now use stern disciplinary measures. God will take the people back to their starting point of slavery in **Egypt** (see above on 7:13-16) or into exile in **Assyria.** Devouring destruction will come upon them, and they will be under a severe yoke.

11:8-9. Here Hosea gives the climactic expression of God's love—and divine suffering as Yahweh ponders the decision concerning the wayward son. Will he treat the son like **Admah** and **Zeboiim**—cities destroyed with Sodom and Gomorrah? No, **his compassion grows warm and tender.** Ephraim has felt some destroying anger, but will not be destroyed. God's apparent inner struggle between wrath and love is over. What marks God as divine is God's holiness, God's unlikeness to vengeful humanity. God's holiness is redemptive love. God can be depended on as one who will not come to destroy.

11:10-11. Therefore God will bring the people back from their Egyptian-Assyrian punishment **to their homes.** They will come quickly, like cubs running to the **roar** of a **lion,** or like **doves,** meaning homing pigeons. Here Hosea may deliberately be using previous warning analogies (cf. 5:14; 7:11; 9:3) to say that God brings good out of what seems to be evil.

11:12–13:16. *Rejected Rebirth and Revival.* Further lessons from its history remind Israel of its continual opportunities for a right relationship with God—and of the consequences of repeated refusals.

11:12–12:1. In contrast to Israel's **lies** and **deceit,** Judah seems to be praised for remaining **faithful** to God. Elsewhere Hosea views Judah as sharing Israel's guilt (cf. 5:12-14; 6:4; 8:14). Thus many scholars have assumed here some alteration by a Judean editor. But perhaps the present text can be understood as referring to Judah's allegiance to the Canaanite god El (see above on 1:4-5) and the "holy ones," the cult prostitutes. Ephraim's foreign alliances—including perhaps Menahem's **bargain** with Tiglath-pileser (see Introduction) and such commercial ventures as exporting olive **oil** to Egypt—exhibit disloyalty to Israel's God. They are like the blighting **east wind** from the desert.

12:2-6. Since **Jacob** in this passage clearly means the northern kingdom, it has been suggested that **Judah** originally read "Israel." From the story of this three events are singled out:

his natal heel-grabbing, a pun on his name (Genesis 25:26);

his wrestling with God at the river Jabbok (Genesis 32:22-30);

his encounter with God at Bethel (Genesis 28:11-17).

These all seem to recommend Jacob's perseverance in his struggles with God. But the all-important concluding word is that similarly by divine help the people should **return** (repent), and then keep **love,** (covenant loyalty), and **justice** and **wait continually** for God. Some commentators, however, view verses 4-6 as a later insertion.

12:7-9. Ephraim is a wealthy **trader,** literally "Canaanite." But **all his riches can never offset the guilt he has incurred** through dishonest dealings. Therefore as punishment Israel must again **dwell in tents** as in the period of the Exodus and desert wandering, commemorated in the autumn **feast** of booths.

12:10-14. Israel has no excuse for waywardness. God has

always provided guidance through the **prophets** with their **visions** and **parables**. The centers of cult iniquity in **Gilead** and **Gilgal** will be destroyed. Their **altars** will become mere **stone heaps,** Hebrew *gallim*, a word play on the place names. The Revised Standard Version places parentheses around verse 12. Many scholars feel that it is an interpolation, perhaps displaced from verses 2-6. It should be noted, however, that Jacob's return from **Aram** involved the building of a stone heap (cf. Genesis 31:43-54) and that the word translated **herded sheep** is from the same root as **preserved** (verse 13).

Moses is the **prophet** by whom Yahweh **brought Israel up from Egypt.** He was probably the one by whom Israel was **preserved,** though some scholars believe the latter reference is to Samuel. By rejecting the prophets Israel has **given bitter provocation** to Yahweh to hold it responsible for its **bloodguilt.**

13:1-3. As the chosen son of Joseph Ephraim was the chief of the ten tribes of Israel (cf. Genesis 37:5-11; 48:14-20; 49:22-26). But ironically, through worship of the supposed god of renewed life and vegetation, he **died** spiritually. Hosea heaps scorn on the piling up of sin as the people make **molten images** and **idols** and in the rites at Dan and Bethel **kiss calves.** Such a society is a ephemeral as **mist . . . dew . . . chaff . . . smoke.**

13:4-11. In appealing tones Yahweh reminds the people that God has been their one and only God from the days of the Exodus. Yahweh pleads the intimacy of the relationship with the people: **You know no God but me, and besides me there is no savior.** They remembered this in the adversity of the **wilderness,** but with prosperity in the Promised Land they thanklessly **forgot** their God. Therefore **like a lion** or a **leopard** or a **bear robbed of her cubs** Yahweh will pounce on them in devouring fury. When God destroys, no earthly thing can save (verses 9-11). Indeed, as the rapid dynastic changes of the last days of Israel testify (see Introduction), God has both **given** and **taken . . . away** kings in **anger** (cf. 8:4).

13:12-14. What is to be done with the huge accumulation of **iniquity?** This dirty pile of evil is to be bagged and **kept in store** to await a final day of reckoning. Its final disposal depends on

Ephraim's own decision. Hosea sadly announces that the people have rejected God's offer of rebirth and revival. The **unwise,** Baal-deluded **son** is not willing to be born again into right relationship with God. The people think themselves alive in Baalism but are actually in the clutches of **Death** in **Sheol,** the underworld cavern of the departed. God would **redeem** the people, but they do not wish it. Hence **compassion is hid** from Yahweh's loving **eyes.**

13:15-16. The nation with its capital, **Samaria,** has sealed its own doom. It began by adding practices of Baalism to the worship of Yahweh. It will end in the atrocities of war. The dreaded **east wind** from the **wilderness** (desert), which dries up everything in the hot summer, is Assyria, which will **strip his treasury of every precious thing.**

G. Promise of Renewal (14:1-8)

The climax of God's word through Hosea's oracles is Yahweh's plea for the people's repentance followed by the gracious promise of healing and freely given love.

This magnificent conclusion—whether the product of Hosea himself or of a thoroughly understanding disciple—is in the form of a liturgy of penitence (cf. 6:1-3). It is composed of the customary three parts: a call to repentance (verses 1-2*b*), a penitential prayer of confession (verses 2*c*-3), and Yahweh's response (verses 4-8).

14:1-2*b*. *Call to Repentance.* The urgent plea is to **return** to Yahweh—to turn away from Baalism or baalized Yahwism. False worship is the reason for their inner guilt and outright disobedience. Not sacrifices but **words,** the sincere utterances of a contrite heart, will permit **return to the LORD.**

14:2*c*-3. *Confession.* The prayer acknowledges and pleads for the removal of **all iniquity**—that is, all inner tendency to wrongdoing, therefore all consequent punishment, therefore all guilt feelings. In place of sacrifices it offers the words called for in verse 2*a*—the **fruit of our lips,** literally "bulls of our lips." Perhaps this implies not merely the animals used in sacrifice but Baalism's symbols of power and fertility, now acknowledged as belonging to Yahweh. The two major sins, international intrigue and idolatry are renounced. **Assyria,** or perhaps its god Asshur (the same word in Hebrew), and the **horses** of Egypt cannot **save.**

14:3e. The punishment cannot be escaped. The nation, already an orphan, is on the way to war and exile. But there is hope that, having confessed, the one time wayward child will again be accepted with motherly **mercy,** or compassion. The Hebrew word implies a mother's womb (see above on 1:6).

14:4-8. *Yahweh's Response.* If God's wayward son will now become completely converted away from Baalism and back to Yahweh, Yahweh will absolve him of his guilt and reverse the sin-caused disasters. Instead of disease there will be healing. Instead of wrath will come a free outpouring of gracious love. Instead of failing fertility will be the fruitfulness that the name Ephraim implies.

Through Yahweh's control of all nature, arid, mountainous Israel will have the **fragrance** and the **wine of Lebanon,** famed for its fertile valley. When Israel will **return and dwell beneath** God's **shadow,** it will find that Yahweh answers and looks after it like a strong, protective, and fruitful **evergreen cypress.** Its **fruit** is not from Baal but from the God of its parents. At last Israel will have learned true knowledge of God.

IV. POSTSCRIPT (14:9)

An ancient reader of the scroll of Hosea adds his word of approval to the prophet's words. As a member of the wisdom school he counsels all future readers to **understand these things.**

THE BOOK OF JOEL

Roland E. Murphy, O. Carm.

Roland E. Murphy, O. Carm.

INTRODUCTION

Author and Date

A dozen men named Joel are mentioned in the Old Testament. None, however, can be identified with the author of this book. We are given no information about this Joel except that he was the "son of Pethuel" (1:1). The familiarity with the temple liturgy shown in the book suggests that he may have been a priest, or perhaps a cultic prophet. However, some interpret the references to priests (1:9, 13 and 2:17) as evidence that the author did not include himself among them. The interest in Jerusalem suggests that he lived in or near this city.

A date in the postexilic period is suggested by

(1) the role of the elders as community leaders (1:2, 14; 2:16),
(2) the concern with ritual and sacrifice (1:13; 2:12, 14),
(3) the relatively small size of the community, which can be assembled in the temple area (2:16),
(4) the reference to Israel as scattered among the nations (3:2),
(5) the acquaintance with the Greeks as a remote people (3:6).

In the twentieth century the only serious challenge to the postexilic date has been a study citing ancient Canaanite cultic practices from Ugarit as evidence for associating the work with a preexilic new year enthronement celebration. This study dates the book as contemporary with Jeremiah, about 600 B.C. But there is no reference to the king, who would be at the center of such a celebration, and so this theory has not won the assent of many scholars.

In the postexilic period references to the temple place the writing after 515. Dependence on later prophets indicates an even later date. (for 2:32 quotes Obadiah 17a and 2:11, 31 reflect Malachi 3:2; 4:5). The rebuilding of the wall (cf. 2:7) and other problems facing Nehemiah and Ezra seem to be already settled. On the other hand the reference to Sidon (3:4), in a passage that may be an addition, indicates that the book was completed before around 345, when this city was destroyed by the Persians under Artaxerxes III. Thus the likely date is the first half of the fourth century.

Unity

The recent trend among scholars is to accept the general unity of the book—with the possible exception of 3:4-8 and maybe 3:18-21. An earlier theory of dual authorship is still favored by some. All would admit that the work divides easily into 1:1–2:27 (a locust invasion) and 2:28–3:21 (judgment on the nations). But the arguments that the sections must be from different authors are much less obvious. There is no reason that the same author could not have interpreted a locust plague as an omen and symbol of the coming day of Yahweh.

Occasion and Message

The event causing Joel's activity is a locust plague that has devastated the land. In the prophetic tradition he interprets this as a visitation from Yahweh, and he urges the Israelites to assemble and mourn. He comes to see the invasion of the locusts as a sign that the day of Yahweh is near and as a symbol of the divine invasion that will characterize that day (see below on 1:15-20). He holds out the hope of deliverance if Israel turns to Yahweh wholeheartedly (2:12-14). The turning point comes in 2:18, when Yahweh "became jealous" for the people. Then

29

follows a series of oracles which assure the people of prosperity, an outpouring of the spirit, and victory over the nations in the final battle, when Yahweh will be a refuge and a stronghold to the people.

Literary Style

The main literary motif is a liturgy of lamentation. But the three chapters present a great variety of literary types:

admonition(1:2-3),

summons to lament (1:5-7, 11-12, 13),

complaints (1:16, 19; 2:17),

alarms (2:1; 3:9),

oracles of assurance (2:19-27),

theological conclusions (2:27; 3:17).

These reflect a varied life setting. The references to priests and sacrifice reveal a cultic background for Joel's activity. However, the different types lose their individuality in the work as it stands. The book is a *literary* composition which combines these various types into a theological interpretation and message.

The literary character is especially seen in the book's so-called "anthological composition." That is, earlier biblical language is adapted to express its ideas. For example:

the paleness of faces (2:6) is from Nahum (2:10);

the trembling of heavens and earth (2:10) is from Isaiah 13:13;

the possibility of Yahweh's repentance (2:14) is from Jonah 3:9.

Joel also draws largely on earlier themes of the day of Yahweh (cf. Zephaniah 1; Isaiah 13; Ezekiel 30; Obadiah). The oracles against the nations rely on Jeremiah 46–51 and Ezekiel 29–32. The threat of an enemy from the north comes from Jeremiah 4–6 and Ezekiel 38–39.

I. The Locust Plague (1:1–2:17)

1:1 *Title.* The name **Joel** means "Yah(weh) is (my) God" or "Yah(weh) is El." Perhaps his father's name, **Pethuel,** means "the young man of God."

1:2-4. *A General Summons.* The call to **give ear** is reminiscent of the style of the wise men (for example Proverbs 4:1) and the Deuteronomic preaching (for example Deuteronomy 4:9). The **aged men,** elsewhere translated "elders" (see verse 14), are the leaders of the Jerusalem community. The appalling event is an invasion by locusts which devastates the land. The four kinds of locust—**cutting . . . swarming . . . hopping . . . destroying**— probably designate the four stages through which the insect evolves. Even in modern times (1915 and 1930) Palestine has been ravaged by such plagues.

1:5-14. *A Summons to Several Classes.* The vines have been destroyed by the locusts and the **drinkers of wine** will be the first to feel the effects of the plague. **Sweet wine** means juice from newly pressed grapes. Both **vines** and **fig trees** are **stripped** by the **nation** of devouring insects.

1:8-10. The entire community, especially the **priests,** is invited to **lament** because the sacrificial offerings in the temple have ceased. The comparison of Jerusalem to a widowed **virgin** is quite poignant. Jerusalem is often called the "virgin daughter" of Judah (cf. Jeremiah 14:17 and Lamentations 1:15). **Grain** and **wine** and olive **oil** were the chief products of Palestine.

1:11-12. The farmers and **vinedressers** are next addressed. These are vitally affected by the destruction of crops and vines and **trees.**

1:13-14. The climax in the series now comes. The **priests,** now bereft of their offerings, are commanded to mourn with the people in the temple on a solemn day of **fast. Sackcloth** was a garment of camel's or goat's hair wrapped about the loins. The wearing of sackcloth is a typical sign of mourning in the Old Testament.

1:15-20. *A Ritual Prayer.* These lines present snatches of the laments which would characterize the **solemn assembly** called by the priests in verse 14.

1:15-16. The great theme of the book, **the day of the LORD,** is now introduced. The term indicates a specific intervention of Yahweh in history. Analysis of the important "day of Yahweh" texts—for example, Isaiah 2:12; 13:6; Jeremiah 46:10; and Amos

5:18-20—shows that the phrase has a rich history and imagery associated with it. The day is a day of battle, and Yahweh is at war with enemies. The imagery probably derives from the conquest of Canaan, when Yahweh intervened to fight for Israel (cf Judges 5:4-31; 7:1-25). Here the day is a day *against* Israel, and the locust plague is its prelude and symbol. In the Hebrew there is a play on the word for **Almighty:** "as mighty destruction from the Almighty."

1:17-20. The ancient manuscripts vary in translating the difficult verse 17*a*. The Revised Standard Version presupposes a plowing under of the seed, or a rotting due to lack of water. At least it is clear that **there is no pasture** for the animals. The "I" in verse 19 can be understood to be the prophet. But it is really the community (which was invited to "cry to the Lord" in verse 14) that speaks. The complaint describes a drought, symbolized by **fire** and **flame.**

2:1-11. *Invasion of Yahweh's Army.* Unlike the summons in chapter 1, this alarm is sounded by Yahweh. It warns of an invasion of a **great and powerful people** on the day of Yahweh. Most commentators interpret this invasion as a continuation of the locust plague. The locusts are Yahweh's **army** or **host,** and they are described as advancing **like soldiers** on the terrible day. Some, however, point out that the invading army is described in terms similar to the divine army which levels Babylon in Isaiah 13. They suggest that Joel is here describing the army which is to attack Israel on the day of Yahweh as in chapter 3.

2:2. The description of the day as **darkness** is similar to Zephaniah 1:15. **Blackness** in the traditional Hebrew text reads "dawn." But in the original Hebrew script, which consisted of consonants only, the two words would have been identical. "Like dawn" gives good sense as a description of the suddenness of the invasion.

2:3-9. The military metaphor is continued in the dramatic description of **warriors** and **soldiers** that swarm over the land. They devastate **the garden of Eden,** as Palestine is here called.

2:10-11. The quaking and trembling of the **heavens** and **earth** are the usual accompaniment of a divine visitation. The **voice** of

Yahweh is God's command for the army to attack. The final question, **who can endure it?** suggests the totally desperate situation on this day. A ray of hope will be offered in the following verses 12-14.

2:12-14. *Deliverance Dependent on Conversion.* Yahweh's invitation to the people to convert is a turning point. Their response is to be a conversion in the style of the Deuteronomic ideal—**with all your heart** (cf. Deuteronomy 30:10). The rending of **garments** is a customary Old Testament ritual of mourning, but it must be sincere. Since verse 12 urges **fasting,** there is no opposition to ritual in itself. However, the prophet strikes out at empty formalism. The motivation for the change of heart is the confession formula of Exodus 34:6, **gracious and merciful,** which is a time-honored characterization of Yahweh.

The question **who knows** is idiomatic for "perhaps he will." God is free to grant mercy and to allow Israel to worship in sacrifice. Unlike prophets before the Babylonian exile, Joel shows great concern about temple worship (cf. 1:9, 13).

2:15-17. *A Summons to National Repentance.* All classes— even the **bridegroom,** who was usually exempted from military service (cf. Deuteronomy 20:7; 24:5)—are summoned on a **fast** day to appeal for deliverance. The **priests** are stationed between the **altar** of burnt offerings and the entrance to the temple. Their prayer indicates the reasons Yahweh should intervene. God's heritage, Israel, is a reproach; the nations blaspheme by questioning, **Where is their God?** Such motifs are frequent in the psalms of lament (cf. Psalm 79:4, 10).

II. THE DAY OF THE LORD (2:18–3:21)

2:18-27. *The Promise of Deliverance.* Though most interpreters place the major division point of the book between verses 27 and 28, verse 18 marks the decisive transition. From this point on there are only words of consolation for Israel. Yahweh's becoming **jealous** for Israel is a turning in their favor, as the following lines indicate.

2:20-22. The **northerner** is the army of invasion. Here it is interpreted in the light of the traditional terminology for invaders (cf. Jeremiah 1:14; 6:1 and Ezekiel 38–39). This enemy will be driven into the wasteland, which spans the desert from the Dead Sea (or perhaps the Persian Gulf) to the Mediterranean. In verse 21 the land is given the assurance that Yahweh **has done great things**—in direct contrast to the **great things** ascribed to the invader in verse 20. This is expressed in the style of the priestly oracle **fear not.**

2:23. Zion is assured of **rain** and the resulting material prosperity. The Hebrew of this verse is obscure. **The early rain for your vindication** is doubtful because this is not the normal meaning for the two Hebrew words, which can be literally translated either as "teacher for justice" or "early rain in due measure." There seems to be a play on the words *moreh* (teacher) and *yoreh* (early rain). Perhaps the blessing of rain will point Israel toward a proper relationship to Yahweh. In any case the promise of the seasonal rains is clear: the **early rain** in the fall and the **latter rain** in the spring.

2:24-27. The promises of blessings on the land are continued: **grain . . . wine . . . oil**—in contrast to the devastation wrought by the locusts, who are here called **my great army** (cf. 2:11). The climax of the promises is found in the "proof" formula of verse 27, **You shall know that I am in the midst of Israel.** Israel will arrive at a deeper realization that Yahweh, the God of the covenant, is present and active in its behalf. This conviction of the divine purpose is derived from the tradition of Second Isaiah (45:2-6) and Ezekiel (39:28). Israel can rely on Yahweh's action in its favor, for this will show that Yahweh is Israel's God, in its midst (cf. 4:17).

2:28-32. *The Outpouring of the Spirit.* The traditional Hebrew text since 1524 has marked these verses as chapter 3 and the rest of the book as chapter 4. The wondrous dealing of God (verse 26) is continued with an outpouring of the **spirit**—a new life and power for weak men and women. The prophet takes up a traditional theme, the giving of the divine spirit, to indicate that Israel will be a people of prophets (**dream dreams . . . see**

visions). There will be directness and spontaneity in every person's relationship to God. Everyone will experience the spirit, as once Moses asked this blessing for all of Yahweh's people (Numbers 11:29).

2:30-32. Accompanying the outpouring are cosmic portents, the usual signs associated with the day of Yahweh (cf. 2:10). To **call on the name of the LORD** is to serve the LORD in the temple liturgy. **Jerusalem** will be the haven for those who **escape** the catastrophic events. Here the prophet consciously refers to the word of Yahweh spoken by Obadiah (Obadiah 17). Those **whom the LORD calls** are the chosen in Jerusalem.

In Acts 2:17-21, the Pentecost speech of Peter, the Septuagint version of verses 28-32 are quoted. The events of Pentecost were seen as part of the pattern proclaimed by the prophet. Verse 28 announces the outpouring for **afterward**. While this is only a vague indication, it appears to follow on the people's conversion. In Romans 10:13 Paul quotes verse 32*a*, **all who call upon the name of the LORD shall be delivered.** Hence, Paul says, there can be no distinction between Jew and Greek.

3:1-15. *Judgment on the Nations.* The perspective now broadens to include **the nations, all** are to be gathered in the **valley of Jehoshaphat** to be judged because of their treatment of Israel. The presupposition is that Judah has been exiled, its **land divided up**—as actually occurred after the fall of Jerusalem in 586—and the people enslaved. The valley of Jehoshaphat has traditionally been located in the Kidron Valley in Jerusalem. But probably it is merely symbolic ("Yah shall judge") and a play on the word for "judge." The judgment on the nations is due to their treatment of exiled Israel. **Lots** would have been cast for prisoners, with no sense of human dignity.

3:4-8. This section has the earmarks of an insertion into the original text. It builds on the idea of trafficking in human beings in verse 3. The context there was the nations, but now a Phoenician-Philistine league is addressed. These peoples are accused of having plundered Judah and of having **sold** Judean slaves **to the Greeks.** The meaning of the questions in verse 4 becomes clear from this plundering and enslavement of the

Judeans. Fittingly they in turn will suffer. They will be sold by the Judeans **to the Sabeans** of the Arabian desert. On the bearing of this passage on the date of the book see the Introduction.

3:9-12. After the digression on verses 4-8 the nations are issued a call to arms. They are to assemble at the **valley of Jehoshaphat.** Isaiah 2:4 and Micah 4:3 are quoted in verse 10: Here the sense is ironically reversed. The journey to Jerusalem has become a military advance—to destruction, not peace—so let them **beat** their **plowshares into swords.** In the enthusiasm of military preparations even the unsoldierly boast of their exploits (verse 10c). The invitation to assemble is repeated in verse 11. But the last line about Yahweh's **warriors**—that is, the members of the heavenly court—may be a gloss (cf. Zechariah 14:5). When all the nations are gathered in the valley of Jehoshaphat, Yahweh will be their **judge,** as in verse 2.

3:13-15. The nations are **ripe** for the **harvest.** Their destruction is described in terms of cutting down the harvest and treading the grapes. As in verse 9 there is no indication to whom the commands of verse 13 are given—to the people of Jerusalem? to Yahweh's warriors of verse 11? The valley of Jehoshaphat is also called **the valley of decision,** for here Yahweh will decide for Jerusalem against its enemies. As in 2:10 the decision will be accompanied by cataclysms in the world of nature.

3:16-21. *Blessings for Judah and Jerusalem.* The proclamation of the blessings is introduced by a well-known metaphor from Amos 1:2: **The LORD roars from Zion.** Now Yahweh's **voice** is against the enemy, God is **a refuge to his people.** The Lord's deliverance of Israel will be a proof that the LORD is the God of Israel, and in Israel (cf. 2:17). The LORD acts that Israel may know its God. God's dwelling **in Zion** makes Jerusalem **holy,** separate from **strangers.**

3:18-21. These verses are possibly a later addition. They describe the paradisiacal blessings of the judgment and deliverance. Yahweh **dwells in Zion.** The LORD brings about the fertility of paradise (verse 18) and the independence of the people over **Egypt** and **Edom,** who are the classical types of Israel's enemies.

The fountain that flows **from the house of the LORD** has its model in Ezekiel 47:1-12, the stream that flows from the temple. This shall **water the valley of Shittim** (that is, Acacia Valley), which is probably the Wadi en-Nar, the continuation of the Kidron Valley in the direction of the Dead Sea. The book ends on the theme of Yahweh's dwelling **in Zion**—an important point emphasized by Joel in his view of the age to come (cf. 2:27, 32 and 3:17).

THE BOOK OF AMOS

Charles F. Kraft

INTRODUCTION

The book of Amos is a collection of the prophetic messages of the first Old Testament prophet whose words are preserved as a book of the Bible. Probably this was the first biblical book to be completed in substantially its present form. It is mostly in poetic form. Prophetic poetry—understood to be God's revelation in the form of spoken and then written oracles—was a unique literary genre in the history of the world's literature. It was first given us by Amos in Israel in the eighth century B.C.

Most of the book is commonly regarded as authentic sayings of the prophet Amos, whether recorded by himself or by disciples. Only the appendix of hope (9:8c-15), coming in stark contrast to the prevailing pronouncements of doom, is regarded by many scholars as added later. Some interpreters also view as additions certain of the oracles against the nations, especially that against Judah (2:4-5), and the "doxologies" (4:13; 5:8-9; 9:5-6). Others consider the doxologies to be fragments of an ancient hymn quoted by Amos.

The Prophet and His Times

Amos was the pioneer of a long succession of prophets. His career is thus of epoch-making importance. His dramatic

appearance on the stage of world history—the conflict with
Israelite officialdom at the royal sanctuary of Bethel—is told in
the one biographical section of the book (7:10-17). That this
herdsman and sycamore-fig pruner did not regard himself to be
a professional prophet seems clear. But it is equally clear that he
felt under divine compulsion to speak (see below on 1:1;
7:14-15). His opening oracles of judgment against the nations
(1:3–2:3) show a remarkable grasp of the history of his world.

Hence he was no country bumpkin suddenly startled into
sermons of warning when he discovered urban wickedness. On
the contrary, as the visions in his book confirm (7:1-9; 8:1-3;
9:1-4), he deliberately declared his unpopular warnings at the
centers of religious and political life in Israel.

Amos' message was to an age of unprecedented postwar
prosperity in the middle of the eighth century. Assyrian invasions
of the preceding century had ceased because of that empire's
internal struggles. In the midst of his long reign (793/92-753)
Jeroboam II of Israel had brought the century and a half of war
with nearby Syria to a victorious end. Amos began in his public
career evidently very late in Jeroboam's reign. By this time Israel
was enlarged to her most extensive boundaries. Judah was
similarly prosperous under Uzziah (or Azariah, 792/91–740/39; see
below on 1:1). An era of luxury like that of Solomon seemed to have
returned. It was to speak to the false presumptions and vile
practices of this heyday that Amos heard God call him.

Amos' Message

Amos' purpose was to penetrate the self-satisfied complacency and reveal the rotten core of the religious and social life of
the leaders of Israel. These people assumed their prosperity to
be evidence of the effectiveness of their cultic observances.
They had been ungratefully false to the faith of their fathers by
turning from Yahweh to Baal. They had repudiated their
parents' obedience to Yahweh's commands by heartless
exploitation in cult center, marketplace, and law court.

Amos foresaw that their rude awakening was at hand. There
was to be a worldwide movement of punishing judgment, a

deadly "day of Yahweh" which would mean the death of the nation at the hands of a God-empowered invading enemy. The situation looked almost hopeless to Amos. But possibly, if they turned to "seek the LORD," and if they "let justice roll down like waters," a "remnant" of the nation might avoid the coming death or exile to a foreign land (5:6, 15, 24).

I. INTRODUCTION: AMOS AND GOD'S WORD (1:1-2)

1:1. *Title.* This prose superscription was written by an editor to introduce Amos' prophetic poetry. More complete than the headings of most prophetic books, it locates the prophet in biblical history. The name **Amos** may mean "burden"—that is, of Yahweh concerning the people Israel.

Among the shepherds may not describe Amos as a typical keeper of a small flock. The Hebrew word used here appears elsewhere only in reference to Mesha king of Moab, a "sheep breeder" who delivered a huge annual tribute of sheep and wool to the king of Israel (II Kings 3:4). A similar Arabic term denotes a breed of sheep. But in early Canaanite literature the word is used of a temple official responsible for as many as two thousand sheep and goats belonging to the shrine. Possibly, therefore, Amos was one of several keepers of Jerusalem or Bethel temple flocks.

His home base was **Tekoa,** a rather prominent Judean highland city ten miles south of Jerusalem. Situated about 2,800 feet above sea level, it overlooked the desolate hills of Judah eastward toward the Dead Sea. But no doubt the requirements of his occupation—for pasturage and for delivery of its produce—led Amos along the main routes to the urban centers of the day. At any rate the **words . . . which he saw**—that is, revelations, not heard, but seen with the inner eye of prophetic perception—were chiefly **concerning Israel,** the northern kingdom, rather than his homeland of Judah.

Amos' prophetic ministry is dated not only by the reigning monarchs (see Introduction) but more specifically in relation to an **earthquake** of such severity as to be long remembered (cf. Zechariah 14:5). Archaeologists have found evidence that Hazor in northern Galilee was destroyed by an earthquake at about this time, but its exact date cannot be determined. In the Hebrew **two years** is ambiguous. It may refer to the duration of Amos' prophetic work or to its date.

1:2. *God's Voice of Judgment.* This opening word is cast perhaps in the form of a brief liturgy, with excellent Hebrew poetic structure. It sounds the keynote of the book. Yahweh speaks with the panic-producing roar of a lion pouncing on the prey (cf. 3:4, 8). Yahweh is speaking from **Zion,** the holy hill in **Jerusalem,** the center of worship for Judah. The LORD'S voice announces immediate doom, the end of prosperity.

As in the drought of Elijah's)ay (I Kings 17:1), the **pastures** will cry out for rain. The **Carmel** ridge, a twelve-mile-long mountain headland on the coast near modern Haifa famous for luxuriant plant life, will lose its fertility. Divine judgment strikes at agricultural prosperity, the means of livelihood. There will be only one outcome—death. Some commentators, assuming that Amos' ministry was confined to the northern kingdom, consider this verse a summarizing couplet by an editor.

II. GOD'S JUDGMENT ON THE NATIONS AND ON ISRAEL (1:3–2:16)

The opening prophetic oracles are a series of pronouncements of doom on neighboring nations (1:3–2:3). They begin with Syria, the nation immediately to the northeast. Amos' hearers only recently recovered from the serious blows of this foe. They must have gleefully greeted the announcement of its imminent destruction. Next, to the southwest, the Philistines, an earlier greatest enemy, are to experience Yahweh's punishing fire. To the northwest Tyre, then to the south Edom, and to the east the Ammonites and Moab—the order forms a crisscross pattern of divine judgment. Its climax is doom on Israel itself (2:6-16). Grim delight over judgment on enemies turns to terror as hearers learn the fate of their own land.

The very regular form of all these oracles may have been

drawn from cultic formulas. They resemble Egyptian texts where curses are first pronounced on surrounding peoples and then on individuals within Egypt. Each oracle begins with the typical prophetic perfect tense, literally "thus has the LORD said." But God's spoken word has continuing effect and thus is properly translated **thus says the LORD.** The repeated expression **for three . . ., and for four** is perhaps taken from wisdom literature (cf. Job 5:19; 33:14; Proverbs 6:16; 30:15, 18, 21, 29). It suggests multiplied **transgressions,** literaly "rebellions," against divine authority.

I will not revoke the punishment is literally "I will not turn it back" or "I will not cause it to return." Most interpreters understand the "it" to refer to the mysterious God-directed punishment which is the inevitable consequence of sin. But if "it" refers to the nation, as seems more natural, then the prophet may be using a figure of speech drawn from a myth of his day about the vegetation god Baal, who was killed and went to the underworld and then returned with the autumn rains. The meaning would then be that Yahweh, the divine power over nature and nations, will never cause the guilty nation to return from its underworld of deserved punishment.

Another possibility is that "return" here means "repent,"—that is, Yahweh will not let the guilty nation repent and be forgiven. Still another is that the word means "restore"—that is, Yahweh will not restore the nation to favor.

Says the LORD not merely marks the end of each oracle. It is a resounding prophetic "Amen." Its omission from the oracles on Tyre, Edom, and Judah has been taken by some as evidence that these oracles are additions to the original words of Amos.

A. ORACLES ON NEIGHBORING NATIONS (1:3–2:5)

1:3-5. *On Syria.* Famed as the oldest city of the world, **Damascus** was the capital of Syria. The devastating wars of Syria against Israel were doubtless vividly remembered by Amos' oldest hearers. They were waged by King **Hazael** and by his son

Benhadad. Gilead, east of the Jordan River and south of Syria, had been the scene of wartime atrocities such as running over prisoners of war with iron-toothed instruments of torture.

1:4-5. The punishment for such cruelty will be:

(1) **fire** destroying the royal citadel;

(2) ruined defenses as the **bar** of the city gate is destroyed;

(3) the death of the royal house or provincial governors (in the Hebrew **inhabitants** is singular, literally "sitter" or perhaps "enthroned one");

(4) return of the Syrians to **Kir,** the eastern Mesopotamian territory, perhaps near Elam, from which God brought them (cf. 9:7)—a fate as horrible as for the Israelites to be returned to Egyptian slavery.

Valley of Aven is literally "valley of vanity" or "wealth" or "idolatry," and **Beth-eden,** is literally "house of delight." Both may be Amos' ironic play on words. On the other hand the Hebrew consonants of Aven can be read as "On," the name of the Egyptian center of sun worship, which was later applied to Baalbek in the valley between the Lebanon mountain ranges. Beth-eden may refer to a northeastern Syrian city-state on the upper Euphrates River mentioned in Assyrian records. Amos' prediction was strikingly fulfilled when in 733/32 the Assyrian king Tiglath-pileser III reduced Damascus to a subservience from which it never recovered.

1:6-8. *On the Philistines.* Turning from northeast to southwest, Amos lays the second curse on Israel's perennial enemy, the Philistines. Perhaps **Gaza** is singled out as the southernmost of the five principal cities lying at the gateway between Egypt and Asia. **Ashdod . . . Ashkelon . . . Ekron** are mentioned. Gath may have been omitted either because of the limits of poetic structure or because it had not yet recovered from its subjugation by Hazael decades before. On the other hand a few scholars have suggested a later date for this oracle because Gath was destroyed by the Assyrians in 711 (see below on 6:2).

The cruelty of mass slave trade, in which not just individuals but whole nations are involved, is the reason for God's curse. Perhaps the reference is to collaboration in slave trade between

Philistines and "Arabs" in the days of King Jehoram of Judah nearly a century earlier (II Chronicles 21:16-17). More probably it is to a more recent event not recorded in the Old Testament. Amos' prediction was partially fulfilled in the overthrow of Gaza by the Assyrians in 734.

1:9-10. *On Tyre.* The object of the third curse is Tyre, chief city of the northwest coastland, Phoenicia. It was fabulously proud and wealthy because of its maritime world trade. The oracle is very similar to the preceding and is brief (there is no parallel to verse 8). This has caused a number of scholars to question its coming from Amos.

1:9e. What was the unremembered **covenant of brotherhood?** King Hiram of Tyre "loved David" (I Kings 5:1) and once, though disappointed, called Solomon "my brother" (I Kings 9:13). But in the ninth century the political marriage of King Ahab of Israel with Jezebel, daughter of a Phoenician king, had results that hardly cemented fraternal relations.

Some regard this reference as not to a broken pact between Phoenicia and Israel or some other nation but to internal conflict in the seventh century, when Tyre twice sided with the Assyrians against other Phoenician cities. If so, this oracle is of course later than Amos. Possibly the phrase is a general reference to inhuman behavior. Tyre was seriously weakened by Nebuchadrezzar's thirteen-year siege in the sixth century. It was finally subdued by Alexander the Great in the fourth.

1:11-12. *On Edom.* In the fourth oracle God's judgment is on Edom, lying south of the Dead Sea. Here is hatred between blood brothers, for Israel and Edom were traditionally descended from the twins Jacob and Esau, whose rivalry was prenatal and perpetual (cf. Genesis 25:19-34; 27:1–28:9; 33:15-17). Tradition also traced the enmity in part to the Edomites' refusal to let Israel pass through their territory on the way from Egypt to the Promised Land (cf. Numbers 20:14-21). But the anger became fiercest over Edom's plundering of Judah after the destruction of Jerusalem in 586. The breach against brotherhood is emphasized in a word play, for the root of the Hebrew word translated **pity** refers to the womb, the place where Jacob and Esau first struggled. The unceasing fierceness of Edom's wrath is like that of a wild beast tearing its prey.

Teman was probably the largest and most important city in central Edom. Bozrah, about twenty miles southeast of the Dead Sea, was the strongest city in northern Edom. Because of this oracle's brevity, its generality, and its particular appropriateness after 586, a number of scholars date it later than Amos.

1:13. On the Ammonites. The fifth oracle most closely resembles the first (verses 3-5). Perhaps the atrocities in **Gilead** of both the Syrians from the north and the Ammonites from the east were connected. However, no specific occasion is known when the Ammonites disemboweled pregnant women in gaining Gilead territory. The Ammonites were traditionally related to Israel (cf. Genesis 19:30-38). They apparently began their wars of aggressive expansion to the west and north in the days of Jephthah in the eleventh century (cf. Judges 11:4-33). Saul's first military exploit was inspired by their threat of gouging out eyes (I Samuel 11:1-11), and they were later subjugated by David. In the ninth century they attacked the Judean king Jehoshaphat (II Chronicles 20:1-23). They paid tribute, perhaps in Amos' day, to King Uzziah of Judah (II Chronicles 26:8) and later to his son Jotham (II Chronicles 27:5).

1:14-15. The Ammonites' capital city, **Rabbah,** or Rabbath-Ammon, is the only Ammonite city named in the Old Testament. It is now modern Amman, capital of Jordan. Amos' predicted doom of **exile** for Ammonite leaders may have occurred at the command of Nebuchadrezzar after Jerusalem's fall in 586.

2:1-3. On Moab. The last oracle against a foreign nation condemns Moab. It rises to a unique climax in condemning the desecration of the **bones** of the king of another of Israel's enemies, **Edom.** Thus Amos is not a nationalist cursing his country's traditional enemies. Rather he is asserting Yahweh's judgment on any nation's cruelty, including sacrilege toward the dead.

Defilement of any tomb or corpse was looked on with horror in the ancient Near East. Many tomb and coffin inscriptions pronounce terrible curses on anyone disturbing their contents (cf. II Kings 23:16-20). Hence deliberately to burn royal bones for the purpose of making lime or plaster was unthinkable sacrilege. The occasion for this act may have been the ninth century war of Mesha king of Moab against the coalition of Israel, Judah, and Edom (II Kings 3:5-27). However, a more recent incident is more probable.

Moab was the fertile tableland east of the Dead Sea. It lay between Ammon on the north and Edom on the south. The Moabites were traditional relatives of Israel (cf. Genesis 19:30-38). Poor relations between Israelites and Moabites, however, continued from the days of the Israelite conquest and resulted in a lack of close relations between these peoples. **Kerioth** was a fortified city of Moab, perhaps the capital in Amos' day. According to archaeological evidence Moab was already declining in this period. It was taken captive by Tiglath-pileser III in 733, and from the sixth century on, it was practically no more.

2:4-5. *On Judah.* The seventh oracle of judgment is against Amos' own homeland. Most scholars regard it as a later addition to the book. Its brief form is exactly like that of the questionable oracles on Tyre and Edom (1:9-12). Its condemnation is in generalities. Its language is akin to that of Deuteronomy and later prophets. Perhaps Amos' denunciation of Israel in the following oracle (verses 6-16) and the rest of the book includes both the northern and the southern kingdoms—**the whole family** of Yahweh's chosen people (3:1). Judah is specifically referred to only here and four other times (1:1-2; 6:1; 7:12; 9:11).

If the passage comes from Amos, the **law of the LORD** probably means the teaching of God's word spoken by the prophets rather than any written law, though the Covenant Code (Exodus 20:23–23:19) may have been in written form long before Amos' day. The perverting **lies** are probably the deceitful ways of idols or false gods.

B. ORACLE ON ISRAEL (2:6-16)

If the people heard Amos' first oracles with either self-righteous gloating or belief that divine retribution was coming upon those who deserved it, they must have become increasingly uncomfortable as his denunciations completely surrounded them. Now the thunder of God's judgment falls on them.

This oracle begins with the familiar pattern. Then in three successive stanzas Amos declares that:

(1) God's judgment will come upon people because of their cruel exploitation of their fellows and their profanation of true worship (verses 6-8).

(2) They have corrupted God's spiritual guides, showing ingratitude for what God has done for them (verses 9-12). Therefore none can escape the imminent doom of the nation of Israel (verses 13-16).

2:6-8. *Exploitation and Profanation.* As in the previous indictments of neighboring nations, cruelty is the chief sin. But with Israel it is not national crimes against other peoples. Within their own society the privileged have exploited the underprivileged. The victims are the **righteous**—the innocent and honest subjects whose rights have been taken away either in lawsuits or in economic deals. They are the **poor**, the **needy**, the **afflicted**, those who are helpless before their exploiters.

Though the poor owe no more than the price of a pair of cheap sandals, the exploiters foreclose mortgage or sell them into slavery (cf. 8:6). Figuratively—or perhaps literally—they brutally grind the head of the poor down into the ground. Or, according to another reading of the difficult text, they are so greedy that they pant after the dust which the poor throw on their heads in their mourning rites.

2:7cd. The charge that son and father resort to **the same maiden**—literally "the girl"—may refer either to secular prostitution or to mistreatment of a slave girl in the household. Most likely, however, it is Amos' way of condemning the practice of cult prostitution. In the nature cult of Baalism the reviving of vegetation after the autumnal rains accompanied the marriage of Baal, the resurrected god of vegetation, with his consort Asherah, who had rescued him from his temporary death in the underworld. Worshipers celebrated this season of hope by orgiastic relations with young men and women employees of the shrine. The female devotees were called literally "holy women." In bitterest sarcasm Amos declares that this supposed holiness of harlotry profanes God's holy name. The **house of their God** may mean a Baal shrine. Or it may mean a shrine where misguided Israelites worship Yahweh with the pagan rites of Baalism.

2:8. Amos goes on to declare that exploitation take place not only in the places of business and law. It is a rot at the core of the religious life. In their shrine revelries **beside every altar** they recline on **garments** the poor have had to pawn (cf. Exodus 22:26-27). The wine they drink has been paid for by taxes, perhaps shrine taxes, laid on the underprivileged.

2:9-12. *God's Revelation Corrupted.* In sharp contrast to what Israel is now doing is what God has done to guard and guide the people. In the past God cleared the holy land for them. The **Amorite** was the pre-Israelite population of Canaan traditionally regarded as giant in stature and strength (cf. Numbers 13:32-33; Deuteronomy 1:28). Yet not just the hearers' ancestors, but they themselves—**you**—receive God's redemption from Egyptian slavery and God's wilderness guidance.

2:11-12. The **prophets** and **Nazirites** are God's gifts as continuing spiritual guides. From the days of Moses on, prophets had been God's spokesmen to reveal divine instructions (cf. Deuteronomy 18:15-22). Nazirites were sacred persons, either consecrated by their parents or self-dedicated, who vowed to live the simple life—letting their hair grow and abstaining from wine, strong drink, unclean food, and contact with the dead (Numbers 6:1-21; Judges 13:2-7). Their loyalty to their vows contrasted sharply with the indulgence of paganized Israel's religious life. Instead of being grateful for God's provisions for the people's welfare, Israel corrupts the very means for spiritual preservation. They make the Nazirites forget their vows and silence the prophets.

2:13-16. *The Judgment of Inescapable Disaster.* The deep hurt in God's heart at the rebellion of the people, may be the point of verse 13a. The difficult Hebrew seems to say literally "I

am pressed under you." Most commentators, however,
interpret it as meaning the inescapable pressure of God's awful
judgment on Israel. Not only will the nation as a whole perish.
Its skilled defenders—the **mighty** and **swift** infantry and
cavalry—will be unable to save even themselves as they strip for
fast flight. **In that day** refers to the "day of Yahweh" (cf. 5:18-20).
The concluding expression, **says the LORD,**—literally "the
utterance [or oracle] of Yahweh,"—is the solemn prophetic
declaration from God.

III. GOD'S TESTIMONIES AGAINST AND WOES UPON THE PEOPLE (3:1–6:14)

The bulk of the book seems to be composed of two series of
prophetic oracles. The first and longest series (3:1–5:17)
proclaims God's thrice repeated testimony against the people:
Hear this word . . . (3:1; 4:1; 5:1). The second (5:18–6:14), much
shorter, is a series of "woes" upon the people (5:18; 6:1; perhaps
6:4). While this is apparently the general structure of these
chapters, it is difficult to find either chronological or logical
thought structure running through the book. Perhaps an editor
has collected Amos' oracles in this general fashion.

A. FIRST TESTIMONY (3:1-15)

Amos' prediction of Israel's imminent doom at once raises
inevitable questions. The country is enjoying unprecedented
prosperity under Jeroboam II. Contrary to the prophet's dour
pessimism, are not God's people reaping the material rewards of
their favored position as the chosen ones? In a series of
testimonies spoken in the name of Yahweh, Amos deals with the
meaning of Israel's unique relationship to God and the reasons
for discerning the signs of disaster.

3:1-2. *Privilege and Responsibility.* The doctrine of Israel's
election as God's own people stems from the tradition of God's

miraculous deliverance of the whole people from Egypt. While Yahweh directs the course of history of all earth's **families** (cf. 9:7) God says to Israel, **You only have I known.** The word "know" here carries any or all of the following meanings: "recognize as covenant people" (cf. Deuteronomy 9:24; Hosea 13:4-5); "experience intimately" as in the closeness of married love (cf. Genesis 4:1); "care for" or "be concerned about" (cf. Isaiah 1:3); and "choose" or "elect" (cf. Genesis 18:19).

Yahweh's choice of the covenant people at Mt. Sinai and Yahweh's subsequent favors have led to a sadly erroneous popular conclusion. Israel believes that as God's darling nation they are enjoying the rewards of favoritism. Amos starts with the same premise that Israel is God's elect nation. But his conclusion is radically different. Such high privilege carries corresponding responsibility for obedience. Israel's multiplied **iniquities**—its guilty and intentional acts of perversity—mark it for the severe punishment which such sin entails.

3:3-8. *Prophetic Certainty, Authority, and Warning.* How does Amos know that punishment is near? By what authority does he speak? Amos replies to such implied questions in the poetic form of the wisdom writers' rhetorical questions (verses 3-6, 8; verse 7 seems to be prose; cf. Proverbs 6:27-28).

3:3-6. Amos' argument begins with a transitional question (verse 3). This perhaps carrying a double meaning: Do not two people seen walking together have at least something in common; have not Israel and its God had a close relationship through the years? The following questions imply both disaster and the fact that an effect has it cause. The lion's roar on sensing the nearness of prey is followed by the cub's growl of satisfaction in eating the kill. The bird's swooping down to the lure of bait is followed by the snap of the trap. The city dweller feels the chill of terror at the blast announcing the approach of an invading enemy.

Amos has cast these questions in the meter of a funeral dirge (see below on 5:1-3). The catastrophe they anticipate comes, not by chance, but as divine discipline and judgment. It is the inescapable result of sin.

3:7-8. It may be a later commentator who adds the prose

statement in verse 7. This states that Amos' message is an example of God's unfailing procedure of revelation. As God's chosen spokesmen the **prophets** can listen in on the **secret** heavenly council planning sessions. The true prophet hears God's lion roar (cf. 1:2). Even though he may be unwilling, by irresistible divine compulsion he must speak (cf. 7:15; Jeremiah 1:6-10; 20:9). This is Amos' authority for warning his people before it is too late.

3:9-12. *Witnesses to Confusion and Destruction.* Using figurative speech Amos calls on the **strongholds** (citadel fortresses), of Israel's enemies to gather round its capital to witness the utter confusion and destruction. The Septuagint has **Assyria** as the normal parallel to **Egypt,** but the Hebrew text reads "Ashdod," a Philistine city. Amos nowhere else mentions Assyria by name, and it would seem strange that an original "Assyria" would have been erroneously changed to "Ashdod." Perhaps here in bitter irony Amos is calling on Israel's past traditional enemies, Philistia and Egypt, to be public observers of God's privileged people's confusion.

3:9c-10. Israel's capital was **Samaria,** the strong-walled hilltop political center originally established by Omri in the ninth century. The city was easily seen from surrounding mountaintops. The **tumults** in its life are the **oppressions** of the poor by unscrupulous exploiters who have gained their wealth by **violence and robbery.** Conscience has been killed. They simply **do not know how to do right**—that is, what is straightforward and honest.

3:11-12. The resulting doom will be siege and conquest by an invading foreign army. Amos is probably speaking before Assyria's first march west under Tiglath-pileser III in 743, but he anticipates the final blow which destroyed Samaria in 722. Using probably a typical shepherd's proverb in verse 12, he describes the scraps left from the invading lion's meal. A hired shepherd might show such bits to his employer to prove that he is not legally liable for what has been killed by a wild beast (cf. Exodus 22:10-13). Amos predicts total destruction (cf. 9:1). What will be left will be only the shreds of former finery, a

corner of a broken **couch** and **part** of a ruined **bed.** The Hebrew word translated "part," apparently related to "Damascus," may refer to inlay work or damask silk cushions.

3:13-15. *Punishment on Sanctuary and Mansion.* The climactic oracle of this first testimony predicts destruction of the religious sanctuaries which presumably provide national security, together with the symbols of material prosperity.

3:13-14. The Lord Yahweh, the **God of hosts** (armies) is speaking. Amos never speaks of Yahweh as "God of Israel" but rather as universal sovereign. Yahweh is Lord not merely of the armies of Israel but of the heavenly armies governing the whole world and composing the divine council (cf. verse 7). Perhaps the divine council is addressed in this oracle, which details events of the judgment on Israel announced previously (2:6-8, 13-16).

Israel is spoken of as the **house of Jacob** because of the patriarch's sacred association with **Bethel,** the northern kingdom's rival sanctuary to Jerusalem (cf. 7:13). **The horns of the altar** may refer to the bull images set up at Bethel by Jeroboam I. That altars had corner projections in the shape of the horns of the bull, symbol of fertility and power, is attested by archaeology. These could be graspd by a fugitive seeking refuge from revenge (I Kings 1:50-51; 2:28). Amos' point is that the symbols of sacred security will provide no refuge from God's awful punishment (cf. 9:1).

3:15. Neither will wealthy material comforts be of any help. The **winter house** was occasionally heated in the cold rainy season of late autumn and winter. The **summer house** was either an upper story open to cool breezes in the hot, dry harvest season or a separate dwelling high on a hill. As verified by beautifully carved idols found by archeologists at Megiddo and Samaria, **houses of ivory** refers to ivory inlays used in furniture and decorated paneling in the homes of the wealthy.

B. Second Testimony (4:1-13)

4:1-3. *Punishment of Corrupt Women.* The second series of oracles beginning **Hear this word** (cf. 3:1; 5:1) opens with a summons to Israel's women. They are sarcastically called **cows of Bashan**—perhaps a proverbial term for the sleek, fat cattle of this fertile tableland east of the Sea of Galilee. While women were occasionally involved in business dealings and thus could be heartless exploiters, Amos pictures fine ladies of **Samaria** as continuously nagging their **husbands,** literally "lords," into exploitation to keep the endless round of feasts going.

4:2-3. Amos uses a play on the word "lord." He declares to these ladies with their "lords" that the real "Lord" Yahweh has vowed the most awful vow possible, by Yahweh's own nature as God. He has vowed that they will find themselves in a procession of captives going out through the breached wall of the city, caught like helpless fish, with **hooks** piercing their lips. The Hebrew expression translated **into Harmon** appears nowhere else. It may be a misspelling of "naked" or "onto the dung heap" or "to Rimmon," a hill east of Bethel where there were many caves and also one of the names for the god Baal.

4:4-5. *The Rebellion of Worship.* In lyrical poetry and with biting sarcasm Amos invites everyone to come to the two chief sanctuaries of Israel and carry on their accustomed sacrificial rituals. But to do so, he says, is not to worship God. It is rather to **multiply** rebellion against God.

On **Bethel** see above on 3:13-14. **Gilgal,** meaning "circle of stones," was possibly a site in the highland north of Bethel. More likely it was the community near Jericho, famous as first encampment of the incoming Israelites under Joshua and important site in the era of Saul (cf. Joshua 4:19-20; I Samuel 11:14-15). It was denounced by eighth century prophets as a onetime holy sanctuary which had become a center of paganized sacrificial cult rites (cf. 5:5; Hosea 4:15; 9:15; 12:11).

In this, his first condemnation of the sacrificial system (cf. 5:21-25), Amos satirizes the elaborate piling up of sacrifices. They are merely public show and a gratification of selfish pleasures in festival merriment—**for so** they **love to do.** His detailed references to the types and frequency of the sacrifices, while not absolutely certain in meaning, may ironically exaggerate popular overzealousness.

Sacrifices were animals slaughtered and eaten in a festival meal with God, priests, and worshipers all participating. Such an occasion would take place no more than three times a year for any worshiper, as it involved making a pilgrimage to the sanctuary.

Tithes, according to the Deuteronomic legislation, were the required annual offering of a tenth of the yield of agricultural products (cf. Deuteronomy 14:22-29). Each year they involved a shared festival meal, and every third year they were to be shared with the landless Levite, sojourner, fatherless, and widow.

Leaven, which produces fermentation, was prescribed in certain late laws for "peace offerings for thanksgiving" to be eaten in convivial meals (Leviticus 7:13). But the older laws clearly prohibited leaven in any sacrifice to Yahweh (Exodus 23:18; 34:25; Leviticus 2:11; 6:17). Amos may mean that the **sacrifice of thanksgiving of that which is leavened** is typical of the participants' concentration on festival enjoyment when they are supposedly to be offering thanksgiving to God.

Freewill offerings, never required by any law, should be the voluntary expression of the worshipers' response to God. But what is the motivation of those who **proclaim** and **publish** such gifts? Cf. Matthew 6:1-16.

4:6-12. *Chastising Experience Unheeded.* This poem was perhaps a ritual utterance at the Bethel sanctuary. Each strophe begins with a declaration of what God has done or will do **to you, O Israel** and ends with the refrain **yet you did not return to me.** God expresses mingled sorrow and judgment that the chosen people have paid no attention to repeated chastisements, which should have caused them to repent. **Therefore,** the conclusion is, . . . **prepare to meet your God, O Israel!** The very indefiniteness is frighteningly vivid. The five specific disasters cannot be identified with any known historical calamities.

4:6. The phrase **cleanness of teeth**—because of no **bread** to put between them—is a striking figure of speech for famine.

4:7-8. A popular belief was that the Canaanite god Baal is the fertility deity responsible for rain and hence abundant crops. On the contrary, it is Yahweh, the controller of nature, who occasionally has delayed the heavy November rains until February so that the farmer has no harvest in April, May, and June. Or God has sent sporadic rains, so that some communities have gone to others' cisterns to get a bit of precious water.

4:9. Complete agricultural failures have been due to **blight** caused by the scorching east wind (cf. Genesis 41:6), the yellowing of crops from **mildew,** and a **locust** plague (cf. Joel 1:4-18).

4:10. The expression **pestilence after the manner of Egypt** may be proverbial for diseases as terrible as the famous plagues before the Exodus (Exodus 7:14–11:10). But the scene here is the tragedy of war, with the youth of the nation slain, the **stench** of unburied corpses, and the capture of cavalry, which the prophets often used as a symbol of pride (cf. 2:15).

4:11. The **brand plucked out of the burning** when God **overthrew some of you** expresses the miracle of anything's having been saved. The diaster is compared to the destruction of **Sodom and Gomorrah,** presumably by earthquake and resultant ignition of released sulphurous gases, asphalt, and petroleum (Genesis 19:24-25).

4:13. *First Doxology.* Concluding the oracle is an exalted description of the God whom Israel is to encounter. This is the first of three "doxologies" (cf. 5:8-9; 9:5-6). Most commentators regard these as additions to Amos. They are written in the language and thought forms of later prophets or wisdom writers (cf. Job 38:4-21; Proverbs 8:22-26; Isaiah 40:28; 45:7-8; 58:14). Some think they may be fragments of an earlier hymn adapted for use in prophetic liturgy. They eloquently characterize the majesty of God. God is the creator of all the universe, whose **thought** is revealed, perhaps through the prophets (cf. 3:7) or through the created world (cf. Psalm 19:1-4). God turns **morning** light into the **darkness** of eclipse or storm.

There may be double meaning in God's treading **on the heights of the earth** (cf. Micah 1:3-4). God, whose mighty steps stride over the mountaintops, can also trample into the ground the "high places" the sanctuaries, of the nature god Baal. The LORD is **God of hosts,**—that is, of all heavenly powers (see above on 3:13-14). This is God's **name**—that is, God's nature and being.

C. THIRD TESTIMONY (5:1-17)

5:1-3. *Virgin Israel's Death*. The third of God's testimonies against the people opens with a funeral dirge over the death of the nation. Perhaps Amos appears in mourning clothes and, accompanied by a musical instrument, sings his elegy in the limping dirge meter of three beats followed by two (verse 2). Cast in the Hebrew prophetic perfect tense, the imminent future event of the nation's death is portrayed as already having happened. The prophet figuratively gazes on the **virgin** corpse lying **on her land,** literally "ground." He speaks realistically in verse 3. In the coming invasion which is God's judgment 90 percent of the Israelite warriors who go into battle from **city** or village (**hundred**) will come out corpses.

5:4-7. *Two Calls to Seek and Live*. Death and life —these are the choice which Israel yet has. Amos is convinced that Israel is practically dead because of its sins. Yet three times (verses 4, 6, 14) he holds out hope for life—a survival possible only if Israel will "seek" the right object.

5:4-5. First God calls, **seek me and live. Do not seek** the traditional sanctuaries, which are doomed. To "seek" God usually means to come to worship at one of God's shrines. But Amos seems to counsel direct encounter with God, getting into right relationship through obedience. Here he uses an ironic play on words. The name **Bethel** (see above on 3:13-14) was also that of a Semitic deity well attested through archaeology (cf. Genesis 31:13; Jeremiah 48:13). Beth-el, "house of God," will become Beth-aven, "house of **nought**"—that is, idolatry or wickedness (cf. Hosea 4:15; 5:8; 10:5, 8). Playing on the sound of the name of the other famous northern sanctuary, **Gilgal** (see above on 4:4-5), Amos declares that "Gilgal shall go into galling captivity" (American Translation, Smith and Goodspeed).

Beer-sheba was a sanctuary twenty-eight miles southwest of

Hebron associated with the patriarchs Abraham and Isaac. To **cross over to** Beer-sheba would be to travel to the traditional southern boundary of the entire land of God's people (cf. 8:14).

5:6. The second summons warns that God's judgment will be a miraculous **fire** (cf. 1:4, 7, 10, 12, 14; 2:2, 5; 7:4). No rain magic of the cult at **Bethel** can **quench** it. The northern kingdom is called the **house of Joseph** because of the importance of the traditional tribal territory of Joseph's sons Manasseh and Ephraim.

5:7. Perhaps the preceding call to seek Yahweh is addressed to **you who turn justice to wormwood.** But the Hebrew is not in the second person. Some interpreters emend it to read "Woe to those who turn . . ." (cf. verse 18 and 6:1) and transpose it to form the beginning of verse 10. Amos never defines **justice** and **righteousness.** He speaks only of their perversion or absence. He seems to use these terms in the sense of the law court and the right or rights of the Israelite citizen. Such righteousness is based on the covenant relationship between Israel and its God, though Amos never uses the word "covenant." He does not need to define righteousness, the well-known duty at the center of Israelite life. He simply deplores its being turned to **wormwood,** an exceptionally bitter-tasting plant (cf. 6:12).

5:8-9. *Second Doxology.* See above on 4:13. As creator and sustainer of all nature, God set in the heavens the constellations, **the Pleiades** and **Orion** (cf. Job 9:9; 38:31). God provides dawn and dusk and the rain cycle (cf. Job 36:27-30). The God who controls all nature also controls human destiny, and so may destroy mere human strength. Some have emended certain difficult Hebrew words in verse 9 to names of other constellations.

5:10-13. *Exploitation of the Poor.* The beginning of verse 10 may be in verse 7 (see above). Exploiters despise those who protest against their injustices **in the gate**—the civic center where the elders and judges held court. But they know that these defenders of the exploited speak the **truth.** The shift to second person in verse 11 may indicate the beginning of a separate oracle. To the previous charges of exploitation (2:6-7)

Amos here adds **exactions,** or extortions, in the grain market and the **bribe** in the law court. He warns that the profiteers will never enjoy the security and luxury of their houses built of expensive **hewn stone.**

5:13. Many interpreters have taken this to be a reader's marginal comment copied into the text. However, the meaning is probably that in the coming **evil time** of God's judgment, the one who has manipulated God and their fellows to their own advantage will find they have not been "successful" (rather than **prudent**). Then they will be shocked into stunned silence.

5:14-15. *Third Call to Seek and Live.* In his final plea for right seeking Amos by implication defines what it means to seek Yahweh (verses 4*b*, 6*a*). It is to **seek good,** to respond in obedience to God. In dealing with people God has shown goodness (cf. 2:9-10) and care for the poor and the afflicted (cf. verses 11-12; 2:7; 4:1). God's people's primary concern must therefore be to seach for **good** rather than evil. These general Hebrew terms refer to the whole range of moral and spiritual possibilities. Here good is pinned down to specific acts of **justice in the gate**—that is, fair dealings in the law court. But it must go deeper. It must be the inner motivation of life. God's people must not simply do good acts and refrain from evil ones. They must **hate evil, and love good.**

Only by such transformation of inner character will it be possible that in the coming judgment a **remnant** will be left by God's grace. This is no doctrine of a righteous remnant. It only expresses the slight chance that there will be some survivors in the coming holocaust (cf. verse 3). Possibly, however, **remnant of Joseph** here means all Israel, viewed as relatively small and unimpressive even in these prosperous days (cf. "he is so small," 7:2, 5). Thus does Amos deny the false illusions of those who proclaim that Israel's present prosperity is evidence of God's presence with them (verse 14*cd*).

5:16-17. *Mourning Rites at Israel's Death.* In this climax of his third series of oracles of God's testimony against the people Amos returns to the funeral dirge meter with which he began it (see above on verses 1-3). In the doom to come, mourning will be heard among all classes of society—both city dwellers in their **squares** (open places for public gatherings) and **farmers** in their fields and usually joyful **vineyards.**

Those **skilled in lamentation** means professional mourners hired for the funeral of any citizen of rank. Possibly it may refer to Baal cult weepers whose wails now fail to bring the dead god of vegetation back to life. As in the covenant ritual of passing between the pieces of the sacrificial animals—symbolizing the death of those who fail to keep the covenant (cf. Genesis 15:7-17; Jeremiah 34:18-20)—and as in the final plague in Egypt (cf. Exodus 12:12-30), Yahweh will now **pass through the midst of you,** in deadly pestilence or in devastating war.

D. FIRST WOE (5:18-27)

As the book is now organized, Amos' series of testimonies against God's people (3:1–5:17) is followed by a climactic pronouncement of woes (5:18–6:14). These depict God's imminent coming as a day of destroying judgment.

5:18-20. *The Day of Yahweh.* In the first woe Amos turns expected joy into lamentation—**light** into **darkness.** This is one of his most important contributions to Israelite prophecy, his reversal of the popular conception of the coming day of Yahweh. He never defines this term, which shows that he is referring to a widely understood concept current in his time. Perhaps it was originally used for an annual celebration of the new year. If such a festival in Israel resembled the well-known Babylonian new year ceremonies, the ritual included re-enthronement of the king, ceremonial victory over all enemies, renewal of the promise of prosperity, and the prediction of fates for the year to come. This day of the glorious coming of Yahweh to bless the people for another year may have suggested the idea of a great day of God's coming to inaugurate a permanent era of bliss.

It is this expectation, supposedly assured by the cultic sacrifices, on which Amos pronounces his first resounding **Woe!** Far from being security for a fugitive from a **lion** and a **bear,** this

59

house of Israel's improper piety contains a hidden venomous **serpent.** There will be no shred of **brightness** in that day. Yahweh will come, not in reward, but in punishing judgment (cf. 8:9-14; Isaiah 2:9-21; Zephaniah 1:7-18).

5:21-27. *The Sacrilege of Sacrifice.* In the most vigorous passage in his book Amos hears Yahweh condemn a cult which assumes that rites without righteousness will continue to buy divine favor (cf. 4:4-5). God despises the **feasts**—that is, the three annual pilgrimage festivals hallowed by law and custom (cf. Exodus 23:14-17). God will **take no delight in** (literally "refuse to smell") the clouds of incense from the **solemn assemblies,** really convivial ceremonies. **Burnt offerings** were the most expensive type. The whole animal was consumed on the altar, leaving nothing as food for the worshiper or payment for the priest. Since verse 22*a* is metrically overlong, this type of sacrifice may be a later insertion.

Cereal offerings were of grain. **Peace offerings** of specially fattened animals were meant to keep amicable relations with the deity. Both were samples of the food eaten by the worshipers in the communion meals. The accompanying **noise of your songs** and **melody of your harps** were the ancient equivalents of our choral anthems, congregational hymns, and organ voluntaries. Surely God does not refuse to **listen** to the sacred worship of his pious people! Indeed yes, declares Amos, because even the most elaborate and devout ritual has no worth in itself. It may be mere religiosity which, however fervent, misinterprets the nature of both God and the covenant relation with men and women.

5:24. Some interpreters see the **justice** and **righteousness** of this key verse as God's deliverance. God will eventually send down saving powers, now delayed by the people's unresponsive preoccupation with their selfishly noisy festivities. Others take them to mean God's awful destroying judgment, not simply in one day of wrath, but in continuing divine "righteous" acts, as powerful and relentless as a **stream** which flows even through the dry season. Perhaps the traditional interpretation is correct. Amos here affirms that the loyalty of God's people is shown, not in elaborate ceremony, but in steady justice in human relationships and righteousness in obedience to God's will (cf. Isaiah 1:10-17).

5:25. It is no new commandment, no new ethical standard that Amos is lifting up. Rather it is a recall to the heart of the covenant, the faith of the fathers in the period of the desert wandering under Moses. Amos, along with other prophets, may have believed that the period under Moses was really a cultless age (cf. Jeremiah 7:21-23). In any case he was convinced that ritual was not necessary, perhaps not really commanded, in that unique time of God's gracious care for people.

5:26-27. These verses may be a later addition to the book. Now, says Amos, cult idols of **Sakkuth** and **Kaiwan,** are carried in syncretistic cult festivals. These were Mesopotamian star deities associated with the planet Saturn. They are carried along in sacred procession, doubtless as lesser gods in Yahweh's train (cf. 8:14). But another sort of procession is forming, to go into **exile beyond Damascus.** If this is Amos' word, and if the Hebrew text of 3:9 is correct (see comment), this is the closest he comes to identifying Assyria as the conqueror he foresees (cf. 3:11-12; 4:2-3; 6:7, 14; 7:11, 17).

E. SECOND WOE (6:1-14)

This second and final woe castigates the proud leaders of all Israel for their false sense of security (verses 1-3) and callous self-indulgence (verses 4-6). It declares that these "first citizens" will become the first of the many to suffer and be carried off into exile (verses 7-14).

6:1-3. *False Security.* Amos here apparently pronounces woe on the leaders of both Israel and Judah—though many have suspected that **Zion,** meaning Jerusalem, is a later insertion. All the **house of Israel** come to these **notable men** in their role as judges. In their eyes Israel as God's chosen is **first of the nations.**

6:2. But how does Israel compare with neighboring **kingdoms?** Probably **Calneh** here refers to a northern Syrian city-state called Calno in Isaiah 10:9. **Hamath the great** was an important city located on the Orontes River. In Amos' day it was the capital of a Syrian kingdom bordering on Israel's northern frontier (cf. verse 14; II Kings 14:25). **Gath** was one of the five Philistine city-states west of Judah. The Hebrew text is somewhat ambiguous here. The expected answer to the question seems to be that none of the nations named compares with Israel in the size of its **territory.** The meaning therefore may be that since Israel is the largest and most prosperous of the states of Syria-Palestine, its leaders have so much the more obligation to be responsible.

The more common interpretation, however, is that these three are cited as examples of kingdoms already destroyed by Assyria. Accordingly, the verse is a warning addressed to Judah by a later prophet which was erroneously inserted into Amos' work. Assyrian records indicate that Calneh was captured around 738 and Hamath and Gath in 711. In Amos' day they had been free from Assyrian attack for nearly a century.

6:3. This verse is addressed to the complacent leaders of verse 1. They refuse to acknowledge the coming of the **evil day** of God's wrath, and in their law courts they render judgments of **violence** rather than justice.

6:4-6. *Irresponsible Indulgence.* The prophet's curse on these leaders continues with an unforgettable picture of self-indulgence. Those who should be Israel's leaders **are not grieved over the ruin of Joseph**—that is, they show no concern over the imminent disaster about to befall their land. Instead they sprawl on luxurious **couches** inlaid with **ivory** (see above on 3:15). They feast on specially fattened lamb and veal (cf. 5:22). They sing drinking songs as they sip their wine from large sacrificial bowls rather than ordinary cups. They apply expensive oil cosmetics to their bodies. **Like David** is not in the Septuagint text. It makes the line metrically too long and may be a marginal comment copied into the text.

6:7-14. *The Final Doom.* These irresponsible leaders will indeed lead when they head the line of those going into **exile.** Their **revelry** will be suddenly ended. The oath of Yahweh is

sworn by himself and nothing is more powerful in the universe. It expresses God's abhorrence of the deceitful people's **pride** (cf. 8:7) and their human achievements such as their military **strongholds.** But no human power can now avert the destruction of their **city**—probably meaning Samaria.

6:9-10. Pestilence will follow war and wipe out all of a household together. One survivor, huddled in the corner of an inner room of a large house, sees the nearest kin come in to find the corpses, to **burn** them in hope of stopping the plague—or, less likely, to burn spices in funeral rites. The terror-stricken survivor will beg that the name of Yahweh not even be whispered lest Yahweh's fury break forth anew.

6:11. The destruction of palace and hovel described in this verse may be caused by earthquake. Or it may result from the razing which archaeology has shown to have been common in ancient warfare.

6:12-13. Israel's tragic conduct is unnatural. Its poisonous pattern of injustice (cf. 5:7) is as futile as trying to race **horses** on a stony cliff or **plow the sea** like farmland. Israel's pride is silly. As examples Amos refers sarcastically to the boasting over Jeroboam II's recapture from Syria of two small cities in Gilead: **Lo-debar** (actually Debir), meaning a "thing of nought," and **Karnaim** (actually Ashteroth-karnaim), meaning "two horns," symbols of **strength** and also of the Canaanite fertility goddess Ashteroth.

6:14. In contrast to such unnatural human pride let Israel look up, for it will see Yahweh coming. This is the emphasis of the Hebrew text. Yahweh will cause oppression by a foreign conqueror which will spread to the farthest ideal boundaries of the chosen people's land. The **entrance of Hamath** was a pass in the valley between the Lebanon and Antilebanon ranges which marked the southern boundary of the territory controlled by Hamath (cf. verse 2).

The **Arabah** was the deep Galilee-Jordan-Dead Sea valley and its continuation south to the Gulf of Aqaba. However, the meaning of the **brook of the Arabah** is uncertain. Perhaps "brook" should read "Sea," as in II Kings 14:25—that is, Amos is ironically quoting Jeroboam II's boast of having enlarged the border of his kingdom to the Dead Sea in the south. On the other hand perhaps II Kings 14:25 should read "brook," meaning the Zered. This flows into the Dead Sea at the southeast corner and marked the southern boundary of Moab, which Jeroboam may have reconquered for Israel. Other interpreters, however, understand this verse as describing the ideal boundaries of all Israel, Israel and Judah together. They therefore make "brook of the Arabah" equivalent to "brook of Egypt" in I Kings 8:65, a stream about sixty miles southwest of Beer-sheba.

IV. Visions and Final Dialogues (7:1–9:8b)

The third section of the book contains a remarkable series of five visions (7:1-9; 8:1-3; 9:1-4). Biography is interspersed in 7:10-17. The concluding oracles of the prophet are given in 8:4-14; and 9:5-8. Many interpreters regard the visions as Amos' account of the experiences which constituted his call to become a prophet (cf. Isaiah 6; Jeremiah 1; Ezekiel 1–3). They therefore assume that these should be read as a prelude to the oracles of the preceding sections of the book. However, in the one clearly biographical section of the book (7:10-17) Amos indicates that he does not regard himself as officially a prophet—despite the fact that God has called him from his daily work to prophesy. It is impossible to say definitively whether the visions describe Amos' call or a succession of experiences during his prophetic ministry.

A. Three Visions and a Biographical Episode (7:1-17)

When God causes Amos to see first the locusts and then the fire, the immediate plea is heeded, and God does not let his people be destroyed (7:1-6). But when Amos is shown the plumb line of judgment against the wall of the nation (7:7-9), he makes no reply. There follows the account of his encounter with Amaziah, the priest of King Jeroboam's sanctuary at Bethel (7:10-17). It cannot be determined whether the third vision was actually closely followed by Amos' encounter and expulsion from Bethel, or whether the sequence in the book is simply editorial, based on the successive references to calamity to befall Jeroboam (verses 9, 11).

7:1-3. *First Vision: Locust Plague.* A scourge of locusts may seem only a natural plague occasionally suffered in the Near East (cf. Joel 1–2). But Amos sees it as God's own warning (cf. 4:9). Possibly the **king's mowings** were the harvesting of the first crop of grass after the autumnal rains, much of which went for taxes. Thus before the spring crop can develop, the locusts are devouring everything, so that the poor man will have nothing.

Verse 2a probably should be emended to read "When they were about to finish. . . ." Amos' plea is not that the locust plague is unjust but simply that God **forgive** the people. **The LORD repented** is the Hebrew way of saying that God's mercy exceeds divine justice. Therefore God's mind may be changed by Amos' intercession.

7:4-6. *Second Vision: Supernatural Fire.* Probably the natural cause of this judgment is drought caused by the scorching summer sun (cf. 4:7; Joel 1:19-20). But this is no ordinary burning heat. Rather it is supernatural fire which devours even the subterranean **deep**, on which the earth rests, and which flows forth in springs and rivers. Hence Amos cries, not "Forgive!" but **Cease!** And, marvelous to relate, God does.

7:7-9. *Third Vision: The Plumb Line.* Amos now sees the LORD **standing beside a wall.** But Amos' eye is not on God but on the plumb line God holds. Seen against this cord with its weight at the end, Israel, God's wall, is obviously so out of perpendicular that it must fall. God's patience is now at an end. There is no chance that God will **again pass by** in forgiveness. Doom will fall on the **high places** (hilltop shrines) **of Isaac**—possibly a reference to religious centers such as Beer-sheba, traditionally associated with Isaac (cf. 5:5). The

65

proud nation will die with the death of the royal dynasty (cf. verses 11, 17; Hosea 1:4).

7:10-17. *Encounter with the Priest of Bethel.* The high priest at the royal religious center reports to King Jeroboam II that Amos is a traitor. **Amaziah** is mentioned only here in the biblical text. Perhaps he fears that Amos has magical power by which his prediction in verse 11 will actually be brought about. Hence **the land is not able to bear all his words,** and Amos must be banished. In his order of expulsion Amaziah declares that Amos may **eat bread**—that is, earn his living—in rival Judah, perhaps at a sanctuary there. But no longer may he speak at Israel's holy **temple** at **Bethel** (see above on 3:13-14).

7:14-15. Amos' reply makes this scene one of the most vivid and important in all Old Testament prophetic books. But the interpretation of Amos' statement about himself varies widely among the scholars. In the Hebrew one can read here either **I am** or "I was." Accordingly some hold that Amos refers to the past, stating that he was not a prophet until called by Yahweh. But the more normal reading is a reference to the present.

Probably Amos recognizes that by **seer** Amaziah refers contemptuously to the well-known court or temple prophet who may profiteer from his profession. Amos declares that he is neither such a prophet nor a member of one of the organized prophetic orders. With high regard for the function of being Yahweh's prophet (cf. 2:11-12; 3:7-8), Amos simply testifies to God's inescapable call. It came to him when as a shepherd he was watching his flocks and herds. His second occupation was in the lowlands where the sycamore-fig trees grow. His job there was to puncture the unripe fruit to make it edible and therefore salable.

7:16-17. Far from recanting, Amos repeats his refusal to be silenced either by officials or by popular demand (cf. 2:12). He predicts details of the imminent disaster. The high priest's own **wife** will be openly ravished by invading soldiers, or perhaps become a prostitute for economic survival. The holy **land** of Yahweh's presence will be sold in **parceled** lots rather than inherited as a united trust. Yahweh's people will be exiled in a land that is **unclean** because it is under the sovereignty of a foreign god.

B. FOURTH VISION AND ANOTHER TESTIMONY (8:1-14)

8:1-3. *Fourth Vision: Summer Fruit*. This vision brings to a conclusion the movements seen in the preceding three. A springtime locust plague and midsummer drought are now followed by late summer's ripened fruit, perhaps figs. The announcement of God's exhausted patience in the plumb-line vision has now resulted in the sentence of doom: **the end has come.** In a play on words of similar sound (indicated in the Revised Standard Version footnote) and, more deeply, in the meaning of **summer fruit** as the last of the harvest Amos sees the end at hand.

There is irony here. In the popular view the harvest of summer fruit at the end of the long dry season is the moment when God's people anticipate the autumn rains with their promise of renewal. Not so, declares Amos. This is not the end of a season but the end of Israel. **In that day** of God's awful judgment now at hand the **temple** or palace **songs** of joy will become howls of lamentation. The mass of corpses will be so stunning that all Israel will fall into a terrified hush (cf. 6:9-10).

8:4-14. *The Final Judgment Day*. In the language of God's previous testimonies against the people—**Hear this** (cf. 3:1; 4:1; 5:1)—Amos now announces details of the awful judgment day ahead. But first he spells out in further detail the exploitation of their fellows which is Israel's rebellion against God and the reason for the coming doom (cf. 2:6-8).

8:4-6. The monthly religious festival of the **new moon** and the weekly **sabbath** require holy celebration. Everyday work must cease on these days. Ironically, the greedy exploiters reluctantly keep holy days and then hurry to cheat their customers. They do so by using faulty measurements—an undersize **ephah** to measure the product they are selling and an overweight **shekel**

67

to balance the customer's silver. They use untrue scales. They sell the sweepings of the **wheat** as good grain.

8:7-9. Yahweh **has sworn by the pride of Jacob** (cf. 4:2; 6:8). He has sworn that the very land producing the grain will suffer earthquake shock as irresistible as the well-known annual flooding of the **Nile** (cf. 9:5). Amos may be speaking figuratively here, or he may mean a real earthquake (cf. 1:1) and an eclipse of the sun such as took place in mid-June 763—a most frightening experience to ancient peoples.

8:10-14. The coming awful day of Yahweh is described in the language of the mourning rites for Baal, the dead god of vegetation. The expected joyous festival period will turn into bitterest **lamentation.** Wearing garments of goat's or camel's hair and shaving the head to produce artificial baldness were traditional mourning customs. Frenzied ritual searching, as in the cult rites for the dead vegetation deity, will be carried on to the very bounds of the earth. But God will be absent. God will send a **word** no more to the faithless people.

From **Dan** to **Beer-sheba** they have turned to false worship. In Dan, as in Bethel, stands an idolatrous bull image (cf. I Kings 12:28-30; Hosea 10:8). Swearing by the **way** or pilgrimage to the southern sanctuary of Beer-sheba may have been customary. More likely the patron deity of Beer-sheba is meant—a reading suggested by the Septuagint and a word with this meaning in the Moabite Stone. Even the capital city Samaria has its patron deity **Ashimah,** later described as imported by Assyrian colonists from Hamath (II Kings 17:30). In the face of such idolatry Yahweh now hides the divine word from the people. **They shall fall, and never rise again** (cf. 5:2).

C. The Fifth Vision (9:1-8b)

9:1. *Destruction of the Temple.* In the previous four visions Amos says, "God showed me." In this climactic one he announced, **I saw the Lord.** But there is no description of God. Perhaps as a mysterious huge human figure (cf. Exodus

33:21-23) God is now at the Bethel temple, standing "upon"—more likely than **beside**—its holy **altar.** The LORD commands one of the heavenly host to ruin the temple, from the column **capitals** holding up the roof to its foundations, until it comes crashing down on the heads of the worshipers. Thus the coming new year festival day of Yahweh ends in doom.

9:2-4. *The Fugitives.* What has been called the practical monotheism of Amos is seen here. Though fugitives from the final doom may flee to the remotest parts of the universe, there is no place where they can escape Yahweh's **hand** or **eyes.** The lower limit of the world is **Sheol,** the subterranean abode of the dead. Its upper limit is the overarching bowl of **heaven,** the sky. Mt. **Carmel** is the wooded, promontory jutting out into the Mediterranean. On the floor of the **sea** is the chained **serpent** (dragon) of creation, Leviathan, or Rahab. The lashing of its tail in its struggle to be free produces monstrous waves. Even as captives in a foreign land (cf. 7:17) the fugitives can expect no protection from the local patron deity.

9:5-6. *Third Doxology.* The inescapable power of the God of the universe is now underlined by this doxology (see above on 4:13). The mere touch of the Lord Yahweh's almighty hand causes the earth to undulate in earthquake waves like the annual Nile flooding (cf. 8:8). By the sound of Yahweh's voice the waters of the sea are drawn up and rained down on the land (cf. 5:8).

9:7-8b. *The Destroying Gaze of Yahweh.* The clearly genuine words of Amos come to a startling conclusion with two searching questions and a final assertion. Amos' hearers must have been pierced to the quick by his questions. Is their status as chosen people of no significance in Yahweh's eyes? Amos is not necessarily referring to the **Ethiopians** because of the color of their skin. He may be affirming that Israel's failure to be loyal to Yahweh (cf. 3:2) means that they are no better than a distant heathen nation.

As master of the destinies of all peoples (cf. 1:3–2:3) Yahweh brought Israel's enemies from their original homelands—the **Philistines** from their home in the sea, Crete and the Aegean area, and the **Syrians** from their former home in northern

Mesopotamia (see above on 1:4-5). Some interpreters hold that Amos' mention of God's care of these peoples suggests that at last, Yahweh's patience exhausted, Yahweh is about to choose a new people. Israel's enemies will replace faithless Israel. At least Amos means that Yahweh's own people by their faithlessness are now deprived of their privilege in God's sight. Hence the **sinful kingdom,** the object of God's devastating gaze, is now to be wiped off the face of the earth.

V. APPENDIX OF HOPE (9:8*c*-15)

Most scholars hesitate to assign the rest of the book, especially verses 11-15, to Amos himself. The contents are almost completely opposite to his clear message of impending doom with no hope (cf. especially 5:2; 8:14). Both in thought and in language this section seems much more likely to be from exilic or postexilic prophets than from Amos in mellowed maturity. The successive themes seem clear: a righteous remnant will survive exile (verses 9-10), David's empire will be restored (verses 11-12), and overflowing material blessings will follow (verses 13-15). The language occasionally turns Amos' own doom predictions to hope.

9:8*c* *An Exception to Doom*. This clause seems to be a deliberate prose addition to the preceding dirge meter. It is meant to soften the terrible blow, or to state that the southern kingdom, Judah, did survive Israel's fall in 722.

9:9-10. *The Righteous Remnant*. The figure of the **sieve** in which the Israel **among all the nations,** meaning in exile, is shaken apparently expresses the turbulence of the experience of captivity in which the sifting of the good from the bad takes place. Though violently tumbled about in God's sieve every **pebble**—every faithful one of the righteous remnant of Israel—will by God's grace be kept from falling to the ground and perishing. But not so, the **sinners of my people.** Some interpreters, however, take the pebbles to represent the sinners.

70

9:11-12. *Restoration of David's Empire.* With the destruction of Jerusalem in 586 David's once glorious "house" (cf. II Samuel 7) became a ruined **booth**, a mere cattleshed or vineyard watcher's hut. But now his empire will be restored to its ancient boundaries. It will embrace all nations **called by my name**—that is, "over whom my name is called" and so designated as "my property." Among these nations is **Edom**, now a mere **remnant**, perhaps because of Arab or Nabatean invasions.

9:13-15. *Blessings of a New Day.* In the golden age to come the famines and disasters of Amos' warnings (4:6-9; 5:11; 8:11) will be replaced by miraculous fertility. The abundance of the crop of grain in May will be such that harvesting will be incomplete at October plowing time. Grape gathering, always completed by October, will still be going on at November grain-planting time. The hills will seem to be melting with flowing **wine.** The final picture is of rebuilt cities, fruitful vineyards and gardens, and the security of being firmly planted in the land—**never again** to be **plucked up** and taken off to exile. This is the exact reversal of the fortunes predicted by Amos (cf. 4:6-9; 5:16-17; 7:17; 8:11-12).

THE BOOK OF OBADIAH

Roland E. Murphy, O. Carm.

INTRODUCTION

Authorship and Date

The Old Testament mentions a number of men named
Obadiah, which means "servant of Yahweh." None of these,
however, can be considered even a probable author of this book.
So we must gain our knowledge of the prophet entirely from his
book.

The book is primarily a denunciation of Edom, the land south
of the Dead Sea (see below on verses 2-4). The Edomites were
conquered by David (II Samuel 8:13-14; I Kings 11:15-17).
Later they continued under the dominion of the southern
kingdom of Judah. They are said to have been ruled by a
governor under Jehoshaphat (I Kings 22:47), though a story told
of this same period refers to a "king of Edom" (II Kings 3:9, 26).
Under the next king, Joram, they revolted (II Kings 8:20-22) and
gained their independence for about half a century. They were
reconquered by Judah under Amaziah and Azariah (II Kings
14:7, 22).

When they succeeded in another revolt against Ahaz (II Kings
16:6) it was merely to exchange masters. Edom soon became a
vassal of Assyria and later of Babylonia. At the destruction of
Jerusalem in 586 the Edomites aided the Babylonians and took

advantage of the opportunity to loot Judah. Under Arab pressure in their own land, they now found the way open to settle in southern Judah and seem to have occupied the area that later came to be known as Idumea. Hebron was their chief city. Archaeological exploration of Edom itself has revealed no trace of settled occupation during the Persian period. In the fourth century this territory came under the domination of an Arab people, the Nabateans. The Nabateans built a great trading empire that lasted through New Testament times.

Most scholars interpret verses 10-14 as referring to the conduct of the Edomites at the fall of Jerusalem in 586. The date of the book, then, falls in the period between 586 and the occupation of Edom by the Nabateans in the fourth century. The book locates the Edomites in their homeland and expresses a memory of their actions fresh enough for deep feeling. Therefore it is likely that the writing comes from early in this period—during the exile or at the beginning of the postexilic era.

Structure

The twenty-one verses make Obadiah the shortest book in the Old Testament. Nevertheless its unity is questioned. The denunciation of Edom is found in verses 1b-14 and 15bc. Verses 15a and 16-21 are a supplement, dealing with the day of Yahweh as a judgment on all the nations and with Israel's restoration. Some think these verses are an addition by a later author.

Relation to Other Books

The book appears in fourth place in the Book of the Twelve (the "Minor Prophets"), immediately after Amos. Perhaps it was placed there because of the mention of Edom at the end of Amos (9:12). Verses 1c-9 are paralleled in a variant form and different order in Jeremiah 49:7-22, and the relationship between the two passages has been much discussed. The present form of the text seems to show mutual influence of one on the other. Perhaps Obadiah is the prior work. Both may have drawn on a third source—possibly preexilic—which contained oracles against

Edom. The similarity of Obadiah to Joel is less striking but worthy of note. Both emphasize the theme of the day of Yahweh. Verse 17*a* is quoted explicitly in Joel 2:32.

Theological Viewpoint

It would be shortsighted to write off books like Obadiah and Nahum as the outpourings of a fanatic nationalism. There is no denying the vengeance which pervades these books, but vengeance was understood as belonging to Yahweh. It is the justice of Yahweh which is described here. It is described as motivated by the crimes of which Edom was guilty. Yahweh's dominion over all peoples demands a reckoning and requital. This notion is deeply embedded in the traditions concerning the day of Yahweh. Indeed Edom comes to symbolize any power hostile to Yahweh (verses 17-21). On the other hand Obadiah is no "servant of Yahweh" after the pattern of Isaiah 53. Any sense of a mission on behalf of the nations is totally absent.

I. JUDGMENT ON EDOM (Verses 1-14)

Verse 1*a*. *Title*. The title of the book is brief—the two words "Obadiah's vision"—without the usual identification of the prophet's family and date.

Verses 1*b*-9. *The Doom of Edom*. Yahweh's **messenger** summons the **nations** to war against Edom. Verse 1*b* does not fit before verse 1*c*. Perhaps it is misplaced (cf. Jeremiah 49:7) or a later addition. **We have heard** perhaps should read "I have heard" as in the Septuagint and Jeremiah 49:14.

Verses 2-4. Yahweh announces Edom's doom. Despite its lofty and supposedly secure position it shall be brought down and made **small.** The description of the Edomites as living **in the clefts of the rock** is a genuine geographical reference to the rocky wastes of their territory. **Rock** (Hebrew *sela*) may be an allusion to the Edomite fortress of Sela (cf. II Kings 14:7). Using this fortress as an acropolis, the Nabateans later built their capital city of Petra around it.

The Edomites occupied the rocky highland of Seir, which lay south of Moab, from which it was cut off by the valley of the Brook Zered. It was east of the Arabah, the deep valley including the Dead Sea and extending south to the Gulf of Aqaba. A large part of the plateau edge is between 5,000 and 5,600 feet high. The whole surface is tilted eastward from the Arabah side toward the desert. Across the plateau from north to south ran the King's Highway, an ancient caravan route which was the lifeline of Edomite trade.

Verses 5-6. This is an ironic lament. The prophet contrasts the minor damage that **plunderers** or **grape gatherers** inflict with the complete pillaging to be visited on **Esau**—that is, his descendants, the Edomites (cf. Genesis 36:9). The disaster is described as already having occurred—a vivid way of declaring that it is sure to come. Edom had considerable **treasures** because of the caravan trade.

Verses 7-9. The ironic tone continues. If even its very **allies**—Moabites, Ammonites, and desert bedouin—are playing Edom false, will not Yahweh **destroy** it with all its **wise** and **mighty?** Verse 7 may refer to the Arab pressure during the sixth and fifth centuries that drove many of the Edomites to settle in southern Judah (see Introduction). Or, if this part is adapted from a preexilic source, it may refer to some threat at an earlier time (cf. Amos 2:1).

Edom was famous for its **wise men** (cf. Jeremiah 49:7), though we know practically nothing about Edomite wisdom. Eliphaz the Temanite (Job 1:11) was probably from **Teman,** a chief city of Edom, about five miles east of Sela. **Mount Esau** means the Seir mountain range of Edom.

Verses 10-14. *The Reason for Judgment.* The crime of Edom against his **brother Jacob**—that is, Israel—is specified in this dramatic passage. Eight times the **day**—of **calamity,** of **distress,** etc.—is mentioned. The day of Yahweh against **Jerusalem,** when the city was destroyed by the Babylonian **foreigners,** was the day of Edom's violence and gloating and looting. Many Old Testament passages testify to the bitter memory of the Edomites' action on that occasion (cf. Isaiah 63:1-6; Ezekiel

75

25:12-14; 35:1-15; Joel 3:19). The bitterness of the indictment is heightened by recalling the brotherly relationship which existed between Jacob and Esau—that is, Israel and Edom (cf. Genesis 25:24-26). Besides looting, the Edomites helped the enemy by capturing **fugitives** from Judah and handing them over to the Babylonians.

Verses 12-14. The series **You should not have gloated,** etc., is literally "Do not gloat," etc. Yahweh is forbidding Edom to do what it has already done—a striking way to intensify the enormity of its sin.

The conclusion of the poem is found in verse 15*bc*. Yahweh declares that the result will be an exercise of the law of retaliation. The Edomites will be punished with **deeds** such as they themselves performed.

II. THE DAY OF YAHWEH (VERSES 15-21)

Verses 15-16. *Judgment on the Nations.* The prophet announces the approach of Yahweh's day of vengeance on **all the nations. You** in verse 16*a* is plural and means the Israelites, in contrast with the singular referring to Edom throughout verses 2-15. As the people of Judah have drained the cup of Yahweh's wrath—a frequent metaphor in the prophets—so now the nations shall drink. The ruin of Edom is turned into the day of Yahweh aginst the nations—just as in Joel a locust plague becomes a symbol of judgment on the whole world.

Verses 17-21. *The Restoration of Judah.* Now **Mount Zion** is pronounced inviolable (verse 17*a*, quoted in Joel 2:32) and **holy. Possess their own possessions** is better translated, as in the Septuagint, "possess those who dispossess them." The **house of Jacob** (Judah) and the **house of Joseph** (the northern kingdom of Israel) will now unite to **consume** the **house of Esau** (Edom). The union of Israel and Judah is a feature of the prophetic descriptions of the messianic age. Edom appears to become a symbol for all of Israel's enemies, all of whom are to be destroyed (cf. Isaiah 34:1-17; 63:1-6).

Verses 19-20. The promise of restoration includes expansion of the boundaries of Judah. The Israelites of the **Negeb** (southern Judah) will take over **Mount Esau** (Edom). Those living in the **Sephelah** (the western foothills) will move into the coastal plain of Philistia. The territory of the former northern kingdom (**Ephraim** and **Samaria**) and **Gilead** in Transjordan will be occupied.

In Halah—a place apparently in Assyria where captives of the northern kingdom were exiled in 722 (II Kings 17:6)—is an emendation of the Hebrew text, which reads "of this host." In either case the meaning is that descendants of the exiled **people of Israel** will be included in the restoration. They will occupy northern Palestine as far north as **Zarephath** (cf. I King 17:9). The identity of **Shepharad** is uncertain. It probably refers to Sardis in Asia Minor, where evidence has been found of a Jewish colony existing in the middle of the fifth century. The ancient rabbis identified it with Spain, so that Spanish Jews came to be called Sephardim.

Verse 21. This concluding verse describes the victorious Israelites. They are to **rule as saviors**—like the judges (cf. Judges 3:9, 15)—from **Mount Zion**. It is the final **kingdom** and reign of Yahweh that is envisioned here.

THE BOOK OF JONAH

Roland E. Murphy, O. Carm.

INTRODUCTION

Authorship and Date

Nothing is known about the author of the book of Jonah. He cannot be identified with the hero of the story, Jonah the son of Ammitai. According to II Kings 14:25 this prophet foretold the reestablishment of Israel's boundaries by Jeroboam II. At that time, early in the eighth century, Nineveh was not the royal residence, nor was Assyria the world power it later came to be. It is likely that this man became the subject of the book much as Job was chosen to be the hero of the book named after him.

The period following the Babylonian exile is the likely date for the writing of the book. Only then would one find in Israel such a strong emphasis on universalism and tolerance toward other nations. Some think that the book was written specifically to oppose the resurgent nationalism and exclusiveness of the Ezra-Nehemiah reform, but its relation to this movement cannot be determined. A postexilic date is borne out by the character of the language and by the view of Nineveh and the Assyrian power as belonging to the remote past. The book was already established as one of the "Twelve Prophets" in the time of Ben Sira (about 180 B.C.). It was also known to the author of Tobit (14:4, 8), though he may have confused it with Nahum.

Literary Form and Interpretation

In modern times the book is not usually interpreted as history. If history were the intention of the author, one would expect names and details. There would be more concern to explain the implausible happenings and the series of remarkable coincidences. The climax of these is the sudden and complete conversion of the Ninevites. There is no opposition, no motivation except Jonah's proclamation of the threat. Yet a tremendous conversion of the entire population of a large city takes place—without leaving another trace in the Bible or in history.

The historicity of the account has been defended primarily because of Jesus' reference to the "sign of Jonah" (Matthew 12:38-42; 16:4; Luke 11:29-32). But the story existed in the Old Testament and this was enough basis for Jesus to refer to it. Interestingly enough, the sign itself was interpreted in several ways in the New Testament era, as a comparison of Matthew with Luke shows.

The allegorical interpretation would make Jonah (meaning "dove") out to be Israel. The disobedient nation is swallowed by the fish (Babylon; cf. Jeremiah 51:34). It is then freed from exile to carry its witness to the Gentiles (repentant Nineveh). Jonah's anger is said to symbolize Israel's impatience at the slowness of the Gentiles to convert.

This allegorical interpretation falls of its own weight. For one thing, Jonah does not come from the fish purified and attuned to the divine will. This is a point against the psychological allegorizing which sees in the fish a fundamental trial from which Jonah emerges a new man. Allegorical interpretation also lies behind the frequent portrayals of Jonah in early Christian art, especially in the catacombs. The scenes show Jonah being cast into the sea and being swallowed, his being spewed out on land, and finally his rest under the plant. These were taken to symbolize death, resurrection, and a blessed immortal rest.

It is not enough to characterize the story as legend or folklore. Even if somewhat similar marvels occur in Greek mythology and elsewhere, there is no question of dependence. At the most there is the folklore motif of a human threatened by a monster, only to be eventually freed. The imaginative style of the legend is certainly present. But the whole thrust of the book goes beyond a mere story and takes on the character of parable.

Its satirical aspect is seen in the picture of a dishonest prophet at odds with the God who commissions him. Its didactic intent emerges from its purpose: God's merciful plans are not to be limited. They include all nations, even Israel's traditional enemies.

This purpose is not a casual lesson. It is skillfully developed by an adaptation of Israel's own traditions and by clever literary devices. The traditions involved are the revelation of Yahweh as "gracious . . . and merciful" (4:2) and willing to "repent" if one will "turn from his evil way" (3:8, 10). At the risk of oversimplifying, one might say that the book is an attempt to interpret these traditions to a later generation.

There are many literary devices. Some are more obvious than others. The four chapters form a diptych: In chapters 1 and 2, the prophet is dealing with foreign sailors who are better than he is. In chapters 3 and 4, the prophet is preaching to Ninevites who understand Yahweh better than he does. The sailors are portrayed as men in fear (1:5, 10) who finally offer sacrifice and fear Yahweh (1:16). This is a typical wisdom saying, for "the fear of the LORD is the beginning of wisdom" (Proverbs 1:7; 9:10). Just so do the Ninevites turn to Yahweh in repentance.

The humorous satire of the book will not disguise the fact that this little work is one of the most important in the Old Testament. There is no greater theological mystery than the mercy of God. The author was brave enough to caricature a narrow-minded Israelite mentality in order to preserve the sovereign freedom of Yahweh. By his insight he anticipated Paul: "Is he not the God of Gentiles also?" (Romans 3:29).

I. JONAH AND THE SAILORS (1:1–2:10)

1:1-3. *A Disobedient Prophet.* The careful reader will not overlook the unusual implications of the very first lines. How could an Israelite prophet be commissioned to preach to the Ninevites? What language would he speak? What authority would he have? Why should there be a mission to the hated Assyrians, the oppressors of Israel? We are in the realm of fiction here. The behavior of the prophet is clearly disobedient. He departs in the opposite direction from Nineveh, boarding a **ship** at **Joppa**, modern Jaffa, bound for **Tarshish.** Many identifications have been proposed for this latter place, which is mentioned often in the Old Testament. Tartessus, beyond Gilbraltar on the southwestern coast of Spain, is the most plausible site.

Jonah's flight is twice characterized as **from the presence of the LORD.** In ancient Semitic thought there was a close connection between the land and the god of the land. But as the story develops, Jonah will acknowledge Yahweh as the creator of the sea (verse 9) and discover that one cannot flee from Yahweh.

1:4-16. *A Ship in a Storm.* The author attributes the storm directly to Yahweh's intervention. The reaction of the sailors, supposedly used to the ways of the sea, is somewhat surprising. They turn to their gods in prayer. Thus the sailors at sea become the counterpart to the Ninevites of chapter 4 on land. In contrast Jonah sleeps. His sleep is interrupted by the "pious" **captain,** who—this is surely not without some irony—urges him to pray.

1:7-12. In the orthodox Old Testament view, misfortune points to some sin. The **lots** single out Jonah as the guilty party. The first question of the sailors in verse 8 is repetitious (cf. verse 7). It is surely unnecessary. Therefore after the lots have indicated Jonah some scholars have assumed it to be a scribe's accidental duplication. Further, verse 10*b* strikes the modern reader as anticlimactic and is viewed by some as a marginal note that came to be copied in the text.

But there is no need to omit these. The incoherence stems from the theological interest of the author, who seems less concerned with details than with setting up situations to serve his purpose. The sailors' question sets up a theological formula as Jonah's answer. His God is the very one who **made the sea** that is now threatening them. The reaction of the sailors—fear of God—is in contrast to the disobedience of the prophet. The artificiality of the story is further indicated by Jonah's calm solution to their dilemma. Like the cargo, he is to be cast overboard.

1:13-16. Again these sailors show a surprisingly deep religious feeling. They do not want the responsibility for Jonah's death. Despite their strenuous efforts, Jonah is finally cast overboard—not without a prayer to be acquitted of his **blood**—and the storm is over. Significantly it is now Yahweh whom the sailors fear and to whom they offer sacrifice!

1:17–2:10. *Jonah Returned to Land.* As always in this book, Yahweh is represented as the direct cause of all that happens. It is Yahweh who **appointed a great fish to swallow up Jonah.** The prophet is not going to be allowed to escape God's commission that easily. The fish has Jonah as his guest for **three days and three nights.** One cannot determine what kind of sea monster the author had in mind.

2:1-9. Inserted here is a thanksgiving psalm which is a classical example of this literary type. The reason it has been used here is doubtless its references to the sea (verses 3, 5). The poem begins with a description of the psalmist's **distress** and an acknowledgment of Yahweh as his rescuer. **Sheol** or the **Pit** was the abode of the dead far beneath the earth amid the waters of the **deep.** Metaphors like these are used especially in the psalms to designate human affliction—sickness or persecution, for example. We do not know the precise trouble in which the author of this prayer found himself. But it led to his being separated from Yahweh's **presence** in the **temple**—the very temple from which Yahweh answered his plea (verse 7). The prayer concludes with a declaration of loyalty, in contrast to idolaters. The psalmist vows to offer his **sacrifice** in the temple.

2:10. Again at Yahweh's command the fish spews Jonah out on the **dry land**—presumably the land he fled from. Thus Jonah is back where he started, and Yahweh begins again.

II. JONAH AND THE NINEVITES (3:1–4:11)

3:1-4. *An Obedient Prophet.* Verses 1-3 are deliberately modeled on 1:1-3. A new moment in the story begins as Jonah now obeys the command of Yahweh to go to Nineveh. Excavations at Nineveh have indicated that its **breadth of three days' journey** is not so great an exaggeration. The Nineveh of old could be envisioned as embracing the so-called "Assyrian triangle," the territory from Khorsabad in the north to Nimrud in the south—a distance of around twenty-six miles. In this area the population suggested by 4:11 is conceivable. Appropriately, one of the mounds which mark the site of ancient Nineveh is called Nebi Yunus ("the prophet Jonah"). Here, among many other sites that claim the honor, the prophet is supposedly buried.

3:5-10. *The Repentance of the Ninevites.* The reaction of the Ninevites is nothing short of astounding. To the possibility of God's forgiveness (**who knows,** verse 9) there is the generous response of the king, the people, and even the beasts. In spite of himself Jonah appears to be the most successful missionary of all time.

The proclamation of the unnamed king of Nineveh contains a whole program of Israelite theology based on Jeremiah 18:7-8. Repentance and conversion from sin moves God to **repent** of the **evil** God intends to inflict. The invitation to the Ninevites that **everyone turn from his evil way** is a phrase often used by Jeremiah. There is a noticeable similarity between the situation here and that in Jeremiah 36. In both the possibility is held out that Yahweh will repent if "every one will turn from his evil way" (Jeremiah 36:7). However, the king of Nineveh is in favorable contrast to the impenitent Jehoiakim.

4:1-4. *The Reaction of Jonah.* Though no prophet ever experienced such a success as Jonah, he is **displeased** and even **angry.** Now his unspoken narrowness begins to reveal itself. He knew Yahweh was "soft," and that he would forgive the Ninevites if they repented. Indeed he tried to **flee to Tarshish** for that very reason—to prevent the Ninevites' conversion.

4:2d. The strong theological flavor of Jonah's reasoning is expressed in this formula, which has a history in the Old Testament going back to Exodus 34:6. Jonah is thus rejecting the Yahweh of the covenant, the God of the fathers, who is consistently described in these loving terms.

4:3-4. Jonah is so disgusted that he asks to die. His request is met by Yahweh's question, **Do you do well to be angry?** or, as it might better be translated, "Are you so very angry?" This same question is repeated in the next scene (verse 9). The repetition seems to be a literary device to heighten the tension—cf. the delaying tactic in Esther's request in Esther 5:3-8. It is also a reminiscence of the prophet Elijah in I Kings 19:4. There is humor in this exchange. The prophet is ready to die, but Yahweh will not allow him to go without teaching him a lesson.

4:5-11. *Jonah and the Plant.* Jonah does not give up the hope that somehow the doom pronounced against Nineveh will still be fulfilled. He takes up his residence in a **booth** outside the city. The question has been raised why Yahweh should make a **plant** (probably the castor oil plant) spring up overnight to provide **shade** for Jonah since he already had the booth. Hence some scholars would insert 4:5 between 3:4 and 5, immediately after Jonah begins to preach to the Ninevites. But this is not necessary in a fictional narrative. Here the religious reaction rather than the reality of details determines the course of events.

4:7-9. Jonah's great joy over the plant does not last long. God sends a **worm** to kill it and an **east wind** (the baleful sirocco) to torment the prophet. An earlier scene now repeats itself. Jonah asks for death (cf. verse 3) and Yahweh asks if he has reason **to be angry for the plant** (cf. verse 4).

4:10-11. The whole point of the story comes here. If Jonah pitied the plant, with which he had nothing to do, should not Yahweh **pity** the people of Nineveh? **Who do not know their right hand from their left** may mean that the entire population of the city is religiously ignorant. But the Ninevites have responded sensitively to Jonah's preaching. The author is more probably adding to the poignancy of the question by an allusive reminder (cf. Isaiah 7:16) that the city contains 120,000 innocent children, not to speak of the **cattle.**

There is simply no answer to this touching question. These final verses constitute the heart of the message. Israel should not presume to limit God's concern only to the people with whom God has covenanted. God's mercy spills out, beyond even the holy covenant, to embrace the Gentiles (cf. Exodus 33:19; Romans 9:15).

THE BOOK OF MICAH

Bruce T. Dahlberg

INTRODUCTION

The name Micah is an abbreviated form of Micaiah, meaning "Who is like Yahweh?" Except for his home and the general period in which he lived, details of Micah's life are unknown.

The Judean town Moresheth (1:1) is presumably the same as Moresheth-gath (1:14). It was probably located about twenty miles southwest of Jerusalem toward the ancient Philistine city of Gath. Micah lived in this relatively small town and was concerned for the small landholder (cf. 2:2). But to assume that he himself was a peasant takes too much for granted. His sophistication and knowledge of public affairs show in his prophetic pronouncements, and suggest that he may have been a person of eminence. Over a century later Jeremiah's contemporaries compared him to Micah (cf. Jeremiah 26:16-19). This fact suggests that Micah may have had access to the royal court in Jerusalem as Jeremiah did.

Historical Background and Date
The book's introductory heading (1:1) identifies Micah's career with the "days of Jotham, Ahaz, and Hezekiah, kings of Judah"—that is, 742-687/86 B.C. This is a much longer period than is reflected in Micah's own prophecies. Jeremiah 26:18-19

identifies Micah's preaching with the reign of Hezekiah (716/15-687/86). It quotes 3:12 in apparent reference to Sennacherib's siege of Jerusalem (701), though the allusion would fit other Assyrian threats as well. The reference may be merely an inference from tradition, however, and is not necessarily accurate chronologically.

More significant is the reference in 1:6-7 to the destruction of Samaria. This capital city of the northern kingdom of Israel fell to Assyria in 722 after a three-year siege. The Assyrian Sargon II asserts that he rebuilt Samaria soon after its fall, but Micah appears to know nothing of a rebuilding. Chapters 1–3 seem to require a date either during the siege or shortly after the destruction of the city—that is, around 725-720 (see below on 1:6-9, 10-16). On the other hand chapters 4–7 undoubtedly come from a period after Micah's lifetime, probably during or soon after the Babylonian exile (586-539).

Micah was a contemporary of Isaiah. Like Isaiah he addressed his message primarily to the leaders of the city of Jerusalem in the southern kingdom of Judah. Amos and Hosea, who preached in the northern kingdom before its collapse, may have been known to Micah, along with Isaiah. His message shows affinities with all three. However, Micah neither mentions his contemporaries nor is mentioned by them.

Authorship and Literary Divisions

According to both subject matter and style the book falls into three divisions: chapters 1–3, 4–5, and 6–7. This can be established on the basis of the chronological data cited above, including the reference in Jeremiah 26:18-19, and their literary unity (see comment). In their present form they appear to be a public manifesto of some kind, conceivably a sermon to be preached.

Chapters 4–5, on the other hand, show a messianic interest which resembles that of exilic and postexilic literature. Also, they mention Babylon (4:10), which succeeded Assyria as the imperial power in Mesopotamia after 605. These chapters seem with almost equal certainty *not* the work of Micah. Rather they must come from an anonymous author or authors in the exilic or postexilic years. The two chapters appear as a later prophetic commentary on the original work of Micah in chapters 1–3.

Chapters 6–7 deal with many of the prophet Micah's themes. But on the whole they are more reflective, and in important respects they go beyond Micah. They seem to be a liturgy of atonement, perhaps arising from meditation on the prophecy of Micah in chapters 1–3.

I. The Crisis of Judah (1:1–3:12)

Except for the introductory heading added later (1:1) chapters 1–3 can be read as a single unified work. They are not merely a collection of separate pronouncements from different episodes in the prophet's career. Instead they are a prophetic sermon intended for Jerusalem and probably preached there. One sign of their literary unity is the thrice-repeated **Hear!** (1:2; 3:1; 3:9). Further marks of unity appear with a comparison of the beginning and ending lines. The focus of attention shifts with a deliberate sweep from Samaria in the north (1:6-9) to Jerusalem and Judah in the south (3:9-12)—a movement anticipated in 1:5, where these two cities are named. In both places attention is directed to the temple (1:2; 3:12), and in both the destruction of the city is proclaimed.

Such patterns in form and theme suggest that chapters 1–3 form a single composition rather than a loose collection of sayings—even though the prophet may well have incorporated some earlier brief pronouncements into this longer work.

1:1. *Introductory Heading.* An editor from a later biblical time has supplied this explanatory introduction. It is similar to those of other biblical prophetic books. **The word of the Lord** is not merely "words from God" but the total situation about which the prophet will speak. The added expression **which he saw** comes from the terminology of soothsaying. Here it alludes merely to the prophet's inspired insight into the meaning of events around him. Neither Micah nor any of the classical

Hebrew prophets were soothsayers. On the historical references see the Introduction.

1:2-5. *Prologue: The Advent of God.* Micah himself begins with a proclamation: God is to appear for a day of judgment. The language, style, and imagery of verses 2-4 have seemed like those of Second Isaiah to some scholars. They have accordingly taken the verses as an editor's introduction to the prophecy of Micah beginning in verse 5. The language, style, and imagery, however, are classic in the Old Testament. There seems no compelling reason to date the verses after the time of Micah or to separate them from verse 5.

1:2. The effect of the opening summons is to get the attention of everyone within hearing, and everyone is meant to **hear.** God will be a **witness against you.** Micah's subject unmistakably involves divine judgment. **From his holy temple** God is bestirring—breaking out of—ordinary confines, as it were.

1:3-4. The notion of the divine judgment's breaking out is carried forward. This passage has been compared with Isaiah 40:3-5. However, there the imagery suggests the building of a road for a military conqueror, whereas here it suggests volcanic action, earthquake, or lightning and storm. Natural and supernatural elements seem intentionally blurred, and the language is figurative. The prophet intends to inspire soberness and awe in his listeners in face of the specific circumstances and events he will go on to describe.

1:5. Micah moves now from the poetic and mythological to the concrete and specific. The **transgression of Jacob** and **sins of the house of Israel** remain yet to be described. These will form the burden of the prophet's message (2:1–3:11). Micah seems to use the names Jacob, Israel, and Judah interchangeably. The transgression of Jacob is in Micah's view first of all **Samaria**— that is, the corrupt society within it. Located about forty miles north of Jerusalem, Samaria was the capital of the northern kingdom of Israel, politically separated from Judah since the death of King Solomon (931).

What is the sin of the house of Judah? follows the Septuagint reading. The Hebrew, "What are the high places of Judah?"

probably should be retained. Micah has already used **high places** (verse 3) to describe the focal point of God's judgment. That is precisely what he anticipates for the "high place" that is Jerusalem.

1:6-9. *Samaria an Omen for Jerusalem.* This passage presumably describes the military destruction of Samaria by the Assyrians. Either it is imminent or it has happened so recently that it can be thought of in the present tense. The Hebrew forms of the verbs here can refer to either present or future time. In any case Micah is addressing not Samaria but Jerusalem (verse 9), using the situation of Samaria as a warning and omen.

1:6. The words here describe literally the methodical obliteration of a city by an ancient military conqueror. These are the actual circumstances that inspire the figurative description of divine judgment in verses 3-4.

1:7. Possibly these allusions to idolatry are an interpolation from a time long after Micah. The prophet does not elsewhere deal with the subject in these three chapters. However, King Ahaz of Judah (735-716/15) had imported an Assyrian altar into the Jerusalem temple before this time (II Kings 16:10-16). Thus Micah himself could have spoken these words advisedly. **All her hires** means the wages of a prostitute. Here it alludes to offerings brought to Samaria's pagan holy places. **To the hire of a harlot they shall return** is Micah's way of saying that these sacred objects and gifts will be carried off to Assyrian temples when Samaria falls. The particular terms used here may be at the same time Micah's contemptuous recognition of ritual prostitution. This was practiced by the pagan fertility cults that competed with the worship of Yahweh.

1:8. It is not clear whether Micah's **lament and wail** and his **going stripped and naked** are meant literally. An exile being deported was made to walk naked in humiliation. Isaiah walked naked to signify approaching disaster (Isaiah 20:2-4). In any case, given the harsh tone and controlled fury of Micah's speech elsewhere, this verse scarcely is enough to justify calling him the "wailing prophet," as has been common.

1:9. Samaria is beyond help. The crisis that confronted it, which it failed to meet, now confronts Judah and Jerusalem.

1:10-16. *The Invoking of Disaster.* Micah now addresses the cities and towns of Judah. A series of taunts and insults makes it seem as if Samaria's fate were descending on them. Micah is not so much spreading an alarm here as himself calling down the Assyrian threat on Judah. So far as we know, it did not materialize at this time. But Sargon's armies remained in southern Palestine to put down a rebellion in the Philistine state of Gaza on the Mediterranean coast (around 720/19) following the conquest of Samaria. This must have made these prophetic curses seem no empty threat to the uneasy inhabitants of Judah and Jerusalem.

1:10-15. The saying **Tell it not in Gath** was proverbial, signifying disaster (cf. II Samuel 1:20). Gath, a Philistine city, was in the line of Assyrian attack should it come. In the Hebrew there is a play on the similarity between the words "tell" and "Gath." Apparently this caught the prophet's imagination, for all the subsequent taunts in these verses attempt some sort of play on word sounds. For example, **-aphrah** sounds like "dust," and **Achzib** like "deceitful thing." So far as they can be located the places named were all in the foothills of western Judah.

1:16. Micah summons the inhabitants of Judah to lament the exile that would be the inevitable consequence of Assyrian occupation (cf. verse 8).

2:1-13. *The Inner Sickness of Judah.* Thus far Micah has spoken of the threat to Judah from without. Now he addresses himself to the threat from within. He cites the subordination of human rights in eighth century Judah to the pursuit of wealth and power. The aristocracy appears incapable of appreciating Judah's precarious position. For Micah the collapse of the state is inevitable.

2:1-5. People with vested commercial and political interests lie awake nights to devise schemes to add to their wealth at the expense of their fellows. Their cleverness enables them to deprive the poor of their few possessions. Micah sees a day of reckoning. Their easy life will be ended abruptly by the invader. Their wealth, even their place in the **assembly of the LORD**, will be taken away.

2:6. Judah's affluent aristocracy is incapable of self-criticism.

They wish to hear preached only what is pleasant, not criticism. Such warnings as were spoken in 1:10-16 are laughed off. The prophet is without honor in his own country.

2:7. Micah responds with amazement to the rejection of his words. **Is the Spirit of the LORD impatient?** he asks. His words are literally: "Is the Spirit of the LORD shortened?" That is, is it possible that Micah's preaching can have so little effect? In **Are these his doings?** the emphasis in the Hebrew is on "these." The sense of the preceding line is repeated: **Do not my words do good to him who walks uprightly?** means, Would not a just man recognize the truth of what has been said? The indifference of Micah's audience is the measure of their moral insensitivity.

2:8. The Hebrew text is obscure in this verse. **With no thought of war** is a plausible rendition. But the phrase can possibly be translated more exactly as "returning from war." The sense is that, the true enemies of the community are these exploiters of the people, not the threats of the Assyrians. The returning soldier confronts worse hardships at home than on the battlefield.

2:9. Even **women** and **children** are evicted from their homes. The picture of the suffering of those who lack economic or social status or any resource for self-defense is a poignant one. Micah's righteous indignation is inspired against a social deterioration in eighth century Judah that was also documented by his contemporary, Isaiah.

2:10. This advice appears to be Micah's ironic consolation offered to the women and children of verse 9. They are better off to leave this unclean place that is doomed for destruction.

2:11. Micah returns to an earlier theme (verse 6)—contentment with preaching which will not disturb these complacent people. For them, Micah says, a drunken man would be about as good a preacher as any.

2:12-13. The apparent optimism of this section intrudes abruptly into the context of Micah's judgment and threat. Most commentators think that it is an interpolation by a pious scribe or editor who found Micah's preaching too harsh. However, the picture given here of **sheep in a fold** and a **noisy multitude of men** is undignified and is not in fact complimentary. Indeed it is reminiscent of the intoxication suggested in verse 11. Further, its expectation that this throng, led by its **king** and with God on its side, would break out of a surrounding siege is naïve. Therefore one must agree with the eleventh century rabbinical commentator Ibn Ezra, who read these lines as Micah's sarcastic ridicule by mimicry of the sort of false preaching for which he shows such contempt in verses 6 and 11. That the words are introduced without any verb of speaking to mark them as a quotation is a practice common in ancient Hebrew.

3:1-12. *God's Departure from the People.* The prophet has finished his case. The divine word has not been heeded. Therefore the people who will have their own way are now to have it altogether. Micah proceeds to give the verdict.

3:1-4. The thought of this passage follows what has gone immediately before. As in 2:12-13 the figure is again that of the sheepfold. But here, rather than being led to safety by their leader, the people are ravaged as if by wild beasts. The **heads of Jacob** and the **rulers of the house of Israel** in fact consume the people they are supposed to guide and protect.

The portrayal of the helpless creature torn limb from limb is reminiscent of the atrocities known to have been perpetrated by the Assyrians on their conquered enemies. As in 2:8 Micah again suggests that the destroyer from without is scarcely distinguishable from the destroyers within.

Judah's rulers have passed the point of return. Repentance can no longer help them. Should the Assyrian threat become a reality, they will discover that they are beyond help (verse 4). This is Micah's explicit rejoinder to those who flatter themselves that **their king will pass on before them, the LORD at their head** (2:13).

3:5-7. Micah spells out the judgment further. Now he attacks those **prophets** who have been willing to underwrite corruption in Judah with their easy promises of divine approval. So long as they are fed they never challenge the status quo. The day of Judah's extremity will discredit them, for they have done nothing to prevent evil. Then they will hold their tongues (verse 7). Micah repeats the judgment pronounced in verse 4. Yahweh will have departed from the people. Judah will discover the eclipse of God. The coming **night** and **darkness** recall the preaching of Amos some years earlier (cf. Amos 5:18).

3:8. The question that has troubled Micah—that his preaching was of so little effect (see above on 2:7)—is now answered. Judah's devastation will be the vindication of his message. The divine **Spirit** has indeed operated through him **with justice and might** through the judgment that has resulted from his message. Isaiah, Micah's contemporary, came to a similar conclusion about his own ministry (cf. Isaiah 6:9-13).

3:9-12. Micah has delivered the burden of his message. Now he swiftly brings it to a conclusion. The final bill of particulars is presented to the **heads of the house of Jacob** and the **rulers of the house of Israel,** the **priests** and the **prophets.** It needs no explanatory comment. Yet all these have still the audacity to claim: **Is not the LORD in the midst of us? No evil shall come upon us.** This is the last outrage.

3:12. Micah's closing words echo the theme with which he began his message (1:2-4, 6-7). The destruction of **Jerusalem** by Assyria, which Micah saw as inevitable, never happened. When the armies of Sennacherib did approach its gates in 701, the Judean king, Hezekiah, bought them off with tribute (II Kings 18:13-16). Nevertheless a century later Micah's words were preserved and remembered. They were recalled when Jerusalem was about to fall to the Babylonian onslaught. At that time Jeremiah was called to take a stand not unlike that of his predecessor, and Micah's words were appealed to in his defense (cf. Jeremiah 26:18-19). Thus these words of Micah spoke to a generation he never knew—a generation that came to understand him better than his own.

II. The Future Restoration (4:1–5:15)

Chapters 4–5 are eschatologically oriented. That is, they are concerned with the "last things," the ultimate outcome of history or at least of the era of history with which the author is concerned. Not until later did biblical eschatology look to the final end of history or beyond history. The expectation here is messianic in the literal sense of expecting a revived political kingdom. It anticipates the restoration of the Davidic monarchy and the temple in Jerusalem, both of which seem here to be known to have previously met their end.

These two chapters must be a later addition to the record of Micah's preaching (chapters 1–3). They were added probably in the exilic or early postexilic period—that is, later than 586, when Jerusalem fell to Babylon. The messianic hope expressed here is quite unlike anything anticipated in chapters 1–3. Indeed it contradicts Micah's preaching altogether. To be sure, Micah could have reversed himself at a later time in his life. Nevertheless the language, imagery, and thought of chapters 4–5 resemble closely other prophetic writings known to be from the Exile or after.

The decisive clue to the later composition of this material is that Babylon rather than Assyria is known as the place of exile (4:10). Though Assyria is referred to (5:5-6), what is said cannot possibly allude to that empire as Micah knew it. Here it is simply the geographical region northeast of Palestine which was known to have been territory of the Assyrian Empire earlier. Such use of the term appears in other late Old Testament writing (cf. Lamentations 5:6 and Zechariah 10:10-11).

However, chapters 4–5 were not appended to Micah's work arbitrarily. At a number of points they echo the language and imagery of chapters 1–3. They appear to have been inspired by Micah's thought and to form a later century's response to him, after study and reflection on his work.

4:1-5. *The Universal Reign of God.* Except for verses 4-5*b* this entire passage occurs also in Isaiah 2:2-5. Its use to begin an appendix to the prophecy of Micah is quite pertinent in a literary sense. Micah's original address ended with an allusion to the **mountain of the house**—that is, the hill in Jerusalem on which the temple stood, which would become a **wooded height** (3:12). Verse 1 now begins in a different vein but with a like reference to the **mountain of the house of the LORD**. The promise that figuratively this mountain will be the **highest of the mountains, . . . raised up above the hills** corresponds antithetically to Micah's own prologue (1:4). Thus it is possible that this poem was composed expressly for this addition to Micah and was inserted later into Isaiah's prophecy.

4:4-5. These lines fill out the picture of peace and general felicity which will characterize the ideal future. The sense of verse 5 seems to be that, whatever the pagan leanings of the surrounding peoples, Judah's fidelity to the one God will abide forever.

4:6-10. *The Return of the Exiles.* It cannot be determined whether these lines are from the Babylonian exile (586-539) or later. In any case they presuppose a scattered community. Their introduction at this point is doubtless prompted by the desire to comment on Micah's earlier prediction of deportation and exile (1:16). This ill fortune is now to be reversed.

4:6-7. The terminology here suggests the forced march of exiles into a distant land. The contrast between their present condition and **a strong nation,** that God will make them, dramatically testifies to Israel's faith in the divine sovereignty over history.

4:8. Using poetic allusions to Jerusalem, the author declares that Judah's lost place among the nations will be restored.

4:9-10. The rhetorical question **Is there no king in you?** looks forward to a time when Israel will again have a king. Some interpreters have supposed that these lines refer to political hardships later in the postexilic period. Accordingly they have tried to find two or more sources combined in chapters 4-5. There seems little evidence for this hypothesis. In a literary sense, at least, these verses owe their present place in the text to the fact that they supply an answer to Micah's prophecy of doom (cf. especially 1:16 and 2:3-5, 12-13).

4:11–5:9. *The New Davidic Kingdom.* In the Old Testament there are at least two occasions during the exilic and postexilic periods when the people of Judah had reason to think that the Davidic throne might soon be restored:

(1) the dispensation accorded around 561 to the exiled King Jehoiachin in Babylon (II Kings 25:27-30);

(2) the appointment of Zerubbabel around 520 as postexilic

governor of Judah under Persian rule. Zerubbabel was a descendant of David who seems to have entertained such aspirations for himself. He was encouraged in this ambition by the prophet Haggai (Haggai 2:20-23). A literal restoration of the Davidic royal house never happened, but the expectation reappears in biblical history. This passage illustrates this hope. Indeed, if it is an exilic prophecy, it may have been one of the early sources that fed this hope.

4:11-13. Presumably the situation is that of Jerusalem (**Zion**) either on or after the occasion of its destruction by the Babylonians in 586. The nations who surround it to gloat over its fate will prove to be like **sheaves** of grain threshed by an ox—that is, by Jerusalem. The prophet thus expects a reversal of the present distress through divine intervention. Judah **shall beat in pieces many peoples.** War as an instrument of God's judgment is more or less taken for granted in biblical eschatology. The peace and felicity described in verses 3-4 is thought of as an aftermath, rather than an alternative, to conflict. The expression **devote their gain to the LORD** is from the language of ancient holy war, in which the possessions of the enemy were utterly destroyed—literally "devoted" to God (cf. Joshua 6:17-19).

5:1. Judah's fortunes are at their lowest before the expected deliverance. The figure of striking its **ruler** signifies the ultimate humiliation. Possibly this is a reference to the exiled King Jehoiachin (II Kings 24:12). Or it may refer to the last Davidic king in Jerusalem, Zedekiah, who was tortured by the Babylonians and presumably perished in exile (II Kings 25:7). Possibly it is a proverbial saying, for **ruler** (*shophet*), literally "judge," plays on the word **rod** (*shebhet*).

In view of the following allusions to the rise of David in ancient times (verses 2-9) the smitten ruler may have originally meant Saul, whose defeat by the Philistines was ultimately reversed for Judah by David. The symbolism of the ruler being struck was taken as a sign of the approach of the messianic age. It appears in Zechariah 13:7, where the context is also Davidic messianism. It is taken up into the New Testament interpretation of the passion of Jesus Christ (Matthew 26:31; Mark 14:27).

5:2. The renewal of Judah will be a reenactment of the events of the golden era of David. Though he is not named, the reference to his birthplace, **Bethlehem Ephrathah,** as well as other details of the verse points unmistakably to him (cf. I Samuel 16:1; 17:12). The Christian tradition saw in this passage a prophecy of the birth of Jesus (Matthew 2:6).

5:3. Judah's deliverance must wait on the birth of the expected heir to David's throne. The connotations of this passage look both backward and forward. It remembers that of eight **brethren** David was the last to be born. But also the present and coming **travail** of Judah—that is, the Exile—is in the prophet's mind. It must continue until the deliverer appears. Indeed the prophet seems to think of it as necessary in order that the deliverer appear.

5:4. These lines compose one of the most beautiful and poignant pictures in all the Bible of the awaited Messiah.

5:5a. The line **And this shall be peace** belongs with the foregoing passage concerning the ruler to come. It may be meant as comment on Micah's indictment of the false prophets who cried "Peace!" (3:5).

5:5b-9. The **seven shepherds and eight princes of men** have been interpreted in various ways. However, it is unnecessary to look beyond the Davidic tradition which dominates this chapter. The meaning is doubtless proverbial in the tradition. David had seven brothers, who, apart from him, were merely shepherds. But all eight, because of him, became "princes of men." The saying expresses the belief that Judah, though presently of little account, will at the coming of the Davidic ruler reign with him in the messianic kingdom. The theme is developed further in verses 7-9 (see above on 4:11-13).

5:10-15. *Purification of the Land.* This passage must be compared with Isaiah 2:6-11. The two passages have an obvious affinity, though the circumstances described there are directly reversed here. The author seems to have drawn on the Isaiah material at this point to portray the coming new age.

5:10-11. In the coming age, when the messianic conflicts have passed, Judah will no longer need to trust in military resources.

The words may be meant as a response to Micah's earlier condemnation of this aspect of Judah's sin (1:13). The parallelism between the two lines of verse 11 suggests that **cities** means fortified cities. This continues the thought of verse 10 that the machinery of war will be abolished.

5:12-14. All the references are to pagan cult practices. **Pillars** here means stone pillars symbolizing the presence of pagan deities. The **Asherim** were sacred objects or images representing the Canaanite fertility goddess Asherah. The occurrence of **cities** in verse 14 seems quite out of context and may be a scribal error for "idols." The whole passage envisions the uprooting of those evils which the earlier prophet Micah condemned (cf. 1:7).

5:15. The thought of this concluding verse returns to the theme of judgment on the **nations afar off** with which the prophecy began (4:2-3). The way the end completes the beginning is a mark of the unity of chapters 4–5.

III. A LITURGY OF ATONEMENT (6:1–7:20)

Biblical scholarship is divided on whether chapters 6–7 are at least in part the words of the eighth century prophet Micah. Certainly it reflects nothing on Micah or on the value of these chapters to say that they probably are the work of a later anonymous psalmist. To be sure, much in them is consistent with Micah's thought as represented in chapters 1–3. But without more evidence than is at hand there is no way to settle the question.

Regardless of authorship, these two chapters together constitute a liturgy of worship—in particular, a liturgy of atonement. Prophetic language and teaching have certainly been incorporated here. Moreover the similarity of 6:1-2 to 1:2-4 and the allusion in 6:16 to Omri, who built Samaria (cf. 1:6-7), suggest that Micah's prophecy has to some degree provided the inspiration for the liturgy.

But in their present form the character of these chapters is on

the whole psalmlike and penitential. There is an orderly
alternation throughout between the speeches of God (6:3-5,
9-16 and 7:11-17) and a penitential response of the worshiper
(6:6-8 and 7:1-10, 18-20). The speeches of God, together with
the poetic summons to judgment (6:1-2), show marked affinities
in style and content to Psalm 50. In a lesser degree the responses
of the worshiper show some affinity with Psalm 49. Compare
Habakkuk 3, which is similarly a psalmlike conclusion from a
source other than the prophet Habakkuk.

6:1-2. *The Summons to Judgment.* The motif of **mountains**
and **hills** is paralleled in the opening lines of each of the two
other divisions of the book (1:2-4; 4:1). This may have something
to do with the addition of this liturgical piece to the book. This
formal opening illustrates a rhetorical declamatory style seen
elsewhere in the psalms and the prophets (See Psalm 49:1;
Isaiah 1:2; Jeremiah 6:18-19).

6:2. Controversy of the Lord is a phrase typical of biblical
prophetic language. It draws on the technical vocabulary of
debate before a judge in a court of law. Much prophetic dialogue
in the Bible shows a "controversy" pattern in its style,
vocabulary, and choice of metaphor.

6:3-5. *God's Saving Acts.* That God addresses Israel as **my
people** evokes one of the most profound ideas in biblical
religion. God chose Israel to be God's "own possession among
all peoples, . . . a kingdom of priests and a holy nation" (Exodus
19:5-6). Allusion to the covenant between God and Israel gives
urgency to the following dialogue. In the collective expression
my people individual worshipers would understand themselves
to be addressed. The question of whether God has somehow
injured or wronged the people is a rhetorical one, capable of
only one kind of answer.

6:4. The priestly and prophetic admonition to the worshiper is
to **remember** what God has done. The deliverance from **Egypt**
remains for Israel the pivotal point in its religion. It provides the
criterion and norm for understanding the power and goodness of
God. Israel's "creed" consists not so much of doctrinal statement
as of this "sacred story," which is the presupposition of its

worship. In verses 4-5 the history of God's dealing with Israel is skillfully recalled.

6:5. The first two lines allude to an attempt by the Moabite king **Balak** to prevent the Israelites from entering the promised land (Numbers 22–24). **Balaam** was the prophet hired by Balak to invoke a curse on Israel. Instead he **answered** with a series of blessings, saying: "The word that God puts in my mouth, that must I speak" (Numbers 22:38).

From Shittim to Gilgal evokes the memory of Israel's crossing the Jordan to enter the promised land after the episode of Balaam. Shittim was the point of departure and Gilgal the point of arrival (Joshua 3:1; 4:19). Shittim was also the location of Israel's encampment during the episode of Balak and Balaam (Numbers 25:1).

6:6-8. *God's Requirements.* Following the liturgical pattern, the worshiper responds to the summons of verses 1-2 and to the recital of God's saving acts in verses 3-5. His question is asked in all solemnity and reverence: **With what shall I come before the LORD?** (cf. Psalm 24:3-6). This passage is often misinterpreted to mean that the offerings named in verses 6-7 are dismissed as without value or meaning. On the contrary they are considered according to an ascending scale of value. The effect is to enhance what is prescribed in verse 8 as the complete offering.

6:6-7. Animals could be sacrificed from the age of eight days on (cf. Leviticus 22:27), but **calves a year old** were of greatest value (cf. Leviticus 9:3). **Thousands of rams, . . . ten thousands of rivers of oil** describes the offering of royalty. King Solomon's dedication of the temple involved such large-scale sacrifice (cf. I Kings 8:5, 63). Oil was used as a libation.

My first-born does not necessarily refer literally to child sacrifice, as many commentators have thought—though this may have been a problem in Israel at certan times. The present context deals with worthy gifts. Thus it is better to understand this line according to the "law of the first-born" (Exodus 13:2, 11-13) and in the tradition of the boy Samuel (I Samuel 1:27-28) and the boy Jesus (Luke 2:22-23). The consideration of a human life totally dedicated to God leads directly to what follows in verse 8.

6:8. These words are among the loftiest in scripture. They give classic statement not only to the prophetic but also to the priestly understanding in the Old Testament of the "whole duty of humanity." They also anticipate a teaching of Jesus relating to right worship (John 4:24).

The liturgical nature of this passage and its context suggest strongly that it is an error to understand these words as a rejection of liturgical ritual in favor of intangible virtues of character. What the passage does say rather clearly is that no particular act of commitment or sacrifice—however magnificent or however great the cost in life—can fulfill God's total claim over the whole of one's life (cf. I Corinthians 13:3). The passage does not reject one's offering (verses 6-7). It does recognize that every offering, however splendid, even to the point of giving oneself, is humble and imperfect.

Justice here translates a Hebrew noun which signifies not only the task of the judge but also the right and duty of everyone according to their particular station and responsibility in life. The king has his justice to perform. The priest, the public official, the teacher, or the parent each has his justice. This understanding of the word is illustrated in the dialogue between John the Baptist and his listeners in Luke 3:10-14. In short, the term "justice" does not define particular duties. It challenges one to learn what is one's particular duty and obligation and to perform it.

Kindness here translates the Hebrew word which the Revised Standard Version in most places renders "steadfast love." It has for its chief connotation loyalty in all human relationships and fidelity to God.

To walk humbly with your God signifies, not personal piety in any narrow sense, but obedience to whatever God requires. This certainly would include worthy worship, including rite and ritual.

The verse has already pointed to the criterion for the life described here: **He has showed you, O man, what is good.** That is, God's saving acts, recited previously, are the standard for the worshiper in this matter. What God has done provides the inspiration for human justice, fidelity, and one's whole walk in life. What God has done suggests what people ought to be and do in faithful response.

6:9-16. *The Failure of Justice.* To recognize what God requires is to recognize how far short of it one has fallen. To hear of God's grace is to hear at the same time a judgment on oneself. With this inexorable logic verses 9-16 develop out of what has preceded. Verse 16*a-c* contrasts explicitly with verse 8.

6:9. The **city** is addressed (cf. 1:6; 3:9-12). This means that each inhabitant of it is addressed. Initially the worshiper responds with prudence: **It is sound wisdom to fear thy name.** In place of **assembly of the city** the literal meaning of the Hebrew should be retained. The line then reads: "Hear, O tribe, for who has appointed it yet?" That is, the wise response described in the preceding line is premature. Until one's guilt is recognized and acknowledged, one cannot stand before the altar. Authentic repentance requires that what follows be heard and acknowledged.

6:10-16. The accusations in verses 10-12 are self-explanatory. As a naming of wrongs they are illustrative rather than exhaustive. Verses 13-15 may be an allusion to specific reversals of fortune or to a dawning sense of guilt (cf. 7:1) or to both. King **Omri** of Israel built the city of Samaria (cf. 1:6-7). His son **Ahab,** whose wife was the notorious Jezebel, was the antagonist of the prophet Elijah in the ninth century. Omri and Ahab were remembered as the opposite of what the king faithful to God should be (cf. I Kings 16:21–22:40). In the present context **walked in their counsels** is the antithesis of **walk humbly with your God** (verse 8). Suffering and humiliation are the realities of judgment, which is nothing abstract. The allusion may be to the Exile, or some other disaster may be meant.

7:1-7. *Confession and Trust.* The worshiper acknowledges the city's desolation as his own, as once Isaiah did in the temple (Isaiah 6:5).

7:2-6. Spiritual cleansing begins in confession. The words of judgment (6:10-12) are repeated and elaborated in the language of penitence. The mood is not self-righteous judgment of others but

103

an acknowledgment of the penitent's involvement in the general human condition (cf. verse 9). Guilt is by nature collective.

7:7. All claim to virtue is laid aside. The worshiper has inquired, "With what shall I come before the LORD?" The worshiper declares now with authentic humility and with trust: **I will wait for the God of my salvation.** Measured by the understanding of what God requires (cf. 6:8) one comes before God with nothing at all.

7:8-10. *Confidence in God's Grace.* Dependent on their own resources the inhabitants of the city could say only **Woe is me!** (verse 1). Dependent now on God they can begin to hope: **When I fall, I shall rise.** Verse 9 expresses an explicit confession: God's **indignation,** seen in the present distress, is just **because I have sinned against him.** There is a radical change from self-approval to trust in God. This is clearly seen in the contrast between the earlier summons to **plead your case** (6:1) and the contentment here to wait on God **until he pleads my cause.**

7:10. Humiliation by the **enemy** (possibly Babylon) was a mark of God's judgment (6:16). Defeat of the enemy will signal salvation. The enemy here, though real, is impersonal. In these words one confronts not moral self-righteousness so much as the psychology of suffering and enslavement (cf. Psalm 137:7-9). The modern reader must not moralize but treat them with understanding.

7:11-17. *The Promise of Restoration.* Hope and expectation have displaced despair. Confession and trust inspire a new vision. Here the psalmist does not dwell on the humiliation of the enemy, as in verse 10, but dwells positively and with enthusiasm on the restoration of the forsaken city. **In that day they will come to you** pictures the risen city presiding over the new order in peace and prosperity. The **River** means the Euphrates. **But the earth will be desolate** recalls the defeat of the surrounding nations that have oppressed Israel (cf. verse 10).

On a small scale Jeremiah 40:7-12 portrays such a revived community at Mizpah following the destruction of Jerusalem in 586. But in general the theme typifies the exilic and postexilic messianic expectation in Israel.

7:14. The language suggests the ideal king in the messianic age (cf. Psalm 78:70-72). **Bashan and Gilead** were former Israelite territory in Transjordan.

7:15-17. Reference to the deliverance from Egypt repeats the theme of 6:4-5, God's saving acts. What God in ancient times began to do, God will one day complete. The extravagant language of verses 16-17 is highly stylized. It intends to recall and to celebrate anew the awesomeness and majesty of the God who delivers the people. It is to be understood in the tradition of the Song of Moses (Exodus 15:1-18), as verse 15 makes clear and as verse 18*a* confirms (cf. Exodus 15:11).

7:18-20. *Adoration and Praise.* This concluding hymn is charged with emotion and deeply moving. It pours out thanks for the forgiveness of sins and the lifting of the burden of guilt. The past is redeemed. Over against the divine judgment proclaimed by Micah (cf. 1:5-6) there appears the overwhelming **love** of the forgiving God. Indeed the jubilant words **Who is a God like thee?** in the Hebrew play on the meaning of the name of the prophet Micah, which means "Who is like Yahweh?" That the **enemy** has been **trodden down** (verse 10) is nothing compared to the knowledge that God will **tread our iniquities under foot.**

7:19cd. Among orthodox Jews it has been the custom since the Middle Ages to visit the bank of a river or other body of water following the synagogue service on the afternoon of Rosh Hashanah (the Jewish New Year). There they repeat this sentence three times while casting crumbs of bread on the water's surface. The ceremony is called *Tashlik,* Hebrew for the opening phrase **Thou wilt cast.** The celebration of God's forgiveness is eminently appropriate for the beginning of a new year and the beginning of a new life. Having offered adoration and praise, the worshiper can depart in peace.

THE BOOK OF NAHUM

Simon J. De Vries

INTRODUCTION

Historical Background

Characteristic oriental reluctance to record their military defeats caused the last three Assyrian kings to leave no record of their empire's decline. The fall of Assyria's capital, Nineveh, however, is the sole preoccupation of the book of Nahum.

The Hebrew kingdoms—Israel in the north and Judah in the south—had suffered more from the harsh and relentless Assyrians than from any other oppressor. For two and a half centuries Assyria had harassed them. The northern kingdom was driven into captivity. Judah was virtually demolished. The kings were forced into rigorously enforced subservience. Now at last Assyria's end was near. As Nahum proclaimed its defeat, he seemed to speak for all Israel and for Yahweh.

Certain verses added to the book after Nineveh's capture turned Nahum's prophecy into a hymn of rejoicing. It is probable that the book became a liturgy for the Jerusalem temple and was first used in an official celebration ceremony between 612 and 609. The latter is the date of Josiah's death. After this the Egyptians, to whom Judah was then forced to submit, would surely have suppressed any open exulting over their expiring ally.

The Book of Nahum

Authorship

We do not know who Nahum was, nor is it possible to locate his home, Elkosh. We can say with assurance only that he was one of Israel's greatest masters of poetic imagery and a thoroughgoing Yahwist. He had strong nationalistic loyalties. Though his oracles abound in motifs from cult mythology, it is difficult to be certain whether he himself had any direct association with the cult.

Composition

The book consists of different materials. Chapter 1 opens with an acrostic, or alphabetic, hymn proclaiming the awesome might of Yahweh manifesting itself in nature. It continues with alternating threats and promises. The remaining two chapters consist mainly of a dramatic description of Nineveh's fall. It is so vividly depicted that some have thought the author to be an actual eyewitness of the event. The linguistic evidence, however, makes it quite certain that he was actually predicting the near future, which he portrayed in highly inspired imagination and overwhelming passion.

The outstanding problems of the book's interpretation are:
(1) the extent of the acrostic hymn;
(2) the identity of the person(s) addressed in the "you" passages;
(3) whether the fall of Nineveh is seen as future or as past.
Scholars have made numerous alterations or corrections in the Hebrew text in an attempt to resolve these problems. Careful attention to form and style, with observation of grammatical niceties and changes in ideology, produces a reasonably clear picture of the book's meaning and composition without numerous changes.

That the ancient translators often failed to comprehend what was before them is understandable. It appears that the materials in this book have undergone an unusually complex process of growth and transformation. The most likely theory explaining this may be outlined as follows:
(1) The prophet or some other person worked out from

ancient models a stirring hymn of Yahweh's theophany, or self-revelation (1:2-8). To this a disciple added a short interpretive application (verses 9-10).

(2) Nahum proclaimed four denunciatory poems against Nineveh shortly before its fall (2:1, 3-12; 3:1-4; 3:7b-15a; and 3:15b-17).

(3) As the doom of Nineveh approached, another disciple brought the poems together. He prefixed the expanded hymn to provide an appropriate introduction, transposed the words "an oracle concerning Nineveh" to the beginning of the book, and introduced editorial transitions, perhaps out of Nahum's own words (1:11, 14; 2:13; and 3:5-7a).

(4) Nahum or a disciple spoke words of promise and exultation (1:12-13, 15; 2:2) and a mock lament (3:18-19) after Nineveh's capture. These were inserted into the existing work as refrains and as a conclusion, adapting the book to liturgical purposes.

(5) The final editor of the Book of the Twelve Prophets filled out the superscription in 1:1.

I. INTERPRETIVE ADDITIONS

1:1. *Superscription.* See Introduction.

1:2-10. *Acrostic (Alphabetic) Hymn with Expansion.* This hymn originally had nothing to do with Nineveh. It may have been written by the prophet, however. Verses 1-8 contain a skillfully composed hymn of Yahweh's self-revelation. It develops the ancient theme of Yahweh's power (**wrath**) in nature and asserts Yahweh's lordship over all peoples, who are reminded that Yahweh is well disposed to all who take refuge in God but unremitting in vengeance on Yahweh's enemies. The beginning is very solemn and ponderous, with its stair-like repetition and strong alliteration. A literal translation would be:

> A God jealous and avenging is Yahweh,
>   avenging is Yahweh and a master of wrath;

avenging is Yahweh against his adversaries,
and wrathful is he against his enemies.

The references to **Bashan, Carmel,** and **Lebanon,** as also those to **sea** and **river,** are adaptations of themes found in Canaanite mythology: Yahweh, not Baal, is the God of the holy **mountains,** the God of fertility. Since the thought and structure of these lines seem so perfectly balanced, it is useless to look for the acrostic in the following sections.

1:9-10. This is one of the most difficult passages in the Old Testament. Numerous alterations or corrections have been proposed. It seems best to take this as a disciple's expansion and to translate it as:

Whatever you may devise against Yahweh
  he will bring to complete destruction,
    so that opposition will not arise a second time;
  for it will become like interlacing thorns and intertwining
    brambles
  which are devoured as completely dried-out chaff.

1:11, 14; 2:13; 3:5-7a. *Editorial Transitions.* Whether or not these verses came from Nahum's own words or any common source, it is clear that a disciple was responsible for placing them where they are. He did this in order to bind the Nineveh poems together and provide them with what he considered a proper introduction.

1:11, 14. A crucial problem is the identification of the person addressed. Hebrew, unlike English, distinguishes gender and number in all pronouns. The **you** in verse 9 is anybody. The **you** in verse 11 (feminine singular) must be Nineveh since cities are regularly feminine. The **you** in verse 14 (masculine singular) has to be the one plotting **evil**—that is, a certain Assyrian king or the Assyrian kings collectively. There seems to be solid reason for observing the text's distinctions in gender wherever possible. Thus verse 11 is to be understood as the charge and verse 14 as the verdict against Nineveh and its king, whose end is decreed in formal juridical style.

2:13; 3:5-7a. These are threats against Nineveh in oracular style, with the formal introduction: **Behold I am against you** (feminine), **says the LORD of hosts.** The first passage summarizes the motifs of the preceding poem (the siege, the **lions**). The second takes up the theme of 3:1-4, developing the motif of the harlot's public ridicule as a formal introduction to 3:7b-15a.

1:12-13, 15; 2:2. *Liturgical Refrains.* These are oracles of blessing for Judah, with formal opening phrases. They were probably interspersed in the material to serve as responses in a celebration liturgy. As such they constitute the latest element in the book—apart from the superscription—together with the mock lament at the end. Nineveh has fallen. And though Assyrian armies remain in the field, Judah's complete liberation seems to be at hand. In 1:12 **they** refers to the evil and villainy of the preceding verse. Read it as "They have been cut off and have passed away." In verse 13 **his yoke** refers to the one plotting evil, who is addressed directly in verse 14. Read "I am breaking . . . am bursting. . . ." Verse 15 is a summons to a victory feast (cf. Isaiah 40:9-11). Because **the wicked** is impersonal, we should read "villainy," as in verse 11. In 2:2 the northern kingdom of Israel will be restored along with Judah.

II. POEMS AGAINST NINEVEH (2:1–3:17)

Some scholars consider this passage to be one long poem. Others remove the transitional material in 2:13 and 3:5-7a. They then rearrange the sections in an attempt to make a unified whole of what is left. It is better to view this remaining material as four separate poems, delivered at a time when Nineveh had not yet fallen. Yet it was so certain to be taken that its capture could be depicted as in progress or even as completed. Here Nahum the poet appears in all his splendor. Strangely, the name of God is not mentioned.

2:1, 3-12. *A Taunt: "The Capture of Nineveh."* This poem consists of a prelude and three strophes, each strophe having three couplets of virtually equal length. The meter is artistically worked out. But the real power of the poem is in its excited movement and vivid imagery.

2:1. Ringing imperatives in this prelude warn Nineveh's defenders of the impending attack.

2:3-5. The attack begins. The descriptions of the invading warriors and their cavalry are like momentary impressions flashing on the mind. The invaders break through the outer wall into the streets. Desperately the confused defenders set up emergency barriers.

2:6-9. The city is taken. Suddenly the river gate is broken open, and the attackers pour through. The **palace** is in consternation. Idols and human captives are led forth, streaming out like the **waters** of a broken **pool,** while the conquerors are urged on to the rich **plunder.**

2:10-12. These verses constitute the taunt proper. Tremendously sonorous and ponderous, three nouns in parallelism symbolize the devastation. Proud and mighty Nineveh is taunted as a **lion** who has taken much **prey** but whose **den** has now been destroyed. For other examples of the lion imagery cf. Job 4:10-11 and Ezekiel 19:1-9.

3:1-4. *A Woe: "The End of the Bloody City."* This is a poem in three short strophes. The charges of bloodthirstiness, mendacity, deceit, and immorality are given as reasons for Nineveh's downfall. **Booty** and **plunder** might better be translated "tearing" and "prey" respectively, recalling the imagery of 2:12 rather than of 2:9. Verses 2-3 return to the rapid and excited style of 2:3-9. Short disjointed lines pile up vivid and gory details, combining them in one overpowering, horrifying picture.

Verse 4 is climactic, stating the great sin of Nineveh for which this disaster has come on her: she is a **deadly,** deceitful **harlot.** Elsewhere Judah is taunted as a harlot (Ezekiel 16, 23), as are Tyre (Isaiah 23:16) and Rome (referred to as "Babylon" in Revelation 17:5, 16). For other examples of the woe form cf. Isaiah 5:8-25; 10:1-4; Habakkuk 2:6-17; and Zephaniah 2:5-7; 3:1-8.

3:7b-15a. A Taunt with Threat: "Nineveh Is No Safer Than Thebes." That this is intended as a taunt is clear both from the introduction supplied by the editor (verse 7a) and from the prelude (verse 7b-c), which rejoices over Nineveh as already fallen. It is taunted for its vain pride in imagining itself safe from divine judgment. Besides the prelude there are two divisions—verses 8-10 and 11-15a.

3:8-10. The strength of Thebes did not protect it. With the Nile waters as its rampart and strong allies at its side it felt secure, yet even it came to experience the terrors of captivity, with little ones murdered and the order of its life shattered. Thebes, lying far up the Nile, was an ancient capital with great prestige. Hence its capture by Ashurbanipal's army in 663 was the worst conceivable blow to Egyptian pride and a crowning triumph for Assyria.

3:11-15a. Nineveh's defenses will likewise fail. In direct address its doom is announced (verse 11). Its warriors are like women, its fortresses like figs falling from a shaken tree. Its gates are thrown open to attack. While its defenders frantically rebuild the walls, the fire and the sword . . . devour.

3:15b-17. A Taunt: "Nineveh Is Like a Locust Horde." This section was directly attached to the preceding because of the catchword *locust*. However, this evokes quite a different image here than in the previous line. Nineveh's merchants, princes (the latter from an Akkadian word perhaps meaning "guardsmen"), and scribes (a Sumerian word perhaps meaning "recruiting officials") have descended like a locust horde. They have stripped every victim bare. But they disappear with the rising of the sun—that is, the destruction of their capital. Though the meter, vocabulary, syntax, and imagery are different from that of the other poems, there is no compelling reason to deny that Nahum wrote this poem.

III. A MOCK LAMENT CONCERNING THE KING OF ASSYRIA (3:18-19)

This is a form of taunt. Perhaps written by Nahum, it was added after Nineveh's fall. That the verbs represent an actual past (not mere projections of the past into the future as in 3:7b) seems likely from the reference to **the news of you**—a report already received. The meter used throughout—three stresses followed by two stresses—marks this as a formal lament. It is used, of course, in bitter mockery, for Judah rejoices instead of weeping.

THE BOOK OF HABAKKUK

Simon J. De Vries

INTRODUCTION

Historical Background

Jehoiakim, the second son of Josiah, was a ruler who hastened Judah's day of final disaster. In the Machiavellian game of politics that he played, he first won and then lost everything. Pharaoh Neco, having killed Jehoiakim's father and deposed his elder brother, offered him the throne at the price of complete subservience. He was willing to comply, for he could gain a free hand for pursuing his ruthless internal policies. But in 604 Jehoiakim was forced to submit to Babylonian control as Nebuchadrezzar drove the Egyptians back to their border. For three years Jehoiakim served him (II Kings 24:1). Then yielding to the enticements of Egyptian ambassadors as opportunistic as himself, he threw off the Babylonian yoke and precipitated the inevitable retribution. He died while Nebuchadrezzar's army was besieging Jerusalem in December, 598.

We gather from the scanty biblical references that Jehoiakim had a character opposite to that of his father Josiah. He allowed the hard-won gains of the Deuteronomic reform to lapse while a new apostasy seized the religious institutions. II Kings 23:37 records that "he did what was evil in the sight of the LORD, according to all that his fathers had done."

Jehoiakim treated the prophets who dared to reprove him with harshness and contempt (cf. Jeremiah 36). He and his retainers apparently forsook morality based on the covenant, oppressing the poor as cruelly as before. Jeremiah was impelled to cry out (Jeremiah 22:17):

> You have eyes and heart
>   only for your dishonest gain,
> for shedding innocent blood,
>   and for practicing oppression and violence.

This is the setting into which the short prophecy of Habakkuk is most probably to be placed.

Authorship

A crucial question must be solved in order to choose among the wide array of possible interpretations of this book. It is the problem of identifying the "righteous" and the "wicked." Careful study reveals that in certain passages the wicked one can be none other than a local tyrant, while in other passages he must be a foreign invader. The righteous are the oppressed local citizenry in the first group of passages and the whole Jewish nation in the second. There is no acceptable solution except to assume that two different authors are involved.

In Habakkuk's original estimate Jehoiakim seemed a greater threat to the true interests of the covenant people than any invading conqueror could possibly be. For this reason he appears to welcome the vision of 1:5-11, in which Yahweh announces the approach of the Chaldeans (Babylonians), whom God is raising up against this presumptuous tyrant.

Thus Habakkuk stands where Josiah would have stood, upholding the terms of the covenant and the now abortive reform. He stands for the simple believer and hence for Yahweh. Though he has affinities with Nahum and the "nationalistic" prophets, he is closer to Jeremiah than many have imagined.

Drastic shifts were constantly occurring in these turbulent times. Habakkuk was soon led to see that the delivering Babylonians could indeed be oppressors of God's people. Soon Nebuchadrezzar loomed as the cruelest tyrant. Yahweh's use of this tyrant became a new problem for the prophet's faith.

In a new vision of Yahweh's power Habakkuk found reassurance that this foreign oppressor would also come under divine judgment (chapter 3). This new emphasis encouraged a disciple of the prophet to refocus the original prophecies against this foreign enemy, giving the book as a whole a strong nationalistic flavor.

This shift in meaning needs to be kept in mind when attempting to evaluate the book's treatment of the problem of theodicy—that is, justification of God's ways. In the original form of his complaint, Habakkuk was thinking only of Jehoiakim. He asks how God can continue even for a while to tolerate this tyrant as he "swallows up" his own pious subjects (1:13). The answer of 2:2-5a concerns this problem. The vision concerning the Chaldeans will surely come to pass at the appointed time. Meanwhile, Habakkuk is given Yahweh's solemn word that the wicked will not finally prevail and that the righteous will live if they only continue faithful.

But the disciple gives the question of 1:13 a different dimension. The wicked one becomes the ruthless Babylonian who oppresses everyone "more righteous *than he*"—that is, every Jew suffering because of persecution. It is now a question of degree. Why does Yahweh allow the more wicked to punish the less wicked?

The Prophet

There is no historical value in the stories about Habakkuk found in the apocryphal legend of Bel and the Dragon (see comment) or in rabbinic tales. We do not know who Habakkuk was or where he lived. His name is not found elsewhere in the Bible. It appears to be non-Hebraic, perhaps being derived from an Akkadian word for a garden plant. We are told only that he was a prophet. We may also infer from Habakkuk's use of cultic forms in his prophecies that he had close associations with cult worship.

Composition

In light of the above considerations, the most likely theory of the book's composition would be the following:

(1) Habakkuk recites the complaint of 1:2-4, and receives the vision of verses 5-11. He recites the renewed complaint of verses 12-13, then goes to his watch post to await Yahweh's answer (2:1). This comes to him in the words of 2:2-5a. He records all this, perhaps for use in the temple liturgy. He also receives a vision parallel to or as part of the one in 1:5-11. This is later inserted by his disciple at 1:14-17.

(2) On other occasions he delivers four woes against the local tyrant (2:6b-17 in its original form).

(3) Habakkuk later experiences the terrors of invasion. Then an old hymn of theophany, or divine self-revelation (3:3-15), becomes a new revelation of Yahweh's power. This circulates for a while separate from the rest of Habakkuk's writing. Liturgical notes are added for use in the temple.

(4) The disciple lived perhaps during Zedekiah's reign (597-586). He modified the original material in chapters 1-2, making changes in the text and adding words of his own.

(5) An editor binds all the material together, including chapter 3. He supplies a superscription, an introduction to the woes (2:6a), and a derisive poem against idols (2:18-20).

(6) The final editor of the minor prophets puts the superscription into its present form.

I. SUPERSCRIPTION (1:1)

Oracle is used to describe all of chapters 1-2, including materials not in the oracular style. Note the emphasis on the visual aspects of inspiration. The Revised Standard Version **of God** is not in the Hebrew text.

II. Habakkuk's Complaint and God's Reply (1:2–2:5)

1:2-4. *A Complaint of Oppression.* This dates from the early years of Jehoiakim's reign. It has the formal marks of a liturgical complaint similar to those found among the psalms. The prophet has been burdened by official corruption within the land and by Yahweh's failure to answer his protests. Verse 2 should probably be translated:

> O Yahweh, for how long have I cried for help,
>> but you do not hear!
> I cry out to you of violence,
>> but you do not deliver.

As **the wicked** (literally "guilty") overwhelm **the righteous** (literally "acquitted, blameless"), covenant law is no longer impartially applied. This lack of justice results in strife, trouble, and violence.

1:5-11, *An Answering Vision: "I Am Raising Up the Chaldeans."* Without formal introduction Yahweh announces the coming of the Babylonians. God has appointed them to be the instrument of judgment upon many **nations,** including the wicked oppressor within Judah. The thought is similar to that of Isaiah 10:5-11. Textual emendations seem to be required in verse 7*b*, which may be read as the specific answer to Habakkuk's complaint in verses 2-4: "From him my judgment shall proceed!"

There is a merging of aural and visual imagery. The poetry falls into three approximately equal strophes. The first contains the announcement (verses 5-6). The second is a description of the Babylonians' rapidity of movement and **fierce** attack (verses 7-8). The third describes the terrifying ease with which they overpower every opponent (verses 9-11).

1:12-13; 2:1. *The Complaint Renewed.* Ancient scribes changed "thou diest not" to **we shall not die.** Because **than he** at the end of verse 13 makes too long a poetic line, it does not belong to the original text. Habakkuk is not satisfied with the vision because it seems far from fulfillment. The knowledge that the eternal God has appointed the **wicked** one for judgment, perhaps in the indefinite future, leaves a vexing contradiction unresolved. Why should so pure and holy a God tolerate the wicked oppressing the righteous even for a moment? This is the burning question Habakkuk takes with him to his watch post. This is probably located in the temple rather than on the city wall or in an open field as popularly visualized. Once again aural and visual imagery are mixed: **look forth to see what he will say.** The Revised Standard Version **what I will answer** should be emended to read "what he will answer."

2:2-5a. An Answering Oracle. Considerable confusion has surrounded an interpretation of this crucial passage. Many scholars have thought that the lines containing the famous words, **the righteous shall live by his faith,** are what Habakkuk is commanded to write. But this is an oracle, not a **vision.** Besides, why would **tablets** be needed for recording so short a message?

Actually the vision that Habakkuk is to write so plainly has already been given. It is the vision of the coming Chaldeans recorded in 1:5-11 (note "look . . . see" in 1:5). Yahweh is now replying to Habakkuk's complaint, assuring him that this vision will not be delayed. It is set for a definite time. Hence he is to wait for it. He is to inscribe it on tablets (metaphorically?) as a permanent reminder and witness.

These words of reassurance are followed by the explanatory oracle of verses 4-5a. Unfortunately, its contents have been badly garbled. We may translate it approximately as in the Revised Standard Version, substituting "wealth" for **wine.** The instability of the unrighteous person's wealth and power is underscored. The righteous are assured that they will live in the surest and highest sense by maintaining their faithfulness (not faith in the New Testament sense). For the New Testament adaptation of this passage, which was so influential on Luther's thinking, cf. Romans 1:17; Galatians 3:11; and Hebrews 10:38-39.

1:14-17; 2:5b. Modifications and Additions. The passage

1:14-17 may be a separate vision or part of 1:5-11. In either case it refers to the Babylonians. Its form identifies it as coming from Habakkuk himself. References to the pagan custom of making **sacrifices** to implements of war, though not to fishing equipment, have been found in ancient texts. The disciple who later viewed Babylon as Judah's greatest enemy (see Introduction) placed this passage here when he added "than he" to verse 13. At the same time he turned verse 17 into a question (the original reading was, "Therefore he keeps on emptying his net"). Perhaps he also altered an original "he makes" in verse 14 to **thou makest.**

These changes made Yahweh directly responsible for the enemy's cruelty. They intensified the problem for which 2:2-5*a* was supposed to be the answer. Accordingly, the disciple added the interpretive gloss in 2:5*b*—a denunciation of the Babylonians—and also touched up the woes that follow.

III. Woes Against a Tyrant (2:6-17)

Verses 18-20 are an editorial addition. But there is no reason to doubt that Habakkuk was the author of the four woes of verses 6*b*-17 in their original form. They all show some evidence of the disciple's rewriting, and it is impossible to recover the original form of verses 12-14. Each woe follows the classic form containing an invective and a threat (cf. Isaiah 5:8-25; 10:1-4; Nahum 3:1-4; Zephaniah 3:1-8).

2:6*a*. Editorial Introduction. This is a badly confused line, for which the Revised Standard Version has as good a translation as any. **Taunt** is a technical term for the woe form. **Scoffing derision** appropriately applies to verses 18-20.

2:6*b*-8. A Merciless Creditor. One of the cruelest forms of economic oppression was the retaining of **pledges** taken in place of unpaid loans or services (cf. Amos 2:8). Here the local tyrant is bitterly denounced and threatened for making himself wealthy with such pledges. The disciple adds words of condemnation for the plundering enemy.

2:9-11. *An Ambitious Builder.* Here the only clear trace of the disciple's rewriting is the line **by cutting off many peoples.** **Forfeited** is literally "sinned against." The best commentary on this passage is Jeremiah 22:13-17. In a time of international crisis Jehoiakim built a pretentious palace with taxes squeezed out of his unfortunate subjects. Thereby he hastened the day of utter ruin. So flagrant is the wrong that the palace's very beams and stones protest.

2:12-14. *A Cruel Conqueror.* Verse 12 seems to recall Micah 3:10. It may have originally referred to Jehoiakim's efforts to glorify Jerusalem at his subjects' expense. Verse 13b is paralleled in Jeremiah 51:58. Because verse 14 is obviously borrowed from Isaiah 11:9 and reflects a universalistic view of God, it has been taken as postexilic.

But probably the disciple is responsible for the entire poem in its present form. Its meaning is that Yahweh's **glory**, filling the whole **earth,** exercises veto power over Nebuchadrezzar's frantic efforts to build **a town** (Babylon?) with the **blood** of his victims, whose labors are **for naught.**

2:15-17. *A Violent Oppressor.* The imagery of drunkenness is probably purely metaphorical, referring to Jehoiakim's cruel oppression. But it was sufficiently appropriate to the broader reference to be left unemended by the disciple. This is the book's most explicit threat against Jehoiakim. The disciple added verse 17b, which is identical to verse 8b.

IV. RIDICULE OF IDOL WORSHIP (2:18-20)

This belongs neither to Habakkuk nor to his disciple but was supplied by an editor. The catchword **woe,** though not in the proper place at the beginning, made it seem to be an appropriate conclusion to the preceding woes. The solemn climax in verse 20 seemed a perfect introduction to chapter 3. The passage has nothing to do with any oppressor, local or foreign, but is a mocking derision of idolatry similar to Isaiah

44:9-20; 46:1-2 and Jeremiah 10:1-4. A better reading for verse 19*a* would be:

> Woe to him who says to a wooden thing, "Awake! Arise!"
> to a dumb stone, "This shall give teaching!"

V. HABAKKUK'S PRAYER (3:1-19)

Chapter 3 shows striking differences in language and conception. It has often been denied that Habakkuk was the author. Scholars have thought that the liturgical notes and the reference to the **anointed** (vs. 13) clearly mark it as postexilic. There can be no doubt that this chapter did circulate separately at one time—the liturgical notes clearly indicate this. But it did not remain permanently detached from the book bearing its author's name.

We have observed several features of Habakkuk's affinities with cult worship. There is no good reason to suppose that he could not have composed this grand-hymn. Recent archeological and linguistic studies have made it clear that the language of chapter 3 is at least as early as that of the other chapters and that some of its imagery goes back to the time of Israel's origins.

As he witnessed the devastation wrought by the Babylonians, Habakkuk was evidently driven to prayer. While he waited quietly for an assurance of Yahweh's mercy, the words of an ancient theophany, or divine self-revelation, similar to Deuteronomy 33 and Judges 5 became the vehicle of inspiration and assurance. It drew from him the most deeply spiritual utterance of this book and one of the noblest in the entire Old Testament.

3:1, 19*b*. *Liturgical Headings.* The introduction contains technical terms similar to those in the headings of the psalms (cf. Psalms 7). Also compare the word **selah** in verses 3, 9, 13 and the words at the end.

3:2. *A Request for Mercy in the Midst of Wrath.* According to its literary form this should be regarded as an integral and essential part of the hymn.

3:3-15. A Theophany: "Yahweh's Combat." This consists of two sixteen-line strophes followed by five-line refrains.

3:3-8. These verses constitute strophe I and the refrain. Magificent language expresses the overwhelming majesty of Israel's God coming from God's traditional home in northern Arabia (Sinai?). God is like the sun, filling the whole **earth** with **his glory,** shaking **the mountains** in wrath.

This is the language of the earliest Yahwistic traditions, set in deliberate opposition to themes from the Canaanite myths. Yahweh, rather than Baal, is engaged in combat with **rivers** and **the sea** (in the Babylonian creation myth Marduk struggled with Tiamat, the primordial sea of chaos).

3:9-13. These verses make up strophe II and its refrain. The actual battle is described in stirring images. All the enemies of Yahweh are vanquished as Yahweh goes forth for the people's **salvation.** The **anointed** one in verse 13 is the Davidic prince.

3:16-19a. The Prophet's Reaction and Response. This is part of the hymn, forming a twelve-line third strophe plus a five-line postlude. But its sources are the prophet's own present experience. Here his inspiration rises to its highest exaltation. The divine manifestation appalls him, leaving him weak and exhausted. But it gives him the calm assurance that however severe the coming trials may be, the almighty Yahweh will surely carry out the purpose against the invaders. These thoughts lead the prophet at the end to rejoice **in the god of** his **salvation.** Whatever he may suffer, whatever may be taken from him, he will continue to be joyful in this great God. Habakkuk is himself a prime example of the righteous one who lives by faith.

THE BOOK OF ZEPHANIAH

Simon J. De Vries

INTRODUCTION

Historical Background

This book has been put at the end of the triad Nahum-Habakkuk-Zephaniah. Chronologically however, it belongs at the beginning. The final editor of the minor prophets was responsible for having made this arrangement. He probably understood the prophet's great-great-grandfather mentioned in 1:1 to be the famous Judean king. Hence he concluded that Zephaniah needed to be placed after Nahum and Habakkuk, in spite of the specific statement dating him in the reign of Josiah (641-609).

It was characteristic of Israel's prophets that they allowed themselves to recede into the background while placing Yahweh's message foremost. Thus most of what we know about Zephaniah is drawn by inference from his prophecy. We are provided with an unusually long genealogy in the superscription, however. Though the prophet himself did not write it, there is no good reason to reject its statement. Other prophetic genealogies go back only to the father or grandfather. This list goes back to the fifth generation. For this reason many scholars agree that Hezekiah must be the king of that name. This would then put Zephaniah within the royal lineage. It would lend special weight to his denunciation of the officials and the king's sons in 1:8—which suggests at least that he was a familiar figure in the royal court.

However, the chronological problems are formidable. However, for those who hold this view, the five generations must be squeezed into the period from around 716 to around 625. If this is not probable, one cannot say that it is impossible.

In any case, various considerations lead us to date Zephaniah's activities not only in Josiah's reign but in the early part of it. Because Baalism and foreign cults are still flourishing (1:4-6), it is clear that the Deuteronomic reform has not yet begun. Zephaniah's freedom in denouncing Manasseh and Amon surely indicates that they have passed from the scene. Josiah is nowhere mentioned (except in a dubious passage, 3:15) and there are references to the officials and king's sons causing dissension or perhaps plotting insurrection (1:8-9). These facts point specifically to the early years, when Josiah was still a lad. At that time he had not yet come to make a public espousal of the reform program. According to II Chronicles 34:3-8, he did not begin to "seek the God of David his father" until the eighth year of his reign. He did not undertake reform measures until his twelfth regnal year, bringing them to fruition in the eighteenth year of his rule, 623/22.

One of the most vexing historical problems pertaining to this period is Herodotus' statement that the Scythians, wild and ferocious marauders from the Asian interior, were sweeping over Western Asia as far south as Egypt about the year 626. Both the Medes and the Assyrians were having trouble with them in this period. Later (around 612) they played an important role in Assyria's downfall. If they did actually approach Egypt, they must have passed through Palestine and Philistia, striking terror into the hearts of peoples living in their path.

There is nothing to confirm Herodotus' statement, however, except an apparent preoccupation with an unnamed menace in the book of Zephaniah and in Jeremiah's early prophecies (chapters 4–6). Identifying this foe with the Scythians begs the very question needing to be solved, but no better identification lies at hand. In any case, it is clear from reading the book that if the prophet were speaking of them, they did not actually attack Jerusalem—though it is quite likely that they would have raided the Philistine coastlands (cf. 2:4-7). Certainly a deliverance from some definite foreign foe was the reason for the hymn of gratitude in 3:14-18.

Authorship

We can be fairly sure that Zephaniah was a cultic prophet. As such he summoned the pious to a solemn assembly in the temple (2:1-4) and led them in cultic celebration (3:14-18). It is generally agreed, moreover, that he had considerable influence in stimulating the Deuteronomic reform, which had strong cultic ties.

This book demonstrates the fact, and sometimes the vitality, of corporate authorship. Zephaniah evidently had a disciple or school of disciples who felt free to adapt his original oracles to new situations. They must have believed that in a real sense they were reincarnating their master, giving his message new life and force. When Josiah died and his reform began to founder—or still later, after Jerusalem had been destroyed (586)—these disciples projected the old messages of doom toward a new future.

Composition

We may reconstruct the composition of Zephaniah somewhat as follows:

(1) In the early years of Josiah's reign and probably shortly before the enemy raid, the prophet delivered a series of oracles, proclaiming judgment

> against all humankind (1:14-18),
> against various foreign lands (2:5-7, 8-9, 12-14),
> against all humankind and Jerusalem (1:2-6; 3:1-4, 6-8),
> and exclusively against Jerusalem itself (1:7-13).

(2) As the menace approached, Zephaniah issued a summons to a solemn assembly at Jerusalem for the purpose of averting destruction (2:1-4).

(3) After the threat had passed, leaving Judah unscathed, Zephaniah led the temple worshipers in a joyful hymn of celebration (3:14-18).

(4) Later, probably during the Babylonian exile, a disciple refocused Zephaniah's oracles of doom and expanded some of them into promises of blessing (glosses, or added interpretations, in 1:9a, 10a, 12a; expansion of 2:5-7; a gloss at 3:5 and additional verses in 3:9-13; a gloss at 3:16a plus 3:19).

(5) Possibly the same, but probably another, author added taunts against Moab and Ammon (2:10-11) and against Nineveh (2:15) and attached the concluding verse, 3:20.

(6) An editor rearranged the book into oracles of judgment against Judah (1:1–2:4), oracles against the foreign nations (2:5-15), and oracles of blessing (3:9-20). He inserted 3:1-8 after the Nineveh oracle because of the direct address to a city common to both. The same person probably added the superscription.

Literary Quality

For the larger part Zephaniah's prophecy consists of beautiful and dramatic poetry. His disciples generally fail to measure up to him in poetic inspiration. But in some respects they surpass him in the loftiness of their spiritual understanding.

I. SUPERSCRIPTION (1:1)

Here is the only place where the prophet is named. His name may have a double allusion to God ("Yahweh is Zaphon"—the holy mountain of the north). Hence it would be an explicit polemic against Baalism (cf. current Phoenician names like Baal-Zaphon). **Cushi** ("Ethiopian") may have been a non-Semite.

II. DIVINE JUDGMENT ON JUDAH AND JERUSALEM (1:2–2:4)

1:2-6. *An Oracle: "The Overthrow of the Wicked."* The contrast between the two strophes of this oracle (verses 2-3 and 4-6)

127

dramatizes its impact upon idolators in Jerusalem. Moving from the greater to the lesser, from the general to the specific, Yahweh first declares judgment on all that has been made and then pronounces doom upon **Judah** and **Jerusalem.** This contradicts the cherished doctrine of Zion's inviolability (cf. Isaiah 37:35), but its force is beyond resisting. If Yahweh is sovereign judge of the whole earth, Yahweh is judge of Jerusalem too. **This place** in verse 4 means "this shrine"—that is, the temple. Fertility rites associated with Baalism were secretly practiced there, along with worship of the Mesopotamian astral deities and human sacrifices to the Ammonite god Malkam (**Milcom** is the "Molech" of I Kings 11:7).

1:7-13. *An Oracle: "The Day of Yahweh on Jerusalem."* For the imagery of this poem cf. Isaiah 2:12-22 and Amos 5:18-20. Zephaniah associates the day of divine judgment with the enemy's approach, announcing that it is very near. **On that day** (verses 9, 10) and **at that time** (verse 12) are from a disciple, who inserted them in order to redirect the prophet's words to a still-distant future.

1:7-9. Strophe I concerns Yahweh's sacrifice and inspection. The **sacrifice** provides an image of blood and slaughter. In **I will punish** the sudden change to the first person demonstrates the prophet's complete identification with Yahweh. The verb may have a wider meaning, however, such as "inspect, call to account" (so also in 1:12; 2:7; 3:7). The officials are indicted for violence and fraud. **Threshold** perhaps designates the pedestal for the royal throne.

1:10-11. Strophe II describes the sound of destruction. The excitement and terror of the approaching invasion are expressed in the form as well as in the dramatic imagery. The foe first comes to Jerusalem's northern and least-protected quarter. There live **the traders** and merchants who deserve to be the first victims of the onslaught.

1:12-13. Strophe III is a judgment on the greedy and complacent. These are the groups living according to the ultimate blasphemy: **the LORD will not do good, nor will he do ill**—a blatant contradiction of Genesis 18:25. Words from Amos

5:11 are borrowed for the picture of devastation. Zephaniah is depicted in Christian art as holding a lamp in his hand.

1:14-18. An Oracle: *"The Day of Yahweh."* This is the source of inspiration for the famous medieval hymn "Dies Irae, Dies Illa" ("Day of Wrath, Day of Mourning"). There is a striking resemblance between verses 7 and 14. Many have held that verse 7 should be transferred to the beginning of this poem, but considerations of form and syntax argue against it. There is nothing in this poem to suggest that it refers solely to Judah—though the general judgment it announces is clearly intended to apply to Judah along with the rest of the nations (cf. 1:2-6).

1:14. In strophe I the **day of the LORD is near.** The Revised Standard Version makes little sense in its literal translation of the second line. The text should probably be emended to read: "Swifter is the day of Yahweh than a runner, it hastens faster than a champion."

1:15-17. In strophe II the day is dreadful. A double triad of three-foot lines produces an overwhelming feeling of doom and desolation. The strong alliteration that is characteristic of Zephaniah's genuine poems is especially striking here. The concluding words make clear that all people are judged **because all have sinned.**

1:18. Strophe III pronounces **the day of the wrath of the LORD** unavoidable. No ransom or bribe can buy escape. There is no second chance or appeal, no exception or exemption.

2:1-4. *A Summons to Solemn Assembly.* Sonorous alliteration, ringing imperatives, and urgent repetitions express the earnestness of this appeal.

2:1-2. Strophe I is a call to the nation. The **shameless nation** is called to show its repentance in a public assembly before the day of wrath breaks on it.

2:3-4. Strophe II summons the humble. In particular, the **humble of the land** are to **seek the Lord**—that is, come to a fast and service of supplication and live a humble and righteous life. The prophet holds out the hope that they may be saved from the coming storm, which is about to sweep over the neighboring territory of Philistia. Some scholars have joined verse 4 to verses 5-7. This ignores not only the poem's form but also the point of Zephaniah's appeal—that with the enemy so close by, Judah's leaders had *better* get scared.

III. DIVINE JUDGMENT ON THE NATIONS (2:5-15)

2:5-7. A *Woe Against Philistia*. Compare this short poem with the woe in 3:1-8. Note that it lacks the invective so prominent there. It is indeed striking and significant that though Zephaniah proclaims Philistia's imminent destruction, he does not denounce it for any crime. Here as elsewhere, the oracular form represents Yahweh as bringing the judgment, though an earthly foe is the agent.

In this poem the disciple's adaptations are particularly apparent. He turned the picture of Philistia as a desolate pastureland into an image of bliss and contentment for **the remnant of the house of Judah,** whose **fortunes** Yahweh promises to **restore** (literally "return their captivity"). Zephaniah's original poem probably read as follows:

> Woe to you, inhabitants of the seacoast,
>   you nation of the Cherethites!
> The word of Yahweh is against you, O Canaan,
>   you land of the Philistines!
> So I will destroy you till no inhabitant is left,
>   and the seacoast shall become pastures,
>   meadows for shepherds and folds for flocks;
>   they shall pasture among the houses of Ashkelon,
>   and shall lie down in Ekron.

2:8-9. A *Threat Against Moab and Ammon*. Judah's eastern neighbors, Moab and Ammon, were traditional enemies. Here Yahweh swears a solemn oath to make their land as empty and desolate as **Sodom** and **Gomorrah**—surely a more severe judgment than that inflicted on the Philistines. This passage

130

should be compared with Israel's taunt in Numbers 21:27-30 and Isaiah's oracle in chapters 15–16. The poem's structure identifies verse 9d as a genuine conclusion. Its reference to a plundering remnant completes the picture of destruction.

2:12-14. *A Threat Against Ethiopia and Assyria.* This poem expresses the scope of Yahweh's judgment. It reaches from the distant south to the remote **north.** Though the major emphasis falls on Assyria's desolation, its specific sin is not stated. **Nineveh** will become more desolate than Philistia (2:5-7), inasmuch as the **beasts** that are to inhabit it are wild animals rather than sheep. Yet it is to be less forbidding than Moab and Ammon (verses 8-9), where nothing is to dwell.

2:10-11, 15. *Taunts Against Moab, Ammon, and Nineveh.* These have been added by a disciple. They appear to date from a time when these enemies had been destroyed. Both begin with the emphatic word **this,** meanig the aforementioned desolations. Verses 15 employs the past tense. Hence Nineveh is already fallen. This is then a taunt similar to Nahum 3:18-19 (cf. 3:7). We may suppose that verses 10-11 likewise refer to the past and are intended to turn verses 8-9 into a taunt. In any case, the universal rule of Yahweh depicted in verse 11 lies in the future.

IV. A WOE AGAINST JERUSALEM (3:1-8)

The Introduction gives the reasons for this poem's present position between the oracles against the nations and the oracles of blessing. Verse 5 is a theologizing interpretive addition. After the introductory denunciation, the charges and specifications are set forth in two six-line strophes, followed by the verdict or threat in a final strophe of four lines. All is artfully balanced and dynamically powerful.

3:2-4. *Charges Against Jerusalem.* Verse 2b in this first strophe is emphatic. In effect it says, *"In Yahweh she has not trusted, unto her God she has not drawn near"*—implying that Jerusalem has followed other gods. Each group among the leaders is indicted. The word here translated **leave nothing**

means "gnaw," possibly interpreted as a description of the gnawing of cubs in contrast to the biting of **wolves**. It means that the rapacious **judges** become ineffectual in administering justice in their proper posts, which they assume in **the morning**.

3:6-7. *Yahweh's Warning Scorned.* In strophe II Yahweh has judged other **nations** in order to teach Judah to repent. But Yahweh's patience has only made the leaders more eager for corruption.

3:8. *Future Judgment of Judah.* Strophe III warns that Judah will surely be included in the general judgment and consumed in the general destruction. **Wait for me** has the same word as is found in Habakkuk 2:3. For the image of Yahweh as **witness** compare Micah 1:2 and Malachi 3:13-15. For the idea of gathering the **nations** for judgment compare Joel 3.

V. Divine Blessing for Judah (3:9-20)

3:19-13. *An Oracle: "Israel's Return and Renewal."* The language and form identify this section as an expansion of the woe against Jerusalem, but it has a definite strophic structure.

3:9-10. Strophe I concerns the purification of the nations. Here is a universalism worthy of Second Isaiah. The nations will learn Hebrew in order to serve Yahweh. Perhaps a clearer reading for **my suppliants, the daughter of my dispersed ones** is "those invoking me among the dispersion."

3:11. Strophe II, concerning the purging of pride from Israel, is an echo of 3:1-7.

3:12-13. Strophe III speaks of the holy remnant. The **humble and lowly** are the holy remnant, by whose righteous living the nation is to be saved from judgment. Theirs is a vicarious repentance. To them is accordingly promised peace and bliss.

3:14-18. *A Celebration Hymn: "Yahweh Is in Your Midst."* Apart from a probable editorial addition in verse 16a, there can be little doubt that this is Zephaniah's hymn for a service of deliverance.

3:14-15. Strophe I is exultant—let **Zion . . . rejoice!** As

Yahweh brought the menacing enemy to carry out judgment, God is responsible for having removed that same menace. In verse 15*b* read "Yahweh rules in your midst." Yahweh is the true **King** in the midst of the people. He has heard the prayer of the humble.

3:16-18. In this second strophe Yahweh rejoices in his victory. Verse 18*b* should read, "I have removed disaster from you."

3:19-20. *Expansions.* Once again the promises to a dispersed remnant and the words **at that time** indicate the work of a disciple. In verse 19*c* the sentence structure requires us to read, "even those whose shame was in all the earth." Verse 20 is a prose-poetry repetition of verse 19. It may be from the same person who wrote 2:10-11, 15.

THE BOOK OF HAGGAI

Roger N. Carstensen

INTRODUCTION

The Prophet

Little is known of the prophet Haggai. Four oracles are
attributed to him, and along with Zechariah he is reported to
have helped the Jews rebuild their temple (Ezra 5:1-2).
Presumably his oracles provided this "help" (Ezra 6:14).

The name Haggai means "festal," which may indicate that he
was born on a feast day. His reference to the previous temple
(2:3) does not necessarily mean he saw it himself, though he may
have been an old man at the time of the oracles. Tradition holds
that he was a member of the "Great Synagogue," the traditional
first college of learned scribes, which the Jews believed carried
the interpretation of the law forward to the later rabbis. This
suggests he may have been influential in the community.

His Times

The book of Haggai is clearly dated in 1:1 to the reign of
Darius I—520 B.C. The return from Babylon led by Sheshbazzar
had occurred about eighteen years earlier (538), soon after
Cyrus' conquest. The people to whom Haggai preached were
poor but not actually destitute. The future of their province
under the insensitive rule of the distant Persian government

showed no prospect of improvement. Drought and disease struck the crops. Evidence of the care of the God who softened the heart of Cyrus was nowhere to be seen. The practices of religion were not taken seriously. The people had made no provision for God to live among them, and God's ancient house lay in ruins. The concept of God's active presence in their community had faded.

In the midst of their discouragement, winds of revolution stirred the air. Cambyses by his campaigns (529-522) had hardened the generous policies of Cyrus. When he died on his way back from a campaign in Egypt, the Persian throne was in jeopardy and the affairs of government in chaos. Darius succeded to the throne in 522. While he proceeded with energy and courage to consolidate his rule, it was several years before it became clear that the empire would survive.

In 520 the issue was still most uncertain. Hopes for national freedom rose throughout the provinces. The building of the temple plus the attempt to put Zerubbabel of the seed of David on the throne was apparently the direction the revolution took in Judah. It would appear that Darius simply carried out the policy of Cyrus, as Ezra 6:1-15 suggests. The building of the temple was allowed to proceed. The crowning of a king, never authorized by Cyrus, was frustrated by means that are unknown.

His Message and Purpose

The central message of Haggai is, "Build the temple!" The house of God has been in ruins while the people have comfortable homes. According to the prophet, this explains the economic and spiritual depression of the struggling community. He holds that a functioning temple will usher in happiness and fulfillment. Haggai's emphasis differs from that of preexilic prophets such as Amos, Micah, and Isaiah, who believed that God's kingdom waits upon justice and righteousness. He insists instead that fulfillment depends upon the proper performance of religious rites. To suppose he was indifferent to the moral and social responsibility of the Jews hardly follows. Rather he saw the primacy of God's demands for *God* over all else.

Haggai was indeed a practical man, but the motive which moved him was hope. People cannot understand the excitement that the project of rebuilding the temple would create unless they are able to sense the great world events which the presence of God would set in motion (2:20-23). The rising of the walls of the sanctuary from the pits of the Jews' despair was the first evidence since Cyrus' decree that God was acting mightily again.

I. SUMMONS TO REBUILD THE TEMPLE (1:1-15a)

1:1-11. *The Summons.* The opening proclamation carries the principal force of the whole book. In practical, concrete terms the prophet outlines the nature, cause, and cure of the Jews' predicament. Haggai shows no suspicion of religious formalism. Nor does he attack immorality and injustice as did most preexilic prophets. It is easy, however, to overdraw the contrast between the earlier and later prophets. The need for the temple was immediate and pressing. For that day, the return to religious responsibility demanded it. Not for six hundred years would the Jews be able to dispense with the sanctuary. Even then much of the life and thought of Judaism would still revolve around memories of the ancient altar.

1:1. Haggai began to prophesy in September, 520. A brief message comes first of all to the governor **Zerubbabel** (literally "seed of Babylon"). Zerubbabel was a grandson of King Jehoiachin taken by Nebuchadrezzar (Revised Standard Version Nebuchadnezzar) to Babylon, and to the high priest Joshua. Joshua was a descendant of the high priest at Jerusalem when it fell in 586. The two leaders were political and spiritual heads of the community.

1:2. The people's unwillingness to rebuild was probably rooted in their poverty. However, they take refuge in the memory that Jeremiah prophesied a seventy-year interval before the Jews' punishment would be complete. Thus they say **the time has not yet come** (cf. Jeremiah 25:11-12; 29:10). There is no evidence that the rebuilding had been started and interrupted years before, as suggested in Ezra, or that Haggai knew of an earlier building ban issued from the royal court (cf. Ezra 3:10; 4:23-24; 5:16). The subsequent message to the people (verses 4-11) insists that putting one's own business above the demands of God is ruinous.

1:4-11. Paneled may be read "roofed." This idea would better fit the destitution of the people than ornately decorated houses. Neglect of the house of God has brought on a depression evidenced in **drought** (verse 11) and inflation (verse 6). People have enough to stay alive, but not to enjoy living. Haggai distinctly teaches that the drought is God's doing (verse 11). Hopes have been blasted year after year, but the erosion of spirit has been even more severe than the shriveling of crops. It is not clear whether the people's misery was due basically to actual poverty or to a dissatisfaction with what wealth they had. Haggai's temple is not simply a place for God's honor and comfort. It looks toward the coming of the Messianic Age, to which the Lord's word, **that I may appear in my glory**, doubtless refers.

Rebuilding the temple is a basic religious duty. However, each person has first to give up at least for a time their private preoccupation **with his own house**. Success depended on community effort. Cooperation the result of the companionship of labor, would form an invisible sanctuary for the divine Presence.

1:12-15a. The Response. The effectiveness of Haggai's preaching is shown by a general response. **The remnant of the people** refers to the returned exiles. That the people **feared before the LORD** is evidence that the prophet was indeed **the messenger of the LORD**. In the tradition of the world's great preachers, Haggai awakens in the people the realization of the presence of God among them. Not all the prophets met with such response.

II. AN ENCOURAGEMENT (1:15b–2:23)

1:15b–2:9. *The Glory of the New Temple.* Haggai sees the discouragement of the people at the modest beginnings of their temple (cf. Ezra 3:12). Characteristically he speaks to the situation when he asks, **Who is left among you that saw this house in its former glory?** Doubtless there were a few who had seen Solomon's temple before it was destroyed. The new building itself may be small—we do not know the dimensions—but the **splendor of this house shall be greater** even than before.

Haggai reminds the people of the covenant faith of Israel. He refers to the LORD who brought them **out of Egypt** and who is about to perform a great new work for the people. The idea of "shaking" **the heavens and the earth** is often used to portray God's judgment in political turmoil. Haggai undoubtedly refers to the disorder of the accession of King Darius, which he interprets to be preparation for the restoration of Israel to its former glory under David (2:21-23). In a political sense, Israel has always been strongest in a period when the great nations of the Near East have been weak.

The immediate promise Haggai holds out is that **the treasures of all nations shall come in** to the temple. The God who made all **silver and gold** will claim it as God's own. God is the chief actor in this view of history. The human function is not to arm one's self and fight, but to create a throne suitable for a victorious God, a treasure chest appropriate to the spoils of triumph.

The victory of the coming of the kingdom is to take place **in a little while.** Haggai does not intend these words to mean a long time—as is clear from his association of the new day with the rise of Zerubbabel (2:20-23). The **prosperity** of verse 9 is often translated "peace" and should therefore not be limited to affluence. This is the profound happiness of God's approval.

2:10-14. *The Holy and the Unclean.* This passage in itself is easy to understand. Haggai simply calls on the priest to witness that it is the unclean, rather than the clean, which is contagious (cf. Numbers 9:6-7). No one knows, however, just why the lesson is included. Many scholars interpret **this people** in verse 14 as the Samaritans who tried to participate in the building. In this case the infectious uncleanness might come from them. However, they are reported to have been previously rebuffed (cf. Ezra 5:1-5). Probably they would have been more directly attacked here.

Whatever the problem is, it apparently is a delicate one. Instead of attacking it head on, Haggai moves by analogy, citing the established sacrificial systems as the rationale of his claim. Perhaps the Jews, who were making the **unclean** offerings, are intended. It may have been that those who never went to Babylon were in some sense unacceptable to God and might compromise the whole enterprise.

Since the **priests** themselves are cited as authorities (verse 11), it could be that Gentiles had at this time already infiltrated the priesthood, as Tobiah the Ammonite did later (Nehemiah 13:4-5). Thus the priests would be cleverly impaled on their own rules. It is also possible that the priests as well as the people had already become involved with foreign women (Malachi 2:10-16).

2:15-19. *Impending Change.* It appears that this passage is misplaced. It should follow the phrase in 1:15*a*, "on the twenty-fourth day of the month, in the sixth month." Some of the reasons are:

(1) There is no apparent connection between these verses and the homily on uncleanness (verses 10, 14).

(2) The frame of reference is properly the drought and poverty of chapter 1.

(3) The dating in verse 18, **the twenty-fourth day of the ninth month,** is probably an explanatory addition, based on 2:10 rather than 1:15*a*. Moreover, it would seem strange that the blessing should not be operating until three months after the work began.

Is the seed yet in the barn? may be intended to read, "Is the seed still diminishing in the barn?" Otherwise one would suppose that failure to plant was the trouble. But the melting away of their resources was the principal problem (verse 16). The prophet declares that the harvest of the **vine, fig,**

pomegranate, and olive will be prosperous once the temple is begun in earnest.

2:20-23. *Zerubbabel the Messianic King.* The promise that the LORD will soon **shake the heavens and the earth** is essentially the same as that made in verse 6. The previous promise emphasizes the wealth to be received (verse 7), while this one emphasizes the overthrow of Gentile power (verse 22). That soldiers should destroy one another, **every one by the sword of his fellow,** is reminiscent of the victory of Gideon and his three hundred men, whose surprise attack threw the Midianites into such a panic that they butchered one another and left the Israelites unscathed (Judges 7:22).

Joshua the priest is not mentioned. Zerubbabel occupies the center of the stage. Haggai foresees that the relaxed power of Persia will permit a descendant of David once more to occupy the throne. He will be the servant of God, bringing the authority of the divine signature into human affairs (verse 23).

History is silent in regard to Zerubbabel, and Joshua apparently is substituted for him in a parallel text in Zechariah 6:11. This would indicate that he failed to fulfill the prophecy. It is quite possible that he was martyred by the servants of Darius when Persian authority was reestablished in all the provinces. Nonetheless, this emergence of the messianic hope, while unfulfilled in immediate history, makes its own contribution to the gathering obsession with the fulfillment of the purpose of God's people.

THE BOOK OF ZECHARIAH

Roger N. Carstensen

Since, for reasons subsequently to be given, it appears that the material in chapters 9–14 is from a writer other than Zechariah, the two sections will be treated separately.

INTRODUCTION TO CHAPTERS 1–8

The Prophet and His Times

Very little is known of the man Zechariah. He was a contemporary of Haggai and similarly concerned with the building of the second temple (cf. Ezra 5:1, 6:14). For the period in which Zechariah lived and the situation to which he spoke, see the Introduction to Haggai. He may formerly have been a priest, for he was sympathetic to the priesthood, especially that of Joshua (3:1-5; 6:13). He prophesied for at least one month concurrently with Haggai (cf. 1:1 and Haggai 2:10, which dates Haggai's last prophecy) and continued for two more years (520-518 B.C.). Haggai emphasized the reversal of material fortune which the completion of the temple will bring. This is broadened in Zechariah. The glories of the messianic age and the wonders of the God of Spirit are to him much more important. Zechariah was a prophet of hope and joy. God was indeed far beyond humanity in glory and majesty, but by the same token God was irresistible. God's victory was the central fact of the prophet's universe.

Visions and Angels

Eight visions constitute the greater part of the material in Zechariah. These are strikingly different from most prophetic utterances. The prophet sees extravagant sights almost impossible to understand unless interpreted—and then often obscure. The figures include animals, people, and angels. They deal with a variety of objects strange to the language of prophecy.

Apocalyptic literature dealt with hidden revelations and with the future. Here, in a series of glimpses of the world under God's control, the reader sees apocalyptic in a partly developed stage. Speaking in cryptic and figurative language, the prophet shows how God's purpose, hidden in the maze of human history, will be manifested and fulfilled.

God did not speak directly to Zechariah. God revealed designs too elaborate and sweeping for ordinary minds to grasp. Thus God sent angels to explain their meanings. The presence of angels emphasizes the transcendence of God. Angelic ministry is most prominent in Zechariah of all Old Testament books. Along with the angels there is a brief but significant appearance of Satan (3:1-2). As the accuser of Joshua the high priest, he plays approximately the same role as in the book of Job (Job 1–2). In these instances he is a servant of God. In I Chronicles 21:1, which is later, he apparently operates as an independent demonic force.

Message

The colorfulness and strangeness of Zechariah's visions make it easy to overlook his concern with moral issues. The introductory pronouncement, "Thus says the LORD of hosts. Return from your evil ways and from your evil deeds" (1:4*b*), must be taken seriously as an underlying theme in the total message.

Zechariah's approach to the building of the temple was not as direct as Haggai's. Zerubbabel, who began the work, shall finish it with the assistance of returned Jews (see below on 4:9; 6:12,

13)—providing they "will diligently obey the voice of the LORD" their God (6:15).

Zechariah seems to identify the role of the Messiah largely with the leadership of Zerubbabel. Here the Messiah seems to be more a sign of the coming of the new age than the agent through which it comes (cf. 9:9-10). The hopes which rested on Zerubbabel as the Messiah, however, were dashed through circumstances no longer known to us. On the other hand, the rising prominence of the high priest Joshua in Zechariah's predictions (3:1-5; 4:11-14) paved the way for the prominence of the priesthood in postexilic Judaism.

Zechariah proclaims the unchanging grace of God. The same inflexibility with which the LORD has punished God will now bless: "As I purposed to do evil to you . . . and I did not relent . . . so again have I purposed . . . to do good" (8:14-15). The horrors of the past prophesy the joys of the future. A God great in punishment is also great in blessing (1:14-17).

I. INTRODUCTORY STATEMENT (1:1-6)

1:1. *Date and Author*. The prophecies of Zechariah like those of Haggai, are carefully dated. No day is mentioned here at the beginning, contrary to Zechariah's custom (1:7; 7:1). But we gather that the first utterance comes two months after Haggai began to preach in the year 520 B.C. The name Zechariah means "the LORD remembers." It is likely that he was the **son of Iddo**—as claimed in Ezra 5:1 and 6:14 and Nehemiah 12:16—instead of his grandson. The appearance of **Berechiah** as his father can be explained as a scribe's misunderstanding of Isaiah 8:2, which notes Jeberechiah as the father of another priestly Zechariah.

1:2-6. *Call to Repentance*. Zechariah draws his text from the past. Those who did not obey the **former prophets** paid the full penalty of their **ways**. But the God who is dependable in punishment is dependable in reward.

In the visions which follow, God is the supreme actor in history. This is the basis of Zechariah's call to repentance. Prophets and kings pass away, but the purposes of God are inescapable. History shall not escape judgment.

II. EIGHT VISIONS OF HOPE (1:7–6:8)

A. FIRST VISION: REPORT OF THE CELESTIAL HORSEMEN (1:7-17)

The date of the first vision—and by implication the following seven—is sometime in late January or February, 519. Swift angels, whose speed is symbolized by **horses,** ascertain that the world is **at rest,** except for the unsettled spirits of the people of God. God's anger hovers over Israel's oppressors. God shall cause the temple to be rebuilt in **Jerusalem** as a seal of the vindication of the people. The appearance of many angels in Zechariah's visions serves to emphasize the increasing sense of distance between God and the people.

1:8. The account of the **horses** seems confused. They probably should appear, as in the Septuagint, in four colors. This would make their number equal the four horns (1:18), four winds of the heavens (2:6), and four colors of horses in the final vision (6:2-3). The number four probably suggests the completeness of the patrol (cf. 2:6).

1:11. The time of universal peace reported by the heavenly scouts is generally supposed to indicate the success of the Persian king Darius in quieting his rebellious provinces (about 520). However, some think it is the peace of Babylon before the rise of Cyrus (about 550). It may be that Zechariah begins with visions of the past wonders of God, which resulted when the fathers repented (1:6). On the other hand, it seems unlikely that Zechariah would portray the immediacy of God's action by reference to the past **rest.** The appeal to return from Babylon in 2:6-13 sounds as though exiles in Persia are still returning and will help in the building (cf. 6:15).

1:11-13. The principal intermediary angel is the **angel of the LORD**. Some suppose that this is the same **angel who talked with** Zechariah, but it seems more likely that the two are separate. The angel of the LORD never speaks to Zechariah. The prophet is a spectator.

1:14-17. Though the patrol reports universal peace, God is filled with unrest. God had been **angry** with the Jews. Now divine wrath burns toward those who have exceeded their commission to punish God's people (cf. Isaiah 40:2). The **nations . . . are** indeed **at ease,** but at ease under the anger of God. The **measuring line** appears to refer either to the building of the temple or to building generally.

B. SECOND VISION: THE FOUR HORNS AND THE FOUR SMITHS (1:18-21)

The first vision made clear that God's compassion for the people and God's punishment of their enemies were part of the same great episode of history. This vision emphasizes the destruction by God's agents of what once seemed indestructible. Perhaps the fall of Babylon is meant, but the prophet may not have been this specific in his meanings. Those who were the agents of terror are themselves to be terrified. The **four horns** are probably symbolic of the powerful nations hostile to **Judah.** The **four smiths** are perhaps supernatural agents intended to protect the Jews from further terror.

C. THIRD VISION: THE HOLY CITY (2:1-5)

The **measuring line** which the man intends to use is not for building. It is for limitation, to mark the city's boundaries so that walls can be built. Some think this man is Zerubbabel. The unidentified **angel** who gives the interpreter news for the **young man** with the line is the angel of the LORD. The Holy City will have no walls because of the greatness of its population and the adequate protection provided by God's presence. The city **without walls** will be safer and more glorious than a city with impregnable fortifications. Its strength is not in impressive numbers but in the presence of the LORD, who as **glory** and **wall** will be the essential temple and its essential defense.

D. INVITATION TO ZION (2:6-13)

The description of the glorious city is followed by two oracles of intense character. The first (verses 6-9), is a sequel to the second vision. It invites the captives to **flee** from **Babylon** and share in **Zion** the **plunder** which will follow the downfall of their enemies. This was prophesied in the vision of the horns (see above on 1:18-21). The second (verses 10-13) is a sequel to the third vision. It celebrates the presence of God **in the midst of** the **people** and the reconciliation of the **nations** as a consequence.

2:6. The **land of the north** generally refers to **Babylon.** The Septuagint reads "will gather you in" instead of **have spread you abroad.** The **four winds** is a conventional phrase for the four points of the compass (cf. 6:5).

2:8. Some difficulty arises with **his glory sent me.** Most suppose the prophet is meant. But Zechariah himself was not sent to the plundering nations. Nor does he ever seem to see himself as an actor in history.

2:10-12. That God shall dwell **in the midst of** the people is the essence of bliss—not only because of the joy of the Presence, but because of the environment with which God is surrounded. In Hebrew thought this was happiness and prosperity (cf. 1:17). Palestine is called the **holy land** only here in the Bible.

E. FOURTH VISION: THE INSTALLATION OF JOSHUA (3:1-10)

The fourth vision clearly supports the priesthood of **Joshua,** who for a time shared the leadership of the little community with Zerubbabel. The priest's authority had been under fire for reasons we may never know. Compare the cleansing of Joshua with Isaiah's experience (Isaiah 6:1-8). It is the ceremonial cleanness of garments that is emphasized here.

3:1-4. The language of verse 1 illustrates how awkward it is to identify the interpreting angel as the angel of the LORD (cf. 1:11). **Satan**—more properly here "the adversary"—has not yet been assigned the character of the devil of the New Testament. He is still one of the servants of God. His function is to uncover the weaknesses of people who are highly regarded by God (cf. Job 1:6-12).

The angel of the LORD is identified here, perhaps accidentally, as the **LORD** (verse 2a). The angel gives the rebuke in the third person, **the LORD rebuke you** (cf. Jude 9). In an interesting restatement the angel identifies this authority as **the LORD who has chosen Jerusalem.** This may mean that the angel is citing the LORD of hosts mentioned in 2:11-12. Thus the angel of the LORD may be speaking of a supreme authority, superior to both the angel and Satan. **Those . . . standing before him** are angels.

3:5. The **turban** was part of the high priest's vesture (Exodus 28:4).

3:6-9. Joshua's commission enjoins him to **walk in my ways** (moral responsibility) and **keep my charge** (official responsibility) in order that he might have the **right of access** ordinarily attributed to angels. The **Branch** no doubt refers to Zerubbabel. But since he is already on the scene, some suppose the phrase may have been added. The **stone . . . set before Joshua** probably is a jewel worn by the high priest which symbolized the removal of **guilt** by intercession.

F. FIFTH VISION: THE GOLDEN LAMPSTAND
(4:1-6a, 10b-14)

Joshua and **Zerubbabel** as priest and prince of the revived community share the power of the presence of God. In the vision they are symbolized by **two olive** trees on either side of the **lampstand.** The **seven lamps** are the **eyes of the LORD.** This light does not simply illuminate; it sees. It is not limited to the sanctuary; it covers the face of the **earth.**

Verses 6*b*-10*a* are omitted from the vision. There is a clear indication of interruption—the question of verses 4-5 is answered in verse 10*b*. There is also shift in content. Possibly it is inserted here because the oil used in the lamp, representative of spirit, coincides with the opening of the oracle to Zerubbabel: "Not by might, nor by power, but by my Spirit" (verse 6*b*).

4:2-4. Precisely how the **lampstand** looked is impossible to determine. The **lamps** are containers with spouts or **lips** to hold the wick. The large **bowl on the top** contains a supply of oil for all seven lamps and probably is connected to them by seven pipes. The **two olive trees** are on either side of the lampstand. Apparently **these** in verse 4 refers to the lamps, for Zechariah asks about the trees later on (verse 11).

4:6*a*, 10*b*-14. If we omit the insertion in 6*b*-10*a* (see below), we read **then he said to me** (6*a*) **These seven . . .** (verse 10*b*). Note that the lamps **are the eyes of the LORD, which range through the whole earth.** In Hebrew thought, God's seeing meant controlling and providing. The question regarding the **olive trees** (verse 11) is, strangely, asked again (verse 12). Information not given in the earlier description is included in the second question. This is the only time a question by the prophet is not acknowledged. The verse may be an addition. The **two anointed** (literally "sons of oil") are generally thought to be Joshua and Zerubbabel.

G. ORACLE TO ZERUBBABEL (4:6*b*-10*a*)

The purpose of this oracle is to encourage **Zerubbabel** to complete the temple. His success in spite of overwhelming odds demonstrates the enabling Presence (vese 9*b*). Having overcome mountainous obstacles, Zerubbabel brings forward the capstone **amid shouts** of joy. The **me** in verse 9*b* is used as in 2:9, 12 to refer to the angel of the LORD **sent** by the **LORD of hosts,** rather than to Zechariah himself. **The day of small things** probably refers to the insignificant beginnings of the building (cf. Ezra 3:12; Haggai 2:3).

H. SIXTH VISION: THE FLYING SCROLL (5:1-4)

Zechariah in this vision sees a large **scroll** which represents God's **curse** on thieves and perjurers. How the curse would operate is not clear, but the idea of cleansing is present. The consuming of the **house** of the wicked portrays the finality of punishment. Stealing and bearing false witness may simply be representative of a much broader list of social sins. But it seems more likely that they were special problems in Zechariah's day.

I. SEVENTH VISION: THE WOMAN IN THE EPHAH (5:5-11)

The vision describes the woman called **Wickedness** imprisoned in an **ephah,** or cask. It is reminiscent of the scapegoat that is sent into the wilderness bearing the sins of the people (Leviticus 16:6-10). By sending the woman away in the cask the guilt of **all the land** will be removed at once (cf. 3:4, 9) and taken to the **land of Shinar**—that is, Babylon. There the abomination of Judah will be worshiped in its own temple.

The ephah was a vessel with a capacity of about six gallons. Apparently the woman **lifted** the **leaden cover** but was **thrust . . . back** by the angel. The **base** on which the vessel would be set was the pedestal on which idols were placed.

J. EIGHTH VISION: THE FOUR CHARIOTS (6:1-8)

Zechariah's first vision was of the horsemen bringing news that the world is quiet but God is disturbed (1:11-13). His final vision likewise contains the sweep of **chariots**—this time bringing the news that God is satisfied (verse 8), and so presumably will be the people. Though the horses represent the **four winds of heaven,** they are assigned only three directions—east is not mentioned. The **north country** refers to Babylonia.

III. ORACLE OF THE THEOCRATIC STATE (6:9-15)

This passage is separate from the series of apocalyptic visions. The oracle as it stands celebrates the crowning of **Joshua** the **high priest** as prince and builder of the **temple.** This makes him in fact a priest-king, which actually was the case later on. There is little doubt, however, that verse 11 originally designated Zerubbabel for the crowning, as verses 12-13 indicate. The absence of Zerubbabel's name from the passage suggests that he never actually ruled. A later editor, aware of the subsequent elevation of the priesthood, may have assigned the promises once intended for the prince to Joshua the priest. Thus he brought the prophecy into harmony with later history.

The evidences that the passage has been altered are:

(1) Zechariah has already indicated that Zerubbabel, not Joshua, will complete the temple (cf. 4:6-10*a*).

(2) The designation **Branch,** or "Shoot," is never used for a priest but for a messianic king (cf. 3:8; Jeremiah 23:5).

(3) The **priest by his throne** is obviously Joshua. One would hardly expect Joshua as priest-king to have another priest beside him.

6:9-10. Verse 9—**And the word of the LORD came to me**—formally opens a new series of oracles. We know nothing else of the three men selected as witnesses to the symbolic crowning or of the **Josiah** to whose **house** they were taken.

6:11-14. **Crown** in verses 11 and 14 is plural in Hebrew. The pronoun **it** in verse 11 and the singular verb form translated **shall be** in verse 14 indicate that only one crown was the original intention. "Zerubbabel" was probably the orignal reading for what is now **Joshua** in verse 11*b* (cf. 4:6-10*a*; see comment above on 6:9-15). The close working relationship between priest and king is reflected in verse 13; 3:8-9; 4:11-14; and Haggai 1:12-15.

6:14-15. The **crown . . . in the temple** suggests temporal power that depends on the spiritual (cf. 4:6). **Those who are far off** refers to Jews returning from their colonies among the Gentiles.

IV. FROM FASTING TO FEASTING (7:1–8:23)

The first vision contained God's message that the time had come for God's anger to be suspended. God's people would know once again the happiness desired for them from the beginning (1:13-17). Just as God has moved from wrath to pity, the mood of the people will change from sorrow to joy. The temple is being rebuilt, and God is at work. In this context to mourn is to blaspheme.

7:1-3. *The Deputation from Bethel.* The building has been in process for about two years when the deputation arrives in 518. The month of **Chislev** was from mid-November to mid-December. The sanctuary at **Bethel** was a center of opposition to Jerusalem. The question the deputation asks concerns the matter of mourning the destruction of a temple now being rebuilt. Should the **fast** regularly observed in the fifth and seventh months (verse 5) over the destruction of Jerusalem and the temple be continued?

7:4-14. *Ineffectiveness of Fasting.* Zechariah deals with the question on a broad scale. Fasting is not a substitute for righteous living in good times or bad (verse 7). The **former prophets** (probably quoted in verse 9) made it clear that religious responsibilities should be socially expressed. But the people **refused** to **hear.** Therefore God would not hear them. God **scattered them** and made their **pleasant land . . . desolate.**

8:1-17. *Restoration of the Whole Order.* The LORD of hosts is once again **jealous** for the people. God will restore **Jerusalem** as a peaceful, prosperous city,.where the aged meditate in peace and children play unmolested. God will gather exiles from **east**

151

and **west** to dwell in Jerusalem. Zechariah encourages the fainting laborers by assuring them the depression is over. Wages and harvests will now be their lot.

8:18-23. *Jerusalem Invites Others.* The delegation asked simply about the fast of the fifth month, which marked the destruction of the temple. But to Zechariah all past catastrophes become prophecies of wondrous good (verses 18-19). The **joy** of good hearts will draw people from all **nations** to the house of God. The watchword is not, "Go there," but, "Come with me" (verses 20-22). Where there is evidence that God is working, people are drawn to the scene: **Let us go with you, for we have heard that God is with you.**

INTRODUCTION TO CHAPTERS 9–14

Authorship

It is now commonly agreed that chapters 9–14 are not the work of Zechariah. Chapters 9 and 12 each begin with the word "oracle," as does the book of Malachi. Since Malachi is anonymous (see Introduction to Malachi) it is possible that Malachi, the last of three similar oracles, was later detached for the purpose of bringing a collection of the prophets up to the significant number twelve.

The following differences in the two sections may be noted:

(1) Chapters 9–14 are largely poetry while the first eight chapters are prose.

(2) Zechariah uses visions extensively. The last section does not.

(3) Zechariah's name does not appear in the last six chapters, contrary to the practice in the former section.

(4) There is also strong emphasis on the possibility of salvaging Israel, a matter of little interest to Zechariah.

(5) The prophets are scorned. Violence and bloodshed are highlighted.

(6) Chapters 9–14 contain no reference to the central theme of Zechariah—building the temple—nor to the leadership of Zerubbabel and Joshua.

(7) The Messiah is a humble king. This suggests the motif of the Suffering Servant of Isaiah 53, which is absent from chapters 1–8.

(8) Chapters 9–14 have their own apocalyptic overtones. Much is made of human depravity and of great battles leading to the subjugation of the world.

This last section, therefore, seems clearly distinct from the first in style and subject matter. Its background, while difficult to identify precisely, certainly does not reflect the day of Haggai and Zechariah.

Message

The materials in this section are linked together only in a general way, and may be from several authors. Thus there is little value in a summary at this point. The general theme is the victory of God over all the nations, leading the world to universal peace. God's own people, though capable of heroism, are largely wicked and misguided. The sheep deserve cruel shepherds (11:7-17). They apparently slay their noblest leader (12:10–13:1).

One God demands ultimately one world. God will not rest until all things are under God's feet. "On that day the LORD will be one and his name one" (14:9b). This victory is inevitable, but as yet it is unrealized. It becomes for the stormy days of developing Judaism a fact towering above all the contradictory appearances of history. God is going to win!

I. THE ORACLE OF THE COMING OF THE MESSIAH
(9:1–11:17)

A. THE WORLDWIDE KINGDOM (9:1-17)

Chapter 9 appears to consist of three separate oracles (verses 1-8, 9-10, and 11-17) which have been gathered together without clear connections. The first seems to be a judgment on Syria, **Tyre,** and **Philistia** culminating in the deliverance of

Jerusalem and Judah. In the second the Messiah suddenly appears as the agent of universal peace. **His dominion** is worldwide. The third oracle speaks of **prisoners** returning to Judah as the Greeks succumb to the Jews in bloody warfare (verses 13-15). Prosperity reigns over the **flock** of God.

To interpret these verses consecutively one would conclude that Syria, Phoenicia, and Philistia will be crushed, presumably by Alexander the Great. As a result Jerusalem will rise again under the Messiah and crush the Greeks in turn. Drawing the exiles back from their dispersion, Jerusalem will set up the universal messianic kingdom. Each of the sections shows a certain unity in itself and should be read first of all for its own meanings.

9:1-8. *The Downfall of Proud Nations.* God will conquer the cities of Syria and Phoenicia—notably **Tyre,** the impregnable fortress in the sea. The Philistine cities will be demoralized at their neighbor's fate and similarly fall (verses 5-6). However, the Philistines will beconverted to God and observe Jewish food regulations (verse 7). The people of God shall never again be **overrun** by an invader.

9:1. The Hebrew text of this verse reads as though God possessed the land of Syria in a benevolent sense and rests in **Damascus.** Though it seems unlikely that the Jews would accept any place other than Jerusalem as a dwelling place for God, other nations also **belong** to God. Tyre is obviously under attack (verse 4). However, **even as all the tribes of** Israel suggests that Syria now belongs to God just as does Israel. The later reference to the acceptance of the Philistines as one of the clans of Judah (verse 7b) compares them to the Jebusites, in whose city (Jerusalem) God does indeed dwell.

9:1-2. Apparently **Hadrach** was north of Damascus. Where the Revised Standard Version reads the **cities of Aram** the Hebrew has "eye of Adam," which makes no sense. The change of one easily mistaken consonant changes Adam to Aram (Syria). Perhaps Damascus was known as "the eye of Aram." **Hamath** is also north of Damascus. The fact that Alexander the Great was the only conqueror up to his time to take the city is a principal reason for supposing that this oracle refers to the advance of the Greeks.

9:5-6. Four of the five traditional Philistine cities are mentioned, with Gath omitted.

9:7. The **blood** of Philistine mouths refers to eating food either unclean in itself or improperly prepared (cf. Leviticus 11:2-23; Deuteronomy 14:3-21). The **Jebusites** were Canaanites of Jerusalem. Their survivors after David's conquest of the city were apparently absorbed by the people of Israel (cf. II Samuel 5:6-9).

9:8. God, standing **guard** in the temple watchtower, will forever guard Judah from invasion. Strictly speaking, the events in chapters 12 and 14 cannot happen following this, for in both cases invaders are described.

9:9-10. *The Humble Messiah.* The Messiah who rides into Jerusalem combines majesty and meekness. He fulfills the requirements of the Davidic king who "shall smite the earth with the rod of his mouth" (Isaiah 11:4b). He also resembles the Suffering Servant, who when he was afflicted "opened not his mouth" (Isaiah 53:7a). David, curiously, is not mentioned at all in chapters 9–11.

That the Messiah comes **riding on . . . a colt** is of particular interest to the Christian world (cf. Matthew 21:1-6, where two beasts are cited, with John 12:14-15). It is possible that Jesus, knowing what had been written, purposely sought a young **ass** on which to ride when he made his final claim to the allegiance of Jerusalem.

9:11-17. *Salvation of the Prisoners of Hope.* As it stands, this warlike section has to deal with a time considerably subsequent to Alexander's conquest. The Jews did not much feel the sting of persecution under Hellenic rule until over a century had passed. The key is verse 13, where **Greece** is mentioned as the destined victim of God's armies. This was probably not Greece itself but the Seleucid dynasty in Syria—one of the four Hellenic subkingdoms emerging from the empire of Alexander.

9:11-13. The antecedent of **you** (in verse 11a) is apparently Zion (vs. 9). Its exiles are to be returned. **Prisoners of hope** is a provocative term especially applicable to Jews. Some think the reference to **Greece** (in verse 13) is an interpolation (see above on 9:11-17).

9:15. This verse is extremely difficult to translate. It is safe to assume a devastating battle is being described.

B. MILITARY EXPLOITS OF THE JEWS (10:1–11:3)

This section consists mainly of a passage dealing with the military exploits of the Jews under their own leaders (10:3-12). It is preceded and followed by brief and apparently unrelated passages (10:1-2; 11:1-3). Of special interest is the return of the ten tribes (verses 6-7) not simply to Jerusalem but as far as the border of ancient Israel (vs. 10).

10:1-2. *Praying for Rain.* The situation here is sharply different from that in 9:17, where there is an abundance of **rain.** It may be placed directly after 9:17 simply because of a common reference to agriculture. The point is simple. Since God alone controls rain, seek it from no other source.

10:3-12. *The Rise of the Soldier.* This passage has been characterized above (see comment on 10:1–11:3). That the **shepherds** are foreign rulers—probably the Ptolemies of Egypt or the Seleucids of Syria—seems indicated by the phrase in verse 4, **out of them.** That is, in the future the leaders of the **house of Judah** will be natives instead of foreigners. They will come **out of** the flock of the LORD. The transformation of a sheep (**flock**) to a war-horse (**steed in battle**) is one of the boldest figures of speech in the Old Testament (verse 3*b*).

Who their own rulers will be—**cornerstone, . . . tent peg,** or **battle bow**—cannot now be known. God continues to be the real combatant (verse 5*b*). **Joseph** refers to Israel, as does **Ephraim.** The dominant mood is one of rejoicing.

10:8-11. God **will signal for** the people **and gather them in.** God will use a whistle as shepherds use to call their sheep together ("whistle" being a variant translation of the word rendered **signal**). The two nations especially noted from which they will return are **Egypt** and Syria, here called **Assyria** according to the habit of later writers. They will come to **the land of Gilead** in the northeast and to **Lebanon** on the northern border of old Israel. The territories of David's kingdom will not hold the new population (verse 10). Harking back to the past, the prophet predicts a miraculous crossing of the **Nile** and probably the Sea of Reeds (or Red Sea; verse 11).

11:1-3. *The Lament of Fallen Leaders.* This passage may stand here simply because **Lebanon** is mentioned in verse 1 and, in a different context, in 10:10*b*. However, it is possible, that the false shepherds of 10:3 are here ironically mourned under the figures of **fallen** trees, **shepherds** minus sheep, and **lions** without a **jungle.**

C. THE DOOMED FLOCK AND ITS SHEPHERDS (11:4-17)

It is exceedingly difficult to make sense out of this section. Attempts to identify events and characters in history have been many and desperate. The correct solution may have been reached, but it cannot be verified. One point is clear. The flock itself, although a victim, is at fault. God's judgments on such people are just and frightening. The sheep shall fall into the hands of their own shepherds.

How this passage related to the foregoing is not clear. The anticipated union of Ephraim and Judah, it would seem, is temporary. It is to be broken after the coming of the Messiah and the establisment of the worldwide kingdom (cf. 9:9-10, 13; 10:6-7). The earlier passages, however, give the distinct impression that the reunion of broken Israel is the climactic event to come at the end of the age (10:6-7). Therefore it may be best to read the main sections of chapters 9–11 as separate accounts of events to occur around the end time—accounts not intended to be put together consecutively.

11:4-7. The **shepherd** is really the LORD, manifesting God's will through the prophet and receiving payment in the temple (verses 12-13). The **staffs** are symbols of shepherd and king.

They represent protection from those who exploited the sheep (**Grace**) and that which prevented the sheep from destroying one another (**Union**).

11:8-12. The **three shepherds** who are **destroyed** cannot be identified. Verse 8*b* indicates that the victimized people rebuff God's shepherd. They are therefore abandoned to **the traffickers in the sheep**—probably foreign rulers or tax collectors who **knew that it was the word of the LORD.** The Hebrew word for **treasury** (verse 13) is quite similar to that for "potter," which is found in the original. The Revised Standard Version is probably correct. God as the shepherd receives the wages (verse 12).

II. THE ORACLE OF TRIUMPH FOR JERUSALEM
(12:1–14:21)

The last chapters of Zechariah are just as difficult to interpret as the preceding. They have as their central theme the triumph of Jerusalem in the coming **day of the LORD.** God does not rescue the people *through* the crisis but *from* it. A great leader has been stupidly slain. God ends the tragedy of errors by invading the earth with the forces of heaven. The mountain ridges of Palestine are leveled, leaving Jerusalem on a lofty pinnacle. The perils of night and winter cease. Putting an end to human pretensions, God rearranges the face of the earth and causes people to acknowledge God in worship. The very horses shall be consecrate; the sacrament may be prepared in a housewife's pots and pans in a time when all things are holy.

A. WOUNDS AND A CLEANSING FOUNTAIN (12:1–13:9)

12:1-9. *Where Ignorant Armies Clash.* Here Jerusalem serves principally as an instrument for God's judgment on all nations. Its powers in war will impress the hostile inhabitants of the countryside of Judah. In verse 4*a* the victory of Jerusalem is attributed to supernaturally induced diseases and consequent panic, a theme expanded in 14:12-15. The **clans of Judah** are the Jews outside the city. The victory of these rural Jews is a reminder to proud Jerusalem that God's people are outside as well as inside its walls (verse 7).

12:10–13:1. Fast on the heels of the triumph over the slaughtered aliens **wails** of grief are heard over the Holy City. Its fairest son lies dead, slain by the hands of his brothers. Why was the victim killed? We cannot tell. The guilty are strangely moved. Enabled at last to weep for someone other than self, they open up an unsuspected fountain for their own cleansing. Their weeping is reminiscent of the **mourning for Hadadrimmon,** a deity; cf. the wailing for the dead god Tammuz (Ezekiel 8:14).

The **mourning** includes all classes of people (verse 14). In some sense each in their aloneness said, "This is what I have done." **A fountain is opened . . . to cleanse them from sin and uncleanness.** 13:1 clearly belongs with chapter 12. **The house of David and the inhabitants of Jerusalem** were guilty of the murder (12:10) and needed to be cleansed.

13:2-6. *The Status of Prophecy.* The darkest hour of prophecy is pictured here. Prophecy was supposed to have ceased, being supplanted by temple oracle and the law of Moses. Therefore to prophesy is to lie. To prophesy **in the name of the** LORD is to blaspheme.

13:2-3. To **cut off the names of the idols** means final destruction. Prophecy had become idolatry, and the idols will not be remembered. Thus prophecy cannot be re-created. The prophet is equated with the **unclean spirit.** Prophecy has become such an abomination that people will be killed by their own parents for returning to the ancient practice.

13:4-6. A certain kind of wound distinguished the prophet in those days, probaby self-mutilation produced in times of ecstasy. Claming to be a simple farmer, the prophet is questioned about the scars on his back. He improvises a desperate explanation. A drunken brawl with his comrades culminated in a few friendly knife fights (verse 6*b*).

13:7-9. *The Purified Survivors.* A good case can be made for moving this oracle to chapter 11, where so much is said about shepherds. In 11:17 a smitten **shepherd** is mentioned, as in verse 7 here. But the shepherd in the former passage deserves his fate and is punished for deserting the flock. In the latter passage it appears that the shepherd is wounded for no fault of his own.

Two themes emerge from this isolated little section: the smitten shepherd and the reclaimed flock. The shepherd who stands next to God (verse 7*a*) is a priest or king. He suffers for his faithfulness, for the sheep do not deserve the care they receive (as is the case in 11:8).

B. Triumph of the Lord of Battles (14:1-21)

The last chapter of Zechariah is typical of the most fully developed apocalyptic in the Old Testament (cf. Ezekiel 38–39; 47). In apocalyptic a final struggle involving all the world may be expected before the last age of peace begins. In such battles God is the real victor.

14:1-5. *The Great Battle and Rescue.* The **spoil taken from you** was gathered in the early defeat, when half of Jerusalem was lost. The LORD is described as a giant whose **feet stand upon the Mount of Olives,** which is **split in two** and becomes a mighty plain (cf. verse 10). **You shall flee** (verse 5*b*) is probaly an editorial footnote based on a scribe's misunderstanding. He must have regarded the verb form **be stopped up** to mean **you shall flee.** The central idea is simply that God shall change the face of the earth for the elect people.

14:6-11. *The Order of Things.* Jerusalem stands now on a lonely eminence. It is the central jewel of a new setting. Inaccessible to all but its friends, it is a haven of perpetual **security.**

14:6-8. The Hebrew of verse 6 is difficult. **Cold nor frost is the** Greek reading. **It is known to the LORD** is probably inserted to refer to the actual day when God will come. The **living waters**

make rain no longer necessary and purify the waters of the Dead Sea.

14:9-10. Verse 9 is the central theme. The LORD will be one **king** over one people, known by one **name. Geba** is ten miles north of Jerusalem. **Rimmon** about the same distance north of Beersheba. This is about the extent of ancient Judah. Apparently the author describes **Jerusalem** by giving the principal corners of the walls, so that the city occupies roughly the area of its early dimensions.

14:12-15. *How the City Is Delivered.* The enemies of Jerusalem will be struck by a horrible **plague** and in **panic** will slaughter one another (cf. 12:4). Some suppose that Judah's **fight against Jerusalem**—odd indeed to account for under these circumstances—means it conquered Jerusalem. This would fit much better with the encouragement of Judah mentioned in connection with the previous panic of 12:4.

14:16-19. *The LORD Is King.* The ultimate subjection of all the Gentile world to the God of the Jews is here attributed to religious observances. The **feasts of booths** was the new year festival, at which time the LORD had traditionally been declared king (cf. Psalms 47; 68; 93). It included a water libation. While **rain** would be denied the nations not making the pilgrimage (verse 17*b*), **Egypt,** who needed no rain, would be afflicted with a **plague.**

14:20-21. *Everything Holy.* These last verses exalt ceremonial over moral holiness. Yet there is something about the expression of holiness in every detail of life that catches the imagination. At last Israel is a kingdom of priests. In every home sacramental bread is broken. The family hearth knows the presence of God. Even the **bells of the horses,** freed from battle, ring to the glory of heaven.

THE BOOK OF MALACHI

Roger N. Carstensen

INTRODUCTION

Date

Several clues in the book of Malachi point to the time of its writing. The restored temple was completed in 515 B.C. It has been in use long enough for the priesthood to become lax and corrupt (1:6). Judah is under the rule of a "governor"—that is, a Persian administrator (1:8). The high rate of divorce and remarriage to foreign women (2:11-16) suggests a time before the governorship of Nehemiah. Otherwise his reform attacking this very problem would surely be mentioned.

The priests are called descendants of Levi rather than of Aaron (2:4). This supports the view that the Jewish community is still under the Deuteronomic (D) Code rather than the Priestly (P) Code. The Priestly Code was introduced around the time of Ezra, who probably followed Nehemiah. Since Nehemiah first arrived in 445, the prophecies of this book were probably composed shortly before this date—that is, about 450.

Author

"Malachi" means "my messenger." The word was evidently placed in the title (1:1) by an editor who took its occurrence in 3:1 to be the author's name. We may use this name for

The Book of Malachi

convenience, but the oracles are actually anonymous and reveal all that is known of their author. It is evident that he was associated with the temple and its cult. His attack on the priests as a class suggests that he was not a priest. But he was at least a cultic prophet—one whose oracles served the cause of the temple and its services.

Malachi differs from most of the preexilic prophets in his attitude toward the cult. They indicted many of the cult activities of their times, not because these were improperly performed, but because they seemed intended as a substitute for morality and justice. But Malachi believes the ceremonies of the cult must be properly performed as reverence proper to God's majesty (1:14). From such reverence will proceed incorruptible justice (3:5). The ideal priest takes God seriously—**he feared me, he stood in awe of my name** (2:5b). Isaiah said, "I cannot endure iniquity and solemn assembly" (1:13c). Malachi would say, "If you really kept your solemn assembly, you could not perform iniquity."

The prophet uses the method of dialogue to present his message. He anticipates and deals with objections by giving reasons for his pronouncements. The demands of God can stand the test of rational judgment. Malachi's arguments illustrate that the later prophets no longer relied simply on the authority of God as God was revealed to them. They appealed primarily to what their hearers already knew.

Setting

In the middle of the fifth century the morale of the small Jewish settlement in and around Jerusalem was at a low ebb. The excitement of the return from exile and of constructing the temple had long since died away. A struggling and poor community, the Jews were losing their identity (2:11). Drought and locusts continually struck the farmers, who were the backbone of the economy (3:10-11).

The worst ills, however, were social. Disintegration of Jewish family life was seen in divorce (2:16) and adultery (3:5). The rich oppressed the poor and victimized the helpless (3:5).

Dishonesty was a key to business success (3:15). The sacred principle of covenant, essential to a responsible society, was constantly disregarded (2:4, 10, 14).

It was bad enough for the country to be overrun by the lawless, but it appeared that God favored them (2:17)! To be cynical, godless, and corrupt was seemingly to enjoy every practical evidence of God's favor. The mood of the hour was "What's the use of trying!" (1:13). The heart of the Jew's predicament was not hard times as such but the loss of the presence of God (3:1).

Priests and people alike were lax in performng their sacred duty—notably sacrifice (1:8) and tithe (3:8). This was obvious evidence that something was wrong with Judah's religion. Ever-increasing latitude in the interpretation of God's demands expressed doubt rather than trust in God's mercy. Disobedience derived from uncertainty.

The priests' teaching function was cynically abused. In part this involved exposition of the traditions of the past and in part the consultation of sacred omens (see below on 2:6-9). Priests forfeited the moral leadership that should have come from the temple (2:9). The failure of the priests in a time of undependable secular authority was a principal cause of the corruption of society.

Message: True Religion Produces Morality

All that the prophet has to say hinges on his conviction that the day is coming when God will act for the people (3:17; 4:3). The day of Yahweh will include the return to Yahweh's temple (3:1), the swift execution of judgment on wrongdoers (3:5), and reward to the righteous (3:17). Evidence for God's justice is already to be seen in judgments outside Israel (1:1-5). Other nations, whether they know it or not, are honoring God in their sacrifices (1:11).

The Levitical priests have failed to keep their sacred covenant of responsibility (2:8). This has caused God to withdraw from the people both the prosperity which is the seal of blessing (2:2) and the divinely supported standards of justice which guarantee a sound social order (cf. 2:9; 3:5, 18). The people have been equally guilty. They have taken advantage of the laxity of their leaders by bringing maimed offerings (1:13), by divorce (2:14), by failing to tithe (3:8), and by oppressing the helpless (3:5).

The message of the prophet is: Return to God, and God will return to you (3:7). More than this, if one meets one's responsibilities to God, the windows of heaven will be opened, and multiple blessings will come (3:10).

Since the priests are custodians of temple and oracle, Malachi calls on them to lead in a return to God (1:5; 2:1, 7). They are challenged. Do they really believe God is there (cf. 1:13; 2:2; 3:1)? Those who do not respect the worship of God will not respect God's commands (1:13; 2:8).

Malachi's belief in the priest as messenger of God (2:7) points toward the end of the institution of prophecy. The prophet will cease to function—not because God no longer speaks, but because God will provide access to the divine word through a cleansed and active priesthood. Once God speaks from the temple, there need be no prophet. The dark sayings and obscure visions of spirit-seized people will vanish in the light of perfect law.

It is not surprising that the next move from the emphasis on a teaching priesthood was a codification of laws to stabilize justice. A half century later Ezra would be a priestly scribe, and his authority would be the law of Moses. Interpreters of the law, not prophets, would become key persons in Judaism. Inspiration must cease with Ezra. The first of two editorial postscripts added to the book (4:4) expresses this reliance on the law of Moses and points to future developments.

I. SUPERSCRIPTION (1:1)

Oracle is literally "burden." **Malachi** is "messenger." One is a messenger because he carries a message from beyond himself, something of more value than anything he could contrive. On the name Malachi, see the Introduction.

II. GOD'S LOVE FOR ISRAEL (1:2-5)

In proclaiming the love of God the prophet offers supporting arguments. To the ancient Jew divine favor was not an abstract proposition or doctrine so much as it was simply the good life. Had times been prosperous, the announcement—in this sense—would have been unnecessary. But times were bad (see Introduction). People were doubting the love of God. Malachi believes their troubles are magnified by self-pity. After all, closely related neighbors, the Edomites, are worse off then they are.

1:2c-4. Of the twin sons of Isaac (Genesis 25:23-26) God chose **Jacob** (Israel) and rejected **Esau** (Edom). Thus Edom at last is tasting the bitter fruit of God's judgment. The misfortune of the Edomites was probably an invasion by the Nabateans (see Introduction to Obadiah). For them there will be no rebuilding.

1:5. Great is the LORD, beyond the border of Israel! has been seen as expressing the tolerance of other peoples which begins to appear in this period. But the context shows that it refers to their rejection rather than their acceptance—that is, God's power to smite Israel's enemies is not limited. This concept of God's universal power, however, points the way to a recognition of God's universal love.

III. FAILURE OF THE PRIESTHOOD (1:6–2:9)

In the postexilic period the Persian government permitted the Jews no king, and the springs of prophecy were drying up. The priest came into his own. Malachi's attack is not on the priesthood as an institution but on the faithless and cynical priests who betray it. They have failed in two respects—prescriptions for sacrifice and public instruction.

1:6-14. *Shoddy Sacrifices.* The point of this passage is that one must not give to God that which does not **honor** God. The priests have failed at the point of their assumed expertness, the prescriptions of sacrificial law (cf. Deuteronomy 15:21). God is holy. God will accept only the unblemished.

1:6-10. In his argumentative fashion Malachi sets out to show that offering defective sacrifices not only violates cultic law but is an affront to decency. Since God is a **father** and **master,** God must be treated with respect. For priests to **despise** God's **name** in this way is blasphemy. No one seeking to win the **favor** of the **governor**—a Persian official—would dream of offering less than the best. Closing the **doors** of the temple and extinguishing the holy **fire** on the **altar** would be far more acceptable than the insult of cheap offerings.

1:11. This claim of worldwide **incense** and **pure offering,** or sacrifice, to Yahweh, whose **name is great among the nations,** is extraordinary in the Old Testament. Some interpreters take this verse to refer to the worship of dispersed Jews, but this seems improbable. In Malachi's time the Jews were not yet scattered **from the rising of the sun to its setting.** Further, the Jerusalem temple was the only legitimate place for Jews to sacrifice. Rather, the meaning must be that the worship which the nations offer to their gods is actually directed to Yahweh.

However, Malachi is not asserting the favorable status of sincere Gentiles before God. He is simply shaming Jews, and in doing so he seems to be commending aliens. He may not intend the inclusiveness and breadth of vision we recognize in his comparison, but it is there all the same.

1:12-14. The priests' cynical boredom is their own judgment on their travesty of ritual (verses 12-13). The layworshiper voluntarily **vows** to give the best of the flock and then breaks the promise by bringing a **blemished** animal. God is a **great King.** The conscience of even the heathen **nations** would not countenance such flouting of God's majesty.

2:1-9. *Irresponsible Instruction.* The faults just described are now laid specifically on the priests. They insult God's **name** by their negligence. The **blessings** which God will **curse** are taken by many to mean the benedictions pronounced by the priests over the worshipers (cf. Numbers 6:22-27). The more probable meaning, however, is the benefits the priests receive for their services, the Levitical tithes and offerings. These will not merely be diminished by the general blight but will bring ill when they are received. **Dung of your offerings** probably refers to the discarded entrails of sacrificed animals.

2:4-5. Here the **covenant** is said to have been with **Levi.** This indicates that the priests, as well as the whole community, are following the Deuteronomic Code adopted in 622 (cf. II Kings 22-23). According to this code all Levites were eligible to be priests. This seems to date the writing before the time of Ezra (see Introduction). Then there apparently was a change to the more complex Priestly Code, in which the priesthood was limited to the supposed descendants of Aaron. Other Levites were permitted to serve only in subordinate positions in the temple.

No **covenant with Levi** is mentioned elsewhere in the Old Testament. Perhaps Malachi means simply the special provision for support of the tribe of Levi (cf. Deuteronomy 18:1-8). "The fear of Yahweh" was the conventional term for "religion" in ancient Israel. Thus **fear** and **awe** here mean, not dread or terror, but reverence and a sense of obedience and even love and joy in God's service.

2:6-9. The word **instruction** here is *torah,* which is usually translated "law"—for example in "law of Moses." It is thus commonly assumed that Malachi is referring simply to the duty of the priests to teach the people the various ordinances of the Mosaic law. This was of course a responsibility of the priests, who were probably the custodians of the few existing copies of the written code. But the language of the passage indicates that it deals primarily with a further duty of the priests—that of securing oracles by the casting of the sacred lots, the Urim and Thummim. In the Deuteronomic Code the priests are made the court of final appeal, from whose verdict no one can deviate (Deuteronomy 17:10-13). In a case where there are not the required number of witnesses the accused and accuser are to be brought to the priests and judges "before the LORD" (Deuteronomy 19:15-19)—that is, to let Yahweh render the judgment through the sacred lots.

That this practice continued after the Exile is shown by the record of a difficult decision in the time of Zerubbabel, which was postponed "until there should be a priest to consult Urim and Thummim" (Ezra 2:63). There are also references to this priestly duty in the Priestly Code (Exodus 28:30; Leviticus 8:8; Numbers 27:18-21).

That Malachi has in mind this function of rendering oracular judgments is suggested by his calling the priest Yahweh's **messenger,** whose **mouth** and **lips,** rather than the written word, are the source of **true** *torah.* Thus he speaks of **your** *torah,* which is hardly a designation of the Mosaic law. He charges the priests with showing **partiality in your** *torah*—that is, they have mishandled justice. In this light we may understand the relation of the integrity of the priesthood to social conditions in the community.

The complaints of injustice in verse 17 may in large part stem from a breakdown in the system of priestly jurisprudence. It is only as the due process of law is corrupted that people are able to oppress their neighbors. Thus the irreverence of the priests is accompanied by social irresponsibility.

IV. CORRUPTION OF MARRIAGE (2:10-16)

When both Nehemiah and Ezra arrived in Jerusalem, the principal social problem they faced was that of "mixed" marriages (Ezra 9:1-2; Nehemiah 13:23-24). The leaders themselves, including one of the principal priests, were guilty of marrying foreign wives. According to Malachi the Jews' guilt is twofold: a religious compromise in marrying a **daughter of a foreign god** and the moral offense of divorcing a Jewish wife to make such a marriage possible.

2:10-12. Malachi cites the fatherhood of God the creator as the reason to avoid foreign wives. Verse 10 is often quoted as a statement of the brotherhood of all peoples. But it is clear that Malachi is thinking simply of God's fatherhood of the Jews, who accordingly must marry within the family. There are obscurities in the Hebrew of verse 12. The idea seems to be that anyone guilty of this sin will find none to aid them in a lawsuit or in offerings in the temple, without which they cannot prosper.

2:13-17. *Divorce.* Here is an exposition of the rationale of marriage. Marriage is a solemn agreement before God. Hence those who divorce their wives are guilty not merely of **covenant** breaking but of blasphemy. Natural ties enforce the relationship, for the **wife** was her husband's first love and has since been his constant **companion.** The Hebrew of verse 15 is difficult. It may refer to the story of woman's creation from the rib of man (Genesis 2:21-24), which gives them one inbreathed **spirit.** This interpretation would seem to apply to marriage among all peoples, since all descend from Adam.

The purpose of a union within God's chosen people is not arbitrary. God desires **godly offspring,** best nurtured by wives of the covenant people. However, if the universal demands of marriage are meant, then marital faithfulness in itself, rather than marriage within Judaism, produces godly children.

That God **hates divorce** suggests that divorce to marry another Jewish wife would be abhorrent to God. It raises the question whether the divorce of a Gentile wife, later demanded by Ezra (Ezra 10:11), would have been required by Malachi.

V. THE COMING JUDGMENT (2:17–3:5)

2:17. *The Justice of God.* The prophet turns from the specific charges he has made to the fundamental attitude underlying the sins of the community. God's justice is being brought into question. Obedience to God's law, in regard to both ceremonial and moral matters, has suffered as a consequence. This question, emerging by the time of the fall of Jerusalem, came to preoccupy not so much the irreligious as the thoughtful and reverent inquirers. It is the question of theodicy: How can God be just and still permit injustice?

3:1-5. *The Coming Messenger.* Though an ancient editor supposed him to be the author of the book (see Introduction) the **messenger,** or "angel," of this passage seems to represent an agent sent by God to **prepare** for God's coming in judgment and grace. Who is he? Will he be supernatural or human? Following what appears to be his identification as Elijah the prophet (4:5) the Christian interpretation has generally identified the messenger as John the Baptist, forerunner to Christ. Malachi, however, may have in mind a reforming or messianic priest (cf. 2:7). If so, the **covenant** may be that with Levi (2:4, 8).

3:2-4. The function of the messenger is to make possible God's return to the temple on a **day** of terrible judgment (verse 2). The priests will be cleansed in the crucible of suffering (verse 3), so that acceptable offerings may be made and God may again bless the people (verse 4). Since this day is not viewed as an end to history (cf. verses 12, 18; 4:3) the unendurable **fire** is probably a poetic exaggeration of the effects of real justice in a kingdom where God rules.

3:5. The meaning may be that God will deal with the wicked. But it seems more likely that the cleansed priesthood is again to carry out the mandate of oracular **judgment** (see above on 2:6-9). If God is not in the temple, oracular judgment will of course be unreliable. Either the sacred omens will not function or an irreverent priesthood will disregard them. The cleansing of the priesthood and restoration of right sacrifices on the day of God's return will guarantee temple justice.

The stroke of divine judgment will at last fall on those guilty of oppressing the innocent: **sorcerers** who victimize by witchcraft; **adulterers** who steal marriage partners; false witnesses; the oppressors who exploit the **hireling,** the **widow,** and the **orphan,** who cannot defend themselves, and the **sojourner,** whose human rights are often ignored. Malachi is here in the tradition of the classical prophetic absorption with social justice. He simply puts the temple and its ritual at the center of a just moral order. When God is in the house, God's household is in order!

VI. NEGLECT OF TITHES (3:6-12)

This treatment of the duty and opportunity of the tithe is the most familiar reference to the subject in the Old Testament. The tithe belongs to God, Malachi declares. To withhold it is to rob

God. Give God what is due and the nation's prosperity will be a worldwide testimony. That Malachi's argument was not entirely successful is shown by Nehemiah's measures to collect and distribute tithes (Nehemiah 13:10-14).

3:6-7. As it stands verse 6 is almost impossible to fit into the context. Its sense may be that the irresistible grace of God alone accounts for the people's survival. Though people act as if God no longer cares whether they obey God's **statutes,** God is as ready as ever to **return** and dwell among them.

3:8-11. The word **nation** is the term ordinarily used of foreigners. Therefore it implies that by **robbing** God the Jews are forfeiting their privilege as the chosen people. The **tithes** and **offerings** to be brought into the temple **storehouse** seem to reflect the laws of the Priestly Code, by which all of the tithes provide support for the priests and Levites (cf. Leviticus 27:30-33; Numbers 18:21-32). This fact does not contradict the other evidence that the book was written before adoption of the Priestly Code (see Introduction). It simply shows that the Priestly Code incorporated customs that had already been developed in practice.

3:10b-12. God asks the people to **test** the divine promises that their obedience will be rewarded. God will **open the windows of heaven**—send abundant rainfall—and **rebuke the devourer**—prevent the coming of locusts. Surplus crops will result. The prosperity of the Jewish community will be a witness to **all nations** of the blessing of obedience to Yahweh. The promises here, as usually in the Old Testament, apply to the people as a whole rather than individually. Presumably if enough of them bring their tithes, the rains will fall and benefit everyone—even those who still withhold their contribution (cf. Matthew 5:45).

VII. JUSTIFICATION OF THE RIGHTEOUS (3:13–4:3)

This last of Malachi's oracles deals further with the question raised in 2:17 about God's justice in relation to the individual rather than the community as a group.

3:13-15. Those who argue with the prophet in his pretended dialogue are asking: "What's the use of serving God?" People who do so seem no better off than their neighbors. In fact the **evildoers** seem to **prosper** more. Even those who defiantly **put God to the test** by flagrant disobedience appear to **escape** punishment.

Walking as in mourning probably refers to an attitude of penitence, possibly when appearing before the Levitical court. On the other hand **arrogant** may describe the assurance with which influential people come before the priests, knowing that a fraudulent oracle will declare them innocent and condemn their victims.

3:16-18. Those who have been expressing doubt about God's justice in verses 14-15 are not the wicked but the pious. It seems almost certain that the Septuagint is correct in reading not **Then** but "Thus" at the beginning of verse 16. That is, Yahweh is responding to the doubt of God's justice by those who have been faithful to God but are losing heart.

The several Old Testament references to God's keeping a **book,** a written record like an earthly king, are a figure of speech. They express confidence that no one of God's worshipers will be overlooked rather than a literal idea that God's memory needs such an aid. Thus the **righteous** may be assured that there is coming a **day** of judgment when God will **spare** them and distinguish them individually from the **wicked.**

4:1-3. Here as in 3:2-3 the catastrophe of the coming **day** of reward for the righteous and destruction for the wicked is expressed symbolically in terms of fire. It is likely that this sort of language was originally used figuratively as a way of describing an event which, while it would transform history, would not terminate it. Later it came to be taken more and more seriously as descriptive rather than symbolic.

It is not certain how far this process has developed with Malachi—whether he thinks of the day as some decisive action by which God will return simple justice to a depraved society or as a literal fire that will destroy all the wicked and leave the righteous to live in happiness. **Stubble,** or dry grass, was a common fuel for the peasant's baking **oven.** The idea of the **sun** with **wings** no doubt comes from artistic representation common in the Near East, especially Egypt, of the sun or a sun god with wings by which he flies across the sky.

VIII. EPILOGUE (4:4-6)

4:4. This postscript appears to be an addition by the compiler of the Book of the Twelve or a later editor. It was intended to tie the whole collection of the minor prophets to the **law of . . . Moses**—that is, the Pentateuch, or first five books of the Bible—which by his time was established as the canonical scripture of Judaism.

4:5-6. This second postscript is apparently another addition by one who wished to identify the messenger of 3:1 as a **prophet,** rather than a priest as in Malachi's thought (cf. 2:7). Probably he considered **Elijah** as available for the assignment because of the record of his being translated rather than dying (II Kings 2:11). His idea caught on. In later noncanonical literature, as well as in the New Testament, Elijah is thought of as returning to prepare the way for the Messiah.

The meaning of the reconciliation of **fathers** and **children** is uncertain. Perhaps family breaches symbolize all the social ills for which the forerunner will offer a last chance of healing before the **great and terrible day.**

THE OLD TESTAMENT
APOCRYPHA

THE FIRST BOOK OF ESDRAS

Charles T. Fritsch

Introduction

This is the first book of the Apocrypha. It is known to Protestants as I Esdras, from the Greek form of the name Ezra. In the Latin Vulgate Ezra is called "Esdras I" and Nehemiah "Esdras II." Those who follow this tradition call this book III Esdras or "Greek Ezra." Unlike most books of the Apocrypha it is not included in the Roman Catholic Old Testament.

Contents

I Esdras is a Greek version of a portion of the historical work of a writer known as the Chronicler, which is represented in the canonical books of Chronicles, Ezra, and Nehemiah. It contains material corresponding to II Chronicles 35–36, almost all of Ezra, and Nehemiah 7:73–8:13a. It also tells a story about a contest of three guards in the court of King Darius I of Persia which is not found in the Old Testament and which clearly is a later insertion into the Chronicler's work. Variations from the Hebrew-Aramaic text consist partly of interpolation and partly of rearrangement. The book tells the story of the last days of the Judean kingdom, the fall of Jerusalem, the Babylonian exile, the returns under Sheshbazzar and Zerubbabel, and the reorganization of the Jewish state under Ezra. No mention is made of Nehemiah and his work (see below on 5:7-46). The abrupt beginning with the account of Josiah's passover and the ending with an unfinished sentence show that this is a fragment of a larger work. The differences in order from the Hebrew-Aramaic text complicate rather than clarify the chronological problems of these books.

Text and Date

The Greek text of I Esdras evidently represents the original Septuagint translation of Chronicles-Ezra-Nehemiah made at Alexandria in the second century B.C. Scholars disagree on whether its variations from these books should be attributed to the translator or to the use of a Hebrew-Aramaic text differing from that later canonized by the Palestinian Jews. They disagree also on the related question of whether the added story of the three guards was composed in Greek or in Aramaic.

As a translation I Esdras is far superior to the literalistic, wooden Greek version of Chronicles-Ezra-Nehemiah, which is found in the present Septuagint. This translation is generally attributed to Theodotion (second century A.D.). The Jewish historian Josephus in the last decade of the first century A.D. used I Esdras in preference to the canonical Ezra-Nehemiah as his source for the Persian period in his *Antiquities of the Jews.* The date of I Esdras therefore must fall somewhere between 200 B.C. and A.D. 90. Since it is definitely related to the early Alexandrian translation in style and vocabulary, most scholars date it around 150 B.C.

I. The Last Days of the Kingdom
(1:1-58)

This chapter corresponds closely to II Chronicles 35:1–36:21 except that verses 23-24 are without parallel there. In verse 34 **Jeconiah** should be Jehoahaz (cf. II Chronicles 36:1).

II. THE RETURN UNDER SHESHBAZZAR (2:1-30)

Verses 1-15 correspond closely to Ezra 1:1-11.

2:16-30. *Samaritan Opposition.* This section corresponds to Ezra 4:7-24, except that Ezra 4:8-10 is missing here. It is even more displaced chronologically than is Ezra, probably because of the insertion of the following story of the three guards. In Ezra the correspondence with the Persian king concerns only the rebuilding of the city and its walls. But in verses 18 and 20 here references to rebuilding the **temple** have been inserted to harmonize with the context. **Coelesyria and Phoenicia** was the province in the Seleucid Empire which included Palestine.

III. THE STORY OF THE 3 GUARDS (3:1–5:3)

This section is unique to I Esdras. Obviously it is a late addition to the Chronicler's history—for example, see below on 4:42-63. It is a fine piece of oriental wisdom literature, describing an oratorical contest among three guards in the court of **King Darius I**, who rewards the one he judges to be the winner. It has been adapted to the history of Zerubbabel (named in the story itself only in 4:13), **who spoke wise words before Darius the king of the Persians** (5:6).

3:17*b*–4:41. *The Oratorical Contest.* The **three young men** make plans for a debate before the king and each one selects his topic. The first contestant debates on the subject that **wine is the strongest** (3:18-24) and the second that the **king is the strongest** (4:1-12). The third, **Zerubbabel,** debates on two subjects **that women are strongest, but truth is victor over all things** (4:13-40). All the people shout: **Great is truth, and strongest of all!** Of **Apame** and **Bartacus** in verse 29 nothing is known.

4:42-57. *Zerubbabel's Reward. Zerubbabel is given a seat next to Darius and is made a* kinsman. More important, he is granted his request to go to Jerusalem to rebuild the city and **temple.** The king writes **letters** to officials to give safe conduct along the way and to supply materials and funds for the construction. Contrast 6:23-26, where after the work has started Darius knows nothing of the authority for it till the decree of Cyrus is located in the archives.

Darius also returns to Zerubbabel the temple **vessels** taken from Jerusalem by Nebuchadnezzar. All this is done in accordance with the vow made by **Cyrus,** which evidently, according to this story, has never been carried out (verses 44, 57; contrast 2:12-15). There is no hint here of a return to Jerusalem in the days of Cyrus (contrast 2:15).

4:58–5:3. *The Conclusion of the Story.* After a prayer of thanksgiving Zerubbabel informs his fellow exiles, who rejoice and join him in the return.

IV. THE RETURN UNDER ZERUBBABEL (5:4–7:15)

5:4-6. *A Group of Returning Exiles.* This is an independent fragment which may have been inserted here as a transition between the preceding story and the list of returnees which follows. There is no explanation for **Joakim the son of Zerubbabel** (cf. I Chronicles 3:19-20; also Nehemiah 12:10, where **Jeshua** is the father of Joakim).

5:7-46. *The List of Returning Exiles.* This passage corresponds closely to Ezra 2:1-70 and Nehemiah 7:6-73a except for variations in the names. In the Revised Standard Version names based on the Hebrew of Ezra and Nehemiah have been substituted in many cases for the Greek forms of I Esdras, which are shown in footnotes. **Attharias** (verse 40) is a Greek transliteration of *tirshatha* ("governor"), found in the parallel verses, Ezra 2:63 and Nehemiah 7:65. **Nehemiah and** probably slipped in here because Nehemiah is called *tirshatha* in Nehemiah 8:9; 10:1.

5:47-73. *The Beginning of Restoration.* Verses 47-73a correspond closely to Ezra 3:1–4:5. Verse 73b is probably a variant of Ezra 4:24. **Two years** is an error, since eight years elapsed between the death of Cyrus (530) and the beginning of the reign of Darius I (522).

6:1–7:15. *The Completion of the Temple.* This passage corresponds closely to Ezra 5–6. On 6:23-26 see above on 4:42-57. In 7:5 completion of the temple is dated **the twenty-third day of the month of Adar** whereas Ezra 6:55 has the third day. There is no clue for determining which figure is original.

V. THE RETURN UNDER EZRA (8:1–9:55)

This passage corresponds closely to Ezra 7–10 and Nehemiah 7:73b–8:13a except for variations in the names in 9:18-36, 43, 48 (see above on 5:7-46). It is significant that here appear together the Ezra materials which in Ezra-Nehemiah are separated by the major section of the Nehemiah memoirs. Some scholars believe that the order here—8:1–9:36 (cf. Ezra 7–10); 9:37-55 (cf. Nehemiah 7:73b–8:13a)—is the original order of the Ezra narrative. They think that the part of the Nehemiah memoirs in Nehemiah 1:1–7:73a was inserted into it, either by the Chronicler or by a later reviser. Other scholars, however, think the reading of the law (9:37-55) originally followed Ezra's arrival in Jerusalem (8:1-67; cf. Ezra 7–8) and preceded the action on mixed marriages (8:68–9:36; cf. Ezra 9–10).

According to either view 9:37a offers a problem. It appears to be a variant of Nehemiah 7:73a and thus to come from the end of the census list of 5:7-46; Ezra 2:1-70; and Nehemiah 7:6-73a. Those who believe I Esdras to be derived from Ezra-Nehemiah cite 9:37a as evidence that the translator or other editor arrived at the order in chapter 9 by simply omitting Nehemiah 1:1–7:72 from his copy of Ezra-Nehemiah.

Other evidences, however, make it more likely that I Esdras and Ezra-Nehemiah represent independent versions of the original work of the Chronicler. Thus scholars have suggested various other explanations for 9:37a. For example, if it was originally the link between the arrival of Ezra in Jerusalem (8:1-67) and the reading of the law (9:37-55), the editor who placed the latter story in Nehemiah 7:73b–8:18 may have omitted this sentence because it so nearly duplicated Nehemiah 7:73*a*.

9:49-55. On **Attharates** compare Attharias in 5:40 and see comment on 5:7-46. The incomplete sentence ending the book (cf. Nehemiah 8:13*a*) shows that we have only a fragment of this version of the Chronicler's history. Possibly the remaining portion included Nehemiah's memoirs, which the Chronicler probably appended at the end of his work.

THE SECOND BOOK OF ESDRAS

Robert C. Dentan

INTRODUCTION

II Esdras is not a continuation or parallel of I Esdras. It is an important piece of apocalyptic literature—dealing with hidden revelations and the final age. In many respects it is comparable to Daniel, Revelation, and such noncanonical apocalypses as Enoch and the Assumption of Moses. However, it makes less use of fantastic imagery than those books and is sharply distinguished from them by its dominant concern with the problem of human suffering. No other book outside of Job exhibits so profound and intensely personal an interest in this subject. Unlike Daniel and Revelation the book seems not to have been written in a time of persecution. It looks back in anguished contemplation on a disaster that has already run its course.

Authorship and Composition

As it now stands the book claims to be the work of Ezra (Esdras in Greek)—a pseudonym such as is conventional in apocalyptic writing. In 3:1, however, Ezra is strangely and impossibly identified with "Salathiel"—that is, Shealtiel, scion of the Davidic line during the Babylonian exile (see below on 3:1-2). The date in this verse and succeeding references to the purported historical situation fit Shealtiel rather than Ezra.

Accordingly some scholars believe, with considerable reason, that the nucleus of the book (chapters 3–10 or possibly 3–13) was originally published in the name of Shealtiel. Only in chapter 14 does Ezra appear in his own character. It is therefore supposed that the addition of this chapter caused the whole book to be attributed to Ezra.

The structure of the book is obscured by the presence of chapters 1–2 and 15–16. These are of later Christian origin and are found only in the Latin version. They are independent compositions and of slight interest. The main part of the book (chapers 3–14) is purely Jewish in character. It consists of seven "visions." The first three of these (3:1–5:20; 5:21–6:34; and 6:35–9:25) are not so much visions as extended conversations of a philosophical character between "Ezra" and the angel Uriel or God. The next three are visions in the strict sense: of the woman who is Zion (9:26–10:59), of the eagle (11:1–12:38), and of the man from the sea (chapter 13).

The final "vision" relates the commission of Ezra (chapter 14). It is so different from all the others that it is considered a later addition to the series. Differences also apparent in the eagle and man-from-the-sea visions may be due to the author's adaptation of varying sources. But more probably they indicate that these sections likewise were editorially joined to the preceding visions.

Date

The date of the basic Shealtiel apocalypse is given as the "thirtieth year after the destruction of our city"—that is, Jerusalem—by the Babylonians in 586 B.C. (3:1). But this is only a dramatic device, for the author's real concern is with the destruction by the Romans in A.D. 70. The thirtieth year, imitated from Ezekiel 1:1, is not to be taken as a precise date, but it points to a time near the end of the first century. The eagle vision was probably written during the reign of Domitian (81-96; see below on 12:22-30). Those who believe it was composed as a part of the Shealtiel apocalypse therefore date this work around 95. The vision of the man from the sea, or its source, seems to come from a time before the destruction of Jerusalem (see below on 13:1-58).

The assumption of twenty-four canonical books in chapter 14 seems to place this unit after the fixing of the Hebrew canon at Jamnia around 85-90. The finished Jewish work (chapters 3–14) would hardly have been borrowed for Christian use after the Jewish revolt of 132-35, which appears finally to have disrupted communication between the two groups. Therefore a date of around 120 seems a reasonable limit for the final editing. Chapters 1–2 are probably to be dated in the second century and chapers 15–16 in the third (see below on 15:1–16:78).

Name

The present name of the book is derived from 1:1, which was not part of the original apocalypse. The book was not included in the Septuagint and therefore not accounted canonical in the Roman Catholic Church. In the Vulgate it appears only as part of an appendix printed after the New Testament, where it is called IV Esdras—distinguished from I and II Esdras, which represent the canonical Ezra and Nehemiah of Protestants, and from III Esdras, which is the Vulgate name for I Esdras of the Protestant Apocrypha. Chapters 1–2 have sometimes been known separately as II Esdras, and chapters 15–16 as V Esdras. The Jewish work (chapters 3–14), or sometimes the whole book, is frequently referred to as IV Ezra or, to avoid confusion, simply the Ezra Apocalypse.

Text

Chapters 3–14 were originally written in Hebrew and subsequently translated into Greek. Both the Hebrew original and the Greek translation are lost, except for a couple of Greek passages quoted in early Christian writers. The entire book exists only in Latin. Chapters 3–14 are also preserved in Syriac, Ethiopic, Armenian, and two Arabic versions, while fragments are extant in Sahidic and Georgian—evidence of the work's once great popularity.

Latin manuscripts of the book are numerous, but contain

many variants and errors. Almost all those now existing are descended from a manuscript of the ninth century. A leaf was cut out of this manuscript, possibly for doctrinal reasons (see below on 7:[75]-45[115], and chapter and verse numbers came to be established for this defective text. In 1875 R. L. Bensly published the missing section, which he found in a hitherto unstudied manuscript, and which harmonized with a corresponding section in the oriental versions. Translations since then have included this material following 7:35, with bracketed verse numbers [36]-[105]. This necessitates an awkward double numeration for the remaining verses of the chapter, 36[106]-70[140].

Religious Interest

The author of the original apocalypse was a fervent, orthodox Jew who believed the world to have been created for the sake of Israel (6:55; 7:11). However, he is remarkable for his broad concern with the whole of suffering humanity (7:[62]-[69]). His immediate problem is the fact that God's chosen people have been subjugated by the impious Romans (4:23). But his mind can never completely separate this from the broader problem presented by the existence of human misery in any form.

A partial answer is found in the universality of sin, caused by the transgression of Adam, who transmitted the disease to all his descendants (3:21-22; 7:48[118]). Even though the power of free choice remains (8:56), most elect to do evil and therefore deserve to perish (7:57[127]-61[131]; 8:3). But the author sympathizes even with sinners (7:18, 46[116]-56]126]), partly because he knows himself to be one (8:35). His pessimistic view of human nature, corrupted by an evil heart (3:26), has striking affinities with the teaching of Paul—as it does his lament that even possession of the divine law is not enough to save Israel (3:22; 9:36).

The continual return to these themes in the first three visions shows the extent of the author's emotional involvement in them. His only comfort comes from the apocalyptic truth that "the Most High has made not one world but two" (7:[50]). Thus the injustices evident in the present age can be corrected in the age to come.

I. THE CHRISTIAN PREFIX (1:1–2:48)

Chapters 1–2 were originally a separate book (see Introduction). They describe the rejection of the old Israel for its faithlessness (1:1-32; 2:1-9) and the choice of a new people, the Christian church, to take its place (1:33-40; 2:10-14). The church is exhorted to joy, good works, and hope of a glorious new age (2:15-32). Ezra has a vision of the redeemed in heaven (2:33-48).

1:1-3. The canonical Old Testament introduces Ezra as a priest and scribe (Ezra 7:1-6, 11; cf. I Esdras 8:1-3, 8). Here he is represented as a **prophet.**

1:4-11. The formula **The word of the Lord came to me** is typical of the prophetic books. Ezra is told to denounce the sins of his people. On **pull out the hair** cf. Ezra 9:3.

1:12-23. God reviews the many blessings bestowed on the chosen people.

1:24-32. Because of Israel's rejection of God, God is going to reject them. Verse 30 reflects Matthew 23:37; verse 32 Matthew 23:34-35.

1:33-40. Ezra is represented as predicting that the place of Israel will be taken by a **people that will come**—that is, the Christian church. The church will then be considered heir to the teaching of Israel's patriarchs and prophets.

2:1-9. These verses reflect the Roman destruction of Jerusalem in A.D. 70. They exhibit an unattractive anti-Jewish spirit—especially verse 7. The fall of the city—the **mother** and **widow** of verses 2-6—and the subsequent dispersion of the Jews are said to be God's punishment for their sins. **Assyria** means Rome.

2:10-14. God now addresses the church as **my people.** It is promised the blessings of the **kingdom** in the coming age. Verse 13 combines Matthew 7:7 and 24:22. Verse 14 is an oblique reflection of Isaiah 45:7.

2:15-32. The church is now addressed as **mother.** It is exhorted to engage in good works and to face the future with joyful anticipation.

2:23-48. In obvious imitation of such passages as Revelation 4; 7; and 14:1-5 Ezra sees a vision of the church's risen martyrs receiving crowns from the **Son of God.**

II. THE EZRA APOCALYPSE: SEVEN VISIONS (3:1–14:48)

The Jewish apocalypse includes chapters 3–14. The first part of it (chapters 3–10) has a philosophical tone quite different from the rest (see Introduction).

3:1–5:20. *Vision One: The Problem of Israel's Suffering.* The ostensible occasion of the visions is the **destruction** of Jerusalem by the Babylonians in 586 B.C. (3:1-2). Actually the author is thinking of the destruction by the Romans in A.D. 70. The situation gives rise to the whole question of the meaning of Israel's suffering and of human suffering in general.

3:1-2. The date **in the thirtieth year** imitates the opening phrase of Ezekiel, the first great book of the Babylonian exile. **Salathiel** is the Greek form of Shealtiel, oldest son of King Jehoiachin (Jeconiah, I Chronicles 3:17), who was taken captive to Babylon in 597 B.C.. He was the father of Zerubbabel (Ezra 5:2), who some hoped would be enthroned after the Exile (cf. Haggai 2:23; Zechariah 4:6-10). As exiled claimant to the throne of David Shealtiel thus symbolizes Israel.

The situation here is clearly that of Shealtiel and not that of **Ezra,** who lived after the Exile when Jerusalem had been rebuilt. Therefore it seems probable that only the name Shealtiel appeared in the original text. The name Ezra was introduced, awkwardly, here and at five other places (6:10; 7:2, 25, [49?]; 8:2), when chapter 14 was added.

3:3-11. The doctrine of "original" sin—that Adam's transgression infected the whole race with a sinful tendency—appears here in Jewish literature for the first time (cf. verses 21-22, 26; 4:30; 7:48[118]).

3:12-27. Even God's **everlasting covenant** with Abraham left Israel burdened with the **evil heart,** inherited from Adam. The evil heart is the rabbinical "evil impulse," which along with the "good impulse" was regarded as a normal part of human nature (cf. 4:30; 7:[48], [92]).

3:28-36. Why did God allow the wicked Babylonians—that is, Romans—to conquer the relatively more righteous Jews?

4:1-12. The angel **Uriel** ("God is my light") is sent to answer the seer's questions. He argues that, since human beings cannot understand even ordinary earthly phenomena, they can hardly expect to understand the plans of God. The seer answers that it would be better not to have been created than to be left thus ignorant.

4:13-25. Uriel argues that every creature must learn to live and operate within its own appointed sphere and not try to comprehend things which lie beyond it (verse 21). The seer complains that it was senseless then to give humans the **power of understanding.** And in any event, he declares, he was not asking questions about ineffable realities but only about a plain historical fact, that Israel has been conquered by the Gentiles.

4:26-32. Uriel goes on to give the final answer. Indeed **this age is full of sadness,** but it will soon pass away to make room for a better.

4:33-52. When the seer asks how soon this will happen, the angel replies that the end is predetermined. It will come when the allotted **number** of the righteous **is completed,** as **Jeremiel the archangel** is reported to have said. The analogy of childbirth shows that the consummation cannot be held back. **Hades** in the original Hebrew text no doubt read "Sheol," meaning the underworld of the dead. Further parables illustrate the truth that the greater part of the present age is past.

5:1-13. The imminence of the end will be marked by omens, and by the growth of iniquity and misery. The **signs** of the end are traditional. Because of differences in style and outlook some scholars think this passage, except verse 13*b*, has been inserted from a different source (see below on 7:26-[44]). If so, 4:52 is probably an editorial introduction to it.

5:14-20. After awaking from the first vision the seer prepares for the second by a seven-day fast. **Phaltiel** is otherwise unknown.

5:21–6:34. *Vision Two: The Coming of the New Age.* His fast completed, the seer prays, complaining at God's unjust treatment of the chosen people (5:21-30). Uriel comes again and once more warns that human understanding is incapable of discovering the divine plan (5:31-37). Beginning in 5:38 God seems to take the place of Uriel for the remainder of this vision.

5:41-55. The seer now introduces a new question: What will be the fate of those who do not live until the new age arrives? God answers that all will be saved simultaneously, for with God there is no past, present, or future (verse 42). It would, however, have been as unnatural for all people to have been **created at one time** as for a woman to **bear ten children** all at once. The reduced stature of the present human race shows that **creation . . . is aging** and hastening toward its end (verses 50-55).

5:56–6:6. The seer asks who will be charged with bringing creation to an end. God answers that just as the world was planned by God, God will end it—without assistance. This seems to be a polemic against certain Jewish, and possibly Christian, ideas attributing creation to intermediaries (cf. Proverbs 8:22-31; Wisdom of Solomon 7:22*a;* John 1:3). It seems also to reject the idea of a coming Messiah (see below on 7:26-[44]).

6:7-10. In answer to another question God declares that the ideal future age will immediately follow the present age, just as **Jacob's hand** attached itself immediately to **Esau's heel** (see below on 7:26-[44]). There will be no intervening messianic time. **Ezra** in verse 10 is probably an interpolation (see above on 3:1-2).

6:11-28. The seer begs to know further **signs** of the end (cf. 4:52–5:13) and is told of additional marvels to come (verses 21-24). Afterward the day of salvation will arrive. Enoch and Elijah will appear (verse 26; cf. Gen. 5:24; II Kings 2:11; Malachi 4:5), and universal righteousness will prevail. On the **trumpet**

cf. I Corinthians 15:52. Some scholars regard verses 13-28 as an interpolation, with verses 11-12 and 29 (cf. verse 14) as editorial transitions (see below on 7:26-[44]).

6:29-34. In an interlude the seer is told to prepare for further visions by fasting.

6:35—9:25. *Vision Three: The Fate of Righteous and Wicked.* This is the longest and most complex of the visions. The seer returns repeatedly to his main argument and is, incidentally, provided with a more elaborate program of things to come (7:26-[44], [75]-45[115]; 8:63—9:12).

6:38-59. The seer asks why, in view of God's purpose in creation, Israel is subjugated to the heathen. The idea that God created the world only for the sake of Israel (verse 55; cf.7:11) is not to be found in the canonical Old Testament. **Behemoth** and **Leviathan** were mythical primeval monsters.

7:1-25. The seer is told to concentrate on the glories of the coming age rather than the miseries of the present, which are due to Adam's sin (verses 1-16). When he continues to express sympathy for suffering sinners (verses 17-18) he is admonished to realize that God is just, for sinners have rejected God's law in full knowledge of the consequences (verses 19-25).

7:26-[44]. On the bracketed verse numbers see the Introduction. Some scholars regard this section, along with 5:1-13a; 6:11-28; and 8:63—9:12, as an interpolation from another document. The ideas are different from those found elsewhere in the book. The seer is told of the coming of the heavenly city and the temporary messianic age (verses 26-29), the resurrection (verse 32), the judgment, hell, and heaven (verses 33-[44]).

The conception of a **four hundred**–year messianic kingdom intervening betweem this age and the one to come is known from rabbinic sources. But the assertion that the **Messiah** will **die** at the end of the period is without parallel. The Latin version, but not the others, interpolates the name "Jesus" in verse 28.

7:[45]-[74]. The seer renews his complaint at the tragic lot of humanity. The divine answer is that sinful souls, being worthless, deserve their fate and should not be lamented (verses

191

[49]-[61]). The seer then argues that animals are then better off than humans (verses [62]-[69]). The answer is that sinful humans freely chose their course. They have finally exhausted God's patience which they had so long enjoyed (verses [70]-[74]).

7:[75]-45[115]. In answer to his question the seer is told of the fate of the wicked and righteous immediately after death. The ideas in this passage seem inconsistent with the conception of a final judgment at the end of the age—found, for example, in verses 32-[44]. The long-lost portion of the Latin text (verses [36]-[105]; see Introduction) may have been deliberately cut out because verse [105] seems to forbid prayers for the dead.

7:46]116]-61[131]. The seer says it would be better if men and women had never been created—or at least had been prevented from sinning. The reply is that free choice is of the very essence of human experience.

7:62[132]–8:3. The seer appeals to the mercy of God. But the only answer is that **Many have been created, but few shall be saved** (cf. Matthew 22:14).

8:4-62a. The seer meditates further on the paradox that human beings, created with such care, must simply perish (verses 4-19a). He prays for God's mercy on those **who have no works of righteousness** (verses 20-36). But God continues to affirm both the justice of divine ways and the depth of divine love. God declares there is no alternative but to accept the decisions human beings make for themselves, however much the result may contradict God's original purpose (verse 59).

The separate title in verse 19b points to the fact that the following prayer (verses 20-36), under the name *Confessio Esdrae,* was often printed separately in the Latin Bible and elsewhere. On **before he was taken up** cf. 14:48 and the Revised Standard Version footnote. The author's skepticism about average person's being saved by **works of righteousness** (verses 32, 36) approaches the mood of Paul rather than of normative Judaism.

8:62b–9:12. Rather curiously, the seer again asks when the end of the age will come. He is given a general summary of things previously said. The passage may be an interpolation (see above on 7:26-[44]).

9:13-25. The seer rejects the warning to concern himself only with the glories in store for the righteous. He continues to lament that more will perish than be saved. God says it has been difficult to save even the righteous few (verses 17-22). He instructs the seer to prepare for another vision by eating **flowers** rather than by fasting.

9:26–10:59. *Vision Four: Zion, Mourning and Transfigured.* The seer has a vision of a woman mourning for her son (9:26–10:4). After he upbraids her for indulging in selfish grief while Jerusalem lies waste (10:5-24) she is suddenly transfigured (10:25-27a). It is revealed that she herself is the Zion who mourns but still is glorious (10:27b-57). The idea that Israel's possession of the law brings no assurance of salvation (9:36) again suggests the thought of Paul. The parable of the woman was probably not invented by the author but adapted from a popular tale. This would account for a certain lack of coherence between story and interpretation.

Zion (10:44) is the heavenly prototype rather than the earthly city. Her **son** (10:46, 49) probably represents the earthly city, now in ruins. The ideal Jerusalem is revealed as still glorious despite the destruction of its earthly counterpart (10:50).

10:58-59. Some scholars consider these two verses to be an editorial transition to the following vision. If so, the original continuation of verse 57 is perhaps to be found in 12:40-50 or 13:57-58 (see comments).

11:1–12:51. *Vision Five: The Eagle.* This vision, with its fantastic animals and mysterious details, resembles such familiar apocalyptic works as Daniel 7–12 and Revelation much more closely than the earlier part of the book. Probably it came originally from a different source and was incorporated by the author of the Shealtiel apocalypse or, more probably, by a later editor (see Introduction).

11:1–12:3a. In a dream the seer sees an eagle with twelve wings and three heads rising from the sea to rule the earth. Successively the wings and then the heads rise to power (11:7-35). Finally a lion comes out of the forest to announce the eagle's doom, which shortly follows.

The eagle represents the Roman Empire, which **came up from the sea** (cf. Daniel 7:3)—that is, from the Mediterranean, as viewed from the east. Both the vision and the interpretation that follows (12:3b-38) have been reworked at least once. Some of the details are unclear, but it is obvious that the wings and heads represent successive Roman emperors. The **opposing wings** are rebellious army officers. The date of this section depends on the identification of the **three heads** (11:23-35), especially the third. Its fall in the near future will inaugurate the last days of imperial rule (12:2-3a; see below on 12:22-30).

12:3b-38. The seer asks for an explanation of the vision. He is told that the eagle is the fourth kingdom of Daniel's vision, the wings and heads are kings, and the lion is the Messiah. The vision is to be preserved in a secret **book.** In Daniel 7:2-8 the **fourth kingdom,** symbolized by the last of four terrible beasts who rise to dominate the earth, is undoubtedly the empire of Alexander the Great and his successors. Here it is taken to refer to Rome. The three preceding kingdoms are then understood as the Babylonian, Persian, and Greek instead of the Babylonian, Median, and Persian. The **twelve kings** are twelve Roman emperors, beginning with Julius Caesar. The **second,** who is to **hold sway for a longer time than any other of the twelve** (cf. 11:13b-17), is obviously Augustus.

12:22-30. The **three heads** are the Flavian emperiors—Vespasian (69-79) and his two sons, Titus (79-81) and Domitian (81-96). Vespasian was the first commander in the war against the Jews (67-69). Under Titus, Jerusalem was captured and destroyed (70). These facts explain the peculiar importance of these kings (verse 25).

Since Domitian is apparently still ruling (cf. 11:23-35) this part of the book can be plausibly dated in his reign—probably toward the end, when he became increasingly despotic. Revelation is usually dated in the same period. On the other hand, since Titus did not die violently, some scholars have dated the original version in the days of Vespasian and assumed it was later reworked.

12:31-38. The **Messiah** is strangely represented as both pre-existent and **from the posterity of David.** The **book** to be hidden from common view is a common apocalyptic idea.

12:39-51. In a curious transitional interlude the seer promises not to forsake his fellow exiles but to return to the city when he finishes his prayers for Zion. These verses bear no relationship to their present context. They probably belong to the original source preserved in chapters 3–10. It has been suggested that originally verses 40-48 followed 13:57-58, which in turn followed 10:57. If so, **seven days** refers to the period mentioned in 9:23, now **past** and exceeded by the **three days** of 13:58. Possibly the transition led to a concluding vision (cf. 10:56) which was omitted when chapters 11–13 were added.

13:1-58. *Vision Six: The Man from the Sea.* The seer dreams of a man who arises from the sea and is met by a great hostile army. He destroys it by a flaming breath from his mouth, after which he gathers to himself a large company of peaceful people. On awaking the seer asks for an explanation. He is told that the man is the Messiah, his flaming breath is the law, and the peaceful company is the ten lost tribes of Israel. This is followed by the usual transition to the next vision (verses 53b-58; see above on 12:39-51).

The conceptions in this vision are so different from those of any of the preceding sections that it almost certainly comes from a different source. Probably it is to be dated before A.D. 70, since the Jews seem to be still living in Palestine. Also there is no allusion to the destruction of the temple, and there is no single great enemy such as Rome.

Something like the figure of a man belongs to the same tradition as the "one like a son of man" in Daniel 7:13. The final battle against God's rule (in verse 5) is a common feature of the apocalyptic tradition. The **great mountain** is interpreted as the heavenly **Zion.** On the Messiah's **flaming breath** cf. Isaiah 11:4 and II Thessalonians 2:8. In the original form of the story this certainly was not understood to be a symbol of the **law,** as it is here interpreted (verse 38). The story of the exile of the **ten tribes** is told in II Kings 17. The remainder of the story told here is entirely legendary.

14:1-48. *Vision Seven: Restoration of the Holy Books.* Only in this section does Ezra, the "scribe skilled in the law of Moses" (Ezra 7:6), appear in something like his historical role (see Introduction). God appears to Ezra and warns him, before he is translated, to prepare himself and his people for the evils of the final time that is near at hand.

Ezra asks for inspiration to rewrite the sacred books that were destroyed in the burning of the temple (verses 19-22). God instructs him to prepare for the task by providing writing materials and choosing scribes (verses 23-26). Then after a general exhortation to the people Ezra drinks a cup of fiery-colored liquid. During forty days he dictates to five secretaries the ninety-four canonical and apocalyptic books of scripture. The obvious purpose of this story is to vindicate the divine authority of the apocalyptic books, which the rabbis tended to view with suspicion.

Like Enoch and Elijah, Ezra is to be translated to heaven, where he will be with the Messiah (verse 9; cf. Revised Standard Version footnote to verse 48). **Thy law** in verse 21 means here the whole of canonical scripture. The **characters which they did not know** are those of the Aramaic, or "square" Hebrew, alphabet, traditionally supposed to have been introduced by Ezra. The **twenty-four books** are those of the Hebrew canon as fixed by a group of rabbis at Jamnia around A.D. 85-90—Samuel, Kings, Chronicles, Ezra-Nehemiah, and the twelve minor prophets each being counted as a single book. The **seventy** are apocalyptic works such as this book, which are here clothed with the full authority of Moses (verse 5) and Ezra. The term "apocrypha" (hidden away) is probably derived from this story (cf. 12:37).

III. THE CHRISTIAN APPENDIX (15:1–16:78)

Though the historical allusions in this section are vague, they refer most naturally to events in the middle of the third century A.D. Unlike chapters 1–2 these chapters contain no distinctive

Christian ideas. But at so late a date they are unlikely to have been taken over from Jewish sources.

15:1-19. Ecclesiastical tradition identifies the seer with Ezra, though he is nowhere named. He is told of evils the Lord is about to inflict on the earth for its wickedness, especially the persecution of God's people (verses 1-11). **Egypt** is threatened with famine and other disasters—very likely referring to a famine that destroyed two-thirds of the population of Alexandria in the time of Gallienus (260-68).

15:20-33. After another denunciation of doom in general terms (verses 20-27) there is another historical allusion (verses 28-33). This is apparently to a Persian attack on the **land of the Assyrians**—the Roman province of Syria—which resulted in devastation of a **portion**, namely Antioch. The **dragons of Arabia** are the armies of the Palmyrene empire of Odenathus and Zenobia, which acted as a buffer between Rome and Persia. The **Carmonians** are the Sassanid Persians, Carmania (modern Kerman) being one of the ancient Persian provinces.

15:34-63. This is a vague prediction that **Babylon**—that is, Rome—will be destroyed by attacks from various directions. **Asia,** probably meaning the Arabs of Palmyra, will suffer the same fate.

16:1-78. This chapter is in large part merely a hodgepodge of apocalyptic ideas and biblical phrases. Only in verses 68-78 does it seem possible to propose a definite historical situation—the persecution of the church by the emperor Decius (249-51).

THE BOOK OF TOBIT

H. Neil Richardson

INTRODUCTION

Tobit is a delightful story of the afflictions of a pious Israelite
and the adventures of his dutiful son. The young man makes a
journey in the company of a disguised angel and returns with a
bride and the means to restore the father's health and wealth.
The book vividly portrays ancient Jewish family life. It also is
important for its religious teachings, which are characteristic of a
stage in the development of post-exilic Judaism.

Contents

Tobit is an exiled member of the tribe of Naphtali living in
Nineveh following the Assyrian conquest of Israel. At the
beginning of the story he is appointed to a responsible position
in the Assyrian government. As a result of his charities for his
fellow Israelites, however—especially his concern to bury the
bodies of those executed and left exposed—he loses both
position and property and eventually his eyesight.

After a quarrel with his wife he prays to God to let him die. At
the same time Sarah, daughter of Tobit's kinsman Raguel, who
lives at Ecbatana in Media, makes a similar prayer. A demon has
killed her seven successive husbands on their wedding

nights. God assigns the angel Raphael to respond to the simultaneous prayers.

Tobit remembers a large sum of money which he placed in the care of another relative at Rages in Media some time before. He gives his son Tobias long fatherly counsel about good conduct and asks him to go for the money. They employ Raphael in the guise of a fellow Israelite as a guide.

After a day's journey the two reach the Tigris River, where the angel advises Tobias to catch a large fish and keep three of its internal organs. On arrival in Ecbatana he directs Tobias to the home of Raguel and suggests marrying Sarah. By use of two of the fish's organs Tobias exorcises the demon. He then sends Raphael on to Rages for the money while he enjoys a fourteen-day wedding celebration.

Raphael, Tobias, and Sarah return to Nineveh with the money and the third fish organ, which Tobias uses to heal Tobit's blindness. When they offer to divide the money with Raphael, he gives them some ethical counsels and then reveals his identity. Tobit is inspired to compose a lengthy psalm of praise. After a long life of charitable deeds he calls Tobias to his deathbed and makes a prediction of the future, including the destruction of Nineveh. Tobias therefore moves to Ecbatana. Before his death at a ripe old age he hears of the fall of Nineveh.

Literary Affinities

The author's dependence on a variety of literature is evident. In the first place he shows acquaintance with books of the Old Testament, including some from all three divisions, Law, Prophets, and Writings. As might be expected, he is thoroughly familiar with the commandments of the Law—especially those in Deuteronomy, but those in Leviticus and Numbers as well. His account of the meeting and wedding of Tobias and Sarah draws on even the phraseology of the stories of Rebecca and Rachel in Genesis 24; 29. His historical setting is drawn from II Kings. There are several evidences of knowledge of the minor prophets, including a quotation from Amos 8:10, and the naming of either Nahum or Jonah—according to the manuscript being read.

Among the Writings, Job has no doubt suggested the general theme of the righteous suffering affliction, and Psalms has furnished a model for Tobit's psalm in chapter 13. A number of the sayings in the speeches of Tobit and Raphael are obviously adapted from Proverbs. Readers familiar with the New Testament will also recognize certain parallels. However, these may be attributed, not to literary influence, but to a common background in the life and thought of Judaism.

The author has also drawn to considerable extent on the book of Ahikar, an Aramaic romance of the fifth or sixth century, about an official in the court of Sennacherib. Because of a false accusation this official suffers various hardships and at length is restored uner Esarhaddon. He mentions Ahikar several times; and brings him into the story as an Israelite who is Tobit's nephew. Both in features of the narrative and in moral teachings there are parallels to the book of Ahikar.

The book also draws on several themes from folklore:

(1) the story of the grateful dead, in which the hero buries a corpse at considerable cost and is later helped to secure a treasure by the ghost of the dead man;

(2) the story of the dangerous bride, in which all the bridegrooms of a princess die on their wedding nights until the hero with the help of a companion slays the dragon who has killed them;

(3) another dragon story, in which parts of a fish have magic powers and a dog helps the hero slay the dragon. Versions of these folk tales were probably known to the author of Tobit through oral tradition rather than written sources. He has skillfully combined these folk themes with the religious ideas and practices of Judaism. The result is an interesting story designed to win readers for its worthy admonitions.

Original Language

The problem of the text of Tobit is very complex. The oldest complete copies of the book are in Greek, in three rather widely differing recensions:

(1) a long form found in the Codex Sinaiticus (fourth century);

(2) a short form found in the Codex Vaticanus (fourth century) and with minor variants in the Codex Alexandrinus (fifth century) and most later manuscripts;

(3) a mixed form, found in a few later manuscripts, in which some chapters follow the short form and the others (chapters 6–13) are apparently a revision of the long form. The second of these textual forms appeared in the manuscripts available to the first English translators in the sixteenth century. Thus it has been used in most subsequent translations, including the Revised Standard Version.

Fragments of the book found in the Dead Sea Scrolls have provided answers to two questions about the text of Tobit which have been long debated. First, the longer recension represented by the Codex Sinaiticus is the oldest. Second, the original language of the book was either Hebrew or Aramaic rather than Greek. The choice between the Semitic languages is still difficult. Characteristic syntax, certain mistranslations, and the Aramaic Scroll fragments point to Aramaic. But a number of exclusively Hebrew idioms and the Hebrew Scroll fragment point to Hebrew. The situation is complicated by the presence of Greek idioms which could scarcely have been suggested by a Semitic original.

The most plausible reconstruction of the process is that the book was composed originally in Aramaic. It was soon translated into Hebrew, and circulated in both languages. The Greek translation was made from the Hebrew. Later it was compared with the Aramaic, corrected at some points, and also revised to improve the Greek style.

The extant text is a result of two stages of translation and is of a character to invite various kinds of editorial revisions—as exemplified by the condensation and revision of the long recension. Therefore judgment of its integrity is difficult. Some earlier elaborate theories of stages by which the book grew in size have been discarded. So has the view that the references to Ahikar are interpolations. A more recent theory that chapters 13–14 were added after the Roman destruction of the temple in A.D. 70 is disproved by the fact that one of the Dead Sea Scroll fragments contains a part of chapter 14—though the possibility remains that these chapters are an early addition.

From the limited evidence at hand it seems more probable that the book as represented in the longer Greek recension is substantially the work of one author. Its textual history is thus one of abridgment rather than addition.

Place of Composition

Most who believe that Greek was the original language of Tobit also assume that it originated in Alexandria, the major center of Greek-speaking Judaism. No doubt the Greek version was indeed produced in Alexandria. But the author of the Aramaic or Hebrew original thought of Egypt as away on the very edge of the world (cf. 8:3).

A few scholars have maintained the book was written in Palestine because of its emphasis on Jerusalem and the temple (1:6-8; 5:13; 13:9-18; 14:5) and on strict observance of details of the law. But its atmosphere is rather that of the Diaspora, the large number of the Jews who after the Babylonian exile lived in many parts of the Near Eastern world outside Palestine (cf. 3:4; 13:3). Jerusalem is simply a conventional symbol rather than a place where Tobit and his family think of living. That many Jews of the Diaspora tended to become lax in their observance of the law is no doubt the very reason the author composed his story. This also explains his exhortation to orthodox Jewish practices.

The most likely places are therefore Syria and Mesopotamia. Antioch in Syria became the capital of the Seleucid Empire around 300 and soon grew to be one of the largest cities of the Near East. It had commercial as well as political relations with the region to the east where the setting of the book lies. Many Jews settled in Antioch and were close enough to keep in touch with Jerusalem. Thus an Antiochian Jew might well write from the standpoint of the Diaspora yet strongly support orthodox Palestinian Judaism.

On the other hand the book shows an interest in the locale of ancient Assyria and Media. This strongly suggests that it was written at some center of Jewish population in Mesopotamia— Babylon, for example. The relatively advanced angelology points to an eastern origin, since this development in Judaism was largely influenced by Persian concepts—for example, seven angels (12:15).

The author erred in locating Nineveh somewhere west of the Tigris River (see below on 6:1-8) and Rages too close to Ecbatana (see below on 9:1-6). But this is not strong evidence against his living in the same region. Such misconceptions were common in ancient times, when there was little opportunity to learn geography except by personal travel.

Date

The author's historical errors are much more significant (see below on 1:1-2, 3-9, 10-20; 14:12*b*-15). They show that his information about the historical setting comes almost entirely from a not too thorough reading of II Kings. The use of the first person in the opening section (1:3–3:6) and the angel's instruction to write a book (12:20) are no doubt intended to represent the story as autobiographical. However, it was clearly written from the perspective of a much later time. Sennacherib's killing of exiled Israelites and refugee Judeans and confiscating Tobit's property was no doubt suggested by the story of his attack on Jerusalem in II Kings 18–19 (with 1:21 cf. II Kings 19:36-37). It is a necessary element of the plot rather than a reflection of the situation at the time of writing.

Otherwise the book gives no hint of persecution of the Jews. Thus most scholars believe it must have been composed before the attempt of the Seleucid king Antiochus IV Epiphanes (175-163) to stamp out Judaism. This persecution struck at the Jews throughout his empire, even though the Maccabean revolt against it was confined to Palestine. More specifically, Tobit's prediction about the temple (14:4-5) mentions no event between its historical rebuilding immediately after the Exile and its promised glorious rebuilding at the end of the age. This seems to antedate Antiochus' desecration of the temple. A pre-Maccabean date is borne out by the absence of theological ideas characteristic of the Maccabean period—for example, resurrection of the dead.

On the other hand many scholars have dated Tobit only a short time before Antiochus' persecution—namely during the first quarter of the second century. This dating is based partly on the similarity of the author's theological and ethical ideas to those of Jeshua ben Sira, author of Ecclesiasticus (about 180). Even more it is based on the assumption that the acquaintance with the books of the Prophets, and some of the Writings, which this book expects of its readers was limited to a small group of priests and scribes in Jerusalem until these books began to be read publicly in the synagogues. Since Ecclesiasticus is the first clear witness to it, this development has generally been placed at around 200.

Now, however, the discovery that the Aramaic language of the three Dead Sea Scroll fragments of Tobit resembles that of Ezra (fourth century) more than that of Daniel (around 165) seems to point to a much earlier date for the book—either late in the Persian period (around 350) or early in the Greek period (around 300). Thus Tobit may evidence general circulation of many Old Testament books a century or more earlier than heretofore supposed.

The Scroll fragments show that Tobit was known and used by Palestinian Jews of the first century B.C. But it failed to make a place for itself in Jewish regard and by the end of the first century A.D. seems to have been completely neglected. Its preservation was due to its inclusion in the Septuagint, which became the Christian Old Testament. Thus it was known and quoted by Christian writers beginning with II Clement.

In later times it became quite popular and influenced liturgy, literature, and art. There are paintings of scenes from the story by such masters as Botticelli, Titian, and Rembrandt. Though placed by the Protestant reformers in the Apocrypha it remains a part of the Roman Catholic Old Testament.

Religious Value

In telling his entertaining story the author seeks to present the noblest teachings of Judaism. God is both just and merciful. God judges rightly (3:2), even though this involves punishing them for their sins (3:3-5). God is merciful and compassionate (3:2; 13:2; 14:5). God has perfect knowledge (3:14). He is a God of power, as indicated by his appellations, who intervenes in human affairs (4:19). God dwells both in heaven (5:16) and in the temple (1:4), and is King (13:6, 7, 15) and Lord (13:4).

In this book Judaism is a personal religion which finds its highest expression in piety, integrity, honesty, and charity. At all times the good Jew prays and observes the Mosaic law with patience and fidelity. Assimilation with non-Jews is avoided by observing the dietary laws and by marrying within one's own family. Proper reverence toward Jerusalem and the temple and its worship is displayed. The good Jew fasts and gives alms, for these good deeds are pleasing to God and bring their own rewards.

"What you hate, do not do to anyone" (4:15) sums up well the morality of the book. One should honor one's parents, shun sexual immorality, and avoid drinking wine to excess. Among good deeds the proper burial of the dead occupies an important place (1:17-19; 2:4-8; 4:3-4; 14:11-13). In these and many other ways the book reflects the conventional theology and ethics of such later groups as the Hasideans and the Pharisees.

I. The Troubles of Tobit and Sarah (1:1–3:17)

1:1-2. *Tobit's Genealogy.* Though **acts** is literally "words" in Greek, it probably represents a Hebrew or Aramaic word meaning both "words" and "acts." **Tobit** is variously spelled in different versions. In the Dead Sea Scrolls fragments it is "Tobi," a form of the Semitic word for "good." Identification of an important person by the naming of several ancestors is found occasionally in earlier parts of the Old Testament but seems to have become especially popular in postexilic times. None of the persons named is otherwise known.

The author attributes the **captivity** of the **tribe of Naphtali** to **Shalmaneser V** (727-722), generally known as the conqueror of the northern kingdom in 722. He overlooks or ignores the record that the tribes of **Galilee** and Transjordan were deported earlier (734) by Shalmaneser's father, Tiglathpileser III. A **Thisbe** in Galilee is otherwise unknown. **Kedesh,** northwest of Lake Huleh, was an important city in the territory of **Naphtali.**

1:3-9. *Tobit's Piety in Palestine.* Tobit's **righteousness** and **acts of charity** are emphasized throughout the story. Here his scrupulous observance of the Mosaic law while still in his native Galilee is described. On **Nineveh** see below on verses 10-20.

Tobit is represented as a **young man** when his tribe **deserted the house of Jerusalem**—that is, the Davidic dynasty—at the division of the kingdoms in 931. Yet he is in his prime when the northern kingdom fell in 722. This is so glaringly inconsistent with the series of regnal statistics in I and II Kings that it can hardly be an inadvertent error. Perhaps the author intends it as a hint at the beginning, matched by the exaggeration of Tobit's longevity at the end (14:11), that the story is to be understood as fiction rather than history.

The reference to the **temple** in **Jerusalem** as the only legitimate place of worship for **all the tribes** reflects the Judean viewpoint after discovery of the major part of Deuteronomy in 622 (cf. Deuteronomy 12:5-14; 14:23-26; II Kings 22–23). The use of **Most High** and other descriptive designations instead of a divine name is common in Aramaic from at least the fourth century on.

1:5-9. *Sacrifice to the Calf.* This is undoubtedly an allusion to the calf cult—the worship of golden calves as images of Yahweh—introduced by Jeroboam I of Israel. According to Deuteronomy 16:1-16 every male Jew must come to the Jerusalem temple three times a year and bring his offerings for the **feasts** of unleavened bread, weeks (Pentecost; cf. 2:1), and booths.

Marriage within the family, understood in its broad sense—for example, with a cousin—is both an ancient and a continuing custom among Semites. It reflects the importance of kinship (see below on 6:9-12). **Deborah** and **Anna** (Hannah) were no doubt chosen by the author with the expectation that his readers would be familiar with the stories of famous women with these names (cf. Judges 4:4-16; I Samuel 1:1–2:21). **Tobias** in the Scroll fragments is "Tobiah," meaning "Yahweh is good."

1:10-20. *Tobit's Piety in Exile.* The author apparently assumes that **Nineveh** was the capital of Assyria when Tobit was first taken there. Actually it became so only under **Sennacherib** (705-681) and his successors. After his deportation Tobit continues his observance of the Mosaic law, especially the dietary rules. However, pilgrimages to the temple in Jerusalem are now presumably forbidden to him.

1:13-15. Historically the "captives" of both Israel and Judah were not enslaved but simply resettled. They were free to prosper according to their abilities in their new homes. A few achieved wealth and positions of influence—Nehemiah, for example. Stories that some rose to high governmental status—as did Daniel and Esther—were popular among the Jews. Thus Tobit is appointed to a responsible office in the Assyrian government, and becomes wealthy enough to deposit a very large sum in **Rages** (Ragae or Rhagae). This was an important city about five miles southeast of modern Teheran, the capital of Iran. **Media** was the region east of Assyria.

In naming Tobit's employer **Shalmaneser** the author was misled by II Kings, which fails to mention that king's death soon after—or perhaps even before—his capture of Samaria. His successor, who carried out the deportation, was Sargon II (722-705), the father of **Sennacherib.**

1:16-18. Sennacherib's **anger** toward Israel was perhaps suggested by the vivid stories in II Kings 18-19. There his representatives' brutal arrogance while besieging Jerusalem during the reign of Hezekiah is told. But why those **fleeing from Judea** should come to Nineveh of all places is a mystery.

Among many ancient peoples the bodies of executed criminals were left exposed to public gaze—**thrown out behind,** or "over," **the wall**—both as an example and as an added disgrace. Later parts of the Old Testament, however, reflect an abhorrence of unburied bodies, left to the wild beasts and birds of prey. Deuteronomy 21:22-23 commands that exposure of a criminal's body be limited to the day of execution and be followed by burial. Thus Tobit's burying of exposed bodies is a religious duty like feeding the **hungry** and clothing the **naked.**

A few scholars have tried to connect the book's repeated emphasis on proper burial (cf. 2:3-9; 4:3-4, 17; 14:11-13) with some historical situation as a clue to its date. But no proposal has proved convincing. Whether its emphasis on this charity exceeds that of its sources is uncertain.

1:19-20. As in the folklore source (see Introduction) Tobit's good deeds of burying the dead bring him undeserved suffering. This reaches a climax in the following specific incident (2:1-10). The rest of the story then describes the working out of the reward for the burial (cf. 12:12-13). It is split between father and son, whose related names symbolize their joint representation of the single folklore hero.

Since Tobit's wife and son are later said to be **restored** to him (2:1), **except** in verse 20 may be a mistranslation of an Aramaic word that in the author's day meant "also." That is, Anna and Tobias are taken along with the **property** and presumably enslaved.

1:21-22. *Relationship to Ahikar.* The account of Senna-cherib's assassination is all but quoted from II Kings 19:37. The story of Ahikar (see Introduction) was quite popular throughout the Near East and was told by the storytellers with many variants. Thus the author could count on his Jewish readers to know about Ahikar yet not question his incorporation into the tribe of Naphtali as another Israelite. Though there is question about the translation **second to himself** (see Revised Standard Version footnote), Ahikar as **keeper of the signet** is able to set the king's seal to any document. He can exert the royal power over the entire **administration** of the Assyrian Empire.

2:1-6. *Another Unburied Body.* On **restored** see above on 1:19-20. **Pentecost,** from the Greek for "fifty," is the Old Testament feast of weeks (Leviticus 23:15-21; Deuteronomy 16:9-11) fifty days or **seven weeks** after passover. This was one of the three pilgrimage festivals, and according to the Mosaic law Tobit should be celebrating it at the temple in Jerusalem. The lack of any hint that he should be there is probably evidence that the author belonged to the Diaspora rather than Palestinian Judaism. Hospitality was one of the primary virtues of the ancient Near East and was especially commanded at a feast. Tobit demonstrates his piety by sending his son to find a **poor man** as a guest.

2:3-6. The religious duty of giving proper burial (see above on 1:16-18, 19-20) is so important to Tobit that he cannot eat until he has saved the body of an unknown fellow Israelite from possible desecration. **Place of shelter** is literally "room" and probably refers to Tobit's own house. He must wait until the feast ends at **sunset** because it is a day of rest, like the sabbath.

According to the Mosaic law (Numbers 5:2; 19:11-13) touching a corpse renders one ritually unclean for a full week, during which one must wash on the third and seventh days. That Tobit **washed** himself without such a delay suggests that Jews of the Diaspora relaxed the requirement. Possibly they had a less stringent rule, like that prescribed for touching the carcass of an animal (Leviticus 11:39-40), by which one would wash immediately and remain unclean only until evening.

The **food** which Tobit eats after moving the body is not that prepared for the feast, which would be holy and could not be touched by an unclean person (cf. Leviticus 7:19-21). The quotation from **Amos** (8:10) has been changed from active to passive, perhaps to avoid ascribing an evil act to God.

2:7-10. *Tobit's Blindness.* Immediately after sunset, which marks the end of the holy day and the beginning of the next day, Tobit hurries to bury the corpse. **Laughed** in the Greek has the sense "derided," which does not fit the context. Probably it represents a Hebrew word which in Old Testament usage had that sense but later under Aramaic influence came to mean "praised." Here it might better be translated "were amazed."

In the Sinaiticus recension, which probably represents the original (see Introduction), verse 9 states that Tobit washed himself again after the burial. He is again **defiled** because of touching the corpse, and presumably will remain so at least until the next sunset (see above on verses 3-6). Thus he sleeps outdoors to avoid passing his uncleanness on to anything he touches in the house.

Verse 10 is a fantastic explanation for the films—that is, cataracts—on Tobit's eyes. According to the Sinaiticus recension they make Tobit completely blind for four years and he is supported by Ahikar (see above on 1:21-22) for two years. Elymais is probably a Greek form of Elam, the province east of Babylonia.

2:11-14. *A Family Quarrel.* The Sinaiticus recension indicates that Anna's women's work is weaving. In his blindness Tobit is suspicious of what goes on around him. In spite of his own charities, he cannot believe the kid is a gift. His honesty will not let him eat what he fears has been stolen, even in their dire straits. Anna's natural reaction is all that is needed to bring Tobit to the depths of despair.

3:1-6. *Tobit's Prayer.* In asking God to let death end his distress Tobit prays in a typical Jewish pattern. He begins with praise of God's justice and mercy and then acknowledges his own sins and those of his fathers, which have brought deserved punishment. The phraseology of verse 4b is a familiar description of the Exile which might occur to a Palestinian author as fitting Tobit's situation. More probably it reflects the viewpoint of an author who is himself among the dispersed (see Introduction). For it is better for me to die than to live is an exact quotation from Jonah 4:3, 8, which the author must have expected his readers to recognize.

3:7-15. *Sarah's Prayer.* Both Tobit and Sarah on the same day are brought to such depths of misery that they ask for death simultaneously (cf. verses 16-17). Both are saved and brought together by the same train of events. Their parallel prayers are a skillful bit of literary artistry that helps to explain the popularity of the book. Ecbatana, the capital of Media (see above on 1:13-15), is modern Hamadan, at the northern foot of Mt. Elvend in western Iran.

The demon is in love with Sarah (cf. 6:14) and therefore kills any husband who attempts to consummate his marriage with her. Some scholars think the name Asmodeus to be derived from that of a Persian evil spirit. More probably it is the Greek representation of a Hebrew word meaning "destroyer." Even the **maids,** who are slaves, openly accuse Sarah of murdering the husbands herself.

3:10-15. Sarah is reduced to the point of suicide but holds back out of consideration for her family. Instead she prays, like Tobit and at the same time, that she may be granted an immediate natural death. Being younger and more hopeful, however, she suggests the alternative of being restored to **respect.** Her reference to marrying a **kinsman or kinsman's son** reflects the author's emphasis on marriage within the family (see comments on 1:5-9; 6:9-12).

3:16-17. *God's Intervention.* In postexilic times there was a growing sense of God's transcendence. This inspired frequent use of such expressions as **presence of the glory of the great God** as a means to avoid portraying God in too human terms. The mission of **Raphael . . . to heal** involves a word play in Aramaic or Hebrew, since the name means "God heals." In view of the author's literary skill it is somewhat surprising that he detracts from the suspense of his story by summarizing here what is to happen.

II. TOBIAS' JOURNEY TO MEDIA (4:1–6:17)

4:1-21. *Fatherly Counsel.* Tobit takes for granted that his prayer for death will be speedily answered. He is concerned about the support of his widow and son, evidently still a teen-ager, and recalls his money on deposit in Rages (see above on 1:13-15). Before telling about it, however, he gives his son what may be his final instruction in ethics and morality—the first and longest of the didactic passages in the book.

The author uses the occasion as an opportunity to set forth certain basic principles of Judaism which he holds to be important. In view of Tobit's expectation of death he starts by reemphasizing proper burial. Tobias' **honor** for his mother (cf. 10:12) must include proper burial for her also.

4:5-11. Giving alms to the poor is strongly enjoined in the laws of Deuteronomy (especially 15:7-11). In postexilic times this grew in esteem as a very meritorious act. Indeed the word generally translated "righteousness" in the Old Testament came to have the specific meaning "almsgiving." Thus **charity delivers from death** in the Hebrew was no doubt an exact quotation from the similar saying about righteousness in Proverbs 10:2*b* and 11:4*b*. Other parts of this chapter are reminiscent of sayings in Proverbs.

4:12-21. The warning against sexual **immorality** sums up a number of passages in Proverbs (cf. 2:16-19; 6:23-29). Verses 12*b*-13*a* reemphasize the importance of marriage within the family (see comments on 1:5-9; 6:9-12). The inclusion of **Noah** as an example is evidently based on one of the legends that were developing about this patriarch in the author's time, for no information about his marriage is given in Genesis.

On verse 13*b* cf. Proverbs 16:18 and 24:30-34. On verse 14 cf. Leviticus 19:13 and Deuteronomy 24:15. Verse 15*a* is a negative form of the Golden Rule (cf. Matthew 7:12*a*; Luke 6:31). A similar saying is attributed to Rabbi Hillel in the late first century B.C., and earlier versions are found in the teachings of Confucius and Aristotle. **Place** in verse 17 is literally "pour" and in the process of translation into Hebrew an original Aramaic word "wine" in this construction could easily be confused with **bread**. "Pour your wine on the graves of the righteous" is found in Ahikar 2:10. Having concluded his instruction Tobit at last tells his son about the money.

5:1-15. *The Employment of Raphael.* The longer Sinaiticus recension (see Introduction) gives fuller details which make this episode somewhat more coherent. Tobias asks how he can identify himself to the trustee and thus be given the money. He also points out that he does not know the way to Media. In his reply Tobit describes the **receipt**, made twenty years earlier, presumably before Tobias' birth. From legal documents of around the same period that have come to light this probably means that Tobit and Gabael wrote a statement of the deposit in duplicate on a single sheet, with the signatures of both parties, and then tore it in two. One half was sealed in the money bags (cf. 9:5) and Tobit took the other. Tobias can now match his half with the sealed half to prove it is genuine.

5:4-8. Instead of accosting a stranger with an immediate invitation to accompany him to Rages, Tobias in the Sinaiticus recension first strikes up a conversation. He inquires where the stranger comes from and then asks if he knows the way to Media. In reply Raphael speaks of many trips there and mentions, as a credible coincidence, having visited Gabael in Rages. Only after learning this much of the man's qualifications does Tobias propose his acting as a guide.

5:9-15. In the Sinaiticus recension the greetings in verse 9 include a moving lament by Tobit about his blindness and a reply by Raphael to take courage because his healing is "near to God"—an apparent mere courtesy with deeper meaning for knowing readers. In response to Tobit's question about his **tribe** Raphael in this usually longer recension simply asks why Tobit needs to know.

The rebuke (verse 11*a*) found in the Vaticanus recension agrees with modern ideas about fair employment practices but not with the author's emphasis on kinship or his portrayal of Tobit as the perfect Israelite. The ancient reader would appreciate the name adopted by Raphael—**Azarias,** the Greek form of Azariah, meaing "Yahweh helps." **Ananias,** or Hananiah, means "Yahweh favors."

The **drachma** was the standard monetary unit of the Greek period. It contained about the same amount of silver as a Roman denarius, said to be a day's wage for a laborer in New Testament times (Matthew 20:2). Mention of this coin, if original, would be strong evidence for dating the book in the Greek period. However, the translators may have substituted it for some Semitic word.

5:16-21. *The Departure.* As Tobias and the disguised Raphael prepare to leave, Tobit prays **May his angel attend you**—a pleasing reminder to readers that they know more than he does about the son's companion. The **dog,** though barely mentioned (cf. 11:4), in later times came to be one of the most popular features of the story. It was always pictured with Tobias in religious art. Since other biblical references to dogs are all derogatory, it has often been said that the ancient Jews did not keep dogs as pets.

On the other hand the fact that the dog was unclean for food (Leviticus 11:1-8; Deuteronomy 14:3-8) did not prevent its use as a domestic animal, to tend the flocks or serve other purposes. With dogs around the possibility that a boy like Tobias would make a pet of one can scarcely be ruled out. Nevertheless the dog is probably not a "human touch" but a vestige from a folklore source (see Introduction) where a dog helped the hero slay a dragon. With **goes in and out** (verse 17) cf. I Samuel 18:16. **Sister** (cf. 7:16; 8:4, 7) is a term of endearment (cf. Song of Solomon 4:9-12; 5:1).

6:1-17. *The Fish.* Since Nineveh was on the eastern bank of the **Tigris river** the two travelers to Media would not cross the river. Possibly the author thought of their route as along its eastern side throughout the first day, or had in mind a tributary. More likely he did not know the exact location of Nineveh, which was not rebuilt after its destruction in 612.

The use of three organs from the magic fish to accomplish only two purposes may be a condensation from a folklore source (see Introduction) where three things were accomplished, or perhaps where overcoming the demon required two stages. Since **liver** was thought in ancient times to cure night blindness **gall** may have been sustituted for an original liver to remove **white films.**

6:9-12. According to Raphael the **law of Moses** requires the marriage of Tobias and Sarah. This may refer to the ruling about the daughters of Zelophehad (Numbers 36:6-9) that a woman who will inherit land because she has no brother must marry within her tribe to avoid any intertribal transfer of land. In the Diaspora, where except in large centers the members of a Jewish community would usually be interrelated, this law may have been interpreted as requiring marriage within the kinship group.

Possibly the author has in mind also the law of levirate

marriage (Deuteronomy 25:5-10), by which the brother of a man who died childless was obligated to marry the widow and beget a son to be the deceased man's heir. This obligation was extended to other kinsmen in the absence of a brother (cf. Genesis 38; Ruth 4). In the ancient Jewish view Sarah would be a widow, even though her marriages were not consummated. But the levirate law actually does not fit this case. It would obligate Tobias as a kinsman of the seven dead husbands, whereas here it is Raguel who is obligated because of Sarah's relationship to Tobias.

There is no law in the Old Testament that would narrow Raguel's choice of a son-in-law to one person, let alone set a **penalty of death** on it. It is not certain that the author is referring to a law known and observed in his own time. He may be hoping his lax Diaspora readers will accept the idea that their ancestors in Tobit's day still followed the example of the patriarchs (cf. 4:12).

6:13-17. Despite the distance the kin in Nineveh and Ecbatana keep in touch, and Tobias has heard of Sarah's jealous demon admirer. Yet Raphael has won his confidence and he accepts without question the instructions for driving off the demon. He is eager to risk becoming his cousin's eighth husband. **Live ashes** no doubt means glowing coals which would cause the fish organs to emit an immediate stench. Along with this procedure derived from a folklore source (see Introduction) Raphael strongly recommends prayer.

III. THE WEDDING OF TOBIAS AND SARAH (7:1–9:6)

7:1-8b. *Arrival at Raguel's House.* Sarah's being the first to meet the visitors is a reminder of the romantic stories of Rebekah, Rachel, and Zipporah (Genesis 24:15-21; 29:9-12; Exodus 2:16-21). **Edna** is a feminine form of Eden, meaning "delight." That Tobias **resembles** his father in appearance as well as in name fits with the joint father-son representation of the folklore hero (see above on 1:19-20).

Some of the phraseology in verses 3-5 is adapted from the story of Rachel (Genesis 29:4-6). **Brother** in verse 4 is probably not literal but a term of affection (cf. verse 8c). Presumably Tobit and Raguel are cousins in some degree. Though Tobias has heard of Sarah (6:13-14), Raguel seems to be learning for the first time of Tobias' existence.

7:8c-15. *The Wedding Ceremony.* In ancient Judaism marriage was arranged by the parents. Therefore Tobias asks Raphael to act in place of his father in proposing for him. On **in accordance with the law** see above on 6:9-12. The wedding ceremony consists of Raguel's **taking** Sarah **by the hand** and giving her to Tobias and then blessing the couple. It is accompanied by the writing of a legal **contract** stating the agreed rights of the husband and especially the wife as well as arrangements about property. Examples of such marriage contracts have been found among Aramaic papyri of the fifth century and later. The **seals** were pieces of moist clay attached to the contract, impressed with the respective parties' signets bearing their identifying designs, and allowed to harden. Archaeological discoveries show that such seals were commonly used on legal documents and in many kinds of business transactions.

The verb referring to the sealing is missing from the Codex Sinaiticus. In the Codex Alexandrinus it is singular, meaning that only Raguel recorded his assent to the agreement. The plural of the Codex Vaticanus is more likely correct but does not identify the parties. Normally a marriage contract was sealed or signed by the two fathers. Here it is perhaps to be understood that Raphael seals it in place of Tobit (cf. verse 8c).

7:16–8:4a. *Victory Over the Demon.* Sarah's distress on entering the bridal chamber, anticipating that Tobias will meet the same fate as her seven previous husbands, and the comforting by her mother provide a skillful buildup toward the encounter with the demon. The climactic scene, however, is rather a letdown, for the action is not described clearly.

Obviously 8:4a is displaced. Tobias must have waited until the **two were alone** before placing the fish organs on the glowing coals. The implication in 8:3 that the demon is already in the room suggests that originally there was a sentence telling of his arrival—perhaps expurgated because it told of his appearing as soon as the couple began to consummate the marriage.

8:3. Defenders of Alexandria as the place where the book was written (see Introduction) have claimed the reference to **Egypt** as evidence supporting their view. They believe that the author was ridiculing his pagan neighbors for their devotion to magic and divination. To the contrary, however, the specification of the **remotest,** literally "upper," **parts** shows that the author is thinking of a faraway place near the rim of the world. Because of Egypt's traditional reputation as a land of witchcraft, as well as a rival at the other end of the Fertile Crescent, he chooses it rather than more recently known eastern and western extremities. The implication that Raphael can bind the demon only after the **odor** of the scorching fish organs has rendered him impotent reflects the influence of Persian dualism—the concept of good and evil spiritual powers engaged in cosmic warfare.

8:4b-18. *Prayers of Gratitude.* As Raphael has instructed (6:17), Tobias calls on his bride to join him in prayer. The opening blessing is the usual invocation in Jewish prayers. Though the Greek of **blessed be thy . . . name** is not identical, it is similar in thought to the opening of the Lord's Prayer (Matthew 6:9).

Sarah's anticipation that Tobias would be killed has aroused sympathy (7:17). Now that the demon has been driven away Raguel's spending the night in digging a grave is a delightful touch of comedy. His prayer on hearing the good news, however, is a beautifully characteristic Jewish expression of thanksgiving.

8:19-9:6. *The Wedding Feast.* Raguel is so joyous that his daughter is at length happily married that he plans a feast of **fourteen days,** twice the traditional length for such a celebration. No doubt he also shares the desire of Rebekah's family to prolong the last days with a daughter leaving for a distant home (Genesis 24:55-56; see below on 10:7c–11:1b). His taking an **oath** indicates the seriousness of his insistence on the lengthy feast.

Though Tobias would not necessarily be bound by what another man has sworn, the **property** promised him in the oath naturally makes him loath to violate it. Yet as a dutiful son he is much concerned about the effect of the delay on his own parents. In this dilemma he sends Raphael to complete his mission of securing the money at Rages.

9:5-6. According to varying reports of Greek historians Alexander's army took ten or eleven days of forced marches for the rugged mountain journey from Ecbatana to Rages. Here the implication is that Raphael—who must travel by human means since he has companionship in both directions—makes the trip each way in a single day. It is evident that the author was unacquainted with the distance and terrain (see Introduction). On the **seals**—presumably lumps of hardened clay enclosing the knots of the cords that tie the **bags** shut—see above on 7:8c-15.

IV. THE RETURN TO NINEVEH (10:1–12:22)

10:1-7b. The Anxious Parents. The poignancy of this scene displays the author's skill in bringing his characters to life. The worried father is **counting each day** and weighing possible explanations for the delay. But the mother dismisses all such calculations and jumps at once to one conclusion, the worst. Yet illogically she keeps watching the **road** for her boy's return. The distress of both is most strikingly revealed in their irritability toward each other (cf. 2:11-14).

Had expired is literally "were filled"—that is, "fulfilled," a Semitic idiom. **Detained** is based on the Codex Sinaiticus, which is confirmed by the Old Latin. It fits the context better than "put to shame" of the Codex Vaticanus (see the Revised Standard Version footnote). The two words are similar in Hebrew and might easily be confused.

10:7c–11:1b. Departure from Ecbatana. The action and some of the phrases of this episode follow very closely the account of Rebekah's parting with her family (Genesis 24:54b-60). In accordance with his oath (8:20-21) Raguel gives Tobias, along with his daughter, who is his sole heir (cf. 3:10; 8:17*a*), **half of his property.** He gives Sarah a final fatherly counsel, extending the law of the Ten Commandments (Exodus 20:12) to her new parents-in-law, who in her new home will become her **parents.** With deeper emotion Edna expresses to Tobias what every mother wants to say to a new son-in-law. On **brother** see above on 5:16-21; 7:1-8*b*.

11:1c-19. *The Healing of Tobit's Blindness.* Though it is passed over quickly, the return journey with wife, slaves, and cattle is necessarily slow. Thus Raphael suggests that he and Tobias **run ahead** to tell the parents of their new daughter-in-law and make preparations. **How you left your father** no doubt refers to Tobit's blindness, for which Raphael has already told Tobias the gall of the fish is efficacious (6:8).

The **dog,** said to have left with them (see above on 5:16-21), is now mentioned again, but still plays no part in the story. In the latest Greek recension (see Introduction), however, verse 6 says that Anna saw the dog running ahead and thus recognized the return of her son.

11:7-19. Tobias receives hurried instructions about the **gall** from Raphael while his mother is running to him. Having feared her son was dead, the mother is **ready to die** herself for joy. Tobias goes on to his blind father and applies the gall to his eyes, whereupon the **white films** are quickly **rubbed** off. When Tobit sees his son again after so many years, he characteristically blesses God for divine **mercy.** He then goes forth, to the amazement of his neighbors and kinsmen, to greet Sarah at the city **gate.** His acceptance of her is important, for Tobias' marriage to her without his having arranged it was a serious breach of custom. Since he and Anna and his brethren in Nineveh could not participate in the wedding feast in Ecbatana, they hold another feast of the usual **seven days.** On **Ahikar** see Introduction and comment on 1:21-22. On **Nadab** see below on 14:8-12.

12:1-22. *Raphael's Departure.* In the folklore source (see Introduction) the grateful ghost offers to help the hero who has buried his corpse for a promise of half the treasure they are to gain. In this story the author has told of Tobit's hiring the angel for modest **wages** and an unspecified bonus for a safe journey (5:14-15). Now he lets the father heartily accept Tobias' suggestion that the bonus be **half of what** has been **brought back.**

By the change from his source he emphasizes not only the generosity of father and son but especially their spirit of gratitude—a virtue he no doubt wishes to teach by the example. He further takes advantage of the narrative situation to put into Raphael's mouth a series of moral and ethical teachings. The passage contains a number of parallels with Proverbs and also with the New Testament.

12:6-10. Before revealing his identity Raphael offers some good counsel. It is right, he says, to **praise God** for God's good works **in the presence of all the living**—that is, publicly—so that others will learn of God's goodness. With the practical caution about keeping the **secret of a king** cf. sayings in the book of Ahikar: "Cover up the word of a king with the veil of the heart" and "A good vessel covers a word in its heart, but a broken one lets it out."

With verse 7b cf. Proverbs 11:27 and contrast Romans 3:8. The combining of **prayer** with **fasting** and **almsgiving** is paralleled in Matthew 6:2-18. **Righteousness** seems out of place in this series. It may be a duplication caused by the change of meaning of the Hebrew word to have the specific sense "almsgiving" (see above on 4:5-11). With verse 8b cf. Proverbs 16:8 and with verse 8c cf. Matthew 6:19-21; Luke 12:33-34; and James 5:3. On verse 9a see above on 4:5-11. With verse 10 cf. Proverbs 8:35-36 and Wisdom of Solomon 1:12.

12:11-22. With the development of the concept of the extreme "otherness" of God came the idea that one of the angelic functions was to bring the prayers of the devout to God's attention. This function was usually attributed to the angel Michael but is here claimed by Raphael also.

On Tobit's burials see above on 1:16-18.

The **seven holy angels** according to Enoch 20:1-8 are Uriel, Raphael, Raguel, Michael, Sarakael, Gabriel, and Remiel. With verses 16 and 21 cf. Matthew 17:6, 8. With verse 19 cf. Luke 24:42-43 and John 21:13. With verse 20*a* cf. John 20:17. The command to **write in a book** the events of the story reflects the growing tendency to emphasize the written word as the revelation of God's will.

V. EPILOGUE (13:1–14:15)

To modern taste the revelation and disappearance of Raphael bring the story to a satisfying conclusion. The following two chapters seem superfluous. Some scholars have therefore viewed them as a later addition. It is true that the psalm of chapter 13 has no relevance to the story and thus may be an interpolation. But to the ancient reader the ending in chapter 14 was a desired assurance that the piety of Tobit and Tobias was duly rewarded by prosperity and long life.

13:1-18. *Tobit's Psalm.* This poem expresses the conventional view that Israel's exile and dispersion are the punishment for its iniquities and when Israel turns to God, God will gather the scattered people to a gloriously rebuilt Jerusalem, to which all nations will come to worship. Jewish theology of the author's time laid considerable stress on the idea that all things come from God—**he afflicts, and he shows mercy.**

The author of the psalm, whether or not the author of the book, identifies himself (verses 3, 6*i*) as one of those scattered in the Diaspora (see Introduction). He addresses readers in like situation (verse 5) and urges them to **turn** to God. **Turn back** (verse 6*k*) translates literally a Semitic verb which may also be translated "repent." The Semitic word underlying **ages** (verse 10*b*) embodies both temporal and spatial concepts—"ages" and "world." **Tent** may allude to the tabernacle of the wilderness but more probably refers to the temple.

The hope that the **nations** (verse 11) would come to Jerusalem to worship the God of Israel became a central feature of the thought of Judaism in the postexilic period. On the glory of the rebuilt city cf. Isaiah 54:11-12 and Revelation 21:18-21.

14:1-15. *Tobit's Deathbed Counsel.* The statistics in this chapter vary greatly in the different recensions and versions and in any case are not to be taken seriously (see above on 1:3-9). When Tobit is ready to die, he calls in Tobias and his grandsons for some final words of advice and a prediction of the future. In place of **Jonah** the Codex Sinaiticus reads "Nahum," which is more appropriate. Nahum is vehement in its description of the destruction of Nineveh, whereas in Jonah the prophecy of the city's destruction is conditional and is averted by repentance of its citizens.

The predicted desolation of **Jerusalem** is its conquest by the Babylonians in 586. The rebuilding of the **house of God**, the temple, **not . . . like the former one** refers to the second temple completed in 515. The **glorious building** is to be in the age to come, when the **Gentiles** will worship the God of Israel (cf. 13:11).

14:8-15. Along with the advice to **leave Nineveh** in anticipation of its destruction Tobit gives some moral counsel. This is illustrated by the examples of **Ahikar** (see Introduction and comment on 1:21-22) and **Nadab,** probably a scribal error for Nadin. In the book of Ahikar the hero adopts his nephew Nadin and persuades the king to appoint the young man in his own place. Nadin plots against his foster father and gets him banished. Later he is duly punished while Ahikar is restored to favor. The **destruction of Nineveh** was accomplished by Nabopolassar, the father of **Nebuchadnezzar,** and Cyaxares the Mede in 612. **Ahasuerus**—that is, Xerxes I—came to the throne of Persia in 486.

THE BOOK OF JUDITH

H. Neil Richardson

Introduction

This book is a fictional account of a victory of the Jews, thanks to the intervention of a woman named Judith who slays the leader of the opposing army. In some respects it resembles the book of Esther. Both books glory in the ruthless destruction of an enemy accomplished by a beautiful woman.

The Story

Nebuchadnezzar has won a great victory in the east. Now he sends his general Holofernes to punish the western nations that refused to join him in the war. Holofernes and his army conquer one after another. At length they begin the attack on the Jews by besieging a fortified city called Bethulia. After more than a month the citizens are in such dire straits from hunger and thirst that they demand that their leader surrender.

At this point Judith, a beautiful, wealthy, and pious widow, enters the story. She upbraids the people for not trusting in God and promises that with God's help she will deliver Bethulia. Making "herself very beautiful, to entice the eyes of all men who might see her" (10:4), she takes a servant girl with her and goes out to the enemy camp.

Holofernes is immediately overwhelmed by her beauty. He

accepts her promise to inform him when the besieged Bethulians forfeit their divine protection by eating the first fruits and tithes set aside for the temple. He invites her to an intimate banquet, at which he drinks too much wine and falls into a drunken sleep. Judith then beheads him with his own sword.

Putting the head in a bag Judith and her maid leave the camp, ostensibly for prayer. They go to Bethulia and announce that God has struck down Holofernes by the hand of a woman. When the enemy soldiers discover that their general is dead, they rush off in disorganized flight with the Jews in hot pursuit. Thus Israel wins the victory. The book closes with Judith's song of thanksgiving and the report that throughout her long life and for many years thereafter Israel had peace.

Literary Character

The book is an excellent example of an ancient short story. The characters are well drawn and the plot moves forward with originality and imagination. The style is bombastic, typical of Jewish and also Greek literature of the period, and the heroine is not introduced until nearly halfway through the story. In spite of this, those who come to the book for the first time find it a fascinating story.

Historicity

Few scholars today doubt that Judith is fiction. Its distortions of history and geography are so many and glaring that they cannot be mere incidental errors in a report of actual events. For example, the opening verse declares that Nebuchadnezzar "ruled over the Assyrians." Actually he was well known as a Babylonian ruler in power after the Assyrian Empire came to an end. His rival in the east, "Arphaxad," is said to have ruled from the fortification of Ecbatana as capital of Media (around 700; 1:1-4) till its capture in 550 (1:14). Holofernes moves his huge army from Nineveh to "Upper Cilicia" in Asia Minor about four hundred miles, in three days (2:21).

Much of the book's Palestinian geography comes from the mind of the author. Many of the localities have fictitious names and cannot be identified. Even Bethulia is unknown, though its description suggests Shechem (see below on 6:10-21 and 7:1-32). So incredible are some of the "errors"—so contradictory to Old Testament records which were well known to the ancient readers—that it is evident the author never intended his book should be viewed as history.

It is possible that the story has some historical basis. With different names and elimination of exaggerations chapters 1–3 might describe an actual invasion of Syria and Palestine by an eastern army. Several possibilities have been proposed. The most likely is a campaign of Artaxerxes III Ochus (358-338) in which a general named Orophernes and a subordinate named Bagoas (cf. 12:11) participated.

The poem in 16:2-17 may well be older than the rest of the book and commemorate an actual deed of valor by a Jewish woman (cf. Judges 4:17-22; 5:24-27). Whatever historical sources the author used, however, most of his book is obviously pure invention.

Date of Composition

Theories about the date of the book have ranged all the way from the seventh century B.C. to the second century A.D. The period on which most scholars now agree is the second century B.C.—specifically around 150, during the latter part of the struggle for religious and political freedom described in I Maccabees.

The statement that Holofernes "demolished all their shrines and cut down their sacred groves" (3:8) can hardly allude to anything except the attempt of Antiochus IV (175-163) to force the Jews to adapt their religion to Greek culture. The reference to Nebuchadnezzar as "god" (6:2) must reflect the claim to divinity in Antiochus' surname "Epiphanes," meaning "manifested one." The pietism of Judith is clearly that of the second century Hasidean movement with its strict observance of the law. The avoidance of fasting on the eve of the festivals (8:6) is an example of the developing Pharisaic oral law during this period.

Language and Place of Origin

The earliest extant text is in Greek, but there is wide agreement that the book was composed originally in Hebrew. The Greek text regularly reproduces Hebrew syntax and idiomatic expressions. Some difficult expressions are best explained by assuming an erroneous translation of the Hebrew. Use of the Septuagint in the Old Testament quotations may be attributed to the translator's familiarity with that version. Jerome refers to an Aramaic text of the book but this was undoubtedly a translation from the Greek—as are later Hebrew versions.

The use of Hebrew points strongly to Palestine as the place where the book was written. Other evidence supports this locale. The references to political administration both of the Jews as a whole and of the citizens of Bethulia reflect intimate knowledge of the governmental structure of Judea in Maccabean times. The book demands precise observance of the Mosaic law and of its extensions in the oral law—which was practicable only within the range of frequent pilgrimages to Jerusalem.

Purpose and Value

Amid the difficult times of the Maccabean struggle for religious and political independence from the Seleucid Empire, many Jews yielded to the pressure to compromise and adopt Greek ways. Others reacted by a stricter dedication to the institutions and practices of Judaism. The author of Judith belonged to this latter group. He sought to encourage his readers to stand fast against the onslaught of Greek culture and pagan religion and to remain loyal in the practice of God's ritual ordinances.

He may well have been a member of the Hasideans, a party zealous for the law. This group supported Judas Maccabeus in the revolt but later broke with his successors when they showed more concern for political than for religious goals. The Hasideans were probably the forerunners of both the Essenes and the Pharisees. But the author of Judith shared neither the

Essene philosophy of retreat to the wilderness nor the pacifism of some of the Pharisees. Rather he believed in fighting the enemy with every available means and expecting God to give the victory.

The book is not accepted as scripture by the Jews. However, it found a place in the Septuagint, which became the Christian Old Testament. It remains in the Roman Catholic Old Testament, though the Protestant reformers placed it in the Apocrypha. Over the centuries it has been quite popular with many, and its heroine is often pictured in religious art.

On the other hand many, even in early times, have criticized its underlying moral principle that the end justifies the means. Though Judith is motivated by the noble aim of saving her people, she uses deceit, enticement to lust, and murder to accomplish it—praying all the while for God's blessing on her acts. The moral dilemma posed by her story has provoked much discussion.

In addition to its main point the book in numerous didactic passages seeks to teach the essentials of ritualistic Judaism. It stresses the power and justice of God and God's concern with the affairs of humans. Though it is not certain whether the author believed in an afterlife of reward or punishment (see below on 16:17), he was strongly convinced of the urgency of obedience to God's will.

I. HOLOFERNES' CONQUEST OF THE WESTERN NATIONS (1:1–3:8)

1:1-6. *Nebuchadnezzar's War on Arphaxad.* The Jews for whom this book was written regularly heard the phrase "Nebuchadnezzar king of Babylon" from II Kings, Jeremiah, and Ezekiel read in their synagogues. Thus an opening sentence calling Nebuchadnezzar (605-562) the ruler of the **Assyrians** in **Nineveh** would give them immediate notice that what follows is not sober history but an amusing tale, possibly disguising commentary on contemporary events (see Introduction).

Insofar as Nebuchadnezzar is intended to symbolize a contemporary persecutor of the Jews, he may represent both Antiochus Epiphanes, the initiator of the effort to stamp out Judaism, and his nephew Demetrius I (162-150), who may have been the Seleucid overlord when the author wrote.

1:1b-4. The homeland of the **Medes** was the mountainous region east of Assyria. The list of their kings known from historical sources includes no **Arphaxad**. The name is the Septuagint form of Arpachshad, which the author probably derived from Genesis 10:22, 24 and 11:10-13 simply because it struck his fancy—cf. **Arioch** (verse 6). **Ecbatana** is modern Hamadan, Iran. According to the Greek historian Herodotus it was built and made the capital of Media by Deioces around 700. Since **cubits** were about one and a half feet, the dimensions of the fortifications here are greatly exaggerated.

1:5-6. Old Testament predictions of **war** between Nebuchadnezzar and the Medes were never fulfilled (Isaiah 13:17-22; Jeremiah 51:11, 28, 34). **Ragae** (Rages; see comment on Tobit 1:13-15) was in the eastern part of Media, the far side from Nebuchadnezzar's empire. **Hydaspes** is the Greek name of the Jhelum River in western Pakistan. This may be a scribal error for Choaspes, or the Karkheh, chief river of Elam, the region east of Babylonia, which was mountainous rather than a **plain**.

There is no mention elsewhere of a king of the **Elymaeans,** meaning Elamites, named **Arioch** (cf. Genesis 14:1, 9; see above on verses 1b-4). The **Chaldeans,** originally from southern Babylonia, were the people of Nebuchadnezzar. Here they seem to be an "error" for the "Assyrians."

1:7-11. *The Call for Allies.* The western nations summoned to aid in the attack on Media include all those around the eastern end of the Mediterranean—from **Cilicia** in southeast Asia Minor to **Egypt** and **Ethiopia** in northeast Africa. **Lebanon** and **Antilebanon** are mountain ranges west of **Damascus.** The **Plain of Esdraelon** is the wide valley of the Kishon River north of Mt. **Carmel** between **Galilee** and **Samaria. Gilead** is northern Transjordan.

Chelous (cf. 2:23) is not mentioned elsewhere in scripture. It was probably a town in southern Palestine. **Kadesh** is the oasis of Kadesh-barnea farther south. **River of Egypt** probably refers, not to the Nile, but to the Brook of Egypt in northern Sinai. Scripture rather than current usage evidently supplied the Egyptian place names: **Tahpanhes** (see Jeremiah 43:5-13), **Raamses** (see Exodus 1:11), **Goshen** (see Genesis 47:27), **Tanis,** Septuagint equivalent of Zoan, probably the later name for Raamses (see Isaiah 30:11), and **Memphis** (see Hosea 9:6).

As an adversary of the people of God, Nebuchadnezzar is "only a man" (see the Revised Standard Version footnote)—a denial perhaps aimed specifically at claims to divinity by the Seleucid rulers (see Introduction).

1:12-16. *The Victory over Arphaxad.* Verse 12 describes again the **territory** of the western nations in somewhat different terms. **Moab** was the land east of the Dead Sea, and **Ammon** was just across the Jordan from Judea. Historically the Median kings Cyaxares (around 625-585) and his son Astyages (around 585-550) conquered an extensive empire extending west into Asia Minor along the northern border of Nebuchadnezzar's Babylonian Empire. **Ecbatana** was **captured** only after Nebuchadnezzar's death, by Cyrus the Persian (550). He took control of the Median Empire and later took Babylon (539) and the Babylonian Empire to create the huge Persian Empire.

To this day in verse 15 is a common Old Testament phrase applied to evidence surviving from the past, but it scarcely fits a person's death. Perhaps it originally read "on that day." Though **one hundred and twenty days** is an obvious exaggeration, prolonged and lavish feasts are known to have occurred among ancient peoples.

2:1-20. *The Commissioning of Holofernes.* Nebuchadnezzar now turns to fulfilling his vow of revenge on the western nations (cf. 1:12). Verse 2b in the Greek reads literally: "and he finished the afflicting of all the earth out of his mouth." The Revised Standard Version reconstruction is based on the assumption that the Greek translator confused two similar Hebrew verbs, "finished" and "revealed," and thus misunderstood the entire clause.

The name **Holofernes** is Persian in form. It may be a corruption of Orophernes, a general sent against Egypt by Artaxerxes III about 350.

2:5-13. This grandiose speech is typical of the author's elaborate style (cf. 6:2-9; 8:11-27). The **number** of troops is probably an exaggeration in keeping with the fictional character of the work. But **thousand** may translate a Hebrew technical term designating a division of the army rather than a number. The Persian kings required gifts of **earth and water** as symbols of surrender. **Your eye** as a figure for "you" is a Hebrew idiom.

2:14-20. The logistical details serve to emphasize the might of Holofernes' army. At the same time they call attention to the impracticability of moving such a large force without modern facilities. The **mixed crowd** refers to the camp followers who have always accompanied armies wherever they went.

2:21–3:8. *Holofernes' Conquests.* On the march **from Nineveh to . . . Cilicia** in **three days** see Introduction. The geography of Holofernes' movements seems confused. **Becti-leth,** otherwise unknown, is described as in the interior of Asia Minor. The author seems to locate **Put and Lud** there also. In the Old Testament they are generally associated with Egypt and therefore were probably in northern Africa. However some scholars take Lud to mean Lydia in Asia Minor and attribute the association to the use of Lydian mercenaries in the Egyptian army at the battle of Carchemish in 605.

Rassis is unknown, but the **Ishmaelites** were well known from olden times as living **south** of Palestine (on **Chelleans** see above on 1:7-11). **Mesopotamia** here refers to the northwestern part, along the upper **Euphrates.** The brook **Abron** is unknown. The reference to **Japheth** (cf. Genesis 10:1-5) is uncertain, and the **Midianites** are another archaism (cf. Judges 6–8). In spite of these contradictory details, however, the general picture is one of conquest and pillage from Cilicia as far south as **Damascus.** Possibly the "errors" reveal, not the author's geographical ignorance, but his cleverness in combining Old Testament allusions with hints his original readers would recognize.

The **wheat harvest,** in early June, dates the sack of the

Damascus area about six weeks after Nebuchadnezzar's order (verse 1)—truly a lightning campaign.

2:28–3:8. On hearing of the southward advance of Holofernes' army the non-Jewish peoples on the **seacoast** of Palestine hurry to surrender unconditionally. In the north **Sidon and Tyre** were famous Phoenician cities. **Sur and Ocina** are unknown but may be corruptions of Dor and Acco. **Jamnia** was west of Jerusalem. **Azotus and Ascalon** are the Greek forms of Ashdod and Ashkelon, Philistine cities further south.

3:8. There was no mention of religion in Holofernes' commission (2:5-13). But now he is now described as attacking the **gods** of the various peoples and demanding that they **worship Nebuchadnezzar only** (cf. Daniel 3; 6). On the possibility that this may be a veiled allusion to the religious persecution and claim to divinity of Antiochus Epiphanes see Introduction.

II. The Attack on the Jews (3:9–7:32)

3:9–4:15. *Judean Preparations for Defense.* In contrast to the speed with which Holofernes has subjugated all the other western nations he now pauses **for a whole month** to prepare for the invasion of Judea. The wait not only allows time for the Jews to prepare to resist but also serves the literary purpose of building up suspense.

Strangely the author views the northern boundary of Judea as the **edge of Esdraelon** (see above on 1:7-11), thus including most of **Samaria** (4:4). This area was not ruled from Jerusalem since the time of Solomon—unless perhaps briefly under Josiah (cf. II Kings 23:15-20)—until it was conquered by John Hyrcanus about 109. That the book was not written so late as that, however, is shown by the reference to the coastal cities as outside Judea (2:28). This area is assumed to be inhabited entirely by Jews, with no mention of the Samaritans. No satisfactory explanation has yet been found.

Dothan was an ancient city a short distance south of

Esdraelon. **Ridge** in the Greek means literally a "saw." Perhaps it refers to the central highland beginning just sough of Dothan, or perhaps it is a textual corruption. **Geba** is probably not the Old Testament city about six miles north of Jerusalem but a town near Dothan. **Scythopolis** was the Greek name of Beth-shan in the Jordan Valley about sixteen miles south of the Sea of Galilee (cf. I Samuel 31:10-12).

4:3. Perhaps the most flagrant historical distortion in the book is the statement that the Jews **had only recently returned from the captivity.** Actually at the date specified (cf. 2:1, 27; 3:10) Nebuchadnezzar was about to exile more of them. On the other hand the reference to the **temple** and its equipment as being **consecrated after their profanation** clearly alludes to the reconsecration of the temple by Judas Maccabeus three years after its desecration by Antiochus Epiphanes. Though Antiochus died soon after this event—if not before—his successors continued the effort to stamp out Judaism until the time when the book was presumably written.

4:4-7. All of the towns named in verses 4 and 6 are apparently expected to defend the **passes up into the hills.** Only **Beth-horon** on the west and **Jericho** on the east can be definitely identified. There is no hint as yet that **Bethulia** (see below on 6:10-21) is to be the scene of much of the story. **Joakim,** in the Hebrew probably Joiakim, is no doubt to be understood as the son and successor of Jeshua, or Joshua, the high priest under whom the temple was rebuilt after the return from the Babylonian exile (cf. Ezra 3; Nehemiah 12:10, 12, 26; Haggai 1:1-2).

Under the successive empires in postexilic times Judea was ruled by governors who were usually foreigners. The high priest came to be the political as well as religious leader among the Jews themselves. Thus when Jonathan the Maccabee as leader of the struggle for independence became high priest (152) he virtually became a claimant to kingship of Judea. In fact some of his successors in the high priesthood took the title of king. The portrayal here of Joakim as chief military commander of the nation may reflect Jonathan's status.

4:8. The word **senate** is derived from the Latin. It translates a Greek word of corresponding meaning—a body of elders. Here it refers to the supreme council of the Jews, later known as the sanhedrin. Composed of priests, scribes, and heads of aristocratic families, the sanhedrin had judicial and legislative functions. There is no evidence that such a body existed before the middle of the third century. Certainly it did not play such an important role as it does here until Maccabean times.

4:9-15. The practices described here were the regular mourning rites of Judaism and indeed of the entire ancient Near East from very early times, as evidenced by Egyptian tomb paintings. Such rites would be observed not only for the death of an individual but in time of national calamity to support prayers for divine pity. On the participation of the **cattle** cf. Jonah 3:8.

Worshipers of Baal annually observed mourning rites for the death of their deity at the beginning of the dry season. No doubt it was in reaction to such pagan practices that Leviticus 21:1-12 greatly restricts mourning by priests and absolutely forbids any show of mourning by the high priest, even for his closest relatives. It seems doubtful, therefore, that Jewish priests would ever approach the **altar** with **sackcloth** and **ashes** as here described.

5:1-21. *Achior's History of the Jews.* Neither the conquest nor the surrender of **Moab** and **Ammon** (see above on 1:12-16) has been reported. Presumably they are to be understood as having come over to Holofernes along with the people of the **coastland** (cf. 2:28–3:7). A foreigner in the area, Holofernes thinks of them all as **Canaanites**—that is, dwellers in the land of Canaan. His lumping them together is to some extent justified, for the Moabites and Ammonites, like the Israelites, shared in some aspects of Canaanite culture. Their languages, like Hebrew, were dialects of the Canaanite language. Historically Moabites and Ammonites aided Nebuchadnezzar by attacks on the Jews (II Kings 24:2).

5:5-21. Since the Hebrew letters *d* and *r* are easily confused, it has been suggested that the original of the name **Achior** may

have been Ahiud, meaning "brother [or "friend"] of Judah."
Verses 6-9a refer to the migration of Abraham. They reflect the
tradition that he came originally from Ur of the **Chaldeans** on
the lower Euphrates River (see Genesis 11:27-28). Another
tradition connects him with Haran in northwest **Mesopotamia**
(see Genesis 11:31-32).

Verses 10-14 summarize the journey of Joseph and his
brothers into **Egypt**, the exodus under Moses, and the
wanderings in the **wilderness**. Verse 15a refers to the conquest
of Transjordan (cf. Numbers 21:21-35) and verses 15b-16 to the
conquest of western Palestine. To the conventional list of
peoples driven out by Israel (cf. Joshua 3:10) the **Shechemites**
are here added—probably an allusion to the Samaritans (see
above on 3:9–4:15).

Verse 17 is a succinct statement of the Deuteronomic view of
history, which explained the Babylonian exile as punishment for
sin (verse 18) and the return as a result of repentance (verse 19).
The Jews' success in their resistance to Holofernes—and, as the
author no doubt wishes to imply, in the Maccabean struggle—
will depend on whether or not they **sin against their God**.

5:22–6:21. *Achior's Punishment.* The author shows considerable literary craftsmanship in portraying the reaction to Achior's
speech. All the Assyrian **officers** and the allies present except
Achior's own countrymen demand his **death**. Holofernes
himself angrily denounces him and his fellow Ammonites as
hirelings of Ephraim—the name of the chief northern tribe,
sometimes used for Israel as a whole. He implies that they have
been bribed by the Jews.

Yet the general is astute enough to see that merely executing
the speaker will not refute the speech and restore the morale of
his troops, especially that of the new allies. Their only
motivation is fear of the divine invincibility of **Nebuchadnezzar**
(see above on 3:8). Therefore he devises a way to show his
disdain for the warning and counteract whatever doubts it has
raised. He will deliver Achior to the Jews so that he may **perish
along with them** and thus discover the falsity of his claim.

At the same time the very vehemence of the commander's denunciation suggests that he himself has been impressed. Thus the author prepares us to be convinced when later Holofernes takes seriously Judith's promise to tell him when the Jews forfeit their divine protection (chapter 11).

6:10-21. The place chosen for Achior to be taken is **Bethulia.** The description of its location and the mention that **Uzziah,** the chief of its three **magistrates,** is **of the tribe of Simeon,** as well as some further clues, suggest that Bethulia is a pseudonym for Shechem (see below on 9:2-4 and 7:1-32). In the author's day this was the principal city of the Samaritans rather than a home of Jews (see above on 3:9–4:15). The Bethulians bring Achior before their local **assembly** for a report. After he tells his story he is **praised** and feasted. The people renew their prayers for God's **help.**

7:1-32. *The Seige of Bethulia.* As Holofernes brings his troops toward Bethulia their number seems to have grown by fifty thousand (cf. 2:5, 15). If the increase is not a textual error, it may be that the allies from Moab, Ammon, and the coastland make up the difference. Whether **Balbaim** and **Cyamon** represent real places or not, they point up the immense size of the army.

The **people of Esau** are the Idumeans, descendants of the ancient Edomites, who in postexilic times inhabited the territory immediately south of Judea. The advice they and others offer to Holofernes would be unnecessary to an experienced general since cutting off the source of **water** was the usual method of attacking a walled city. It was in precisely this manner that Samaria was captured by the Assyrians in 722. There is some evidence for identifying the places named in verse 18*b* with sites near Shechem (see above on 6:10-21).

7:19-32. The suffering from lack of water causes the citizens to urge surrender. Verse 28 states the ancient belief of Israel, reflected often in the Old Testament, that punishment of individual faults results in collective punishment. Uzziah promises to capitulate if God has not given them help in **five more days.**

III. JUDITH'S PREPARATIONS (8:1–10:10)

8:1-8. *Introduction of Judith.* The heroine of the story now makes her belated entrance. Her name **Judith** is the feminine form of Judah or Judas and may be intended to suggest a counterpart to Judas Maccabeus. Though the only Judith mentioned in the Old Testament was a foreign woman (Genesis 26:34) the name in the author's day meant "Jewess." Thus it would symbolize the nation personified (cf. chapter 16, especially verses 2-5). Perhaps Judith was a well-known legendary figure before this book was written.

8:1b. Most of the names in Judith's fictional genealogy are taken from the Old Testament. Probably in the original Hebrew all of them were so derived. Only the last three, however, represent the Old Testament personages named. **Salamiel, son of Sarasadai** is the Greek form of "Shelumiel the son of Zurishaddai," leader of the tribe of Simeon during the wilderness wandering (Numbers 1:6). **Israel** is of course Jacob. Simeon belongs in the list as Judith's tribal ancestor (cf. 9:2) and may have been originally included. On the other hand the author may have chosen to omit him because the Old Testament does not reveal from which of his sons Zurishaddai was descended (Genesis 46:10; I Chronicles 4:24). The naming of some of the ancestors after such famous persons as **Joseph . . . Gideon . . . Elijah** suggests that Judith has some of the characteristics of these heroes.

8:2-4. Judith is a **widow.** The account of her husband's **overseeing** workers in the **barley harvest** likens him to Boaz (cf. Ruth 2). His name, **Manasseh,** is that of the largest of the northern tribes. It may be intended to symbolize Judah's widowhood since the fall of the northern kingdom, or possibly it alludes to the location of Bethulia in Manassite territory (see above on 3:9–4:15). **Balamon** has the same consonants as Belmain (4:4) and thus may represent the same Hebrew name. But the place it designates is uncertain.

8:5-8. The description of Judith's punctilious and prolonged observance of mouring rites serves to establish her pious character. This account provides authentic insights into such practices at the beginning of the Pharisaic movement. The observance of the **day before the sabbath** and before other special days is not mentioned in the written law. Thus it shows the development of the oral law of which the Pharisees were such strong proponents. Judith's beauty and wealth make her an appealing romantic figure capable of promoting the author's ideals of piety.

8:9-36. *Rebuke of the Elders.* The reader should not jump to the conclusion that it is Judith's wealth that enables her to **summon** Bethulia's three **elders** and upbraid them while they meekly listen and then apologize. Apparently the author has in mind rather her reputation for **wisdom** as the basis for her privilege. Since he puts into her mouth the chief lesson he wants to teach, her criticisms of the **ruler** must be accepted as right whereas those of her fellow citizens are **wicked words**. Obviously **Uzziah** was originally included in verse 10 (see the Revised Standard Version footnote) since he is later the spokesman (verses 28-31, 35).

8:11b-27. The elders have promised to **surrender** unless God acts **within so many days.** Judith's view is that they are trying to **put God to the test,** to hand God an ultimatum. But **God is not like man** and cannot be **threatened** into changing plans.

Unlike their ancestors, who suffered a **catastrophe**—the Babylonian exile—because of their apostasy (see above on 5:5-21), the Jews now are free from idolatry. They can have confidence that God will not forsake them—a relevant and important message during the Maccabean conflict. All Judea is depending on the Bethulians to ward off the attack and save the **temple.** God is thus **putting** them **to the test,** as God did the patriarchs (cf. Genesis 22:1-14; 29:15-30). **Mesopotamia in Syria** means the northwest part of Mesopotamia, inhabited by Syrians—that is, Arameans. God's purpose is not **revenge** but education.

8:28-36. Uzziah admits the truth of Judith's statement. But he explains that he was **compelled** by the people and that he must keep his promise. The only hope he can see is a **rain** to relieve

237

the water shortage. Judith, however, declares she will take action herself. The **rulers** give her their blessing without knowing what she will do.

9:1-14. *Judith's Prayer.* The mourning rites are intended to reinforce Judith's plea for divine aid in her undertaking. It is a typical prayer of the time, appealing to God by recalling God's past deeds and by extolling God's virtues. The tribe of **Simeon** was allotted territory in the south within that of Judah (Joshua 19:1-9). Apparently it was absorbed into Judah in early times. Here, however, Judith and Uzziah (6:15), and perhaps the whole population of Bethulia, are Simeonites living in the north.

The explanation may lie in the allusion to the sack of Shechem by Simeon and Levi to avenge the rape of Dinah (verses 2-4; cf. Genesis 34). Whereas in the ancient story Jacob criticized their action, Judith praises it in all its ruthlessness. If Bethulia represents Shechem, an aspect of the relation between Jews and Samaritans is undoubtedly symbolized here. But the meaning is uncertain (see above on 3:9–4:15).

9:5-14. God determines the course of all events. Judith implores his aid against the attackers whose ultimate aim is to **defile** his **sanctuary**—no doubt an allusion to Antiochus Epiphanes' setting up a pagan altar in the temple in Jerusalem. **Deceit of my lips**, literally "my lips of deceit," is a typical Hebrew expression.

Many have deplored the morality of Judith's prayer for blessing on a deceit. Others have justified her course as the only means of defense for herself and her people against a pitiless aggressor. In such a situation, they claim, she is acting as God's agent and has God's blessing. Certainly her invocation of God as the **helper of the oppressed** is in line with prophetic theology, and God's doing so by means of war and violence is the usual Old Testament portrayal. So here as elsewhere the author follows the principle that the end justifies the means.

10:1-10. *Judith's Departure from the City.* Lying **prostrate** full length on the ground is a characteristic posture for prayer among both ancient and modern Semites. If the people of Bethulia could have foreseen the outcome, they would no doubt have gladly contributed their scanty supply of drinking **water** to provide a bath for Judith. But the author mentions it without explanation, suggesting that he forgot this detail of the situation. Verses 3-4 provide an interesting picture of how ancient Jewish women adorned themselves (cf. Isaiah 3:16-23).

Judith is also concerned about taking along food and especially **vessels**—bowls, plates, cups, and other utensils for cooking and eating—so that she may continue her pious observance of the law by eating only "clean" (*kosher*) food while in the enemy camp. Thus prepared, she and her servant girl go to the **gate** and are let out with the blessing of the three **elders**.

10:11-23. *Into Enemy Custody.* Judith and her maid are soon found by an **Assyrian patrol.** They identify themselves as **Hebrews**—the term for Israelites generally used by outsiders in the early books of the Old Testament. Fugitives volunteering information would usually be given careful treatment and interrogation. But such is Judith's beauty that she is given an escort of a **hundred men** and taken directly to the commander's **tent.** Its bed, with posts (cf. 13:6-9) supporting a richly ornamented **canopy,** or net to keep out insects, is true to life, as confirmed by other literature and contemporary art.

11:1–12:9. *The Meeting with Holofernes.* The general greets his beautiful captive with courteous assurance of her **safety.** Judith replies with conventional flattery. Then she reminds him of what **Achior** said and confirms it as **true,** that the Jews can be overcome only if they **sin.** Now, she says, they are about to do so, and for this reason she has **fled** from them.

In her explanation of the laws of Judaism which are about to be broken the author emphasizes the importance of their strict observance, especially the **first fruits** (cf. Exodus 23:16; Leviticus 23:15-22; Deuteronomy 16:9-12) and **tithes** due the **priests . . . at Jerusalem** (cf. Leviticus 27:30-31; Deuteronomy 14:22-29). Judith promises to tell when the Bethulians break these laws and thus become powerless to oppose an advance on Jerusalem. To do so she must leave the camp **every night** for prayer—a practice she must establish to make possible her later escape.

Beguiled by her **beauty**, Holofernes is too easily convinced of her **wisdom** on his behalf. When he offers her **some of his own food** she insists that she must eat only what she has brought. She promises with double meaning that God will act before her **supply runs out**. The need for her food bag, like her habit of going out each night for prayer and bathing—that is, ritual ablution to remove the defilement of her contacts in the pagan camp—prepares the way for her escape. At the same time this emphasizes her piety.

12:10–13:10a. *Holofernes' Banquet.* The wait till the **fourth day** for further meeting with Holofernes provides Judith and her maid the needed time to accustom the Assyrian **guards** to their pattern of nightly trips outside the camp carrying their food bag. No doubt the author intends that Holofernes' delay is to be understood as not merely fortuitous but an answer to Judith's prayer, to protect her virtue if not her life. Now that the stage is set she can accept with **joy**—in which the reader of course sees the deeper meaning—the invitation to an intimate dinner with Holofernes brought by **Bagoas** (see Introduction).

12:16-20. Holofernes is quite overwhelmed by both Judith's charms and her elation over being in his company—which of course has a different basis than he supposes. He is so smitten that he is not bothered by her refraining from all except her own food and drink. In fact the effect is to make him drink the more. **Since I was born . . . since he was born** points up the contrast of the two characters.

13:1-10a. Perhaps the author might have achieved more suspense in his climactic scene if Holofernes were not already **overcome with wine** by the time the **attendants** leave the two **alone**. His emphasis, however, is less on an exciting story than on Judith's trust in God. She dramatically prays for **strength** to perform the assassination—a plea that strongly points up the moral problem of the book (see above on 9:5-14).

After the decapitation Judith takes the **canopy** (see above on 10:11-23) to prove the identity of the **head** (cf. verse 15), which she hands to the **maid** to put into the **food bag**. This scene was popular with medieval and renaissance artists—for example, the painting by Lucas Cranach, friend of Martin Luther, in which the guileless, prim expression of Judith is in striking contrast to the gory head of Holofernes.

V. VICTORY FOR THE JEWS (13:10*b*–16:25)

13:10*b*-20. *The Return to Bethulia.* The regular practice of Judith and her maid to leave the camp every night for prayer and the appearance of their food bag have become familiar to the guards. The two are now able to escape without challenge and make their way back to Bethulia. There Judith's **voice** is recognized in the dark, and the gates are opened to let the women in. A crowd quickly gathers, including the **elders**. All are suitably **astonished** and grateful at the sight of the enemy general's head.

Blessed art thou, our God is a common formula with which many Jewish prayers begin. With Uzziah's address to Judith compare Genesis 14:19-20 and Judges 5:24. Since in Hebrew the words "head" and "leader" would probably be the same, the phrase **strike the head of the leader of our enemies** may represent an early textual error of duplication. The original may have read "strike the leader of our enemies."

14:1-10. *Achior's Confirmation.* The order in this section seems to be disarranged. Logically Achior should verify the head's identity (verse 6). Judith should tell the full story of her exploit to the people (verse 8*b*) before she proposes a military venture based on it (verses 1-4), since her plan calls for immediate action (verse 11). This order is found in the Vulgate, where verses 6-9 precede verses 1-4, and may represent the original. Verse 5, not found in the Latin, is probably an editorial attempt to connect the disordered parts. Verse 10, which even in the Latin remains as an interruption between the military plan (verses 1-4) and its execution (verse 11), may also be an interpolation. It contravenes the law against an Ammonite's joining the **house of Israel** (Deuteronomy 23:3).

The **parapet** in verse 1 was a small wall built on top of the main defense wall, behind which the soldiers could stand. Judith's prediction that the enemy will **flee** in panic on discovering the leader's death may be based on the demoralization of the Moabites when Ehud assassinated their king (Judges 3:15-30). However, Old Testament accounts of such panic among Israel's enemies are common enough that the original readers would scarcely question her confidence.

14:11–15:7. *Rout of the Enemy.* Just as Judith has foreseen, the Jewish sortie at **dawn** precipitates discovery of the headless body of Holofernes. The resulting turmoil while the men are still **in the tents** half awake sends the huge army into terrified flight. The allies **camped in the hills**—that is, the Edomites and Ammonites (7:18)—also flee. The Bethulian soldiers hurry in pursuit, while messengers are sent to the other fortified cities on the **frontiers** to rally all the Jewish forces to join in.

Probably in the original Hebrew all the places named were from the list in 4:4, 6. **Those in Gilead** (east of the Sea of Galilee) **and in Galilee** (west of the lake) are Jews living in these Gentile regions. They take up arms against the fugitives passing by on the way to their homeland.

15:8-13. *Blessing of Judith.* The mighty victory brings the **high priest** and the members of the **senate** from **Jerusalem** to congratulate Judith and bless her for her **singlehanded** achievement for the nation. In the extended plundering of the enemy camp Judith is given the **tent of Holofernes**, where her great deed was done, and all its **furniture**.

Victory dances such as described in verses 12-13 are well known both in the Old Testament and in other ancient literature. **Branches** is literally "thyrsi," the wands tipped with pine cones and ivy leaves carried by worshipers of Dionysus. They are said to have been used by Judas Maccabeus' followers in celebrating the rededication of the temple (II Maccabees 10:7). However, the original Hebrew may have referred to the branches traditional in Jewish celebrations. The use of **olive wreaths** is a Greek custom without Old Testament parallel.

16:1-17. *A Song of Thanksgiving.* This hymn of praise summarizes the whole story in typical Hebrew poetry. The introduction states that Judith composed it, but it is more appropriately sung by **all the people** since it refers to her in the third person. Many have pointed out that the literary style of the poem is superior to that of the prose story. This difference and the reference to the **Medes** as allies of the invader suggest another author. It is possible that an independent story and poem were combined by an editor. But it is more likely that the story is based on the poem, the author having filled in details out of his imagination. The poet shows his acquaintance with Old Testament poetry, especially the Psalms. But the introductory and concluding expressions of praise (verses 2-3, 13-17) are appropriate even if not distinctively original. The narrative section is imaginative and vivid.

16:4-12. If the poem is earlier than the rest of the book, the enemy may not have been identified in it as **Assyrian**. This pseudonym was probably the invention of the prose author. **Titans** and **giants** are terms from Greek mythology. Here they are merely the translator's rendering of such Hebrew terms as Nephilim, Anakim, and Rephaim (cf. Genesis 6:4; Numbers 13:33; Deuteronomy 2:20-21). **Sons of maidservants** probably refers to slaves. However, it might have the literal sense "sons of young women"—that is, mere boys.

16:13-17. With verse 14 cf. Psalms 33:6-9 and 104:30. With verse 15 cf. Psalm 97:4-5. Verse 16 might seem to indicate sympathy with such prophetic denunciations of the sacrificial cult as Amos 5:21-24; Hosea 6:6; Isaiah 1:11-17; and Micah 6:6-8—a view at odds with the prose author's concern for precise observance of the ritual law. But as conventionally stated here, and understood by the pious in Maccabean times, the thought is merely that **sacrifice** is but a **small** part of the observances required of **one who fears the Lord**—that is, one who obeys his law. That the author of the book should include such a statement is therefore not incredible.

Verse 17 has aroused much discussion. It may refer to an apocalyptic **day of judgment** on which the bodies of Israel's enemies will be consumed by **fire and worms**. Or it may indicate a judgment after death with punishment literally lasting **for ever**—a concept that began to develop during the second century. A definitive solution seems impossible.

16:18-25. *Conclusion of the Story.* On reaching Jerusalem the people engage in the proper purificatory rituals and then offer sacrifices. Judith donates the booty secured from Holofernes. The celebration lasts **three months** (cf. 1:16). In earlier times Judith's reward would have been remarriage and a number of children. But the author considers an extended widowhood more appropriate. He notes her distribution of **property** in accordance with the law (Numbers 27:11) as a final example of her piety. With verse 25 compare Judges 5:31*c*.

THE ADDITIONS TO THE
BOOK OF ESTHER

H. Neil Richardson

INTRODUCTION

The Greek Septuagint version contains six passages, ranging in length from seven to thirty verses, which are not found in the Hebrew text. These expand the narrative at the beginning and end and at three intermediate points. In his Latin translation Jerome worked from the Hebrew text. He added these extra passages from the Septuagint as an appendix, with notes of their places in the story. In so doing he put the ending from the Septuagint in its proper place following that from the Hebrew. Then he went back to pick up the other passages in the Septuagint order.

By the time chapter divisions—and later verses—were added to the Vulgate, Jerome's notes had dropped out. The numbers were applied to the whole book in this confusing order. These were retained when the Protestant reformers relegated to the Apocrypha the part not in the Hebrew. In the Revised Standard Version Apocrypha, the six passages comprising the Additions to Esther are restored to their Septuagint order, with notes of their relation to Esther. Thus the "book" begins with 11:2 and the numbers 10:4–11:1 come at the end following 16:24.

Late in the nineteenth century a scholar devised an alternate plan of identifying the six passages by the letters A-F. These letter designations, which are not noted in the Revised Standard Version, have been used by many scholars in writing about the material. Therefore they are included in parentheses following the boldface references in the commentary below.

Inconsistencies in story details and differences in general viewpoint and literary style make it hard to believe that any of the additions can be the work of the author of Esther. Authorship by the Septuagint translator, though sometimes assumed, also seems unlikely. The colophon (11:1) by attesting to the genuineness of the work as translated implicitly denies any supplementation in the process. Thus the additions are best attributed to otherwise unknown authors—perhaps six or more different persons, as suggested by the inconsistencies and stylistic differences among them.

There is no clear historical allusion by which any of the additions can be dated. The earliest evidence of acquaintance with them is around A.D. 90 in the retelling of the story of Esther by the Jewish historian Josephus. He paraphrased or even quoted all the additions except the first and last, which probably were not congenial to his purpose. The two purported royal decrees (13:1-7; 16:1-24) were clearly composed in Greek. They therefore must date from after the Septuagint translation, which probably was made a short time before 77/76 B.C. (see below on 11:1). On the other hand Semitic idioms in the other four passages suggest that they are translations from Hebrew or Aramaic. Thus they may have been added to Esther before the Septuagint translation was made.

The purpose of the additions is twofold:
(1) to add interest to the story by supplying more details at selected spots;
(2) to provide the religious element so strangely lacking in the Hebrew text.

In neither respect are they very successful. The narrative details are mostly unrealistic and contribute little to the understanding of either plot or character. The religious references, it is true, name God, call on God in prayer, and attribute favorable events to God's action. But since they are used to express the same vindictive spirit toward Gentiles found in the Hebrew text, they do little to raise the religious level of the book. Like most of the Apocrypha the Additions to Esther are included in the Roman Catholic Old Testament.

COMMENTARY

11:2–12:6 (A). *Mordecai's Dream.* There are two parts to this addition—the description of Mordecai's dream (11:2-12) and the narrative of his saving the king's life (chapter 12). They may be separate units which happen to have been placed together. The introduction (verses 2-4) duplicates Esther 2:5-6. **Second Year** is inconsistent wth the third year in Esther 1:3. **Artaxerxes** is the Septuagint translator's interpretation of the Hebrew name now known to represent rather Xerxes. Probably he had in mind Xerxes' son Artaxerxes I (465-424), whose second year was 134 years after **Nebuchadnezzar** took away the Jewish **captives** in 597.

11:5-12. The dream and its features—**tumult upon the earth**, the **two dragons**, and the conflict between the forces of good and evil—are characteristic of the apocalyptic writing during the Maccabean and Roman periods (see Introduction to Second Esdras). An interpretation of this dream, perhaps by another author, appears in the final addition (10:4-9). There the **two dragons** are said to symbolize Mordecai and Haman, and the **river** Esther. But it is not certain that these meanings are intended here. It is clear, however, that the **righteous nation** is the Jews. **Ready to perish**, they have **cried to God** and will be saved by God. This is in contrast to the Hebrew text, where they win the victory by their own strength and the favor of the king.

12:1-6. This episode duplicates Esther 2:21-23 with some variations. Here Mordecai himself hears the plotters and informs the king directly. He is rewarded, and incurs the enmity of Haman for this deed. **Gabatha** and **Tharra** are Greek versions of variant Hebrew forms of Bigthan and Teresh. **Bougaean** is also a Greek representation of a Hebrew corruption of the word meaning Agagite (cf. Esther 3:1).

13:1-7 (B). *The First Edict.* This purports to be the text of a letter sent out by the king. It orders the destruction of an unnamed people who will be identified in **letters of Haman**. It contradicts the account in Esther 3:10-12, where Haman uses the king's signet ring to send out a single letter in the king's name. This of course specifies the Jews (cf. Esther 4:3). The erroneous date for the massacre, the **fourteenth** of **Adar** instead of the thirteenth (cf. Esther 3:13; 8:12; 9:1, 17), suggests that this edict may have a different author from the second edict (chapter 16), in which the correct date is given.

13:8-14:19 (C). *Prayers of Mordecai and Esther.* These are typical Jewish prayers of the first century B.C., in which God is extolled as creator and ruler of the universe and savior of Israel. Mordecai's mention of Abraham and the Exodus refers to the two early events in the life of Israel in which God entered into significant covenantal relationship with the people. His explanation of his refusal to **bow down** to Haman (13:12-14) indicates that he would not bow to any human being—a position he must have abandoned on being presented by Esther to the king (Esther 8:1-2). There is nothing in the Old Testament to prohibit a Jew from making the customary obeisance to a ruler or other superior.

14:1-19. Verse 2 describes well-known **mourning** practices of ancient times. These were the customary reinforcement of prayer for divine mercy in time of great affliction. Esther's references to the history of Israel as the scene of God's activity (verse 5) and to the people's sin as the cause of their captivity (verses 6-10) are good Old Testament doctrine. On the Jews as God's **scepter** (verse 11) cf. Psalms 60:7 and 108:8.

Her declaration that she detests being married to a Gentile and even wearing the crown which symbolizes her **proud position** accords with strictly orthodox Judaism in the days of the Maccabees. So also does her claimed refusal to eat with Gentiles, including even her royal husband. However, the evidence of the Hebrew text is against the truth of this claim (cf. Esther 2:9, 18; 5:5; 7:1).

15:1-16 (D). *Esther's Approach to the King.* This passage follows the preceding prayers in the Septuagint. Generally it is regarded as a separate composition. It takes the place of Esther 5:1-2, which briefly describes Esther's coming to the royal hall and being received at once by the king.

This expanded account builds on the fear previously expressed by Esther because of the alleged law making an unsummoned approach to the throne a capital offense (Esther 4:11). In highly exaggerated style it portrays the king's initial anger, which turns to solicitude when Esther faints from fright. The three references to God are conventional. They reveal no religious outlook rising above the secularity of the Hebrew text.

16:1-24 (E). *The Counter Edict.* This is a purported copy of the decree issued in the king's name by Mordecai to counteract the allegedly irrevocable decree of Haman calling for destruction of the Jews (cf. Esther 8:8). Actually it does revoke the previous order (cf. especially verse 17). Here Haman is identified as a **Macedonian** rather than an Agagite (Esther 3:1), who has attempted to turn the Persian Empire over to the Macedonians (verse 14). This is an anachronistic allusion to the conquest of Alexander the Great, since in the time of Xerxes and Artaxerxes the Macedonians were not militarily significant. The Jews are here pictured as great defenders of the Persian Empire.

God is referred to as the ruler of human history. God is responsible for the turn in events that has thwarted Haman and destined the appointed **thirteenth day of . . . Adar** (see above on 13:1-7) to be a **joy to his chosen people**. Even the Persians are ordered to observe Purim (verses 22-23).

10:4–11:1 (F). *Interpretation of Mordecai's Dream.* This explanation of the vision described at the beginning of the Septuagint (11:5-11) is an allegorical treatment. Whether it precisely represents the meaning intended in the previous description of the dream is questionable. Here the name Purim is plural, though in the Hebrew text it is based on the use of only the singular Pur, or lot (cf. Esther 3:7; 9:24, 26). This may have suggested to the author the idea of **two lots**. He plays on the word "lot," which means not only the object cast to determine a course of action but also destiny.

11:1. This colophon dates the arrival in **Egypt**—that is, Alexandria—of the Septuagint translation of Esther. The year intended is doubtful because all the kings of Egypt for about three hundred years were named **Ptolemy** and were married to their own sisters, most of whom were named **Cleopatra**. The probable date is the **fourth year** of either Ptolemy VIII Soter II Lathyrus (114/13) or Ptolemy XI Auletes (77/76). The latter is more likely. Possibly the translation was made only a short time earlier.

It is attributed to **Lysimachus**, a resident of **Jerusalem** but possibly educated in Alexandria. The book is here called the **Letter of Purim**. The declaration that it is **genuine** implies that Lysimachus translated precisely the Hebrew or Aramaic text lying before him, which may have included all the additions except the two edicts (13:1-7; 16:1-24; see Introduction).

THE WISDOM OF SOLOMON

Robert C. Dentan

INTRODUCTION

Name and Character

Without dispute the Wisdom of Solomon is the most appealing and important of the Old Testament apocryphal books. It belongs to the general category of wisdom literature. But it differs from the older wisdom books, particularly Proverbs and Ecclesiasticus, in that it abandons the use of the brief, pithy, didactic epigram in favor of long, sweeping arguments more in the style of the literary essay. In this it shows both its different purpose and the different cultural environment in which it arose.

The purpose is no longer to prepare the young for service in an ancient and stable society. Instead the Wisdom of Solomon attempts to preserve a transplanted way of life and thought in an alien environment. The new cultural setting was plainly that of Hellenistic Egypt. The large Jewish community there was in danger of losing its identity because of the rivalry of Greek philosophy and the attractions of a relaxed morality.

Ecclesiastes in the canonical Old Testament illustrates the kind of erosion to which ancient Hebrew faith was subject in this period. It can hardly be an accident that 2:1-5 provides so accurate a summary of the argument of that curious book. It was just this kind of argument—that life is short, meaningless, and without hope, and that God is indifferent to justice and sound morals—that the Wisdom of Solomon was written to refute.

If the author specifically meant to combat the destructive thesis of Ecclesiastes, this aim would largely explain his use of the pseudonym "Solomon." Ecclesiastes had been composed in Solomon's name, and it was only fitting that its rebuttal should be launched with the same authority. In view of the fact that the book was written in Greek and is suffused with the atmosphere of the Hellenistic world, the alleged Solomonic authorship can hardly have been taken very seriously even by its original readers.

Contents

The books falls into three main parts. Each is unified within itself, though their relationship to each other is not entirely clear.

(1) Chapters 1–5, addressed to Jews, depict the contrasting life and final destiny of the righteous and the wicked.

(2) Chapters 6–9 are addressed at least rhetorically to the kings of the Gentiles. They extol wisdom as the unifying principle of the cosmos as well as the guide of individual life.

(3) Chapters 10–19 survey God's direction of Israel's history. Strangely, in this part the figure of wisdom plays an explicit role but is scarcely mentioned after chapter 10. The continuity is interrupted by two important digressions. 11:15–12:27 tells how God punishes the wicked in ways appropriate to their sins (although God is also merciful, 11:24-26; 12:19-22). Chapters 13–15 discuss the origin of idolatry and its moral consequences. This last division, though occasionally reaching a high level, is on the whole vastly inferior in content and tone to chapters 1–9.

Unity and Language

Various parts of the book differ in style and tone. This has caused some scholars to suppose that more than one hand was involved in its composition. The style of chapters 1–5 is definitely more Hebraic than the rest of the book. It has been sometimes thought that this section (or alternatively chapters 1–10) was originally written in Hebrew, possibly in Palestine. According to this theory, these chapters were translated into Greek by another author, who then composed the rest of the book in the same language.

In spite of the undeniable differences between the sections, however, the similarities in style, vocabulary, and ideas still seem to most scholars at least as impressive as the differences. In the absence of decisive proof to the contrary it would appear best to treat the work as the product of a single author writing in Greek. His initial interest, seen in chapters 1–5, is unmistakable. But it is quite possible that other sections of the book were added by him at later times and in somewhat different circumstances. This would sufficiently account for the apparent inconsistencies in form and style.

The abrupt ending of the book has led some to suspect that either its conclusion has been lost or the author left his work unfinished. It is more likely, however, that the book is complete, even though it ends somewhat lamely for modern taste.

Place and Date of Composition

It is hard to imagine that this work was written in any other place than Alexandria in Egypt. This was the greatest center of Jewish life in the Hellenistic world, the city where the tension between traditional Judaism and Greek culture was both most acute and most intellectually productive.

As to date, the book clearly represents a later development in wisdom literature than Ecclesiasticus, which is usually dated about 180 B.C. On the other hand Philo Judaeus, another Alexandrian writer whose career roughly spanned the first half of the first century A.D., attempted a Hellenistic-Jewish synthesis in ways far more complex and subtle than those of the Wisdom of Solomon. A date of around 50 B.C. would thus seem most suitable.

Importance

The author of the Wisdom of Solomon was in a general way acquainted with the art, literature, and philosophy of the Greek world and obviously much attracted to it. He was also a loyal son of Israel and, in intention at least, thoroughly orthodox. His purpose was not to denature Judaism but to defend it. What is remarkable is the freedom with which he uses Greek terms and ideas to express what he conceives to be the essence of Old Testament faith.

He thus became the first to achieve some kind of rapprochement between those two great cultures, so different from each other and yet both so basic to western civilization—the Greek and the Hebrew. Philo Judaeus would later follow in his footsteps, and so would the Alexandrian Christian fathers Clement and Origen. So, to a greater or lesser degree, did most of the great thinkers of the Christian church.

In the New Testament itself one can see the movement taking shape, particularly in the letters of Paul and in Hebrews. It seems probable that Paul was familiar with the book even though he never quotes it as scripture. Cf. Romans 1:19-32 with chapters 13-14. Also note that Ephesians 6:13-17 also seems clearly dependent on 5:17-19. Hebrews 1:3 is influenced by the language of 7:26. Many other passages of the New Testament show a direct relationship to the Wisdom of Solomon—or share in the intellectual climate which produced it.

Thus the book is important as a monument in the general history of apologetics and theology. It is also important for at least three doctrines, fundamental to much of later Jewish and Christian thought, which appear in its pages for the first time:

(1) the immortality of the soul, in contrast to the older Hebraic idea of the resurrection of the body (1:15-16; 3:1-4);

(2) death and all other evils as the work of the devil, who through jealousy tempted Adam and Eve in the garden of Eden (2:24);

(3) wisdom in a genuinely metaphysical sense (not merely poetically, as in Proverbs and perhaps in Ecclesiasticus) as

God's agent in creation and the continuing bond between
God and the universe.
The consequences of these developments for New Testament
Christology can hardly be exaggerated (cf. 7:22–8:1 with John
1:1-4; Colossians 1:15-17; and Hebrews 1:2-3).

I. THE REWARDS OF THE RIGHTEOUS AND THE
WICKED CONTRASTED (1:1–5:23)

1:1-15. *Invitation to Seek God, Wisdom, and Life.* The
address in verse 1 to the **rulers of the earth** (cf. 6:1) is merely
formal. "Solomon" would of course be expected to address his
equals. The audience actually in the author's mind consists of
wealthy, educated Jews in Alexandria who were in danger of
losing their faith. The author states his thesis here in general
terms. **Righteousness** is advantageous, in spite of the arguments
of skeptics. Through the practice of truth and righteousness one
can prepare the way for the attainment of wisdom (verse 4).

1:6-15. In verses 6-7 wisdom is identified with God's **Spirit**
(cf. 7:22-30; 9:17). The conception of the Spirit in verse 7 seems
derived from the Stoic idea of the world soul. Verse 12 warns
that unrighteousness is punished by **death** (eternal death, as the
subsequent argument makes clear). According to verses 13-15
God is not the author of death. God's creation, and all that
conforms to God's will, is made for life and immortality.

1:16–2:24. *Death Comes From Sin.* God never meant that
men and women should die. Death was the result of sin.

2:1-20. An imaginary conversation of apostate Jews describes
the philosophy which the author intends to refute. The
argument in verses 1-5 that a life is brief and meaningless is very
close to that of Ecclesiastes. One can hardly avoid the conclusion
that the author has this book particularly in mind (cf.
Ecclesiastes 3:19-22; 4:2-3; 7:2-3; 9:2-6, 11-12). The following
verses draw more far-reaching conclusions from this pessimistic
philosophy than Ecclesiastes does (cf. Ecclesiastes 9:7-10). It

was inevitable that the admirers of that book should go far beyond the sober opinions of their master.

2:6-20. Verses 6-9 advocate an unrestrained, pagan type of hedonism. Verses 10-11 express contempt for the helpless and proclaim that **might** is right (cf. 15:12). Verses 12-20 use language that suggested to the early church the circumstances of the Crucifixion. They declare war on **the righteous man**—the good, law-abiding, traditional Jew. From verses 16 and 18 it is evident that the fatherhood of God was an element in contemporary Jewish orthodoxy.

2:21-24. Their argument was based on a faulty premise. They failed to realize that in a future life righteousness will be rewarded. Verse 23 concludes, from the fact that humans were made in God's **image** (Genesis 1:26-27), that they are by nature immortal. Death was **the devil's** work. For the first time in the history of Jewish thought Satan is identified with the serpent of Eden (cf. Genesis 3:4, 19).

3:1–5:23. *Judgment After Death.* The death of the righteous is only an illusion. In reality they will possess everlasting felicity, share in the government of God's kingdom, and enjoy God's **love**.

3:10-13a. The wicked have nothing to look forward to—in this life or a life to come.

3:13b–4:6. There is blessing for the **barren woman** or the **eunuch** who is righteous. The ancient Hebrew view was that many children were the reward of righteousness. It now becomes necessary to refute this view and assert that in some circumstances it is better to remain childless (cf. Isaiah 56:3-5; Matthew 19:12). The many children of the wicked will be despised (3:17; 4:3-6) and will have no immortality (3:18). Righteousness is better than many children.

4:7-19. It was also the ancient Hebrew view that righteousness was usually crowned by a long life. Since the author cannot deny that the righteous often die young, he must redefine **old age** (verses 8-9) and demonstrate that the long life of the wicked is profitless (verses 16-19). Verses 10-15 refer to the example of

Enoch (Genesis 5:24). On the absence of his name see below on
10:1-4.

4:20–5:14. When the last reckoning comes, the wicked will
realize the superior wisdom of the righteous person's life.
Verses 4-13 represent the wicked's sorrowful condemnation of
their own way of thinking and living.

5:15-23. In contrast the final judgment will bring triumph to
the righteous. The picture of the Lord battling for the righteous
in verses 17-20 is based on Isaiah 59:17. The language is echoed
in Ephesians 6:11-17. Verses 21-23 describe the devastating
fury with which God will destroy their enemies, who in effect
will have destroyed themselves.

II. THE PRAISE OF WISDOM (6:1–9:18)

The destruction threatened against evil rulers in 5:23
provides an opportunity for "Solomon" to speak. He now
appears for the first time clearly speaking in his own person
(6:22; 7:1-30). He appeals to the kings of the earth to learn true
wisdom, which he acquired and is prepared to expound to them.
While the author may hope for some Gentile readers (6:1-11),
there can be little doubt that his audience is still primarily a
Jewish one.

6:12-20. *The Nature and Function of Wisdom.* Wisdom is
pictured in language highly reminiscent of Proverbs and
Ecclesiasticus. Verses 17-20 are in the form of a chain argument.
Wisdom brings people to immortality and participation in God's
kingdom (verse 20; cf. 3:8; 10:10).

6:21–7:22a. *How Solomon Acquired Wisdom.* Solomon tells
of his own experience. In verses 1-6 he describes his birth and
makes it clear that his wisdom was not due to any unusual native
endowments. He obtained her through prayer (verse 7; cf. I
Kings 3:9), realizing how important it was to possess her (verses
8-14). God (God's wisdom) was the source not only of Solomon's
good judgment but also of his skill and scientific **knowledge** (cf.

I Kings 4:32-33). Wisdom was God's agent in creation (verse 22*a*; cf. Proverbs 3:19; 8:30).

7:22*b*–8:1. *Detailed Description of Wisdom*. The remarkable description of wisdom in verses 22-23 is made up of terms borrowed in large part from Greek, especially Stoic, philosophy. Obviously the author wishes to show that whatever words might be used to describe such Greek philosophical concepts as the *logos*, or world soul, might also be used to characterize the biblical concept of wisdom. The importance of this entire passage for the development of New Testament Christology has been noted in the Introduction. Wisdom is the source of universal order (8:1).

8:2-21. *How Solomon Sought to Win Her*. Solomon fell in love with Wisdom and set about obtaining her for his **bride**. In verse 7 the **virtues** she teaches are the four recommended in Platonic and Stoic philosophy. She conveys private knowledge (verse 8), inspires respect among counselors (verses 10-12), gives **immortality** (verse 13) and skill in government (verses 14-15). Verse 19 teaches the Platonic doctrine of the preexistence of the **soul** (cf. 15:8). Wisdom cannot be acquired by effort; she can only be given by God (verse 21). This thought provides the transition to the prayer that forms the whole of chapter 9.

9:1-18. *Solomon's Prayer*. Cf. 7:7. The parallel use of **word** and **wisdom** in verses 1-2 prepares the way for the identification of the two in New Testament Logos Christology. The idea of the **copy of the holy tent** in verse 8 is presumably derived from Exodus 25:9, 40. The conception in verse 15 of the **perishable body** that **weighs down the soul** is Platonic, not Hebrew (cf. II Corinthians 5:1, 4).

III. How God Directed the Destinies of Israel
(10:1–19:22)

The rest of the book is an exposition of early Old Testament history, mainly the Exodus. It shows how wonderfully God exercised control over nature and events for the instruction and deliverance of the people.

10:1–11:1. *Wisdom the Protector of the Nation's Ancestors.* Wisdom makes her last appearance in this section. In the remainder of the book God is the director of history. It may be, however, that the author intended the theme stated here to be understood as implicit in the rest of the story as well.

10:1-4. Wisdom played a part in the lives of Adam, Cain, and Noah. The curious omission of names in the stories and allusions in the Wisdom of Solomon has often been noted (cf. 4:10-15; 12:3-11; 14:6; 15:14; 18:21). The anonymity helps create a sense of mystery and solemnity.

10:5-8. The **nations** were **confounded** at Babel (Genesis 11:9). Wisdom **recognized** Abraham and **rescued** Lot.

10:9-14. The precise phrase **kingdom of God** is said to occur here for the first time in Jewish literature—though the idea is much older. The reference is presumably to Jacob's vision at Bethel (Genesis 28:12). Verses 13-14 refer to Joseph.

10:15-21. Wisdom brought about the Exodus. The **servant of the Lord** in verse 16 is Moses. Wisdom is identified with the pillars of cloud and fire (verse 17; cf. Exodus 13:21). **They sang hymns;** cf. Exodus 15:1-18, 20-21.

11:1. This is the last significant mention of wisdom. The word occurs later only in 14:2, 5. **A holy prophet** refers to Moses.

11:2-14. *Treatment of Israelites and Egyptians Contrasted.* A constant theme in the remainder of the book is the comparison between the plagues suffered by the Egyptians and the corresponding blessings enjoyed by the Israelites (verse 5). In this passage the contrast is between the **water** from the **rock** which quenched the thirst of the Israelites (verses 4, 7) and the water turned to **blood** which afflicted the Egyptians (verse 6).

11:15–12:27. *God's Punishment and Kindly Correction.* This digression explains how God's punishments are fitted to human sins. A basic theme in this part of the book is that one **is punished by the very things by which he sins** (verse 16; cf. 12:23, 27; 16:1). **The Egyptians worshiped animals** instead of God. They were therefore punished by plagues of animals (frogs, gnats,

259

flies, locusts). Because God is omnipotent, having **created the world out of** preexistent, **formless matter** (verse 17, a Platonic idea), God could have sent great, terrifying animals instead of little, annoying ones (verses 17-19).

11:23–12:2. God's punishment is always tempered by mercy. God's love is universal (cf. 12:13). God's punishments are gradual and intended to lead people to repentance (cf. 12:10, 20).

12:3-27. The wickedness of the Canaanites merited the worst punishment (verses 3-6). Yet God treated them with forbearance, although God knew them incapable of changing their ways (verses 10-11). On **wasps** cf. Joshua 24:12. Verses 12-18 reaffirm God's omnipotence and justice. Verses 19-22 declare that God's love and patience are examples to be imitated. Verses 23-27 are a transition to the next discussion.

13:1–15:19. *The Nature of Idolatry.* Nowhere does the author show more understanding than in 13:1-9. Here he distinguishes one form of paganism, the worship of the elements or heavenly bodies, from mere idolatry. To worship things which are a part of God's creation and are by nature beautiful and strong is a worthy impulse. It is blameworthy because it stops short of its true object (verses 3-5), but it is relatively forgivable (verse 6). The argument from the **beauty** and **power** of the creation to the beauty and power of the Creator (verses 1, 3-5, 9) is Platonic. Paul echoes this argument in Romans 1:19-20.

13:10-19. There is no excuse, however, for those who worship objects made by their own hands. The argument, with its devastatingly accurate account of how images are made, is similar to that in Isaiah 44:9-20. It reaches a climax in verses 17-19, which picture the folly of begging favors from an object that obviously knows nothing of them.

14:1-11. What folly it is to pray for safety at sea to the **wood** of an idol—even though one rightly trusts the wood of a **ship,** built and navigated by divinely given wisdom. This is illustrated by the example of Noah in verses 6-7. Those who pretend to manufacture gods deserve to be punished (verses 8-11).

14:12-21. The author considers the problem of how so irrational a practice as that of idolatry could have originated. He arrives at a rather sophisticated answer. It began innocently enough, he thinks, in the desire for an image of a departed loved one (verse 15) or a faraway ruler (verse 17). In the end the image became an idol and received the name of "god" (verse 21).

14:22-31. From idolatry came immorality. The bad theology of the pagans was the **cause** of their licentious lives. Verse 27 summarizes the thought (cf. verse 12). Paul's argument in Romans 1:24-32 is like this and probably dependent on it.

15:1-6. Israel knew the **true** God from the beginning. Thus it is saved from the temptation to idolatry.

15:7-13. The supreme folly is to worship molded, ceramic gods. How can a person made out of **clay** suppose one can make a god of clay (verse 8)! The point of view of the idolater in verse 12 is identical with that of the apostate Jews in 2:1-11. Such idolatry has no excuse because those who practice it obviously know better (verse 13).

15:14-19. Of all idolaters the Egyptians are the worst. In verses 14-17 the author is probably thinking of the Egyptians of his own time, whose culture seemed so attractive to many of the Jews. In verses 18-19 he prepares to resume the historical comparison which was interrupted at 11:15.

16:1–19:22. *Resumed Contrast of Israelites and Egyptians.* The rest of the book completes the series of comparisons begun in 11:2-14. It tells how the Egyptians and Israelites were treated in such different ways, even though in most instances God was making use of the same natural objects or forces. God's control over nature is such that God can use the same things to bring punishment to foes and blessings to friends.

16:1-4. The Egyptians, who worshiped **animals** (15:18-19), were **tormented** by them (cf. 11:15-16). The Israelites, on the other hand, were given animals (**quails**) to eat (Exodus 16:13).

16:5-14. The people of Israel were for a short time punished **by the bites** of poisonous snakes, after which healing was provided (verses 7, 10; Numbers 21:6-9). The Egyptians were bitten by other vermin with **no healing** available. The bronze snake, however, had no magic power. The healing was through God's **word** (cf. verse 26).

16:15-23. The Egyptians were destroyed by a rain of **hail** from heaven (Exodus 9:24-25). The Hebrews were fed by a rain of manna (verse 20; Exodus 16:14-18). **Snow and ice** in verse 22 refers to the appearance of the manna.

16:24-29. This is another digression on how the universe supports the moral order. The whole world is an instrument in God's hand for the punishment of the wicked and the protection of the virtuous (cf. verse 17c; 19:6). Verse 28 may refer to some sectarian custom of saying prayers before dawn.

17:1-21. The story of how darkness came over Egypt is told. This chapter is an illustration of the author's vivid imagination—and also his tendency to let rhetoric obscure the course of his argument. The account is an elaborate paraphrase of Exodus 10:21-23. The emphasis in verse 12 on **reason** as the source of courage is Greek. This idea is the entire theme of IV Maccabees, another typical Hellenistic-Jewish work. When the author speaks of the moral darkness of the Egyptian world (verses 2-3, 21), he is no doubt thinking of contemporary Alexandria as much as the ancient Egypt of the pharaohs.

18:1-4. In contrast **light** was given to Israel. Not only were the Israelites not affected by the darkness which covered Egypt (Exodus 10:23). They were also accompanied on their later journeys by the pillar of fire (Exodus 13:21-22). Occasionally the author uses traditional language that suggests a narrow view of God's attitude toward the Gentiles (see 12:10-11). But such passages as verse 4, which makes Israel merely a mediator of God's truth to the rest of the world, are far more indicative of his real opinions (cf. 11:24).

18:5-25. The children of the Egyptians were killed in punishment for the death of the Hebrew **children** (verses 5-19; cf. Exodus 1:16; 12:29). Later, in the desert, death threatened the Israelites (Numbers 16:44-45). **A blameless man** (Aaron, verse 21) was able to avert the danger through **prayer** and **incense** (Numbers 16:46-48). Jewish tradition believed that the decorations on Aaron's **robe** (Exodus 28) symbolized the divine omnipotence. Each part represented a part of the universe (verse 24). The "destroyer" of Exodus 12:23 is described in verses 14-16 as God's **all-powerful word . . . , a stern warrior.** This magnificent passage is partly based on I Chronicles 21:16. It is one of the principal sources of the account of the activity of the divine Word in Revelation 19:11-15.

19:1-12. While the Egyptians met a strange death in the sea, the Israelites had an equally strange journey through the desert (Exodus 14:21-31).

19:13-22. *Concluding Remarks.* The Egyptians' doom was just **punishment** for their inhospitality. They had treated the Israelites, their **guests,** as viciously as long before the Sodomites had treated the guests of Lot (verses 13-17; Genesis 19:1-11).

19:18-22. Like a musician playing on the strings of a **harp** God transmutes the elements at will and plays a divine tune on the universe (cf. verse 6; 16:17, 24). Verse 22 is a concluding doxology.

ECCLESIASTICUS OR THE WISDOM OF JESUS THE SON OF SIRACH

Edward Lee Beavin

INTRODUCTION

Author and Date

Ecclesiasticus is one of the most highly regarded and widely used books of the Apocrypha. It is the only one in which the author reveals his name (50:27). Jesus the son of Sirach (Greek), or Jeshua ben Sira (Hebrew), was a sage or wisdom teacher who lived in Jerusalem early in the second century B.C. From the evidence in 50:1-24 (see comment) the date of his writing can be fixed within narrow limits. Scholars generally believe it to be around 180 B.C.

The Title

The original title of the book is unknown, since none of the Hebrew copies preserve the opening passage. The Greek manuscripts introduce it as "Wisdom of Jesus the Son of Sirach" or simply as "Wisdom of Sirach." Since the third century A.D. it has been known in the Latin versions as "Ecclesiasticus"—generally taken to mean "The Church Book." Presumably it was so named because it is the longest or most important of the

264

deuterocanonical books—that is, those which the church accepted though they were not a part of the Hebrew canon.

While some ancient authors refer to a Hebrew version of the book by the name "Parables," or "Proverbs," or "The Proverbs of ben Sira," it is more likely that the original was called "The Wisdom [or "Instruction"] of ben Sira."

Text and Versions

Though Aramaic was the common language in the second century B.C. in Palestine, ben Sira wrote in Hebrew, the literary language. His grandson made a Greek translation of the book from a Hebrew copy soon after 132 B.C. (see below on the Prologue). Jerome used a Hebrew copy in making his Latin translation for the Vulgate around A.D. 400. After that the Hebrew versions dropped from sight until the beginning of the twentieth century.

Through that long interval the Greek versions multiplied. Even now these are regarded as the basic texts. They are extant in two major groups which differ significantly. A responsible modern translation cannot woodenly follow any single text. In addition there are two Syriac versions extant. One of them was probably translated from a Hebrew copy and is quite useful in places. The other seems to have been translated from a Greek version. Other rather numerous versions of the book—for example, Old Latin, Coptic, Arabic—are for the most part paraphrases of the Greek or Syriac and are not very helpful.

Our century has seen a dramatic and important reintroduction of Hebrew texts of ben Sira's book. In 1896 a genizah (a storeroom for worn-out or discarded manuscripts) was discovered in a synagogue in Old Cairo. By 1931 the sifting through its many old manuscripts had produced five Hebrew fragments of Ecclesiasticus, covering about two-thirds of the book. These are medieval copies, dating from around the eleventh century, and their worth has been widely disputed. Some hold that they basically preserve the Hebrew original. Others believe that they are retranslations from Greek back into Hebrew. More recently the Dead Sea Scroll discoveries have contributed to the solving of this problem. Among them are a scroll of Ecclesiasticus containing 39:27–44:17 and two fragments (6:20-31; 51:13-20). These early Hebrew copies tend to confirm the authenticity of the Cairo fragments.

The Revised Standard Version translation of Ecclesiasticus is based principally on an edition of the Septuagint which reflects the texts of the earliest Greek manuscripts. But the translators also used later Greek manuscripts which present a somewhat longer version. In several places they have included the expanded readings in footnotes. They also carefully considered the Hebrew texts from Cairo. The Dead Sea texts were not available to them.

Nature and Content

Ecclesiasticus belongs to the category of wisdom literature. It consists of moral and religious instruction and of practical counsel, offered for the most part in a number of "essays" or brief discourses. These are not the terse, highly polished aphorisms which fill most of Proverbs or the long, involved discourses of Job. They stand somewhere in between, being more in the nature of Proverbs 1–9 or Ecclesiastes. In addition the book includes maxims, hymns, prayers, psalms of praise, autobiographical allusions, and eulogies. It may well be a revised and partially structured edition of ben Sira's oral teaching to his students.

Its content is so diverse, however, that no brief summary of it can be given. The book naturally divides itself into two parts (chapters 1–23 and 24–50), each of which begins with a treatise on wisdom. A few units of some length are easily distinguishable. But beyond these the work defies all attempts to outline it in any logical or systematic manner.

Wisdom and the Law

Ben Sira was a scholar and teacher. His life, activity, and thought bridged the gap between the earlier wise men who produced Proverbs and the later rabbis of the Talmud, the commentary on Jewish oral law and tradition. Like the more ancient sages he teaches a wisdom which has developed out of practical experience and observation. It is human-centered, though it reveres God as the source of all wisdom.

Ben Sira makes paramount their dictum that "the fear of the LORD is the beginning of wisdom" (Proverbs 9:10) and interprets it as they did. Fundamentally this means an awesome, reverent acknowledgment of God as creator and sovereign. It includes a commitment to God which involves seeking, trusting, following, and praising God, and eventuates in a life of personal piety. Like the earlier sages ben Sira stresses the rewards that come to one who possesses such wisdom—joy, well-being, and long life. He holds to the doctrine of retribution, confident that the wicked must suffer punishment. He shares their belief that reward and punishment are allotted in this life, for the grave is one's end. Like the authors of Proverbs he personifies wisdom as one who beckons people to follow her. He adopts the concept of Proverbs 8:22-31, which speaks of wisdom as the first product of God's creation.

In other respects, however, ben Sira's thought is very unlike that of the more ancient wisdom teachers. His emphasis is on things not found in Proverbs—the law, the election of Israel as the especially beloved people of the Lord, the Davidic monarchy, and the eternal nature and great importance of the Aaronic priesthood. This difference arises from the fact that ben Sira seems the first to take seriously the identification of wisdom with the law. This is the unique feature of his book and his greatest contribution.

Wisdom *is* the law, "the book of the covenant of the Most High God . . . which Moses commanded us" (24:23). To ben Sira this means fundamentally the Pentateuch—the first five books of the Bible—and primarily its moral rather than ritual prescriptions. But he uses the word "law" in a broader sense, too. It includes all written scripture and the interpretations of it which were being developed. How does one attain wisdom? he asks. By listening to the wise and by meditating on the law (6:32-37).

This identification of wisdom with the law contains two basic implications which distinguish ben Sira from the Old Testament wisdom writers and establish his affinity with the later rabbis.

(1) It makes central *learning*—the study, interpretation, and exposition of scripture and the preservation of traditions.

(2) It takes seriously the major features of Hebrew religious faith and life as these are presented in scripture.

Any thorough attempt to explain what ben Sira meant by "wisdom" would elicit a many-faceted definition. But he himself reduced the many to two:

> All wisdom is the fear of the Lord,
> and in all wisdom there is the fulfilment of the law (19:20).

The one aspect reflects his heritage from the wise men of Proverbs. The other anticipates the development of rabbinic Judaism.

I. THE PROLOGUE

The Prologue is not an integral part of ben Sira's own book but a prefatory statement attached to the Greek version. It is important in that it introduces the Greek translation, witnesses to the developing of the canon of scripture, and testifies concerning the nature and purpose of ben Sira's efforts.

There is no valid reason for denying that ben Sira's own grandson prepared the Greek translation or for doubting the information relating to its date. The **thirty-eighth year of the reign of Euergetes** can refer only to Ptolemy VII Euergetes II Physcon, who ruled around 170-117 B.C. Thus the translation from Hebrew into Greek was made in the years following 132 B.C.—a date compatible with the conclusion that the original was written arund 180 (see below on 50:1-24). The translation was made **for those living abroad**—the Jews of the Diaspora living in Alexandria, whose natural language was Greek. The grandson feared that the Hellenistic culture which surrounded them might obscure their appreciation for Hebrew values—that is, for **living according to the law.**

II. First Treatise on Wisdom (1:1-30)

1:1-10. *The Origin of Wisdom.* This poem contains little that is new. In many respects it may be regarded as a typical wisdom writing. It has three main points:

(1) The Lord is the ultimate source of wisdom (verses 1, 4, 8-9*a*). Obviously ben Sira is thinking of Proverbs 8:22-31, which speaks of wisdom as the first of God's creations. The two lines of verse 4 are synonymous parallels; no distinction should be made here between **wisdom** and **prudent understanding.**

(2) The Lord alone knows wisdom fully (verses 2-3, 6). That God's works are so great as to baffle human beings is a frequent theme in Ecclesiasticus, as in the Old Testament. In the cosmological view of the Hebrews the **abyss** was the subterranean deep, an especially mysterious place.

(3) Humans can know wisdom only as it pleases God to bestow her as a **gift** (verses 9*b*-10). The meaning of verse 10 parallels that of 24:6-8: wisdom is made available to everyone in limited measure, but she is fully supplied to Israel.

1:11-20. *The Nature of Wisdom.* Here ben Sira declares the essential nature of wisdom—**the fear of the Lord.** This phrase was a favorite of Old Testament writers too, and doubtless underwent a long development of meaning. In Ecclesiasticus it is especially rich and full. Here it carries no connotation of terror or trembling dread. Basically it means a reverent recognition of God as the Lord of life and a willingness to live under the obligation which this awareness entails.

1:11-13. These verses could well be a homiletic expansion of Isaiah 11:2-3. But what is said here has many counterparts in Proverbs 1–9 and in Deuteronomy. In verse 11 **is** means "brings" or "results in."

1:14-20. Verse 14*a* recalls such passages as Job 28:28; Psalms 111:10; and Proverbs 1:7; 9:10. **Beginning** may mean starting point or chief part. Either sense is balanced by **full measure** in verse 16—cf. **crown** (verse 18) and **root** (verse 20). Verses 14*b*-15 can be taken to mean that since wisdom's **eternal foundation** rests in Israel (cf. 24:8-9) she is both the inheritance and the legacy of faithful Israelites (cf. 4:16). The rewards listed in verses 16-20 are frequently specified in wisdom literature (cf. Proverbs 3:13-18).

1:22-30. *The Marks of Wisdom.* The heart of this passage, and the logical transition from the preceding, is verse 27. Ben Sira is doubtless reflecting on Proverbs 15:33. He defines the **fear of the Lord** as **wisdom and instruction** (cf. 19:20; 21:11) and identifies **fidelity and meekness** as traits of the wise person.

1:22-26. One who is properly humble avoids **unrighteous anger** and exercises self-control (cf. Proverbs 14:29; 29:22). By waiting patiently for the **right moment** to speak one wins praise from others (cf. 4:20, 23; 20:7). Such a godly person produces **wise sayings** from the **treasuries of wisdom,** but the **sinner** has no appreciation for this. One who desires thus to tap the treasuries of wisdom must **keep the commandments** (cf. 19:20*b*; 24:23; Ecclesiastes 12:13). Then wisdom comes as the Lord's gift.

1:28-30. The wise person does not **disobey** (cf. 2:15), avoids the **divided mind,** is not a **hypocrite** (cf. 32:15; 33:2), and shows no **deceit.** This list of vices, each a denial of steadfast loyalty, seems to reflect Psalm 12:1-4. The **divided mind** (literally "double heart") is that which is not totally committed to God but seeks to serve two masters. With verse 30*a* cf. Matthew 23:12. On **your secrets** see below on 27:16-21.

III. EXPOSITIONS ON FIDELITY AND HUMILITY (2:1–4:20)

These passages further illustrate the characteristics of the wise person described in 1:27.

A. THE ENDURANCE OF TRIALS (2:1-18)

It is possible that this chapter alludes to the second century struggle between those who wished to adopt Hellenistic culture and the orthodox "pious" who resisted it. If so, the **calamity** in verses 1-5 is the Hellenistic threat, and the **sinner who walks along two ways** is the man who is Jewish in religion but Greek in cultural preference. They **who fear the Lord** (verses 7-11, 15-18) are they who adhere to Jewish values only.

2:1-5. *Testing by Affliction.* The Old Testament offers various answers to the riddle of human suffering. One is that suffering is a form of divine discipline. A closely related concept is that suffering is a form of testing or trial. Ben Sira employs both interpretations, though here the element of trial predominates. **My son** is the teacher's normal form of address to the wisdom student in this book, as in Proverbs and in ancient Near Eastern wisdom books generally. **Do not be hasty** means not to be fearful but to respond to the situation with poise. **Men** and **gold** are alike in that neither is acceptable until **tested**.

2:6-11. *Trust in the Lord.* These verses repeat the plea for steadfastness, echoing the thought of Habakkuk 2:4—"the righteous shall live by his faith." They add an assurance of God's help and reward (cf. 34:13-17). Verse 6 is similar to Proverbs 3:5-6, and even more so to Psalm 37:3*a*, 5. The promise of God's **help** recalls Psalm 46:1 and the exhortation to **hope** Psalm 71:5. Verse 9 defines the **reward** as **good things, . . . everlasting joy and mercy,** perhaps under the influence of Psalm 103:4*b*-5*a*. "Everlasting" means, not eternal, but constant or enduring.

The **ancient generations** are the fathers of old (cf. Psalm 22:4-5). The last two questions of verse 10 may be based on Psalm 37:25. In essence they affirm that the righteous are inevitably rewarded and the wicked punished. The language and thought of verse 11 (cf. 17:29; 18:11-14) derive from Exodus 34:6-7*b*.

2:12-14. *Woe to the Faltering.* Ben Sira denounces those who are weak through shallow commitment (**timid hearts . . . slack hands;** cf. 22:18) or through divided loyalties (**walks along two ways;** see above on 1:28-30). They cannot endure trials.

2:15-18. *The Response of the Righteous.* In contrast verses 15-16 describe the response of **those who fear the Lord.** Verse 17 repeats the theme of humility (1:22-27). Verse 18 fits the

271

context awkwardly. It could more naturally follow verse 11, but there is no manuscript evidence for that. The first two lines are based on David's remarks to Gad in II Samuel 24:14. Apparently the meaning is that it is better to receive punishment from the Lord than from other humans. **His mercy**, which is as great as **his majesty**, will temper God's punishment (but cf. 16:11-14).

B. Honoring Parents (3:1-16)

This is the first of three expositions on proper humility. All carry out the theme that meekness is one of the Lord's delights (cf. 1:22-27). It is a commentary on the fifth commandment (Exodus 20:12; Deuteronomy 5:16). Verses 1-9 adopt a positive approach, verses 10-16 a negative. With the entire passage cf. 7:27-28. **Kept in safety** is ben Sira's paraphrase of the "promise" of the commandment. It means essentially **long life** but includes other attendant blessings. Like the commandment itself and other Old Testament passages ben Sira insists on the mother's **right** along with the father's.

3:3-4. *A Means of Atonement.* These verses, together with verses 14-15, suggest one of the most interesting and significant features of ben Sira's thought. The honoring of parents is a means of winning atonement for oneself. That is, deeds performed in obedience to this commandment accumulate as credits or merits which may be used, now or in the future, to help "cancel out" one's sins. The same holds true for deeds of almsgiving (see below on verses 30-31).

Perhaps this belief developed out of an interpretation of Proverbs 16:6: "By loyalty and faithfulness iniquity is atoned for." At any rate Daniel 4:27 most explicitly teaches the same point of view. In later times the doctrine was highly developed and widely held—so much so that early Christians found it necessary to deny it pointedly (cf. Luke 17:10; Galatians 2:16; Ephesians 2:8-9). Ben Sira insisted, however, that no means of atonement was efficacious apart from genuine contrition and repentance (cf. 5:5-6; 34:26; 35:3).

3:5-9. *Other Blessings.* The persons who honor their parents receive further blessings. A son's obedience to the Lord relieves his mother's anxiety over the quality of his life (verse 6b). True honor includes both **word and deed** (cf. Matthew 21:28-31). The stability of a son's newly founded household is affected by the approval or blame of his parents (verse 9).

3:10-16. *Warning Against Disrespect.* On verses 10-12 cf. Proverbs 15:20; 17:6; 23:22. **Lacking in understanding** may mean unlearned but probably suggests the mental deterioration of an aging parent. Verses 14-15 reaffirm verses 3-4 (see comment). **Kindness to a father,** shown in obedience to the commandment, removes one's sins as **fair weather** melts away **frost.** Some manuscripts indicate that verse 16a may have had "despises" instead of **forsakes** and that verse 16b may have read "whoever curses his mother angers the Lord."

C. THE ATTITUDE OF HUMILITY (3:17-29)

Ben Sira exhorts his students to be humble. The Hebrew text of verse 17 reads: "Walk in your wealth humbly [most wisdom students were young aristocrats, people of some means]; then you will be loved more than he who gives gifts." That is, a humble wealthy person is more loved than a proud one, even though the latter distributes gifts freely. On verse 18a cf. Matthew 20:26-27. On verse 18b cf. Proverbs 3:4, 34. On verse 20b cf. I Corinthians 1:26-29.

3:21-24. *Humility in Scholarship.* Ben Sira warns his students against the arrogant presumption that they can know more than God pleases to reveal to them. He counsels them to limit their attention to the law (verse 22a), which is itself more than they can understand fully (verse 23b). Speculation about secret, **hidden** things, which are really beyond their abilities to know, will only involve them in error as it has other **hasty** (presumptuous, conceited?) questioners.

What was this hidden knowledge against which ben Sira warns? Most scholars believe that it was the speculations of

273

Greek philosophy. Another possibility, however, is early esoteric doctrines which the rabbis developed. These doctrines were not to be taught in public. They could be imparted only to one student at a time. They centered on two subjects: cosmological speculation, based on Genesis 1, about what was before, behind, above, or beneath the first day of creation; and theosophical speculation based on the visions in Ezekiel 1; 10.

3:26-29. *Afflictions of the Proud.* The **stubborn mind** stands in sharp contrast to the humble. The **end** of life brings blessing and honor to one who fears the Lord (cf. 1:13; 2:3). But to the **proud** it brings **affliction**, for he accumulates **troubles** as the **sinner** accumulates sins. There is no deliverance for him such as is available to those who call on the Lord (cf. 2:10*d*-11).

3:29. This concluding verse ties the passage together. The **intelligent man** is the antithesis of both the presumptuous (verses 21-24) and the stubborn (verses 26-28). He desires only to listen to wisdom utterances and to reflect on them (cf. 6:32-37; Proverbs 2:2).

D. ALMSGIVING AND EMPATHY (3:30–4:10)

This is the last of the three expositions on humility. Ben Sira teaches that it properly expresses itself through concern for the poor (cf. 7:32-36; 29:8-13).

3:30-31. Like the honoring of parents **almsgiving atones for sin** (see above on 3:3-4). It is another specific illustration of obedience to the law (Deuteronomy 15:7-11). **Kindness** in verse 14 and **almsgiving** here are in Hebrew the same word. Elsewhere it is most frequently translated "righteousness." In verse 14 it carries the general sense of attitudes and acts of "rightness," but here it is used in the specific sense of giving alms.

4:1-6. Cf. Deuteronomy 15:7-11 and Proverbs 3:27-28. The **poor** person's **living** is defined in 29:21 as food and drink, clothing and shelter. On verse 1*b* cf. 29:8. On verse 4 cf.

Matthew 5:42. On verse 5 cf. Proverbs 28:27. On verse 6 cf. Exodus 22:22-23; Deuteronomy 15:9; and Proverbs 17:5.

4:7-10. Rabbi Hillel (late first century B.C.) used to say, "Separate not thyself from the congregation." This meant, make oneself a part of the community by sharing its joys and sorrows. That is what ben Sira is saying. One should show the appropriate attitude toward both the **great man** and the **poor**. It has been suggested that the original Hebrew in verse 8*b* may have meant: "Respond to his 'Shalom!' [literally "peace," the traditional Hebrew greeting] gently"—that is, do not ignore the poor person and refuse to return their greeting (cf. 41:20*a*). Verse 9 means to work for the just acquittal of one being **wronged** by a false accusation in court (cf. verse 27*b*). Verse 10 says to show a father's concern toward **orphans** and a husband's concern toward their widowed mothers.

IV. THE PURSUIT OF WISDOM (4:11–10:5)

A. THE REWARDS OF WISDOM (4:11-19)

The rewards here promised to one who follows wisdom are often mentioned in scattered passages throughout the book. On verse 11 cf. Proverbs 4:8*a*. On verse 12 cf. Proverbs 3:18; 8:17, 35; and the Wisdom of Solomon 8:16-18. **Seek her early** means to give her first priority. Verses 13*b*-14 are very obscure. The language is much like that of 24:8, 10, where **place** means Israel and **minister** refers to the temple service. But these meanings make no clear sense here. Perhaps the idea is simply that God and wisdom are so closely interrelated that God's blessing is wherever she is. Whoever serves wisdom serves God and whoever loves her God loves.

On verse 15*a* cf. Proverbs 8:15-16. On verse 15*b* cf. Proverbs 1:33. On verse 16*b* cf. 1:15; 44:10-13. Wisdom's **discipline** of those who follow her recalls the Lord's testing of God's followers in 2:1-5 (cf. 6:20-21). Her **secrets** are the knowledge and understanding which she has to offer.

B. Excess and Deficiency of Humility (4:20–6:4)

The truly wise person shows neither too much humility nor too little. Too much leads to self-effacement or self-abasement (4:20-29). Too little leads to pride (4:29–6:4).

4:20-28. *Excessive Humility.* Wisdom involves a sense of timing, the ignoring of which will **bring shame**. Of course not all shame is bad. One ought to feel shame at some things, and this proper sense of it brings **glory** to the person (cf. 41:17-23). But the shame mentioned in verses 20b-21a and illustrated in the following verses is improper (cf. 42:1-8).

4:22. Too much shame may lead one to sin. It makes one afraid to stand up for the right. When one lets wrong go unchallenged because of fear of offending the parties involved, one actually harms oneself (cf. verses 9, 27b).

4:23-25. A second example of improper humility is being ashamed to speak out or to share one's counsel when doing so would make a contribution (cf. 20:30-31). Verse 24 is qualified by verse 25 (cf. 5:12; 11:7).

4:26. Excessive humility is also exemplified by those who are **ashamed to confess** their **sins**. They may as well confess, because they could as easily stop a river's flow as have their sins pass unnoticed by God. Elsewhere ben Sira urges confession and repentance (21:1, 6). He assures the penitent of God's willingness to forgive (2:18; 16:11-12; 17:24; 18:11-14).

4:27-28. Verse 27 is almost a restatement of verse 22. To defer to a slave and to **show partiality to a ruler** just because of rank are wrong. Both are acts of self-abasement which deny the right, or **truth**, for which one should **strive**.

4:29-31. *Arrogance.* Ben Sira censures **reckless . . . speech** and attitudes of tyranny, carping, and grasping, all of which reveal a lack of humility. Verse 29 might be paraphrased: "Do not speak more than you perform, but let your deeds match your words" (cf. 23:7-15; Ecclesiastes 5:2-6).

5:1-8. *Self-Reliance.* These verses treat the sin of misplaced confidence. Neither **wealth** nor personal **strength** can offer security. Whoever relies on these neglects proper humility before God, and thus incurs punishment. Ben Sira does not deprecate wealth itself (cf. 31:8) but warns against its dangers (14:3-10; 26:29–27:3; 31:1-2, 5-7).

5:4-8. Ben Sira quickly reviews three wrong attitudes:

(1) Some do not repent because they see no need to. Because they **sinned** and nothing **happened**, they assume that nothing will happen. In reply ben Sira argues (from Exodus 34:6) that punishment is certain but is delayed by the Lord's slowness **to anger** (cf. Exodus 34:6).

(2) Others sin continually, but are **confident** that **atonement** can be easily won (see above on 3:30-31; cf. 24:25-26).

(3) Still others find false security in God's abundant **mercy** and willingness to **forgive.** Ben Sira points out that God's **wrath** is as real as God's **mercy** (cf. 16:11-14). In verse 7 he urges immediate repentance instead of delay **from day to day.** On verse 8 cf. Proverbs 10:2; 11:4.

5:9–6:1. *Insincerity of Speech.* Failure to have the proper attitude of humility causes sins of speech. Sometimes pride will not let one keep silent but drives one to speak out at every opportunity (verse 9). But instead of speaking consistently (verse 10), deliberately (verse 11), and thoughtfully (verse 12), one speaks "opportunistically," saying whatever the occasion seems to demand (verse 9). This is a type of **double-tongued** speech and follows naturally from being double-minded (see above on 1:28-30). On verse 11 cf. 11:7-8. On verse 12 cf. 20:6. On verse 13*a* cf. 27:4-7; Proverbs 18:21; and Matthew 12:37. On verse 13*b* cf. 14:1; 22:27; and 23:8.

5:14–6:1. Slander (cf. 28:13-16) is another type of **double-tongued** speech. The **slanderer** deserves a thief's punishment because, having ambushed the victim, the slander steals the victim's reputation. In summary, one whose pride leads to speaking insincerely becomes an **enemy** to others (5:15–6:1).

6:2-4. *Sensuality.* The fourth example of pride is one who is abandoned to a passionate life. The Greek and Hebrew texts of verse 2 differ markedly. The Greek yields no satisfactory sense. It seems better, therefore, to interpret the verse from the Hebrew text, which may be paraphrased: "Do not let passion rule over you, thinking that it will increase your vigor." It has instead the opposite effect, destroying your virility and making you an object of ridicule (verses 3-4).

C. FIDELITY IN FRIENDSHIP (6:5-17)

6:5-7. *Choosing Friends.* Verse 5 offers a contrast to 5:15–6:1. Speaking with a double tongue causes enmity but speaking pleasantly **multiplies friends** (cf. 20:13; Proverbs 16:21, 23). For **courtesies** the Hebrew reads "those who say peace"—that is, those who greet you with the traditional salutation (see above on 4:7-10). This fits well with verse 6a. While one should seek a peaceful relationship with **many**, one's closest confidants should be few indeed (cf. 8:17; 9:14; 37:7-15). Any prospective friend should be tested (cf. 19:4a).

6:8-13. *False Friends.* Some are "fair-weather friends" only, disappearing in time of **trouble** or loss (cf. 37:1-6; Proverbs 19:6). Among true friends a **quarrel** remains a private matter. The false friend, however, publicizes it, seeking to **disgrace** his fellow (cf. 27:16-21; Proverbs 25:8-10).

6:14-17. *The True Friend.* In contrast a **faithful friend** is invaluable (cf. 7:18), adding happiness and health to life (cf. 9:10). A true friend is a gift from the Lord and is to be regarded as oneself.

D. ATTAINING WISDOM (6:18-37)

Cf. 4:11-19; 14:20–15:10; 39:1-11.

6:18-22. *Working for Wisdom.* To obtain wisdom one should begin in **youth** (cf. 25:3). Then knowledge will increase through time, as did ben Sira's (24:30-31), and flower in old age (cf. 25:4-6). The figure of the farmer in verse 19 teaches that while one must work for wisdom's **produce**, the labor seems little in comparison with the richness of **her good harvest** (cf. 24:19-21).

The simile of wisdom as a weight-lifting **stone** suggests again her severe testing (cf. 4:17). The weak drop her quickly because the value of carrying her is not immediately clear to them (verse 22*b*). In the Hebrew verse 22 seems to play on a word which can be read both as "discipline" (Greek **wisdom**) and as "withdrawn," hence **not manifest.**

6:23-31. *Submission to Wisdom.* After addressing his student in a familiar pattern (verse 23) ben Sira counsels submission to wisdom. He uses the figures of a slave and a yoke bearer. The illustration of the slave (verses 24, 29) seems clearly to have been inspired by Psalm 105:16-22, which recalls how Joseph was sold as a slave. The **fetters** and the **collar** were Joseph's to wear, for the Lord was testing him.

Ben Sira's speaking of wisdom as a **yoke** (verses 25, 30) is a very rich figure. The later rabbis referred to the law as a yoke. Indeed they called the recitation of the Shema (Deuteronomy 6:4-5: **Hear, O Israel . . .**) the receiving of the yoke. That is, in saying these words one proclaims the sovereignty of God and takes upon oneself the obligation of obedience to God's law. This is what ben Sira is saying. He even uses words from the Shema in verse 26. To him wisdom and the law are the same thing; he identifies them explicitly (cf. 19:20; 24:23).

6:28-30. One who bears the yoke then finds **rest** (cf. Jesus' use of the figure in Matthew 11:29-30). **At last** all of wisdom's **fetters** cease to be burdens and become the joy and glory of life. The **strong protection,** the **glorious robe,** and the **golden ornament** may have been inspired by recollection of the signet ring, fine linen garments, and gold chain which Pharaoh bestowed on Joseph as the reward for his wisdom (Genesis 41:42).

The **cord of blue** again suggests the law. In Numbers 15:38-39 the Israelites are told to wear cords of blue on each tassel of their garments as a reminder of it. The **crown of gladness** (cf. 1:11; 15:6) recalls the crown which wisdom bestows in Proverbs 4:9.

6:32-37. *The Way to Wisdom.* On the practical level how does one attain wisdom? In two ways, ben Sira says: by listening to the **wise** (verses 33-36) and by reflecting on the law (verse 37; cf. 3:29; Proverbs 2:2; 18:15; 22:17). Ben Sira often encourages the youth to attend the **elders** and the sages (cf. 8:8-9; 9:15; 25:3-6).

On verse 35 cf. 18:28-29. Meditating on the law (verse 37) culminates in the Lord's gift of wisdom (cf. 14:20-21; 15:1; 32:15*a*).

E. WARNINGS AND PRECEPTS (7:1–9:16)

7:1-17. *Warning Against Presumptuousness.* After a general introduction (verses 1-3) ben Sira draws illustrations from practical life. He warns his students against pride and the inevitable punishment which follows it.

7:4-7. Avoid self-exaltation (cf. Proverbs 25:6-7; Luke 14:8-11; 18:9-14) and political ambition. Those who actively seek a judgeship may find that they cannot execute the office. Or they may yield to its temptations (cf. 4:9, 27), thus incurring **disgrace**.

7:8-10. Presumptuous persons do not hesitate to repeat a sin. They are confident that they can easily placate God by offering many sacrifices. Ben Sira denounces such repetition of sin (cf. 5:5; 34:25-26). He denies that a sacrifice offered in this spirit could be acceptable to God (cf. 34:19; 35:12; Proverbs 21:27). Forgiveness necessitates steadfastness in **prayer** (cf. 21:1) and the giving of **alms** (see above on 3:30-31).

7:11-16. Ben Sira warns against insensitivity to the poverty-stricken (verse 11), lying, verbosity, hatred of manual **labor** or **farm work**, and association with **sinners**. These bring quick punishment from God (cf. 5:7; 16:11).

7:17. In contrast to such pride ben Sira exhorts his students to humility. There is a marked difference between the reading of the Hebrew and Greek texts (see the Revised Standard Version footnote). The Hebrew suggests that one should be humble because the fate of all humans is death and the dissolution of the body. The Greek refers, not to the natural end of all people, but to the **punishment of the ungodly.** That the Hebrew text is to be preferred is supported by the nearly parallel thought in 10:9-11.

7:18-36. *Duties Toward Various Persons.* Ben Sira greatly values friendship (cf. 6:14-17). The location of **Ophir** is disputed, but its **gold** was of fine quality. Verse 19 resembles Proverbs 31:10. The Hebrew text of verse 19a reads "reject not," meaning "do not divorce" (cf. verse 26; 26:1-4, 13-18). The disciplined **servant** is mentioned again in 33:30-31. Their **freedom** is that which is due them by law after six years of labor (cf. Exodus 21:2; Deuteronomy 15:12-18).

7:22-25. Verse 22 mentions the only nonpersonal relationship in the list. As in Proverbs 27:23-27 the profit motive underlies one's concern for **cattle**, though the element of kindness to beasts may not be altogether absent (cf. Proverbs 12:10; Deuteronomy 25:4). In all probability verse 23 alludes to sons (cf. 30:1-13) since **daughters** are the subject of verses 24-25. Ben Sira regards daughters as especially troublesome (cf. 22:3-6; 42:9-11). The father's duty is to discipline them most strictly and to arrange **marriage** for them.

7:26-28. Verse 26 can be interpreted several ways. Perhaps it simply means to divorce an evil **wife** (cf. 25:26) but not a good one (cf. verse 19). Here one's duty to one's **parents** (cf. Exodus 20:12) rests on gratitude. In 3:1-16 the motivation is almost entirely the selfish desire for blessings.

7:29-31. Ben Sira advises regard for the Lord's **priests**. He commends the practice of giving them certain portions of the sacrifices and offerings (cf. 45:20-22). This is commanded in Exodus 29:27-28; Leviticus 7:31-36; and Numbers 18:8-20 as a concession to the priests, who could not be otherwise gainfully employed. On the whole ritualistic matters do not loom large in ben Sira's thinking, but he has an extraordinary appreciation for the priesthood (cf. 45:6-22; 50:1-21).

7:32-36. At first sight verses 32a and 33a seem to be a simple repetition of the plea for almsgiving (3:30-31; cf. 29:8-13). But more than that is involved in this passage. The rabbis employed a concept which they called "deeds of kindness" and sharply distinguished such benevolence from almsgiving. It can be seen that in Ecclesiasticus this doctine of "deeds of kindness" is already beginning to take shape.

Such deeds include preparation or burial of a corpse (cf. 38:16; Tobit 1:17), emphatic mourning (cf. 22:11-12; 38:17; Romans

12:15), and visitation of the sick (cf. Matthew 25:36; James 5:14-15). In 17:22; 35:2; and 40:17 ben Sira uses the words "almsgiving" and "kindness" to denote the two principal branches of charity.

8:1–9:16. *Proper Relationships.* Prudent people avoid quarreling with the **powerful**, the **rich**, and the **chatterer**. They know that the right is often overshadowed by strength, wealth, and words (on verse 3*b* cf. verse 10; Proverbs 26:20-21). They avoid the **ill-bred** and show proper respect to the penitent, the elderly (cf. 3:12-13), and the dead. The meaning of verse 4*b* is given by 22:3*a*; cf. 23:14.

8:8-9. One should heed the **sages** and the **aged** (cf. 6:34-36; 25:4-6). It is possible that their **discourse** refers to the "oral law," which circulated alongside the "written law" (the canonical scriptures). In general it was exposition and commentary on the written law, passed along through a chain of tradition. In the early Christian centuries it was reduced to written form, now preserved in the Talmud. By the time of ben Sira the oral law probably had begun to assume a definite form. **Answer** in verse 9*d* means true counsel to one in need.

8:10-19. These verses treat persons and situations which the wise person should avoid:

(1) association with a **sinner** or an **insolent fellow**, who will use **your words** against you;

(2) lending to the strong (cf. 29:4; such a lender will soon learn the meaning of "might makes right");

(3) giving excessive **surety** (cf. 29:20; Proverbs 6:1-5);

(4) suing a **judge** (cf. verses 1-3);

(5) traveling with a **foolhardy fellow**;

(6) association with a **wrathful man** (the **wilderness** is open country, the uninhabited area between towns);

(7) sharing confidential matters with a **fool** or a **stranger** (cf. 6:6*b*; 9:14; see below on 27:16-21).

Divulge in verse 18 comes from a verb meaning to "bring forth a child"—that is, you do not know what "offspring" he may produce from your words.

9:1-9. Ben Sira praises the good wife (26:1-4, 13-18). Yet for the most part he is suspicious, antagonistic, and even openly hostile toward women (cf. 25:16-26; 26:6-12; 42:14). These verses concern proper conduct toward them. One should be neither **jealous** of his wife—lest the jealousy itself produce the thing feared (verse 1)—nor overly submissive (verse 2). To keep company with the **loose woman** or the **woman singer** is to risk entrapment (cf. Proverbs 7:22-23; 22:14; 23:27). Gazing at a **virgin** invites penalty (cf. Deuteronomy 22:28-29). Consort with **harlots** can lead to loss of money (cf. Proverbs 5:10; 29:3). Verse 7 recalls Proverbs 7:7-12. On verse 8*a* cf. 25:21 and Proverbs 6:25. Verse 8*b* refers to the wife of **another** (cf. 41:21*c*). On verse 9 cf. 19:2-3 and 26:22. **Destruction** as the adulterer's punishment is figurative. The death penalty of Leviticus 20:10 and Deuteronomy 22:22 was not enforced in ben Sira's time (see below on 23:22-27).

9:10-16. These verses conclude the rather lengthy section begun in 8:1. On friendship cf. 6:14-17 and 7:18. Verses 11-12 treat a proper relationship toward the **sinner** (cf. 7:16). Though it is certain that the sinner's **end** will be punishment, verse 11*b* indicates that no one knows when or in what form it will come. On envying sinners cf. Psalms 37:1-2; 73:3, 17 and Proverbs 24:1.

Verse 13 counsels caution in the presence of rulers (cf. Proverbs 16:14; 20:2). Ben Sira may well be speaking from personal experience here (cf. 51:1-7). The **city battlements** were the topmost fortified walls, a place of great danger. Finally he advises one to know which **neighbors are wise** and **consult** only with them (cf. 8:17). One should limit **discussion** to the law (cf. 2:16*b*; Psalm 1:2) and **glorying** to the **fear of the Lord** (cf. 10:22).

F. Wisdom in Rulers (9:17–10:5)

9:17-18. Just as the finished product witnesses the **skill** of the **craftsmen**, so **speech** testifies to the ruler's wisdom or lack of it (cf. 4:24; 5:13; 27:6-7).

10:1-5. The subjects reflect the personality of the **ruler**. The

wise magistrate—that is, king—**will educate** (discipline) **his people**. Under his **well ordered** rule the **city will grow**. But an **undisciplined king will ruin** his subjects. All this is strictly controlled by the Lord, however. No king can be wise and successful apart from the Lord's gift of wisdom. In verse 5 **scribe** reflects the Greek text's misunderstanding of the original Hebrew word "law maker" or "law enforcer"—that is, ruler (see the Revised Standard Version footnote).

V. REFLECTIONS ON PRIDE AND WEALTH (10:6–15:10)

A. EIGHT DISCUSSIONS ON PRIDE (10:6–11:28)

At first sight these passages appear to treat widely diverse subjects. In the past they have not been regarded as a literary unit. It may be, however, that they are a series of homiletic expositions based on the Prayer of Hannah in I Samuel 2:1-10. If so, these passages are surely among the earliest recognized homilies on scripture.

In brief the Prayer of Hannah proclaims the uniqueness of God, denounces human pride, asserts God's knowledge of every person's deeds, and declares that God controls the fortunes of each life as God controls life and death itself. Each of ben Sira's discourses elucidates one or more of these points. But the underlying theme of the whole section is the inappropriateness of human pride. Presumably the location of the expositions in the book is due to the content of 10:4-5 immediately preceding, which reminded ben Sira of the closing sentence of the psalm in I Samuel.

10:6-18. *Warning Against Pride.* This first discourse teaches that the vicissitudes of private and national life are due to the sin of pride. Anger, **insolence, arrogance, injustice,** and greed are all forms of pride. These cause nations to rise and fall (verse 8; cf. verses 15-17) as do individuals (verses 13c-14; cf. 7:11b). On the whole these verses seem to be based on I Samuel 2:3. The specific content of verse 6 may derive from Leviticus 19:17-18.

10:9-11. These verses reflect I Samuel 2:6. They stress the impropriety of human pride in the light of the lowly human nature. As a creature of God one is **dust and ashes** (cf. 17:32). Human life at best is brief and one's fate is death (see above on 7:17).

10:12-13b. Verse 12 teaches that the **beginning**—that is, the essence (cf. 1:14)—of pride is the refusal to recognize one's dependence on God. To **depart from the Lord** is to deny the Creator. Verse 13ab means that when persons begin to feel pride, they sin. If one continues in it, sins are piled up (cf. 3:27; 5:5).

10:13c-18. Since the Lord controls the government of the earth (verses 4-5), the Lord debases proud rulers and **nations. Them** in verse 13cd means the **rulers** of verse 14a. God elevates the **humble in their place.** With these verses cf. I Samuel 2:4, 8, 10. Verses 14-17 also resemble Isaiah 40:15-17, 23-24. Verse 18 returns to the thought of verses 9-11.

10:19-25. *The Truly Honorable.* These verses are inspired by I Samuel 2:7-8. Who deserve **honor?** ben Sira asks. **Those who fear the Lord**—that is, who keep the **commandments** (cf. 1:26-27; 19:20). Those who do not are **unworthy** of it. People honor **their leader,** but the Lord honors followers (verse 20). Whatever one's station in life, the highest **glory** derives from fear of the Lord (verses 22, 24; cf. 1:11; 9:16; 25:10-11). Despising the **intelligent poor man** or honoring the sinner is therefore wrong. A wise person, even though a **servant,** should rule over **free men,** and a **man of understanding** will accept this as a proper relationship (verse 25; cf. Proverbs 17:2).

10:26–11:1. *The Exaltation of the Humbly Wise.* This third discourse is based on I Samuel 2:3, 7-8. Ben Sira reminds his students that exaltation or debasement is the Lord's prerogative, not the individual's own. He explains that the proper **humility** which glorifies one involves honest self-appraisal (verse 28). Ostentatious **display of . . . wisdom** and boasting in **want** are prideful forms of self-exaltation. They can no more be justified than can self-abasement (verse 29).

Verse 27 is an elaboration of verse 26b (cf. Proverbs 12:9).

Intelligent persons accept their station in life, confident that they are **honored** though poor. But such persons will be even more honored when the Lord elevates them to a seat **among the great** (11:1; instead of "great" the Hebrew text reads "princes").

11:2-6. *Deceptive Appearances.* Ben Sira warns against the pride which trusts in present **appearance,** oblivious to the fact that the Lord can mysteriously reverse human fortunes. This passage expounds I Samuel 2:4-5, 7-8. One should trust neither looks, size, nor dress (verses 2-4). Verse 2 recalls I Samuel 16:7. Verse 3 may have been a popular proverb (cf. Proverbs 30:24). **Fine clothes** as an illustration of false pride may have been suggested by Isaiah 47:1-2. Verse 4*b* repeats the theme of 10:26–11:1 that self-exaltation is improper. Only the Lord exalts (cf. I Samuel 2:7). Human beings cannot understand the reversal of fortunes spoken of in verses 5-6 (cf. 10:4, 14; I Samuel 15:24-28; 16:6-13). It results from the Lord's knowledge (I Samuel 2:3*c*).

11:7-9. *Impudent Speech.* This concise discourse is the fifth in the series on pride. It expounds I Samuel 2:3. The need to be considerate in passing judgment is stated elsewhere (see 5:11-12; 19:13-17). Verse 9*a* recalls Proverbs 26:17.

11:10-13. *Against the Self-Made Person.* This passage is perhaps based on I Samuel 2:7-8. Ben Sira condemns the false pride by which one seeks to be enriched by one's own efforts. The person who is overanxious in pursuit of wealth fails to find it. Instead they incur inescapable punishment (cf. Proverbs 21:5*b*; 28:20*b*). Presumably the reason is that haste leads one to commit ethical crimes—oppression and dishonesty, for example. Yet in contrast the Lord can elevate from a **low estate** the **slow** and the poverty-stricken.

11:14-20. *Wealth No Security Against Death.* In the seventh exposition ben Sira warns against prideful reliance on wealth. The Lord's reward is the only security. In effect verse 14 combines Deuteronomy 30:15 and I Samuel 2:6-7. Verses 15-16 (see the Revised Standard Version footnote) elaborate verse 14 and may have been a part of the original text. Only that which the Lord confers on one is enduring. The wealth which one attains through one's own efforts cannot secure one's life (cf. I Samuel 2:9).

11:21-25. *Wealth No Security Against Loss.* This passage is closely related to the two preceding. Verses 10-13 concern one who tries to attain wealth but cannot. Verses 14-20 describe one who attains it but dies with it. These verses concern one who attains it but loses it. Verses 21-22 repeat the thought of verses 17 and 20, that God's **blessing** is constant and reliable (cf. Proverbs 23:17-18). Just as **quickly** as the Lord can **enrich** the poor, however, the Lord can impoverish the wealthy.

Some wealthy people look for new sources of wealth (verse 23). Others relax to enjoy their gains (verse 24; cf. 5:1). In their pride both fail to recognize the nearness of the **adversity** to which the Lord can reduce them. When it comes, past **prosperity** is not of much comfort (verse 25; cf. verse 27; 18:25-26).

11:26-28. *Conclusion of the Discourses on Pride.* These verses are really pertinent to the whole series of expositions begun in 10:6. Ben Sira does not believe in the Pharisee's doctrine of resurrection. He believes that God's rewards and punishment must come to the individual in this life. At times, to be sure, retribution is delayed (cf. 5:4). But even if it is delayed to the last day of life, it will come then. Thus not until the **day of death** can one be certain of God's final judgment concerning one's life.

The saying **Call no one happy before his death** was apparently a commonplace in the ancient world. The Hebrew text of verse 28*b* reads: "A man will be known through his latter end," which in essence repeats verses 26-27. The Greek suggests that if one does escape retribution before death, it will be visited on **his children** (cf. 40:15; 41:6-7).

B. Warnings Against Exploiters (11:29–13:13)

11:29-34. *The Stranger.* There is danger in admitting a stranger into the family circle (cf. Proverbs 24:15). Their **mind** is set to entrap the host and to probe the host's **weakness**. They turn even one's virtues into faults (verse 31). If they find a **spark**—minor flaw—they fan it into flame. On verse 32*b* cf. Proverbs 1:11. On verses 33*a* and 34*b* cf. Proverbs 6:18-19.

12:1-7. *The Unworthy Recipient of Alms.* Elsewhere ben Sira unreservedly praises almsgiving (cf. 3:30–4:6; 29:8-13). Only here does he warn against giving to the **ungodly**. The reason is that a gift to such a person will not be rewarded, as would a gift to the righteous one (verse 2). On the contrary it will be used against one (verse 5). Furthermore withholding a gift helps God to punish the sinner (verse 6; contrast Romans 12:19-21).

The general, rather bland statement of verse 3 may have arisen from a misunderstanding of the Hebrew text, which may be paraphrased: "No good comes to him who helps the wicked, for this is not a valid act of almsgiving." The rabbis also knew that harm could come from indiscriminate giving, but generally they discounted this.

12:8-18. *Enemies.* When people are prosperous, people flock around them. It is impossible to distinguish a true friend (cf. 6:5-13). In **adversity,** though, an **enemy** is easily identified. He is the one waiting to take advantage of the unfortunate (cf. verse 17*a*; Proverbs 14:20; 19:4-7). The Hebrew text of verse 9*a* reads: "When one prospers even his enemy is his friend"—a more natural reading in the context.

One should guard against the enemy's deceptive appearance (cf. 27:22-23; Proverbs 26:23-25), for this wickedness will show itself just as surely as corrosion will appear on an unpolished bronze **mirror.** But polishing will keep the corrosion away (verse 11*cd*) and vigilance will keep an enemy's wickedness from beclouding one's life. Should one suffer misfortune, however, the enemy will take advantage of it (verse 17). Previously hidden hostility will then be quite apparent in acts of scoffing derision (verse 18).

13:1-8. *The Rich.* Verses 1-3 introduce the discussion of the rich (verses 4-8) and the powerful (verses 9-13). **Will become like him** would better read as in the Hebrew "will learn his way." It is not that association with a **proud man** makes one proud, any more than touching **pitch** makes one "pitch-like." The point is, as the following verses show, that touching pitch stains one. Whoever associates with the proud will be **defiled**—that is, will suffer evil by them. In any such association the poor and the weak get the worst of it (verse 2). Rich wrongdoers complain as if they had been wronged. Poor victims must apologize as if they had committed the wrong (verse 3). Verses 1-2 are much like verses 15-20. Verse 3 is like verses 21-23.

13:4-8. There is an interesting comparison between these verses and 7:22. The **rich man** will treat you like cattle, keeping you only if you are profitable to him. Though he pretends concern for your needs (verse 6) his only real interest is in what he can get from you. Should you accept an invitation to dine on his rich foods you will be impoverished by having to return the favor (cf. Proverbs 23:1-3, 6-7). Having thus deceived and **humiliated** you he will openly **deride you.**

13:9-13. *The Powerful.* Verses 9-10 stress the need for tact in the presence of the **powerful man.** The chief content of the passage is the warning in verses 11-13 against the ruler's interrogation by which he seeks to exploit you. The questioner **will not hesitate** to use your information to inflict punishments. Wise persons, aware of danger, will be restrained in their answers. Since verses 9-10 are so similar to Proverbs 25:6-7, verse 11*cd* may have been inspired by Proverbs 25:2*b*, "The glory of kings is to search things out." If so, ben Sira gives the line an interesting twist of interpretation.

C. WEALTH (13:15–14:19)

13:15-20. *Social Incompatibility of Rich and Poor.* This passage expands the thought of verse 2. In human relationships, as in those among animals, likes attract (cf. 27:9*a*), unlikes repel, and the strong **prey** on the weak. In verse 15 **his neighbor** is misleading. It means the person who is **like himself** (verse 16*b*). On verse 20 cf. Proverbs 29:27.

13:21-23. *Society's Preference for the Rich.* These verses expand verse 3. The public measures one by economic status. The rich can say or do no wrong, the poor no right. Cf. Proverbs 14:20; 19:4, 7; and Ecclesiastes 9:16. Contrast ben Sira's assertion that it is not right to despise an intelligent poor man (10:23).

13:24-14:2. *The Joy of a Clear Conscience.* In the passage above, ben Sira has spoken as if "rich" and "unrighteous" were synonymous. He knows, however, that wealth is not in itself bad. In verse 24a he offers the needed corrective (cf. 31:8-11). It is not wealth that makes persons happy, nor **poverty** that makes them sad—contrary to the popular view (verse 24b). It is the condition of the **heart**—the moral and spiritual life—which reflects in **his countenance** (cf. Proverbs 15:13).

Scholars are the single exception, he explains. They scowl, not because they are sinners, but because thinking is such hard work! The happy person is one who avoids **sin** and the guilty conscience which it causes (14:1-2). To **blunder** with the **lips** is to express the evil of one's mind (cf. Mark 7:18-23).

14:3-10. *The Unhappy Rich.* Wealth brings no joy to the **stingy man** (verses 3-8, 10) nor to the **greedy**. His **property** is of no use because it does not satisfy him (cf. Ecclesiastes 5:10). The folly of the miser who dies and leaves wealth to others (verse 4) is a favorite theme in wisdom literature. The **grudging** in spirit is actually harmful, whether the misers ignore their own needs or those of others (verses 5-8; cf. Proverbs 11:17). Even if they seize another's property the **greedy** cannot be happy.

14:11-19. *Proper Use of Wealth.* The wise use whatever wealth they have to make life pleasant for themselves and others, realizing that they must die. This passage appears to be a discourse on Psalm 49, even though the general subject of the psalm is a rebuke of those who foolishly trust in wealth. Ben Sira reinterprets its major theme.

14:11-16. The wise know that **death will not delay** forever and that at death they will descend to **Hades** (cf. Psalm 49:9b, 11a, 14; Ecclesiastes 9:10) where there is no **luxury**. Hades is not hell but the Hebrew Sheol or the Pit—the abode of the dead, conceived of as a gloomy, underground chamber. It is the common destination of all people, though not a place of punishment or reward. The **decree** or covenant **of Hades** is God's order which consigns a person there (cf. 41:3).

While no one knows the exact day of their death (verse 12*b*) they do know that they are "appointed for Sheol" (Psalm 49:14). They must leave their property to others (cf. verse 4; Psalm 49:17). Therefore the best course is to give what one can to oneself, to the Lord, and to others. In turn one should receive what comes, all the while practicing a kind of beneficent self-deceit by which both flippancy and morbid brooding concerning their ultimate fate are avoided (verse 16*a*; cf. Ecclesiastes 5:18-20).

14:17-19. Like **all living beings** a person will **become old** and **die**. The **decree** or covenant of death, stated in Genesis 2:17, applies to all **generations** and to every person.

D. Intimate Association With Wisdom (14:20—15:10)

This passage should be read with Proverbs 8:32–9:6.

14:20-27. Ben Sira repeatedly counsels close association with wisdom (cf. 4:11-19; 6:18-37). Here he uses three figures of speech to suggest the student's proper approach to her. She is choice game which the **hunter** should stalk. She is a woman against whose **house** the hunter should encamp. She is a lush tree in whose **boughs** the hunter should nest for **shelter**. The Hebrew of verse 26*a* reads: "He builds his nest in her foliage."

15:1-6. To live intimately with wisdom means to keep the **law**. The one who does this will enjoy her rewards, which are refreshments (verse 3; cf. 24:19-21), security (verse 4; cf. 24:22), exaltation (verse 5; cf. 4:11; 11:1; 21:17), joy (verse 6*a*; cf. 1:11; 6:31), and an enduring reputation (verse 6*b*; cf. 39:9).

The figure of wisdom as a **mother** is used elsewhere only in a Hebrew fragment of 51:13-20 discovered among the Dead Sea Scrolls. The figure of **bread** and **water** in later times was frequently applied by the rabbis to the law.

15:7-10. In contrast to those who keep the law the **foolish** and the **sinful** cannot find wisdom, for her paths are justice and righteousness (cf. Proverbs 8:20). Neither can they rightly praise God, who is the source of wisdom. Apparently these verses are ben Sira's interpretation of Proverbs 27:21*b*, "a man is judged by his praise." It has been suggested that those denounced here are hellenizing Jews, who have neglected the law in the pursuit of Greek culture.

VI. SIN AND WRATH: REPENTANCE AND MERCY (15:11–18:14)

A. HUMAN RESPONSIBILITY FOR SIN (15:11-20)

15:11-13. No one should argue that the Lord causes people to sin. Such a thing would be impossible for two reasons. First, the Lord does not want a person to be sinful. Second, hating sin, the Lord would never deliberately bring it about. In verse 13*b* the Hebrew text is preferable: "and will not bring them upon those who fear him."

15:14-16. If humans sin it is their own responsibility, for God **created** them with the **power of choice**. Human **inclination** or "impulse" (Hebrew *yetzer*) here means the free will which each person possesses to govern their own conduct. By it they may choose between **fire and water**—opposite types of conduct, which are essentially obedience and disobedience to the **commandments** (see above on 10:19-25).

Later the rabbis developed an important and intricate theological doctrine in which they distinguished two *yetzers* within each person—the impulse to good and the impulse to evil. They conceived each of these as an innate drive competing for dominance in the person's life. These refinements were not fully known to ben Sira, but in 37:3 he does lament the creation of the "evil imagination"—that is, impulse.

15:17-20. The Lord does not determine whether one chooses obedience to the law, which leads to **life**, or disobedience, which leads eventually to **death**. But the Lord carefully observes the choice.

B. The Certainty of Retribution (16:1-14)

God cannot let wickedness go unpunished. Ben Sira offers five illustrations of the inevitability of retribution. One (verses 1-4) is based on his own personal experience (verse 5a). The others (verses 6-10) are drawn from his knowledge of history (verse 5b).

16:1-4. Against the usual view, which highly valued numerous **children**, ben Sira argues that quality is better than quantity. **Ungodly sons** are no cause for rejoicing and will not survive. **One** righteous son is preferable to a **thousand** godless ones, for he can build a city (verse 4a; cf. 10:1-5; 40:19a). The **lawless** will bring on its ruin (cf. 21:3; Proverbs 11:30).

16:6-10. As wickedness bursts into flame **in an assembly of sinners** (cf. 21:9), so God's **wrath** breaks out on a sinful **nation**. For example, **the ancient giants who revolted** were destroyed in the Flood (cf. Genesis 6:1-4). The city of Sodom perished for its sin (verse 8; cf. Genesis 19:12-25). A nation **devoted to destruction** (presumably the Canaanites) was destroyed. And Moses' followers who complained of hardships in the desert died before they could enter the Promised Land (Numbers 11:21; 14:22-24).

16:11-16. Retribution was sure in the past, and it is no less so in the present. God's **mercy and wrath** are equally real (see above on 5:4-7). Each person receives **according to his deeds.** Verse 14 is subject to two interpretations. Perhaps it means God will exert every effort to be merciful (cf. 2:11; 17:29). Yet in the last analysis one's deeds determine the issue—a paraphrase of Psalm 62:12. Or it may mean God will not fail to credit one with every good deed performed (see above on 3:3-4), just as God will not fail to punish one for every sin. It is uncertain whether verses 15-16 were a part of the original text (see the Revised Standard Version footnote). They recall God's punishment of the Egyptians (Exodus 5:2; 10:21-23; 11:7) as another example of past retribution.

C. The Folly of Expecting to Escape God's Notice (16:17-23)

The fool (verse 23) thinks that God does not judge according to deeds because in so vast a universe the individual is too insignificant for God to notice (cf. Isaiah 40:27-28). Verses 18-19 may be ben Sira's reply to the question in verse 17. More probably they continue the fool's statement by declaring that God is involved with the larger forces of nature rather than with individuals. **Highest heaven** is probably a rhetorical superlative, as in Old Testament usage, rather than an expression of the later concept of heaven as having distinct levels or stages (cf. II Corinthians 12:2). On **abyss** see above on 1:1-10.

16:20-22. The Greek text suggests that God's **works** are so great that they surpass all human understanding. Besides no one knows if or when God's **justice** will express itself in retribution. And at any rate God's **covenant**—that is, decree (cf. 14:12, 17)—will not be felt for a long time yet. The Hebrew text follows more closely the thought of verse 17 and may be paraphrased: God does not notice me or observe my ways (verse 20). If I sin no one sees it; if I deal falsely in secret no one knows it (verse 21); if I perform righteous works no one declares it. What hope is there? For God's retribution is remote and uncertain (verse 22).

The sharpest difference between the two is that the Hebrew more pointedly denies both God's punishment of sin and his reward of righteousness. That ben Sira specifically deals with each of these points in 17:20, 22 suggests that the Hebrew text is closer to the original here.

D. God's Concern as Shown in Creation (16:24–17:14)

16:24-30. *Creation of the Cosmos.* After a brief introduction ben Sira affirms that God created the cosmos. God arranged an

eternal order by which its various parts have their **divisions** and **dominion**. He refers, of course, to light and darkness, the firmament, the waters, the luminaries, etc. (Genesis 1:3-19). These **neither hunger nor grow weary** nor **cease from their labors** (cf. 43:10), in contrast to humans and animals. God **filled** the **earth** with **good things** (food for the creatures) and with living beings, which **return** to the earth at death. Cf. Psalm 104.

17:1-14. *Creation of Human Beings.* In this section ben Sira deals more directly with the skeptic's denial that God is concerned for humans.

17:1-10. God **created man . . . in his own image** so that humans have **authority** over the animals (cf. Genesis 1:26-28; 9:2; 2:7), though after a **limited** lifespan they die. God gave all people physical attributes—the **five operations** of verse 5 (Revised Standard Version footnote) are the five senses. They have mental capacity, so that they can see God's **works** and **praise** God for them.

17:11-13. *Creation of the Covenant.* This is the climax of the passage (cf. 45:5). In the revelation at Sinai (verse 13; cf. Exodus 19:16-20) God entered into **covenant** with Israel (cf. Exodus 24). God **showed them his judgments**—in a general sense the law as a whole; in a more specific sense the commandments of Exodus 20–23. Thus God gave them the law which confers on them both **life** and **knowledge**. Cf. Deuteronomy 4:6, which may be the basis of what is often said to be ben Sira's major contribution to wisdom literature—his identification of wisdom with the law (see below on 24:23).

17:14. This is a summary of all the commandments. Perhaps the first line refers to the Decalogue (Exodus 20:1-17) and the second line to Exodus 21–23 or Leviticus 19:18*b*. Cf. Jesus' summary in Matthew 22:35-40 and the summary in the form of the Golden Rule in Matthew 7:12 and Luke 6:31.

E. THE CERTAINTY OF GOD'S JUDGMENT (17:15-24)

The fool is wrong in assuming that the fool is hidden from the Lord (verse 15; cf. 16:17). God knows human ways, especially

those of **Israel**, the chosen people (cf. 24:12). Verse 17 is awkward in the context. Its presence is understandable on the assumption that in this passage ben Sira is thinking of Deuteronomy 32:6-10. If so, verse 17 is a paraphrase of Deuteronomy 32:8-9.

Every sin which a person commits is known to the Lord and will be requited when the Lord arises for judgment (verses 20, 23). Similarly every good work will be remembered, for the Lord regards **almsgiving** as **like a signet** ring—the rich and beautiful symbol of royalty (cf. 49:11). **Kindness** is something especially precious (see above on 7:32-36). After mentioning repentance as a condition of returning to the Lord's favor ben Sira closes the subsection with an allusion to Isaiah 40:29-31, as he began with an allusion to Isaiah 40:27-28 (see above on 16:17-23).

F. REPENTANCE AND FORGIVENESS (17:25–18:14)

17:25-28. *An Exhortation to Repent.* The sinner should **forsake** sin and **turn to the Lord** (cf. 4:26; 5:7; 21:1, 6). The one who dies because of sin can no longer praise God as can the living (on **Hades** see above on 14:11-16). Such praise is one of the primary purposes of life (cf. 17:10).

17:29–18:14. *Assurance of Forgiveness.* Ben Sira closes this major section (begun in 15:11) with the assurance that the Lord is aware of human weaknesses. Therefore the Lord is patient and merciful toward people.

17:29–18:10. The Lord is characterized by **mercy** and **forgiveness**. The Lord is the eternal creator, who controls the stars (17:32*a*; cf. 16:26–17:14; 42:15–43:33). God **alone** is **righteous**, and God's great **works** and great **mercies** are beyond human comprehension. In contrast, human beings are mortal, weak and unknowing (18:7-8), and inclined to **evil** (17:31*b*). **His good** and **evil** alike are inconsequential in comparison with God (18:8*b*). The text of 17:30 is uncertain. The Syriac reads, "But it is not like this in man [that is, man is not merciful and forgiving,

as God is], nor is God's thought like that of the sons of men."
Using this reading cf. 17:25-30 with Isaiah 55:6-9.

18:11-14. Human beings are weak and the duration of their
life short—**their end will be evil** means they are destined to die.
Therefore the Lord is **patient,** merciful, and forgiving (cf.
17:29). The Lord tries to help people by rebuking, training, and
teaching them. He is compassionate to all who **accept his
discipline** and his judgments.

VII. Discretion in Behavior (18:15–23:27)

A. Caution (18:15-29)

18:15-18. *Giving Charity.* Ben Sira greatly values almsgiving
(see above on 3:30-31). But here he warns against offending the
recipient by ungracious **words** (cf. 41:19*d*, 22*d*). Indeed, if a
choice must be made, a kindly **word** is preferable to a **gift,** for it
can better allay the **heat** of humiliation. Of course the ideal
response would be **both**—a kind word and a generous gift (verse
17*b*). **Dim** eyes expresses grief or pain.

18:19-29. *Foresight.* The prudent person takes careful
precaution against various happenings. On verse 19*a* cf. 5:11-12;
11:7-8; 33:4. On verse 19*b* cf. 30:21–31:2; 37:27-31. Self-exami-
nation makes one aware of one's sins. Thus when the Lord
comes for **judgment** one can readily confess them and be
forgiven. Verse 21 means: **Humble yourself** lest you fall **ill,** and
repent lest you sin.

18:22-24. Ben Sira repeats the demand of Deuteronomy
23:21-23 for prompt payment of a votive offering or gift. If one
promises a gift when one makes a vow, it ought to be paid. Not to
pay would be a sin. And while **death** atones for sin—an axiom of
rabbinic theology—it is better to avoid the sin altogether. One
should make a vow deliberately, not rashly (verses 23-24; cf.
Proverbs 20:25).

18:25-29. The **wise man** is cautious in that he does not let
affluence blind him to the imminence of **poverty** (verses 25-26;

cf. 11:24-28). Nor does he sin, though there may be ample opportunity to do so (verse 27). The original meaning of verses 28-29 is uncertain. The Revised Standard Version translation might be paraphrased: The intelligent person recognizes the wisdom of what I have said, will praise me for it, and will be able to teach wisdom (cf. 21:15*ab*).

B. Self-Control (18:30–19:19)

Ben Sira warns against surrendering to the temptations of lust and appetite (18:30-33), wine and women (19:1-3), gossip (19:4-12), and premature judging (19:13-19).

18:30-33. *Lust and Appetite.* On **appetites** cf. 23:6, where "gluttony" is the same Greek word. On **laughingstock** cf. 6:4. Elsewhere ben Sira warns against **luxury** as destructive of health (37:29-31), of unsure duration (11:19, 24-25), and leading to poverty (13:7). On **beggar** cf. 40:28-30. The Hebrew text of verse 33 reads: "Be not a squanderer and a drunkard, else there will be nothing in your purse." If correct, this indicates that the verse should be read in close conjunction with 19:1.

19:1-3. *Wine and Women.* Ben Sira, with the Old Testament generally, extols the delights of wine drunk in moderation. But he deplores overindulgence (cf. 31:25-30)—here, because it leads to poverty (Proverbs 21:17; 23:21). Verse 2 links **wine and women** as twin evils (cf. Proverbs 31:3-5). On yielding to the temptation of illicit sex and consequent punishment cf. 9:2-9 and 23:16-26.

19:4-12. *Gossip.* Self-control is also needed to avoid the sin of gossip. People who prattle what they know to just any listener (verse 4*a*; cf. 8:17-19) harm themselves. What they say will be used against them (verse 9; cf. 13:8-13). Except in a case where it would be sinful to withhold information one should never repeat another's conversation (cf. 41:23; Proverbs 25:9*b*-10). Inability to restrain one's speech is the mark of a **fool** (cf. 20:19-20; 21:26*a*).

19:13-19. *Premature Judgment.* Verses 13-17 seem to reflect

Proverbs 25:8-9*a*, as verses 4-12 do Proverbs 25:9*b*-10. Proper self-control prevents the hasty assumption of another's guilt. One should first investigate the case and then if necessary reprove the **friend** or **neighbor** (cf. 11:7). The accused may be innocent or their conduct may be excusable. On the evils of **slander** cf. 5:14; 28:13-26. On verse 16 cf. James 3:2. The **law** referred to in verse 17 is that of Leviticus 19:17. Verses 18-19 (Revised Standard Version footnotes) occur in only a few manuscripts. Verse 19 alludes to the doctrine of **immortality**, which ben Sira does not accept.

C. DRAWING PROPER DISTINCTIONS (19:20–20:31)

19:20-30. *Wisdom, Cleverness, and Ignorance.* True wisdom is the **fear of the Lord**. It expresses itself in the keeping of the law. Other types of **knowledge**, which do not involve the fear of the Lord, cannot rightly be called wisdom—for example, that possessed by **sinners** or the **cleverness** used for **abominable** ends. Indeed a pious ignorant person is better than a shrewd sinner.

Some clever people are very exact about minor details yet on the whole are **unjust**. They keep the letter of the law but violate the spirit of it. Others cleverly use **kindness** for ulterior motives (cf. 11:29-34; 13:3-7). Or they adopt a deceitful attitude, pretending disinterest to get the best of you (verses 26-28; cf. 12:10-12, 16-18). One way to guard against such a person is to pay careful attention to his **appearance** and mannerisms. These reveal much about true character (cf. 13:25; 27:22). Verse 21 (Revised Standard Version footnote) is found in only a few manuscripts and interrupts the context.

20:1-8. *Speech and Silence.* These verses appear to continue 19:13-17. At times it is better to remain **silent** than to **reprove**. But at other times it is better to speak out than to remain silent and harbor anger. Besides, the offender may recognize and confess **his fault** and be kept from punishment. In no case, however, should **judgments** be executed **by violence**.

20:5-8. There are various reasons for silence. Sometimes fools are silent because they know nothing—though this silence may be interpreted by others as wisdom (verse 5*a*; cf. Proverbs 17:28). The wise may be silent because they lack sure knowledge of the case (verse 6*a*; cf. 5:12) or because they know that it is not an appropriate time for speaking (verses 6*b*-7*a*; cf. 1:23-24; Ecclesiastes 3:7). The **fool** or **braggart** fails to appreciate the virtue of silence (cf. Proverbs 10:19).

20:9-17. *Appearance and Reality.* These paradoxes teach that things are not always what they seem. Normal expectations are not always fulfilled (cf. 11:12-13, 23-25). The **gift** in verse 10 is one which is given, not received. On verse 11 cf. 10:14; 11:5. The fool's **courtesies** cannot be taken at face value. They are calculating ways to get the greatest possible return on their investment. Having given **little** they complain if they do not receive **much**.

20:18-31. *Inappropriate and Proper Speech.* The fool's speech is inappropriate because it neglects the element of proper timing (cf. 19:11-12; 20:7). In the Syriac version verse 19 reads: "As the fat tail of a sheep [a choice portion] eaten without salt, so is a word not spoken in season." It is possible that the Greek translator misunderstood the original reference.

20:21-23. Some people remain sinless because they lack the means to sin (verse 21; cf. 19:28). But there are those who sin by refusing to speak. Through a sense of false **shame** they remain silent or feign ignorance (verse 22; cf. 4:20-21). Others sin by speaking out rashly, making **promises** which they cannot expect to keep.

20:24-26. Lying is a form of perverted speech (cf. 7:12-13; 25:2; Proverbs 12:22). Like slander it can be compared with thievery (cf. 5:14). **Shame** and **disgrace** accompany the liar (cf. Proverbs 13:5).

20:27-31. In contrast to all these the wise speak sensibly. They do not hide their wisdom (verses 30-31, repeated in 41:14-15; cf. 4:23), but cultivate it (verse 28*a*). Thus they earn advancement and the opportunity to win pardon for sin. Nonetheless they need to be warned against bribes that would **blind** them to injustice and **muzzle** their reproof of it. Verse 29*a* is a near quotation from Deuteronomy 16:19.

D. Warnings Against Sin (21:1-10)

21:1-7. Ben Sira exhorts his students to repentance and confession in prayer. He assures the humble that they will be heard by God and **speedily** vindicated (verse 5; cf. 35:13-17). Sin is deadly and the **proud**, unrepentant sinner will be destroyed (on sin as a lion cf. 27:10). Verse 7 seems awkward in the context and its original text is uncertain. The Greek text seems to mean that the proud (or boastful) person is famous but the wise person is more sensitive to the need for forgiveness.

21:8-10. These verses reaffirm the fact that sin leads to death. To amass a fortune unjustly is in effect to prepare one's own grave (cf. 5:8). The **assembly of the wicked** (cf. 16:6) can be ignited to destruction by a mere spark. On the **smoothly paved** road of the sinner cf. Proverbs 14:12; 16:25 and Matthew 7:13. On **Hades** see above on 14:11-16.

E. The Wise Person and the Fool (21:11–22:18)

21:11-28. *A Contrast.* The wise person and the fool stand in sharp opposition—in their attainment and appreciation of knowledge (verses 11-15, 18-19, 21), in their **speech** (verses 16-17, 25-28), and in their conduct (verses 20, 22-24).

21:11-15. The meaning of verses 11-12 is similar to that of 19:20-23. Instead of **his thoughts** the Syriac reads "his *yetzer*" (see above on 15:14-16), which may be correct. There are two kinds of **cleverness.** In a good sense it is the ability to learn (cf. 6:32), or perceptiveness (cf. 34:10). In a bad sense it is shrewdness used for ignoble ends (cf. 19:23, 25). The wise person's knowledge grows through life (verse 13; cf. 6:18), as did ben Sira's own (cf. 24:30-31). The fool despises a wisdom **saying** but the wise one applauds and develops it (cf. 6:32-37; 18:28-29).

On **flowing spring** and **broken jar** cf. Proverbs 10:11*a* and Jeremiah 2:13.

21:16-24. The fool's story is a heavy **burden** to bear (cf. 8:15). But **intelligent** speech brings delight and respect (cf. 15:5; 39:9-11). Wisdom is as nothing to a fool, who regards **education** as heavy **fetters**, but to the wise these shackles become an **ornament** (cf. 6:24, 29-31). In verses 20, 22-24 the boorishness of the fool is contrasted with the cultivated manners of the wise (cf. 19:30; 31:12–32:13).

21:25-28. Here again the contrast is in speech habits. The text of verse 25*a* is quite uncertain. One manuscript reads: "Babblers declare what is not theirs"—that is, what they do not really know (cf. 21:18). This contrasts well with the wise, who weigh their words carefully (cf. 16:25; 28:25).

Fools speak before thinking and wise people think before speaking (verse 26; cf. 4:24; 5:13). Verses 27-28 warn against two types of foolish speech. He who **curses** another lays a curse on himself. The **whisperer** (deceiver? slanderer?) actually harms himself (cf. 19:4*b*). **Adversary** in verse 27 represents the same word as "Satan." Originally the Hebrew word meant a slanderer or accuser. Probably here it means simply a human enemy.

22:1-18. *The Undisciplined and the Foolish.* Ben Sira values work (cf. 7:15; 38:24-34). But except for a section on idle slaves (33:24-28) he speaks only in verses 1-2 of the **indolent**. In Proverbs this is a major theme.

22:3-6. The discipline of children is a favorite subject in this book (cf. 7:23-25; 16:1-3; 30:1-13). In the ancient world generally a **daughter** was valued much less than a son. Besides being especially troublesome (cf. 42:9-11) she could not perpetuate the family, bring income into it, or support her parents in old age. But nowhere else is this attitude expressed more forcibly or succinctly than in verse 3*b*. On verses 4-5 cf. 7:22-28; 42:9-11. An **impudent daughter** probably means one who fails to show proper discretion in sexual matters (cf. 26:11).

22:7-15. Teaching a fool is as useless as trying to mend a broken pot. Even the **dead** man is better off than the fool. The traditional period of **mourning** was **seven days**. One should avoid close association with the foolish (cf. 27:12), for it is like being burdened with a heavy weight (verses 14-15; cf. 8:15; 21:16; Proverbs 27:3).

22:16-18. The wise have a **mind firmly fixed** but fools have a **timid heart.** One follows **reasonable counsel** and stands unafraid. The other follows a **fool's purpose** and yields in **fear** (cf. 2:2, 12-13). The exact connotation of the words in verse 17*b* is unknown and the precise point of comparison is unclear.

F. The Preservation of Friendship (22:19-26)

The value of friendship is extolled in 6:14-17; 7:18; and 9:10. True **friendship** will survive many blows—a quarrel, even if it is taken to the point of battle (verse 21), and open opposition (verse 22). But it cannot survive the sneaky attacks listed in verse 22*c* (cf. 23:8), of which none is worse than the **disclosure of secrets** (cf. 27:16-21; 41:23; Proverbs 11:13; 20:19; 25:9). The maintenance of friendship demands fidelity even though the friend suffers **poverty** and **affliction,** or hostility (verses 23, 25; contrast 6:8-12; 37:1-5). Verse 24 interrupts the context.

G. Sins of Speech and Lust (22:27–23:27)

Ben Sira prays that he may be delivered from sins of speech and lust (22:27–23:6). He then warns his students about the former (23:7-15) and denounces those who surrender to the latter (23:16-27).

22:27–23:6. *A Prayer for Deliverance.* The prayer begins with a near quotation of Psalm 141:3 and an allusion to the thought of Proverbs 21:23. Elsewhere ben Sira emphasizes the **mouth** as the cause of sin or the means by which sin of the mind or heart is given expression (5:13; 14:1; 23:8; cf. Proverbs 18:21). He prays that **discipline** may control his unintentional errors and his willfulness to sin, lest they bring about his downfall. Logically verse 1 should follow verse 3. The mistakes and sins of verse 3 are the proper antecedents of **their** and **them** in verse 1.

23:4-6. The conclusion of the prayer asks for deliverance from **lust** (cf. 6:2-4). The phrase **haughty eyes** suggests pride, but the root expression is "lift up the eyes." In some other instances this clearly connotes sexual desire (cf. 26:9; 41:20*b*, 21*c*; Genesis 39:7). Similarly **gluttony** here derives from the expression "appetite of the belly," which could mean sexual passion (cf. 18:30).

23:7-15. *Sins of Speech.* A general statement in verses 7-8 mentions reviling and arrogance as sins of speech (cf. 22:22). Then ben Sira centers his attention on frequent, thoughtless swearing. The **Name** is the personal name of God, Yahweh. From well back in the Old Testament period this sacred name had been held in such reverence that its pronunciation was avoided. The priest was permitted to utter it in giving the benediction (Numbers 6:23-27; cf. 50:20). But in most other cases a substitute, most frequently Adonai, "Lord," was used instead. From this substitution in reading the Scriptures aloud has come the use of "the LORD" for Yahweh (or "the Lord GOD" for Adonai Yahweh) in the Revised Standard Version and other English versions of the Old Testament.

Of course in making an oath "Yahweh" had to be pronounced, because the oath was validated by invoking the deity by name. In the Old Testament the most common oath forms are "As Yahweh lives" and "May Yahweh do so to me and more also if . . ."

23:12. The **utterance . . . comparable to death** (or "clothed in death" as most manuscripts read) may mean either blasphemy—that is, cursing God or denying God, God's work, or God's name—or lewd, vulgar speech, which is the topic of the following verses.

23:13-15. One who uses obscene language is an undisciplined child. Such speech in the presence of noble people disgraces one's parents, for it reflects one's training and education (cf. 3:1-16; 8:4).

23:16-27. *Sins of Lust.* Ben Sira denounces the fornicator (verses 16-17), the adulterer (verses 18-21), and the adulteress (verses 22-27).

23:16-17. Verse 16 begins with a numerical introduction. This was a stylistic device perhaps originally intended to aid memory. The **fire** of passion consumes the lustful (cf. 6:2-4). **Bread** is a euphemism (cf. Proverbs 9:17).

23:18-21. Ben Sira everywhere advocates faithfulness in marriage, though he does not hesitate to counsel divorce if conditions warrant (cf. 7:26; 25:26). It is noteworthy that in his view the adulterer sins because he **breaks his marriage vows** rather than, as in earlier times, because he wrongs the woman's husband or father. The adulterer errs in thinking that he can conceal his sin. God's **eyes** are bright and perceive **all** one's **ways** (cf. 16:17-23; 17:15, 20; Psalm 33:13-15; Proverbs 15:3, 11).

23:22-27. Ben Sira frequently speaks out against the adulteress and the harlot. But here the specific concern is with the woman who bears a child through an adulterous relationship. She thus commits a threefold wrong (the **law** is that in the Decalogue, Exodus 20:14; Deuteronomy 5:18). Such a child could not be expected to live, or if it did live could not be expected to have a prosperous life (cf. 40:15). The woman's punishment involves arraignment before the **assembly** of her town and **disgrace**. The absence of any reference to death here and in verse 21 indicates that the harsh penalty for adultery prescribed in the Pentateuch was not enforced in ben Sira's time (cf. Leviticus 20:10; Deuteronomy 22:22). On verse 27 cf. 25:11 and 40:26-27.

VIII. ATTRACTIVE AND HATEFUL THINGS (24:1–36:17)

A. SECOND TREATISE ON WISDOM (24:1-34)

24:1-22. *A Hymn in Praise of Wisdom.* This is the second of two principal poems praising wisdom (cf. 1:1-10). Each stands at the beginning of a major section (see below on verses 30-34). After the introduction in verses 1-2 wisdom speaks of herself in the first person.

24:1-2. Personified wisdom praises **herself** on earth and in heaven. In the context **her people** must mean Israel. **The assembly of the Most High** and **his host** refer to the divine council, the ministers of God who surrounded God's throne in the heavens.

24:3. Wisdom was the first of God's created things (cf. verse 9; 1:4). Obviously ben Sira is thinking of Proverbs 8:22-31, where this is taught. But he also seems to have in mind the creation accounts in Genesis. In Genesis 1:1–2:4*a* God creates by speaking. Thus ben Sira says wisdom **came forth from the mouth of the Most High.** In Genesis 2:4*b*-25 a mist covers the earth before other things are created. So wisdom speaks of herself as **like a mist.**

24:4-7. These verses describe the omnipresence of wisdom. As the Lord's companion she is present wherever God is present—in the **pillar of cloud** which was with Israel (cf. Exodus 14:19-20; 33:9-10) and in the **vault** (the dome) **of heaven,** the **abyss** (see above on 1:1-10), the **sea,** and the **earth.** These four are enumerated in Proverbs 8:28-29.

24:8-12. Wisdom now speaks of **Israel** as her particular dwelling place. In a sense she is found in other nations too, for they have their wisdom and wise people. But God **assigned** her especially to Israel. While it is appropriate to what ben Sira says elsewhere, verse 9 seems to interrupt the thought here. It is understandable, however, when one sees that in writing these verses ben Sira is thinking of Jeremiah 10:11-16. That passage mentions the Lord as establishing the world by wisdom. **Creator of all things** and the references to **Jacob** as the **portion of the Lord** and to the Lord as Israel's **inheritance** are inspired by Jeremiah 10:16. Since the whole passage in Jeremiah contrasts the Lord's eternality with the perishability of idols, ben Sira is led to make brief reference in verse 9 to the eternality of wisdom.

As wisdom was present in the worship of God from the early **tabernacle** (cf. Exodus 33:9-10), so also she became **established** in the later temple service in Jerusalem. It is clear that ben Sira is thinking of wisdom as the law (cf. verse 23).

24:13-17. Wisdom speaks of how, having taken **root** in Israel, she flourished in its sweet soil. The figures suggest strength, beauty, pleasantness, and fruitfulness.

24:19-22. In these final lines wisdom invites those who will to eat of her **produce** (cf. 15:3). As the opening lines of the poem are inspired by Proverbs 8:22-31, these are inspired by Proverbs 9:1-6. There wisdom, having established her house, sets out food and drink and issues her invitation. On verse 20 cf. Psalm 19:10 and Proverbs 24:13-14.

The reference to wisdom's **help** and to her protection from **shame** in verse 22 may reflect the contrast between those who work with their idols, only to be shamed by them (Jeremiah 10:14), and wisdom who works with people so that they cannot **be put to shame.**

24:23-29. *Wisdom and the Law.* **All** this means wisdom and what is said of her in the preceding hymn. It is to be equated with the **law which Moses commanded us as an inheritance for the congregation of Jacob** (quoted from Deuteronomy 33:4). This may be the most important saying in ben Sira's book. Whether he was the first to make explicit the identification of wisdom and the law (see above on 17:11-13), he was the first of those whom we know to take seriously its implications.

By "law" he means, not the Pentateuch only—though it is primary—but all scripture. By equating law and wisdom he fully integrates wisdom and wisdom literature with the priestly, prophetic, and historical concerns of Israel as they are expressed in scripture. Later writers were quick to make use of this identification. It became a general assumption underlying rabbinic thought. It is almost a commonplace, for example, to find the rabbis quoting a biblical passage which mentions "wisdom" and applying it as if it said "law."

This is not to rule out other definitions of wisdom. For ben Sira wisdom is still "the fear of the Lord" (see Introduction and comment on 1:11-20). But this is a subjective definition. Objectively wisdom is the keeping of the law (cf. 19:20; 21:11).

24:25-29. One who knows the law is filled with wisdom as rivers are full at the time of high water. Four of these are the rivers said to flow from Eden (Genesis 2:10-14). To these is added a reference to the **Jordan** (cf. Joshua 3:15) and possibly to the Nile. By a slight emendation of the Hebrew text "go forth like the Nile" may be read for **shine forth like light**. Such is wisdom's depth, however, that no one can know her completely (cf. 1:2-3).

24:30-34. *Ben Sira's Wisdom.* Ben Sira continues the figure of wisdom as **a river** to describe his own personal experience. At first his wisdom was only an irrigation ditch, but it grew greatly in volume and depth. In a second figure of speech he compares his instruction to the brightness of the sun at **dawn**. Verse 33 clearly shows that ben Sira regarded his **teaching** as inspired. He expected his book to be added to the still growing canon of Hebrew scripture. Verse 34 is repeated in 33:17.

This passage can have several interpretations:

(1) At first he studied only for himself. But as his wisdom grew he felt compelled to teach others.

(2) Initially he was concerned only with his small circle of students. Later he was led to write for all people.

(3) Originally he intended to write little. But as his knowledge increased he found it necessary to add to his earlier writings.

Of these interpretations the last is the most appealing. **Again** in verses 32-33 might indicate that ben Sira found it necessary to add a second volume (chapters 24–50) to his original book (chapters 1–23).

B. MISCELLANEOUS OBSERVATIONS (25:1-11)

25:1-6. *Pleasant and Hateful Things.* Mention of the **adulterous old man who lacks good sense** brings on a digression on the beauty of **wisdom in the aged** (cf. 8:6-9; Proverbs 16:31; 20:29).

25:7-11. *Ten Who Are Blessed.* Verse 7*b* seems to promise a list of ten praiseworthy people. But the Greek text counts only nine—two each in verses 7, 9, 10 and three in verse 8. The

Hebrew and Syriac texts add as the tenth (following verse 8a): "[he who] does not plow with an ox and an ass"—that is, one wise enough not to mix unnatural things (cf. Deuteronomy 22:10). The inclusion of the **man who lives to see the downfall of his foes** admittedly falls short of the highest ethical ideals. But Ecclesiasticus, like Proverbs, simply does not attain great heights of altruism toward enemies.

25:9-11. The list rises to a climax in the mention of the man of **good sense**, the man of **wisdom**, and the man **who fears the Lord**. At first sight these appear synonymous—as indeed they usually are in the book. But here the man of wisdom must be one who is prudent or knowledgeable yet is not a God-fearer (cf. 19:24b). Thus he is still inferior to the one who feared the Lord. The latter alone possesses true wisdom (see above on 19:20-30).

Some manuscripts remove the apparent duplication of "good sense" and "wisdom" by giving verse 9a as "happy is he who has gained a good friend." Whether this represents the original text is uncertain. On verse 11 cf. 10:24 and 23:27.

C. HAPPINESS AND UNHAPPINESS IN MARRIAGE (25:13–26:27)

25:13-26. *The Evil Wife.* The list of four vicious things in verses 13-15 introduces the section on the evil wife. Clearly **wound** and **wickedness** relate to her, and the Syriac could be correct in reading "a woman's wrath" in verse 15b. The confusion between **venom** and "head" (verse 15; see the Revised Standard Version footnote) is due to the fact that in Hebrew they are the same word.

25:16-26. On verse 16 cf. Proverbs 21:9, 19. Ben Sira elsewhere warns of the dangers of **woman's beauty** (9:8; 42:12) but praises the beauty of the **good wife** (26:16-17; 36:22). His reference to Eve (verse 24) as the cause of human sin and mortality is the earliest such doctrinal interpretation of Genesis 3. The figure of an **outlet to water** may be taken from Proverbs 17:14. The suggestion of divorce in verse 26 rests on the law of Deuteronomy 24:1. **Separate her** is literally "cut her off from

309

your flesh," since in marriage they are one flesh (cf. Genesis 2:24).

26:1-4. *The Good Wife.* To ben Sira a good wife and a happy marriage are among life's greatest joys (cf. 7:19; 25:1, 8; 36:22-24; 40:19, 23). It is significant that monogamy seems to be assumed in the happy marriage. His possible allusions to polygamy are always in contexts of tension and trouble (see below on verses 5-6). On this section and verses 13-18 cf. Proverbs 31:10-31. A good wife is regarded as a **blessing**—that is, a gift or favor from the Lord. **Rejoices** literally says "makes fat"; cf. verse 13.

26:5-6. *The Jealous Wife.* Of four frightful things the worst is a **wife** jealous of another. Conceivably the **rival** could be another woman outside the marriage relationship. More probably she is another wife of the same husband (cf. 37:11*a*). Doubtless monogamy was the normal pattern of marriage in ben Sira's time. But the old practice of polygamy—motivated by political reasons, or by love, lust, or the desire for sons—may not have been infrequent. The second wife was called by the technical term "rival," which comes from a root meaning "show hostility." Leviticus 18:18 and Deuteronomy 21:15-17 state laws relevant to the "rival" problem.

26:7-12. *More on the Evil Wife.* The evil wife irritates and stings (verse 7). The **drunken** or harlotrous wife is especially troublesome. On verse 9 cf. Proverbs 6:25. In verse 10 **daughter** means wife.

26:13-18. *More on the Good Wife.* Ben Sira celebrates a wife's **charm** and **beauty**, which shine brightly and gladden **her husband** (cf. 36:22). The **holy lampstand** is the seven-branched menorah which stood in the temple. The text and meaning of verse 18*b* are uncertain. Some manuscripts read "so are beautiful feet on firm heels." While there is no manuscript evidence for it, a more natural analogy would be for **pillars of gold** to refer to legs and a **base of silver** to feet.

26:19-27. *More on Marriage Relations.* These verses (see the Revised Standard Version footnote) occur only in two Greek manuscripts and the Syriac and Arabic versions. Their authenticity is not established, and they contain little that is not said elsewhere. Verses 19-21 exhort faithfulness to one's wife. The meaning of verse 22*b* can be seen from the description of such a **tower** in II Maccabees 13:5-6.

D. An Isolated Observation (26:28)

This verse which lists three grievous things, is similar in style to 25:1-2, 7-11.

E. Sins and Sinners (26:29–28:26)

26:29–27:3. *Dishonesty in Business.* In commercial transactions it is easy to seek a petty advantage and to overlook a shady deal. Indeed, devotion to the Lord is the merchant's only protection against the temptation to dishonesty and its resultant calamity. Other warnings against dishonest wealth are found in 5:8 and 21:8.

27:4-10. *A Digression.* The surest **test of a man is to hear him reason**. What he says reveals what he thinks and what he is. Shaking in a **sieve** or firing in a **kiln** reveals any coarseness or any inner, hidden flaws. Verses 8-10 affirm in effect that one reaps what one sows. On verse 8*b* cf. 6:31. On verse 10 cf. 21:2.

27:11-15. *Sinful Talk.* Fools are unworthy associates (verse 12; cf. 22:13; Proverbs 14:7). Their speech is inconsistent and sinful. On verse 13 cf. 19:30 and 21:20. On verse 14 cf. 23:11. Their **abuse** of the godly is mentioned again in verses 28-29.

27:16-21. *Betrayal of Secrets.* Cf. 22:19-22. Ben Sira greatly values friendship. He regards the sharing of secrets as the final step in the attainment of intimacy (cf. 4:18; 8:17-19). The violation of a friend's **secrets** is the ultimate breach of fidelity.

27:22-29. *Deceit.* One who **winks his eye**—a frequent Old Testament figure of speech—is a deceiver. He speaks sweetly but plots to use **your words** against you (cf. 12:16). **Even the Lord will hate him,** however, and his punishment is sure. With the proverbs of verses 25-27 cf. Psalms 7:15-16; 9:15-16 and Proverbs 26:27. Verses 28-29 seem poorly connected with what precedes. Their inclusion can be understood on the assumption that ben Sira is thinking of Psalm 35:15-26. There the psalmist prays for God to take vengeance on those who "wink the eye" and "conceive words of deceit," mocking and rejoicing as they anticipate his downfall.

27:30–28:7. *Vengeance.* **Anger and wrath** are treated more fully in 28:8-12. The mention of them here serves only to introduce ben Sira's comments on **vengeance.** The law affirms that vengeance belongs to the Lord and is not the individual's right (Leviticus 19:18; Deuteronomy 32:35). A man's part is to **forgive** one who wrongs him, so that in turn God will forgive his own sins.

This is a remarkable passage, in that it so clearly anticipates New Testament teachings. These verses are apparently quite genuine, though it is easy to see why some have suspected them as a Christian interpolation. One should **overlook** an unintended offense (verse 7). One should be deterred in one's own sinning by remembrance of coming **death** and of the **commandments.**

28:8-12. *Strife.* These verses are for the most part a restatement and expansion of ideas expressed in Proverbs to the effect that anger produces strife. For example, cf. verse 8 with Proverbs 15:18; verses 8*b*-9 with Proverbs 29:22; verse 10*ab* with Proverbs 26:20-21; verse 10*d* with Proverbs 18:23. The mouth's ability to inflame or quench anger is also noted in Proverbs 15:1.

28:13-26. *Slander and the Evil Tongue.* Apparently ben Sira knows the evil consequences of **slander** from personal experience (cf. 51:2, 5-6). He has spoken of it earlier (5:14). Verse 15 seems to refer to noble wives who have been divorced and **driven** from their homes because of slander. Therefore it may be correct to regard verse 16 as a reference to the husband who will never know the **peace** of a well-ordered home until he learns to ignore slander.

28:17-26. The evil **tongue** is a vicious instrument, worse than a **whip** or **sword**, which brings heavy, inescapable hardships. In Hebrew **edge of the sword** is literally "mouth of the sword." Indeed the peace of death is **preferable** to the trouble caused by the evil tongue. Genuine piety is the only defense against it (verses 21-23). One should therefore guard the **mouth** as carefully as one does **property** (cf. 16:25; 21:25). By one's mouth one may become a sinner (cf. 14:1; 23:8; 25:8) and thus be subject to the evil tongue of others.

F. BORROWING AND LENDING (29:1-28)

29:1-7. The law provided for giving financial help to those who need it by loan without interest (Exodus 22:25; Leviticus 25:35-37). In actual practice this provision was frequently disregarded. Ben Sira sanctions such loans and encourages responsible repayment (cf. 4:31). He knows, however, that many persons take advantage of a lender. Some humbly petition for a **loan**, then default in **repayment**, to the creditor's loss.

29:8-13. Nevertheless one should run the risk and help the needy, for three reasons:
   (1) the **commandment** requires it (Deuteronomy 15:7-11);
   (2) unused funds are subject to loss anyway (verse 10);
   (3) if the debtor does not repay, your act can be regarded as **almsgiving**, for which the Lord will repay you (see above on 3:30-31).
Verse 11*a* in the Syriac version reads: "Lay up for yourself a treasure of righteousness and love."

29:14-20. Proverbs regards suretyship with virtual horror (cf. Proverbs 6:1-5; 11:15; 22:26-27). Ben Sira encourages it as an act of kindness—on the condition that one should not assume an obligation beyond one's means (verse 20) or participate in the practice for hope of **gain**. Verses 15-18 warn against letting one's **surety** suffer loss.

29:21-28. Borrowing another's hospitality is as bad as borrowing money. Either may lead to shame (verse 28). It is better to be self-reliant though **poor** than to be an unwanted visitor. Such a visitor has to perform menial tasks, suffer reproach, and yield place to a more **honored** guest (verses 24-27).

G. Causes of Joy or Sorrow (30:1–31:11)

This section teaches that disciplined children, health, and financial independence are sources of joy in life. Undisciplined sons, sickness, and the love of wealth cause sorrow.

30:1-3. *Children.* The disciplining of sons is of major importance (cf. 7:23; 22:3-6; 42:5b). The rod wielded in love has a prominent place in it (cf. Proverbs 13:24; 23:13-14; 29:15). Nonetheless ben Sira's concern in this passage is not so much the good of the child as the joy or grief that the child can bring to the father. Cf. 3:1-16, where the son is advised to honor his parents primarily to secure blessings for himself.

30:14–31:2. *Health.* Ben Sira declares that **health** is better than **wealth**, and **death** than **chronic sickness** (cf. 41:2). The **afflicted** cannot enjoy the **good things** which wealth provides. In verse 18 some manuscripts read "before an idol" for **upon a grave**. Placing food on a grave as a sacrifice to the dead was apparently a pagan practice and seems to have been forbidden by the law (Deuteronomy 26:14; but cf. Tobit 4:17). Bel and the Dragon ridicules the practice of placing food before idols. The Letter of Jeremiah 6:27 regards gifts to idols and to the dead as equally foolish. Verses 18-20 recall Psalm 115:5-6.

30:21–31:2. Ben Sira believes that life should be enjoyable (cf. 14:11, 14, 16). He praises **gladness of heart** (cf. Proverbs 13:12; 15:13; 17:22). He warns against excessive **sorrow** (cf. 38:18-20) and other responses which would tend toward emotional illness. The text of verse 25 is quite uncertain. Perhaps it originally said something akin to Proverbs 15:15b: "a cheerful heart has a continual feast."

31:3-11. *Wealth.* The effect of wealth can be either positive or negative. It brings sorrow to those who are **devoted to it** (cf. Proverbs 11:4a, 28a; 28:20; I Timothy 6:9-10). But it is a source of blessing to those who use it well (cf. 13:24a). Some people remain sinless simply because they lack the means to sin (20:21). The clever, deceitful person will sin if given the opportunity (19:28). But this **rich man** remains **blameless** though he has both the means and the opportunity to sin (verses 8, 10). Instead he uses his wealth for **charity** (see above on 3:30-31).

Verses 3-4 appear to be popular proverbs which ben Sira cites as an introduction to this passage. Their relation to verses 5-7 is clearly seen if one supposes a "nevertheless" between verses 4 and 5.

H. TEMPERANCE AND GOOD MANNERS (31:12–32:13)

It was expected that the wisdom student should become a person of culture. The type of teaching included in this section is characteristic of Near Eastern wisdom. It may well have been an important part of the curriculum in the wisdom schools, where presumably most of the students were young aristocrats.

31:12-22. *Against Gluttony.* The similarity of verse 12 to Proverbs 23:1-2 suggests that **a great man** is better than "a great table" and that the figure of the "throat" is well interpreted by **greedy** (see the Revised Standard Version footnotes). **Greedy eye** is literally "evil eye," which in the Old Testament has nothing to do with black magic but is a symbol of stinginess, envy, or greed (cf 14:8-10). Verses 14-18 are well summarized in 41:19c, "Be ashamed of selfish behavior at meals." On verse 15a cf. 6:17. On verses 19-21 cf. 37:29-31. In verse 22c **industrious** seems out of place. The context appears to demand "modest" or "moderate." Perhaps the meaning is "be industrious in heeding my instruction."

31:23-24. *The Good and Bad Host.* As they stand these verses are a digression. They shift from the guest to the host. Most commentators are agreed, however, that the Greek has missed the point. Originally the verses concerned the good guest who praises the liberality of the host and the bad guest who complains against the host.

31:25-30. *Temperance in Drinking Wine.* Ben Sira, with the Old Testament generally, praises the delights of wine drunk in **moderation** (cf. Psalm 104:15; Proverbs 31:6-7). But he deplores overindulgence and stresses its evil consequences (cf. 19:1-2; Proverbs 20:1; 23:29-35).

31:31–32:13. *Proper Behavior at Banquets.* Banquets are made for laughter and joy, music and wine. Thus inappropriate topics should be avoided (verse 31). Friendliness, kind modesty, and lack of ostentation should be the order of the day for the **master**, the elders, and the younger guests alike. The true source of all **good gifts** should be remembered. It is possible that this suggests formal grace at meals, based on Deuteronomy 8:10.

I. Stability Under the Law (32:14–33:6)

The law is a firm support to one who trusts it fully. But it is an unsettling influence on the hypocrite.

32:14-17. The serious wisdom student gives the Lord first priority in life and accepts the Lord's hard discipline (cf. 2:1-5, 15-18). Since the student **seeks** (studies) **the law**, it becomes a part of the student's very being, producing right thoughts and **deeds**. In contrast the **hypocrite**—that is, the person of divided loyalties, finds the law a hindrance. Hypocrites shun its teaching, reinterpreting it to suit themselves.

32:18-23. The wise do not approach life overconfidently. They carefully deliberate each act (cf. 37:16), seeking to do what scripture demands. But the **insolent and proud man** is not so deliberate. He does not **fear** that he is about to transgress against the law.

32:24–33:3. Unlike the hypocrite the wise person finds in the **law** a strong protection and a trustworthy resource. **Urim** and Thummim were oracular devices employed in ancient times to determine the Lord's answer to questions. Their use after the time of David is not clearly indicated. Indeed ben Sira feels that they are no longer needed—the Lord's will can be confidently known through the law.

33:4-6. Ben Sira exhorts his students to **prepare** carefully and to teach with steadfast consistency (cf. 5:10-11). Verse 5 suggests the inconstancy of the fool's mind, which is ever changing (cf. 27:11). The point of verse 6 is that a **stallion** shows no steadfast affection to any one master. Similarly the fool is no true friend of the law.

J. OPPOSITES (33:7-15)

All days are alike in that they are lighted by the **sun. All men** are alike in that they are **from the ground** (cf. Genesis 2:7). Yet God has **distinguished** the sabbath and the other religious holidays. Likewise God has **distinguished** human destinies. Some God has **exalted** (Israel) and among these he has exalted some even further (the priesthood; to be **brought near** technically means to minister as priest). Others he has debased (non-Israelites, especially Canaanites; cf. Genesis 9:25).

The figure of the **potter** suggests the Lord's power and prerogative over men and women. It is used rather often in scripture (cf. Isaiah 29:16; Jeremiah 18:4, 6). But verse 14 does not say and cannot mean that God makes some people sinners (cf. 15:11-20). Men and women themselves choose different types of life, and their choice makes them as **opposite** as **good** and **evil** or **life** and **death**. On verse 15 cf. 42:24.

K. A FATHER'S DUTIES (33:16-31)

33:16-18. *An Interlude.* Ben Sira regards himself as the **last** of a great line of teachers (cf. 24:30-34). The Lord's **blessing** is the gift of wisdom.

33:19-23. *Toward His Estate.* A father should protect his financial independence by not distributing his estate too soon. To become dependent on his heirs would be a disgrace.

33:24-31. *Toward His Slaves.* Verse 24 virtually puts the slave into the same class as a beast, but the slave was a chattel, regarded as a thing. On the whole ben Sira's views are quite lenient and merciful (cf. 4:30; 7:20-21). Strict discipline is enjoined for the sake of obedience and industry (cf. 42:5c). But nothing excessively cruel or unjust is permitted (verse 29). The difference between verses 30-31 and verses 24-29 perhaps rests on the distinction between the good and the wicked servant. But the Syriac text may be correct in identifying the servant of verses 30-31 as "an only servant." Buying a servant **with blood** means with money gained at your own hard labor. Cf. the Pentateuchal laws on slavery, especially Exodus 21:2-6, 20-21, 26-27 and Deuteronomy 15:12-18.

L. Grounds of Hope (34:1-17)

34:1-8. *False Grounds.* The fool is often excited or elated by **dreams**. But if he rests his hopes on them, he is likely to be disappointed. Dreams are nothing (verse 2)—or are only reflections of the fool's foolishness (verse 3b; cf. Proverbs 27:19). They cannot disclose anything that is **true**. False or lying dreams are denounced in Jeremiah 23:25-32; 27:9 and Zechariah 10:2. All forms of divination and sorcery are forbidden in Deuteronomy 18:9-14. Of course ben Sira has to make allowance for God-given dreams, but he much prefers the truth of the **law**. This entire discussion seems to have been inspired by Deuteronomy 13:1-5.

34:9-17. *True Grounds.* In a personal comment ben Sira extols the education and maturity which result from travel and a broad acquaintance with the realities of life. On the basis of his own education and experience he affirms that the Lord is the surest ground of **hope** and of one's firm **support** (cf. 2:6-13).

M. Worship of the Lord (34:18–36:17)

34:18-26. *Unacceptable Worship.* Following the highest insights of the prophets and the sages of Proverbs, ben Sira teaches that atonement for sin cannot be won by the mere mechanics of ritual performance. The sacrifices of the **ungodly** are unacceptable (cf. Proverbs 15:8; 21:27), even if offered in great numbers (cf. 7:9). To sacrifice **from what has been wrongfully obtained**—for example, from assets which really belong to the **poor**—is a heinous crime. On withholding **wages** cf. Leviticus 19:13; Deuteronomy 24:14-15 and Tobit 4:14. Similarly fasting is not a proper act of worship if repeated sins cancel out its good effect (cf. 5:5).

35:1-11. *Acceptable Worship.* The most meaningful type of **peace offering** (commanded in Leviticus 3) is the keeping of the **law.** The spirit underlying the gift of **fine flour** (Leviticus 2) and the **thank offering** (Leviticus 7:12) finds more genuine expression in acts of charity (verse 2; on **kindness** and **alms** as technical terms see above on 7:32-36). There is no **atonement** without repentance (see above on 3:3-4). In essence ben Sira here restates the prophetic interpretation of sacrifice. The prophets criticized the substitution of the ritual act for the larger concerns of ethics and morality.

35:4-11. Nonetheless ben Sira cannot ignore the institution of sacrifice itself. After all it is commanded in the law and must therefore be observed. Verse 4 is quoted from Exodus 23:15 and Deuteronomy 16:16, where each Israelite is ordered to sacrifice three times a year. Ben Sira recommends a **cheerful** and generous participation (cf. 7:31).

35:12-20. *The Lord's Justice and Mercy.* As one who is just, the Lord cannot accept a **bribe** or **unrighteous sacrifice** (cf. 34:18-20). God cannot **show partiality** in favor of one who has wronged the poor (cf. 34:18-22). Instead the Lord mercifully heeds the afflicted (verses 13*b*-15), the righteous (verse 16), and the **humble** (cf. 21:5).

35:18-20. The subject suddenly shifts to Israel, to whom the Lord will be merciful and for whom the Lord will take **vengeance** against the **unrighteous**—that is, the Greeks—as the Lord did against other **nations** in time past.

36:1-17. *A Prayer on Behalf of Israel.* The prayer follows naturally 35:18-20 and continues its theme. God has shown holiness in the restoration of Israel after the punishment of the Babylonian exile. Thus ben Sira prays that God show Israel divine greatness by punishing the **nations**.

The thought of verse 4a is a favorite of Ezekiel (cf. Ezekiel 20:41; 28:25; 36:23). Verse 6 pleads for God to act **anew** as God acted in Israel's deliverance from Egypt. The present **enemy** is the Greeks. In verse 8b the Hebrew and Syriac read: "For who may say to thee, 'What doest thou?' "—suggesting that God can avenge Israel at any time God wishes. The words of the proud, self-reliant **enemy** (verse 10b) are words which the Babylonians used to say (cf. Isaiah 47:8, 10).

36:11-17. These verses repeat the often expressed wish that the scattered **tribes** of Israel might be reassembled and might again control all of Palestine, with **Jerusalem** as a focus of active worship. **In the beginning** (verse 15) means the same as **first-born** (verse 12). The **blessing of Aaron** (verse 17) is found in Numbers 6:24-26.

IX. PROPER DISCRIMINATION (36:18–42:14)

36:18-20. These verses introduce a series of passages which counsel proper discrimination, or proper discretion, in various areas of life. Each verse may have been a popular proverb. Similar forms of verse 19 occur in Job 12:11 and 34:3.

A. SOCIAL RELATIONSHIPS AND BEHAVIOR (36:21–39:11)

36:21-26. *Choosing a Wife.* Marriage is better than bachelorhood (verses 25-26). But one should use careful discrimination in choosing a wife (verse 21). The best wife is one that is both beautiful and modest (cf. 26:1-4, 13-18). **A helper fit for him** comes from Genesis 2:18.

37:1-6. *Choosing a Friend.* Verses 1-4 are much like 6:7-13 and contain little that is new. On **evil imagination**—that is, impulse to sin—see above on 15:14-20. Verses 5-6 are close to

22:23-26. The Hebrew text of verse 6 reads "in war" for **in your heart** and "when you take spoil" for **in your wealth.** This makes the verse an elaboration of verse 5*b*.

37:7-15. *Choosing a Counselor.* Proper discrimination will help one to avoid a counselor who is motivated by self-interest or prejudice (verses 7-11). The **rival** in verse 11*a* is probably the second wife in a polygamous marriage (see above on 26:5-6). Rather one should favor a **godly man** who has one's own interest at heart. Better yet is the **counsel** of one's **own** reason or conscience. In either case one should also **pray** to God for guidance.

37:16-26. *The Speech of the Wise.* Verses 16-18 may be paraphrased: Thought precedes action. The expression of thought in speech determines the fortunes of one's life, whether for good or evil. The meaning of verse 18*c* is more clearly presented in 27:6-7. The Hebrew of verses 17-18*a* may be translated: "The roots of the mind's reasoning produce four branches"—though the four are really only two: good-life and evil-death (cf. 15:17; 33:14).

37:19-26. The text of these verses is very confused. Ben Sira is apparently distinguishing four types of wise people. The speech of the first two types produces evil:

(1) one who can guide others by wisdom, but whose own life is less than a success (verse 19);

(2) one who is a skillful speaker yet does not prosper because the Lord has not been favorable with the gift of true wisdom and one's thought therefore lacks content (verses 20-21).

The speech of the following two types produces good:

(3) one whose words accurately reflect **understanding** and bring one personal reward (verse 22);

(4) the truly wise, who gives **trustworthy** counsel to others and receives the people's **praise**; though one's life may be relatively short, one will have an enduring reputation in the life of the nation (verses 23-26; cf. 39:8-11).

37:27-31. *Matters of Food.* Proper discrimination should guide the choice of foods and proper discretion the amount (cf. 31:19-22).

38:1-15. *Treating Illness.* The **physician** is to be honored because **the Lord created him**—that is, his profession. His skill is a gift of the Lord (verses 2*a*, 14), and his value is recognized by **great men** (verses 1, 2*b*, 3). Verse 5 is an allusion to the sweetening of the **water** of Marah (Exodus 15:23-25). In verses 6-8 **he . . . his . . . him** all refer to the Lord and **them** to the **medicines**—the medicinal herbs of verse 4.

38:9-15. Careful attention to the subject of illness discloses four proper steps in treatment. All presuppose the customary interpretation that illness is a result of sin.

(1) Prayer (verse 9). Steadfast prayer is needed (cf. 7:10; 21:1), since the Lord is the true healer.

(2) Repentance (verse 10). This is basic to all forgiveness and healing (cf. 18:21; 21:1, 6).

(3) **Sacrifice** (verse 11). Ritual matters do not loom large in ben Sira's thinking. This is one of the few places where he stresses sacrifice (cf. 7:31; 35:4-10; contrast 35:1-3). The reference is to sacrifice as commanded in Leviticus 2.

(4) Consulting a **physician**, who is regarded as the Lord's instrument of **healing** (verses 12-15). Verse 15 seems to speak disparagingly of the **physician**, but this is not the original intent. The Syriac text reads: "He who sins before his Maker shall be delivered into the hands of a physician." This simply restates the view that illness is a result of sin, and this is the sense in which the Greek should be taken. A much later rabbinic saying puts it: "The door which is not opened for charity will be opened to the physician." Still the Hebrew text reads: "He who sins before his Maker is presumptuous before a physician." That is, only the sinner despises the physician's skill—a sense which fits well what ben Sira says in verses 1-8.

38:16-23. *Mourning.* The difference between proper and improper **mourning** should be recognized. The **body** should be properly prepared and buried. Verse 16*d* in the Hebrew says: "Do not hide yourself when he becomes a corpse."

One should also indulge in the ritual **lament**. Ben Sira's mention of **one day, or two** in mourning, when the traditional period was seven days (cf. 22:12), may indicate that in actual practice the time varied greatly. Or perhaps he refers to certain required rituals which could be completed in the shorter period, leaving the remaining days for informal expression. Indeed the whole tenor of his advice seems to stress ritual more than actual psychological involvement in grief. His warning against excessive sorrow (verses 18-20, 23) is much like 30:21-23. On the finality of death (verse 21) cf. 14:16-19 and 41:3-4. Verse 22 is a word of counsel from the dead.

38:24–39:11. *Craftsmen and the Wise Person.* **Leisure** for study is an absolute necessity for those who aspire to be wise. The farmers, engravers, smiths, and potters make society possible and maintain its structure; yet they cannot become leaders of the people, judges, or teachers. The portrait of the ideal scribe or wisdom student (39:1-11) makes no mention of gainful employment in a craft or trade. Apparently ben Sira himself pursued none. The later rabbis, however, usually had an occupation.

39:1-3. The ideal scribe or wisdom student is a student of scripture. Hebrew scripture (the Old Testament) includes three well-defined sections: the Law, the Prophets, and the Writings. In verse 1, as in the Prologue, the first two are clearly distinct, but the third section is not yet firmly delimited. Ben Sira calls it **wisdom**. The Prologue refers to "the others" or "the rest." One would expect that what ben Sira knew as "wisdom" included at least Job, Psalms, and Proverbs. Verse 2*a* may well be an allusion to the developing oral law, which was to be preserved in memory (see above on 8:8-9). However, verses 2-3 refer not so much to legal interpretations as to the type of wisdom found in Proverbs.

39:4-5. The wise person will be one of stature and of broad experience and will be devoutly religious.

39:6-11. Verse 6 is a reminder that wisdom is a gift of the Lord, a matter of the Lord's favor, without which none can be wise (cf. 6:37; 51:17). **Secrets** in verse 7 means the knowledge of the Lord, revealed in the law and available only to the Lord's intimates. Verses 8-11 are an expanded restatement of 37:23-26. **It is enough** means his reputation suffices.

B. GOOD AND EVIL THINGS (39:12–42:14)

Some of the various topics treated in this section are regarded as good and some as evil. Others are either good or evil, depending on conditions or circumstances.

39:12-35. *The Lord's Good Works.* This passage contains a psalm of praise, blessing, and thanksgiving to the Lord for the goodness of all the Lord's works. But the exact structure of the passage is unclear. Most commentators regard verses 12-15 as an introduction, verses 16-31 as the text of the psalm, and verses 32-35 as an epilogue. The Revised Standard Version punctuation and arrangement, however, suggest that verse 16 alone is the psalm and verses 17-35 are a series of further expositions on it. A third possibility is to regard verses 12-17*b* as the introduction, since verses 12*a*, 14*cd*, and 16-17*b* are in essence repeated in the epilogue (verses 32-35). This would leave verses 17*c*-31 as the psalm itself.

39:16-31. However the structure is understood, the content of the passage affirms the goodness of all God's **works.** Since God is omnipotent (verses 16*b*, 17*c*-18) and omniscient (verses 19-20) no one can question the Lord's works or the good purpose which the Lord has for them (verses 17*ab*, 21, 33-34).

Some of God's works are obviously **good,** though they can be perverted into **evil** by **sinners** (verses 24-27). Other things which appear to be evil (verses 28-30) are in reality good, since they are God's willing instruments of just punishment (verse 31). Both **blessing** and punishment are well within God's power (verses 22-23). In verse 22 instead of **a river** and **a flood** the Hebrew text reads "the Nile" and "the River," meaning the Euphrates. Both are known for frequent, extensive flooding.

39:32-35. As noted above, these verses are repetitive. Cf. verse 32 with verse 12; verses 33-34 with verses 16-17*b*; verse 35 with verse 14*cd*.

40:1-11. *Suffering.* Ben Sira's acquaintance with the harsh realities of life convinces him that hardship (verse 1), mental anguish (verses 2, 5-7), and physical suffering (verse 9) are the lot of all people. For **purple and a crown** the Hebrew text of verse 4a reads "a turban and plate" and thus includes high priest as well as king (cf. Exodus 28:36-37). Suffering mars one's life from birth to death (verses 1, 11). **Mother** is of course the earth. Perhaps verse 11b should read as the Hebrew: "what is from above [returns] on high." The reference would be to one's breath rather than to any idea of life after death.

Ben Sira is involved here in a rather serious conflict of thought. Usually he affirms the basic theological stand of Proverbs that sinners suffer but the righteous reap rewards. But here he has to admit that life itself seems to ignore the doctrine. How explain the suffering of the righteous? Elsewhere he interprets it as the Lord's testing, or as the Lord's disciplining for their good (2:1-5). But that will not suffice here. All he can do is claim that suffering afflicts the evil much more than other people (verse 8)—that in fact it is for them that these **calamities . . . were created** (cf. 39:25).

40:12-17. *Enduring and Transitory Things.* Dishonesty and ill-gotten gain will soon pass away (verses 12a, 13, 14b; cf. 5:8). Honesty and wisely used wealth endure (verses 12b, 14a; cf. 31:8-11). The **children** of sinners (in the Hebrew text the sinner himself) will not be productive, for their rootage is shallow (verses 15-16). **Plucked up** in the Hebrew text reads "dried up." The idea is that as soon as the stream recedes, the **reeds** will perish. Charity **endures** and is abundantly fruitful (on **kindness** and **almsgiving** see above on 7:32-36). In the Hebrew verse 17a reads: "Kindness, like eternity, shall never be cut off."

40:18-27. *Joys of Life.* These verses form a list of eighteen of life's delights, culminating in the **fear of the Lord** (see above on 1:11-20). Almost all are discussed at greater length elsewhere in the book. The **self-reliant** in verse 18 is one who is independent. The Hebrew text in verse 20b reads "friends" for **wisdom**. In verse 23 it reads "a prudent wife" for **a wife with her husband**.

40:28-30. *The Beggar's Life.* This is an example of one of life's evil things (cf. 29:21-28).

41:1-4. *Death.* Death can be either an evil or a good. But it is inevitable and final and should be accepted without fear. On **Hades** see above on 14:11-16. The Hebrew text of verse 3 carries the meaning: "Remember those who have lived before you and those who come after; all alike share the decree . . ."

41:5-13. *Memorials.* At death sinners are survived by ungodly children whose **posterity** will **suffer reproach** and will ultimately die out (cf. 40:15; contrast 26:21). Thus death is truly the end of everything for the sinner. Even a **good** person's **life** is short at best (cf. 17:2; 37:25), but a good reputation **endures.**

41:14–42:8. *Kinds of Shame.* Verses 14b-15 are repeated from 20:30-31. The distinction between a proper sense of shame (41:17-23) and an improper one (42:1-8) was drawn in 4:20b-21. It is illustrated in 4:22-27 and 20:22-23.

41:17-23. Almost all the twenty things listed in this passage are discussed elsewhere.

42:1-8. Specifically the things of which one should not be ashamed fall under five heads:

(1) The **law** and the **covenant**. This may be directed against "hellenizing" Jews.

(2) Justice to the innocent party in a case, even if in general they are **ungodly**, meaning a Gentile (cf. 4:9).

(3) Honesty in business (verses 3-5a, 7). The Hebrew text of verse 4a could be rendered "of accuracy with scales and balances, and of testing measures and weights."

(4) **Discipline** in the home.

(5) Correction of the **foolish.** In some manuscripts verse 8b refers to the aged man who is accused of sexual impropriety (cf. 25:2).

42:9-14. *Woman's Wickedness.* These paragraphs conclude the section on good and evil things.

42:9-11. The troubles which a **daughter** brings on **her father** are also noted in 7:24-25 and 22:3b-5 (cf. 26:10-12, though there "daughter" probably means "wife"). Quite possibly **hated** in verse 9 refers to the less liked of two wives. **Laughingstock to . . . enemies** occurs also in 6:4 and 18:31 in contexts denouncing lust.

42:12-13. In the Hebrew text these verses are closely related to the preceding. Still speaking of the daughter, verse 12 says:

"Let her not display her beauty to any man or converse with married women." Verse 13 means "lest she learn the wickedness of their ways." But in the Greek texts these verses are sharply set off as a body of advice to men concerning the wickedness of women in general. Verse 12a repeats the counsel of 9:8 and 25:21, which is not applicable, however, to one's own wife (26:16-18; 36:22).

42:14. This verse is the climax of ben Sira's deprecation of women.

X. Praise of the Lord of Nature (42:15–43:33)

In addition to hymns celebrating God's creation of wisdom (1:1-10; 24:1-22) Ecclesiasticus includes several other creation poems which extol God's greatness (16:26–17:14; 18:1-10; 33:7-15; 39:16-31). This is the most lengthy. It falls quite naturally into three parts: an introduction (42:15-25), a catalogue of some natural objects and forces (43:1-26), and a summary conclusion (43:27-33).

A. Introduction (42:15-25)

After a single prefatory statement (verse 15ab) ben Sira speaks of God's creating by fiat (verse 15c; cf. 39:17c; Genesis 1) and of the pervasiveness of **his glory**, which is like that of sunlight. Even the angels are unable to declare the fullness of God's **works** (verse 17). God is eternal (verse 21b) and all-knowing (verses 18-20). On the **abyss** see above on 1:1-10. On God's ability to know human thoughts cf. 23:19. God's **wisdom** is complete (verse 21). God's works are enduring (verse 23a; cf. 16:27). They are sufficient **for every need** (cf. 39:21, 33-34), and **obedient** to divine control (verse 23b; cf. 16:28; 39:31). Though they are distinct, they work together harmoniously (verses 24-25; cf. 33:15).

B. A CATALOGUE (43:1-26)

This list of God's natural wonders is similar to several others—for example, Job 36:24–38:38; Psalms 136:4-9; 148; and Song of the Three Young Men 35-60.

43:1. *The Firmament.* In ancient Near Eastern cosmology the firmament was the arch or dome of the skies. It was conceived of as a solid substance which held up the waters above it. The luminaries moved across it.

43:2-5. *The Sun.* Ben Sira pictures the sun at dawn, heralding the new day, at blazing midday, and toward evening as it follows God's **command**.

43:6-8. *The Moon.* Verse 6 is quite difficult, but apparently the Revised Standard Version makes the best of a confused text. The moon appears at its proper **season**, to mark the **times**—that is, months (cf. Genesis 1:14). The Jews followed a lunar calendar. As an **everlasting sign** it is a symbol of permanence. It marks the time for the observance of the religious festivals. The major ones—Passover in the spring and Ingathering in the fall—began with the new moon. Numbers 28:11-15 specifies offerings for the time of the new moon, and many religious-social gatherings were held at that time. **The month is named for the moon** in that the same Hebrew word means both "new moon" and "month."

43:9-12. *The Stars and the Rainbow.* On the idea of the stars standing according to the Lord's **command** cf. 17:32; Psalm 119:91; and Isaiah 40:26. Genesis 9:13 records the creation of the rainbow.

43:13-15. *Snow (?), Lightning, Clouds, Hail.* The Hebrew text refers to hail rather than **snow** in verse 13. Lightning is an instrument of God's **judgment**.

43:16-17*b*. *Thunder and Storm.* The order of these lines in the Hebrew text is 17*a*, 16, 17*b*. Verse 16*a* describes the effect of thunder rather than of earthquake as some have interpreted.

43:17*c*-20. *Snow, Frost, and Ice.* Cf. Psalm 147:16-17. The fact that in the Palestinian hills snow falls on an average only three days a year adds to the sense of wonder which it causes. Its whiteness or cleanness is a frequent figure in the Bible. To the ancient mind frost also seemed to fall from heaven. In the Hebrew text verse 19*b* reads "And produces thornlike blooms"—a reference to sparkling **pointed** ice crystals on the plants.

43:21-22. *Drought and Dew.*

43:23-26. *The Sea.* On verse 23*a* cf. Job 26:12*a*. In verses 24-25 ben Sira seems to have been thinking of Psalm 104:25-26. Verse 26 is a concluding statement to verses 1-25, which declares that God orders and sustains creation. **His messenger** is the wind.

D. CONCLUSION (43:27-33)

Designating God as **the all** is certainly no suggestion of pantheism. Ben Sira's meaning is that God is indescribable and unfathomable. Even the angels are unable to recount God's works (cf. 42:17). Since God is **greater than all his works** human beings cannot expect to **praise him** adequately. At best our knowledge of God's works is shallow or fragmentary (verse 32). The creator of **all things** also created **wisdom** (verse 33) and bestowed her as a gift on the **godly** (cf. 1:1-10; 24:1-17). This verse is the connective link between the long poem just concluded and that which immediately follows.

XI. IN PRAISE OF FAMOUS MEN (44:1–50:29)

This long section is a natural sequel to the hymn in praise of the Lord of nature (42:15–43:33). Just as all God's works testify to God's power and praise God through their obedience, so Israel praises God through its life. In a sense Israel is the climax of God's creation, as in 16:26–17:14. Ben Sira reviews Israel's history by offering individual eulogies of its worthy persons. But his praise of them is rightly understood as also a praise of the Lord who **apportioned to them great glory**. Wisdom itself was a part of God's creation, and Israel's greatness was possible only because the Lord granted wisdom as a gift to these godly men (43:33).

44:1-15. Introduction. In verse 1 **our fathers** is synonymous with **famous men.** In Hebrew this is "men of piety" or "loyalty." In verse 10 the same phrase is translated **men of mercy. In their generations** means in chronological sequence. Verse 2 means that their possibility for greatness was itself a gift of God (cf. 33:11-12). Verses 3-6 list several types of people who lived in the past—kings, warriors, counselors. They all were **honored** by their contemporaries, but only some are remembered and still praised in later times. Others are completely forgotten.

These in verse 10 means these whom ben Sira is about to enumerate in the following chapters. Their memory endures and their children still **stand by**—that is, live within—the covenant promises which were made to them.

44:16. Enoch. Scholars have long been puzzled by the fact that Enoch is twice mentioned in the list of famous men (see 49:14). It is now apparent, however, that this was not originally the case. The best Hebrew text and the Syriac version do not include verse 16 at this point, but begin the list of worthies with Noah (verse 17). It now seems that verse 16 has been modified and transposed from 49:14 (see comment), perhaps by those who especially admired Enoch and felt that he deserved to head the list.

44:17-18. Noah. Ben Sira recalls that because Noah was **righteous** and blameless he was spared from the great **flood** (Genesis 6:9–8:19). On the covenant with Noah cf. Genesis 8:20-22 and 9:8-17.

44:19-23. Abraham, Isaac, Jacob. Verse 19*a* is based on Genesis 17:5. The patriarch's name is there changed from Abram to Abraham, which is explained as **father of a multitude.** The addition of **great** may have been inspired by Genesis 12:2: "I will . . . make your name great."

The covenant in his flesh refers to the rite of circumcision. **He was tested** alludes to the proposed sacrifice of Isaac in Genesis 22:1-14. The promise of verse 21 refers to that in Genesis

22:16-18. **From sea to sea and from the River** (the Euphrates) **to the ends of the earth** is a traditional description of the ideal extent of Israel's territory. **Isaac** is a particular illustration of the general statement in verses 11-12 (cf. Genesis 26:3-5, 24). He gave the **blessing** of the firstborn son to **Jacob** (Genesis 27:28-29; 28:3-4), who in turn blessed each of his **twelve** sons (Genesis 49:28).

45:1-5. *Moses.* Verse 1 seems to be based on Exodus 11:3. Verse 2*a* refers to Exodus 4:16 and 7:1, in which Moses is told that he will be "as God" to Aaron and Pharaoh. Since the Hebrew *Elohim* can mean "God," "gods," "angels," or "holy ones," depending on the context, the Greek rather timidly rendered the last.

Verses 2*b*-3*b* refer to the plagues which Moses brought on Egypt (Exodus 7–10). Verse 3*d* is based on the story in Exodus 33:18–34:8. In response to Moses' prayer "Show me thy glory" God declines to disclose the fullness of the divine being but does reveal the divine character as being gracious and merciful. Ben Sira teaches that **faithfulness** and **meekness** are qualities in which God delights (see above on 1:22-30). It is for these that God chose Moses. This is based on Numbers 12:3, 7, where "entrusted" is a form of the verb "be faithful." Verse 5 recalls the revelation at Sinai (see above on 17:11-13).

45:6-22. *Aaron.* The extraordinary attention given to Aaron in this passage and to Simon in 50:1-24 shows the importance which ben Sira attaches to the priesthood. Aaron the Levite was Moses' **brother**. He was the first priest, the founder of the **priesthood**. God vested the institution in him and his descendants (cf. Exodus 28:1-4; 29:9).

45:7*c*-13. This detailed description of the priestly vestments is based on Exodus 28. **Splendid vestments** and **superb perfection** in Hebrew involve the words "for glory and for beauty" in Exodus 28:2. On the oracular devices **Urim and Thummim** see above on 32:24–33:3. An **outsider** is any person not descended from Aaron.

45:14-17. Moses' anointing of Aaron is described in Leviticus 8:10-13. But in verse 15 ben Sira is apparently thinking of

Exodus 40:13-15, which also mentions that he shall "serve as priest" in a "perpetual priesthood." Deuteronomy 10:8 says that the Levites were "to minister to him and to bless in his name." The content of the priestly blessing is given in Numbers 6:24-26.

It has been suggested that verse 14 refers to the cereal offering which the priest offered daily in his own behalf (cf. Leviticus 6:19-24) and verse 16 to the burnt offering and cereal offering made **for the people** (cf. Leviticus 1–2). Verse 17 lists the rights and responsibilities of the priests in addition to the temple service. They are teachers and expounders of the law (cf. Deuteronomy 31:9-13; 33:10). They have authority in judging certain difficult cases (cf. Deuteronomy 17:8-12; 21:5).

45:18-22. Verses 18-19 recall Numbers 16. That passage refers to two unsuccessful rebellions by **outsiders**—that is, those not of Aaron's family.

45:20-22. Verses 20-21 speak of the dues which belonged to the priests, since they could not be gainfully employed otherwise (cf. Numbers 18:8-19). Also, the Levitical priests were not given property in the Promised Land (cf. Numbers 18:20; Deuteronomy 10:9; 12:12).

45:23-26. *Phinehas.* Ben Sira's statement about Phinehas in verses 23-24 is based directly on Numbers 25:6-13. Verse 25 interrupts to compare the **covenant** of the kingship (cf. 47:11) with that of the priesthood. Ben Sira's strong insistence that Phinehas was in the true line of descent of the priesthood of Aaron seems to be some type of apologetic. However, the details of it are obscure. Perhaps it has to do with the authority of one of Simon's successors (cf. 50:1-24), to whom verse 26 is addressed.

46:1-10. *Joshua and Caleb.* Deuteronomy 34:9-10 explains that on Moses' death the leadership of the people passed to Joshua. **Successor of Moses in prophesying** reflects Moses' being called a prophet in that passage. As a **great savior** Joshua lived up to **his name**, which means "Yahweh is salvation." In taking **vengeance** against Israel's **enemies** he saved the nation and won for it **its inheritance** (cf. Joshua 11:23).

The language of verse 2 is borrowed from the description of

the capture of Ai (Joshua 8, especially verses 18-19). But if the Greek text is correct in reading **cities** (the Hebrew has the singular) the reference is also to the series of conquests recorded in Joshua 10:28-39. Each of these was won "with the edge of the sword." Verses 4-6 celebrate Joshua's victory at Gibeon (Joshua 10:6-14).

46:7-10. The background of verses 7-8 is Numbers 13–14. When the congregation murmured, Joshua and Caleb alone supported Moses and Aaron. Thus they survived to enter the Promised Land while **six hundred thousand** died in the wilderness (cf. 16:10; Numbers 11:21). Later **Caleb**, aged but strong, requested the **hill country** of Hebron (Joshua 14:6-14). In turn he passed it on to **his children** (Joshua 15:15-19; Judges 1:11-15). Verse 10*b* alludes to the repeated designation of Caleb as one who "wholly followed the LORD."

46:11-12. *The Judges.* Ben Sira speaks collectively of the heroes of Judges. He expresses the hope that their **memory** may continue to live in their descendants—the meaning of **may their bones revive** (cf. 49:10). Verse 11 seems to exclude Gideon, who was involved in **idolatry** (Judges 8:27) and Samson, whom the Lord left because he disclosed his secret to Delilah (cf. Judges 16:20).

46:13-20. *Samuel.* Ben Sira recalls that Samuel was known as a **prophet of the Lord** who was faithful and **trustworthy** (cf. I Samuel 3:20; 9:6). The longer Hebrew form of verse 13 notes that he also acted as a priest. He was a judge whose efforts helped to bring relative peace (cf. I Samuel 7:12-17). It was he who **established the kingdom** by anointing Saul (I Samuel 10:1) and David (I Samuel 16:13) as kings.

46:16-20. Verses 16-18 relate to Israel's victory over the Philistines at Mizpah (cf. I Samuel 7:7-11). Since the Phoenicians were not involved in that struggle, **people of Tyre** must be regarded as an error for "enemy." Verse 19 is a remembrance of Samuel's address to the people in I Samuel 12:1-5. Verse 20 refers to the story in I Samuel 28:3-19 in which the dead Samuel is conjured from Sheol by the medium at En-dor. He predicts Saul's death and Israel's defeat by the Philistines.

47:1-11. *Nathan and David.* Nathan plays a prominent role in the narratives of II Samuel 7:1-17; 12:1-15; and I Kings 1:5-48. Ben Sira is especially interested in him because he helped continue the prophetic succession between Samuel and Elijah.

47:1*b*-7. David was chosen from Jesse's sons and set apart for the kingship just as certain choice portions of the **peace offering** are reserved for sacrifice (cf. Leviticus 3:3-5). While yet a youth he killed the Philistine **giant** and won the people's praise (cf. I Samuel 17; 18:7). As king he defeated many **enemies**, especially the **Philistines** (II Samuel 5:17-25; 8:1).

47:8-11. But David is remembered for more than his military exploits. It was he who provided for the worship of the Lord in Jerusalem. Verse 9 recalls I Chronicles 16:4-7. Verse 8 is a brief summation of the song in I Chronicles 16:8-36. In verse 10 ben Sira alludes to David's provision for daily praises, both **morning** and evening, and for the observance of the **feasts** (I Chronicles 23:30-31). On David's **sins** cf. II Samuel 12:13; 24:10. The **covenant** is the promise that David's dynasty would continue (cf. II Samuel 7:12-16).

47:12-22. *Solomon.* According to I Kings 4:21 Solomon's territories were extensive, but **fared amply**, literally "lived in a broad place," refers rather to prosperity. His prosperity included **peace** and provided the opportunity to build the temple in Jerusalem. This was not a reward for his own righteousness, for he sinned, but **because of him**—that is, David. This is an illustration of how the prosperity of the righteous remains with their descendants (cf. 44:10-13).

47:14-18. Solomon's wisdom was God's gift to the young king (cf. I Kings 3:7-12). It was expressed in **parables . . . riddles . . . songs . . . proverbs . . . interpretations** (probably based on I Kings 4:32-33; Proverbs 1:6) and won for him an international reputation. The reference to Solomon's wealth reflects I Kings 10:21-22, 27.

47:19-22. Ben Sira seems to criticize Solomon for being overly submissive to **women**. But his words may also imply that these were forbidden foreign women whose gods Solomon favored (cf. I Kings 11:4-8). This is given as a reason for the division of the monarchy just following Solomon's death (cf. I Kings 11:9-13). Even so, the covenant with David was kept (cf. verse 11; II Samuel 7:15-16). His **descendants** were not completely cut off.

47:23-25. *Rehoboam and Jeroboam.* Ben Sira's reference to Rehoboam is derived directly from I Kings 11:43–12:17, which offers a second interpretation of the cause of the divided monarchy (cf. verses 19-21). Rehoboam shows **folly** and lack of **understanding** in refusing to follow the advice of the elders (cf. I Kings 12:8, 13) who counseled him to lighten the burden of Solomon's forced-labor **policy.** The **sin** in which Jeroboam involved **Ephraim**—that is, the northern kingdom of Israel— was improper worship (I Kings 12:28-33). The **vengeance** which **came upon them** was conquest by the Assyrians in 722 B.C.

48:1-11. *Elijah.* Verses 2-9 are a series of allusions to the Elijah stories in I, II Kings. The **famine** is that of I Kings 17:1; 18:1. Verses 2*b*, 7-8 refer to his visit to **Sinai** (synonymous with **Horeb**) in I Kings 19:8-18. There Yahweh commanded him to anoint **kings** over Syria and Israel and Elisha as his prophetic successor. Elijah **shut up the heavens**—that is, prevented rainfall (cf. I Kings 17:1)—and **three times brought down fire** (cf. I Kings 18:30-40; II Kings 1:9-12). Verse 5 refers to the story in I Kings 17:17-24 (on **Hades** see above on 14:11-16). Verse 6 refers to II Kings 1:2-17*a*.

Verse 9 recalls Elijah's translation into heaven (cf. II Kings 2:11). He and Enoch were remembered as having escaped death. Therefore it is not surprising that both later became the subjects of an enormous amount of legendary material. **It is written** points to the expectation of Elijah's return (Malachi 4:5-6). The texts of verse 11 are so poorly preserved that it is impossible to be sure of its meaning.

48:12-14. *Elisha.* The account of Elisha's becoming Elijah's successor is given in II Kings 2:9-15. In speaking of his boldness before rulers ben Sira is apparently thinking of his challenge of Jehoram of Israel (II Kings 3:13-14), of a Syrian king (II Kings 6:15-16, 18), and of an unnamed Israelite king (II Kings 6:33–7:1). Verses 13*a* and 14*a* refer to the collection of remarkable stories of Elisha in II Kings 2–8 (especially 2:19-24 and 4:1–6:7). Verses 13*b* and 14*b* recall the revival of the dead man at Elisha's grave (II Kings 13:20-21).

48:15-16. A Historical Interlude. Ben Sira interrupts his praise of the ancient heroes to note again the fall of the northern kingdom, Israel, to the Assyrians in 722 B.C. Verse 15*ef* refers to the survival of the southern kingdom, Judah, where the Davidic monarchy continued in accordance with the covenant with David (cf. 47:11, 22). Verse 16 sums up the scripture appraisals of the Judean kings.

48:17-22*b*. Hezekiah. Hezekiah's strengthening of Jerusalem against Assyrian attack is described in II Chronicles 32:5-6. **Hezekiah fortified** is a play on words between the king's name, which means "Yahweh strengthens" and the first word of II Chronicles 32:5, literally "he strengthened." Verse 22 contains a similar play between Hezekiah and **he held strongly.** The rest of verse 17 refers to the drilling of the Siloam tunnel. In this incredible engineering feat workmen dug through 1,749 feet of **rock** to bring **water** from the Spring of Gihon to the Pool of Siloam (cf. II Kings 20:20). Verses 18-21 contain numerous allusions to the account of the Assyrian threat against Jerusalem (**Zion**) in II Kings 18:13–19:36 and Isaiah 36:1–37:37.

The reading of verse 18*a* (see the Revised Standard Version footnote) is a capsule summary inspired by the first and last verses of the story in II Kings. **The Rabshakeh** was an Assyrian court official. Instead of **made great boasts** some manuscripts read "blasphemed God" (cf. II Kings 18:35; 19:6, 22). On verse 22*ab* see above on verse 16.

48:22*c*-25. Isaiah. Isaiah is remembered for **his vision** and for the sign which he gave to Hezekiah when **the king** was ill (cf. II Kings 20:8-11). The sign was given to confirm the promise that Hezekiah would recover and live fifteen additional years and that the Lord would defend Jerusalem against the Assyrians (cf. II Kings 20:6). Still later Isaiah foresaw the coming Babylonian conquest (verses 24-25; cf. II Kings 20:16-18; Isaiah 39:5-7). But he **comforted** the people by announcing the end of the exile (cf. Isaiah 40:1-2; 42:9) and the glory of the rebuilt community (cf.

Isaiah 61:1-7). Ben Sira of course recognizes no distinction between the eighth century Isaiah of Jerusalem and the sixth century Isaiah of the Exile. By his time Isaiah was regarded as a single book.

49:1-3. *Josiah.* Ben Sira joins other biblical writers in praise of Josiah (on verse 3 cf. II Kings 22:2; 23:3, 25). Under the inspiration of the newly discovered book of the law (cf. II Kings 22:8-20) he instituted widespread reforms in his kingdom. **He was led aright in converting the people** would refer to II Kings 23:2-3, but the Hebrew text reads: "He was grieved at our backsliding"—a reference to II Kings 22:11-13. Verse 2*b* highlights a major feature of the reforms—the removal of every trace of improper worship (cf. II Kings 23:4-20, 24).

49:4-6. *Another Historical Interpretation.* The Babylonians captured Judah and burned Jerusalem in 586 B.C. and the Davidic monarchy **came to an end.** Ben Sira's comment on **David and Hezekiah and Josiah** shows that he was influenced by II Kings (see above on 48:15-16; of the Judean rulers after Hezekiah, II Kings praises only Josiah). But his interpretation of the fall of the city and the subsequent exile as a fulfillment of the **word of Jeremiah** may also show that he was influenced by the Chronicler's work (cf. II Chronicles 36:21).

49:7. *Jeremiah.* When Jeremiah persisted in saying that the city would fall to the Babylonians, he was beaten, imprisoned, and thrown into a cistern to die (cf. Jeremiah 37:15; 38:6). The rest of verse 7 reflects Jeremiah's call (cf. Jeremiah 1:5, 10).

49:8-9. *Ezekiel.* Verse 8 alludes to Ezekiel's **vision** (cf. Ezekiel 1; 10). The text of verse 9 is so uncertain that interpretation amounts almost to guesswork. On the basis of a doubtful Hebrew text some scholars believe that the verse is a reference to Job (in Hebrew "Job" and "enemy" are very similar words) or to the mention of Job in Ezekiel 14:14, 20.

49:10. *The Twelve Prophets.* In Hebrew scripture the twelve prophets (Hosea through Malachi in the Old Testament) are regarded as one book and follow Ezekiel in order. On the figure of verse 10*ab* see above on 46:11-12.

49:11-13. *Postexilic Heroes.* Zerubbabel and Jeshua (or

Joshua) are remembered for having built the second **temple** in Jerusalem (cf. Ezra 3:2, 8-9; 5:2; Haggai 1:14; Zechariah 4:9; 6:12). Ben Sira also remembers the mention of Zerubbabel as **like a signet** ring (Haggai 2:23). He does not speak of the messianic (monarchal) expectation which that figure suggested in the time of Haggai and which otherwise surrounded Zerubbabel and Jeshua (cf. Zechariah 3:8; 4:14; 6:11-13). He makes much of the eternal nature of the Davidic monarchy (for example, 45:25; 47:11, 22). But he never features the hope for the restoration of the monarchy, even in his prayer for Israel (36:1-17).

49:13. Under Nehemiah's direction the **walls** and **gates** and gate **bars** of Jerusalem were rebuilt. That he also rebuilt the people's **houses** is apparently an interpretation of Nehemiah 7:4. The absence of any reference to Ezra is the most glaring omission in ben Sira's list of famous men. Elsewhere the priest-scribe Ezra was regarded as the greatest leader after the Babylonian exile. Some have suggested that perhaps Ezra and Nehemiah have been fused together in ben Sira's memory. Others believe that since Ezra's thought developed into later Pharisaism, while ben Sira shows certain "Sadducean" tendencies, his oversight of Ezra was deliberate. Still others say simply that the lack of any reference to Ezra is a mystery.

49:14-16. *Heroes Before the Flood.* Having enumerated the heroes from Noah to Nehemiah, ben Sira now works backward from Enoch to **Adam.** Verse 14 may well have contained four lines originally, two of which have been modified and transposed to 44:16 (see comment). Perhaps the verse originally said:

Few like Enoch have been created on earth,
An example of knowledge to all generations (cf. 44:16*b*);
He walked with the Lord,
And also he was taken up personally (or "from the earth," as the Greek says).

The verse is an interpretative rendering of Genesis 5:24: "Enoch walked with God; and he was not, for God took him." "Few" (line *a*) represents the Herew text and is probably more correct than **no one.** For "knowledge" (line *b*, meaning the knowledge of God) the Greek mistakenly read repentance (see 44:16*b*). **Pleased** (44:16*a*) is based on the Septuagint text of Genesis 5:24, but "walked with" (line *c*) is supported in the Hebrew text. Ben Sira knew the tradition that Enoch's perfection enabled him to escape death. The words "few" (line *a*) and "also" (line *d*) may reflect the remembrance of Elijah's similar experience (cf. 48:9).

Enoch and **Joseph** are likened in that by tradition Enoch's body was translated and Joseph's was especially **cared for** (cf. Genesis 50:25-26; Exodus 13:19; Joshua 24:32). **Shem** (cf. Genesis 9:26) and **Seth** (cf. Genesis 4:25-26) were **honored** because, according to the Hebrew text, they were "visited" with the sacred name Yahweh. The Hebrew text reads "and Enosh" for **among men.** Adam is honored above all.

50:1-24. *Simon.* The long section in praise of famous men, begun in 44:1, climaxes in a eulogy of the recent **high priest** Simon. Ben Sira remembers Simon for having directed certain repairs and fortifications (verses 1-4) and for his leadership in an observance of the Day of Atonement (verses 5-21).

Who was this high priest Simon? Scholars seem now to think that Simon the **son of Onias** (Johanan in Hebrew) was high priest from around 225 to shortly after 200 B.C. The Jewish historian Josephus (late first century A.D.) calls him Simon (or Simeon) II, though it is doubtful that there ever was a Simon I. It seems likely also that he is to be identified with Simon the Just (or the Righteous), who in rabbinical literature is said to have been an important link in the transmission of the traditions from the time following Ezra to the later rabbis.

50:1-4. The Revised Standard Version is probably correct in considering verse 1*a* a reference to Simon rather than to Joseph (see the footnotes to 49:15 and 50:1). **In his life** indicates that Simon is no longer living at the time ben Sira is writing. His repair and fortification of the **temple** and **city** fit well into the historical period immediately following 199/98 B.C., when the Seleucid King Antiochus III the Great seized control of Palestine from Ptolemy V of Egypt. It is likely that this work was done soon after Antiochus' victory and with his consent. Indeed Josephus so indicates.

50:5-21. This description of the temple worship on the Day of Atonement is obviously that of an eye-witness. But ben Sira forgoes the details of the ritual acts—he seems to overlook some of them altogether—to concentrate on the radiance of Simon himself (verses 6-10). He does mention Simon's coming out from the **inner sanctuary**—literally "house of the veil"—the Holy of Holies, to which only the high priest had access, and he only on the Day of Atonement.

Simon puts on the regalia normally worn by the high priest. He goes to the **altar**, and from his assistants receives the parts of the sacrificial beasts, which he offers for himself and the people (cf. Leviticus 16:24-25). Then follows the drink offering, specified in Numbers 28:7-8 in connection with the daily sacrifices. The **trumpets** sound (cf. Numbers 10:2, 10) and the people prostrate themselves in **worship**, which involves singing and prayers.

The climax of the service is Simon's pronouncing of the priestly benediction (Numbers 6:24-26). **Glory in his name** involves the fact that the divine name Yahweh was actually pronounced aloud by the high priest in this blessing (see above on 23:7-15).

50:22-24. As they stand in the Greek text these verses could be a fitting conclusion to the whole section in praise of famous men. But the Hebrew text of verse 24 reads: "May his love abide on Simon, and may he keep him in the covenant of Phinehas; may one never be cut off from him, and may his offspring be as the days of heaven."

Simon's son and successor, Onias III, was deprived of the high priesthood in 175/74 B.C. when his brother Jason bought the favor of King Antiochus IV Epiphanes (cf. II Maccabees 4:7-10). Within three years, however, Jason himself was outbid by Menelaus (cf. II Maccabees 4:23-26). Smoldering resentment over Jason in the Jewish community flared into outraged riot over Menelaus. This led eventually to the Maccabean revolt.

Ben Sira reveals no knowledge of the loss of the priestly office by Onias III, or of the subsequent events. Yet his unusual stress on the importance of the true priestly succession seen in 45:6-26 reveals dire premonitions that the office is threatened. The knowledge of Simon's fortifications and the unawareness of the deposition of Onias III indicate terminal dates of 198-174 for ben Sira's writing. Most scholars suggest a date near 180.

50:25-26. A Fragment. These two verses, in the literary style of 25:2 and 26:5, denounce the Idumeans, the Philistines, and the Samaritans. **Mount Seir** is the chief mountain range in the former land of Edom southeast of the Dead Sea. In the Old Testament it is often used as a synonym for the nation of Edom. Long before ben Sira's time the Edomites had been driven from their land by the Arab Nabateans and lived in southern Palestine (Idumea), where they encroached on Judah's territory. Ben Sira is probably using traditional terminology to refer to these Idumean neighbors rather than to the Nabateans who in his day actually lived on Mount Seir.

The Philistines were traditional enemies of Israel. By ben Sira's time they had been largely absorbed into Phoenicia and were receptive to Hellenistic influence. The Samaritans existed as a separate **people**, though **no nation**, who worshiped in a rival temple built on Mount Gerizim near **Shechem.** Ben Sira may have felt that they also were too kindly disposed toward the Seleucid kingdom.

50:27-29. Colophon. The author signs his book, adding a commendation of its content and a blessing on the reader. There are several minor differences between the Greek and Hebrew texts in these verses. Perhaps the most important is that the Hebrew of verse 27*ab* reads: "Wise instruction and apt [?] proverbs I have written . . ." This may account for the fact that the word "proverbs" or "parables" occurs in some of the ancient titles by which the book was known. On the author's name see the Introduction.

XII. APPENDIX (51:1-30)

In the Greek text, which the Revised Standard Version basically follows, this chapter contains a psalm of thanksgiving (verses 1-12) and an acrostic poem relating to wisdom and instruction (verses 13-30). The Hebrew text includes a thanksgiving liturgy quite similar in form to Psalm 136. Additionally, at the end of the chapter there is a doxology—present in variant form in a few Greek manuscripts—and a second colophon, similar to 50:27*b*.

It has been customary to accept ben Sira as the author of at least the two poems which the Revised Standard Version includes. But discovery among the Dead Sea Scrolls of a first century Hebrew text of verses 13-20*a* and two words of verse 30 calls this assumption into question. This text clearly shows that at least this portion of the poem has been extensively modified in the Greek version, and even more so in our other Hebrew copies. It contains no reference to prayer, the temple, or to glorifying the Lord who gives wisdom. Instead it is an allegorical, erotic account of a young man's intimacy with wisdom, who is personified as his nursing mother and then as his teacher and mistress.

The Dead Sea text is contained in a collection of psalms which claim to be written by David. The members of the community who copied the Dead Sea text knew ben Sira's book. They could scarcely have attributed this poem to David if it had been a part of ben Sira's book as they knew it. This evidence suggests, therefore, that the poem was written by some other wisdom teacher. It was affixed to ben Sira's book, presumably because it was so similar in content.

If indeed the acrostic poem of verses 13-30 is a later addition, one is also led to speculate on the origin of the psalm of thanksgiving in verses 1-12. It would be a natural assumption that the colophon in 50:27-29 marked the end of ben Sira's work. Thus it is possible that the psalm of thanksgiving was also added later from another source, one point of attraction being ben Sira's statement in 34:12 that he has "often been in danger of death."

51:1-12. *A Psalm of Thanksgiving*. The psalm is filled with the phraseology of the biblical psalms. The author sings praise to God for having delivered him from some mortal danger. One can only guess as to the details of his difficulty. But unless the language is figuratively veiled it would seem that enemies maliciously slandered him before a **king** (verses 2, 6; the Hebrew omits **to the king**). Their charge is punishable by **death** (verses 5-6; on **Hades** see above on 14:11-16). Though he was innocent (verse 4) he received no human help (verse 7) but was delivered by the Lord after he had prayed (verses 9-12).

An interesting point is the designation of the Lord in the Greek text of verse 10 as the **Father of my lord.** What does "my lord" mean? Suggestions include:

(1) an error for "my life," as in 23:1, 4;
(2) a reference to the priest-king of Israel, as in Psalm 110:1, "The LORD says to my lord," or by an extension of meaning to the nation itself;
(3) a later Christian rephrasing of the verse to make it refer to Jesus.

Admittedly all these are quite tenuous.

51:13-30. *An Acrostic Poem*. This concluding passage is an alphabetical acrostic—a poem structured so that the verses or lines begin with the successive letters of the Hebrew alphabet.

51:13-22. According to the Greek text this first part describes the search for wisdom by a youth. **From blossom to ripening grape** means from childhood to manhood. This young man appreciated the necessity for thorough dedication and self-discipline (verses 15c, 18, 19ab, 20ab), but he knew also that ultimately wisdom comes only as the Lord's gift. Therefore he prayed for her (verses 13b, 14a). Having received her, he praises God (verses 17, 22). Much of this is like what ben Sira says elsewhere—the allusion to his travels (cf. 34:11; 39:4); the value of seeking wisdom in youth (cf. 6:18); the need for discipline (cf. 4:17-19); prayer to God and praise for God's gift of wisdom (cf. 39:5-6).

51:23-30. In this last half of the poem a wisdom teacher invites prospective students to come to his **school**. This is the earliest known occurrence of this term—literally "house of study"—which later became the common name for advanced schools of biblical studies. Verse 25 indicates that no tuition was charged. Apparently this is to be taken literally, though in later times there was sometimes a charge.

Verses 26-28 are quite similar in thought to 6:18-31—verse 28 should be taken figuratively, much in the sense of 6:19. Verse 29 seems clear enough. But in the Hebrew text it reads: "May my soul delight in my circle of students, and may you not be put to shame in praising me," which may have been the original meaning. Verse 30 urges the students to be diligent in study, so that they will be ready when the Lord visits them for judgment (cf. 18:20*a*).

BARUCH

Stanley Brice Frost

Introduction

This book is sometimes designated I Baruch to distinguish it from the Apocalypse of Baruch, which is then called II Baruch. It consists of three parts (1:1–3:8; 3:9–4:4; and 4:5–5:9) which can be recognized as originally independent. The book is extant in Greek and in several translations from the Greek. But almost certainly at least the first two parts were composed in Hebrew.

The First Part

This is a letter containing a prayer of confession (1:15–3:8). It has a historical introduction (1:1-14) which claims that Baruch, the secretary of Jeremiah (cf. Jeremiah 36), wrote the letter in Babylon at the time of the fall of Jerusalem in 586. The exiles sent it to Jerusalem with the request that the prayer be used in the services there. They also, it is said, paid for sacrifices to be offered on behalf of Nebuchadnezzar and his "son" Belshazzar (see below on 1:10-14).

This work was clearly not written by Baruch, because he was evidently in Jerusalem at the fall of the city (cf. Jeremiah 32:12-16) and went afterward to Egypt (cf. Jeremiah 43:5-7). It repeats the mistake of the author of Daniel in calling Belshazzar the son of Nebuchadnezzar (cf. Daniel 5). Also, the liturgical prayer is strongly dependent on the prayer in Daniel 9:4-19. Therefore it must be dated after Daniel, which was written around 165 B.C. Accordingly some scholars assign it to the Maccabean period (see Introduction to I Maccabees).

The content, however, suggests a time when the Jews were under foreign domination—that is, after 63 B.C., during the Roman period. Its purpose is to say: "Baruch and his contemporaries saw the need to submit to Gentile conquerors, and to pray for them. We urge you to do the same." More specifically it requests sacrifices and prayers for a ruler and his son who have just destroyed Jerusalem.

If we look for a time when such a message would be relevant, it may be found immediately following A.D. 70, when Titus completed the capture and destruction of Jerusalem after his father, Vespasian, had returned to Rome to become emperor. In such a time this piece might well be written by a Jew living in Rome or some other metropolitan center—perhaps Antioch in Syria. Its purpose would be to urge submission to the Emperor Vespasian and his coregent son Titus—"and we shall serve them many days and find favor in their sight" (1:12).

Thus this part of the book is probably to be dated during the reign of Vespasian (69–79) or of Titus (79-81). It hoped to heal the breach between the Jews and Rome by becoming a part of synagogue liturgies. There is evidence that in some areas it became for a while part of the liturgy of lamentation on the ninth of Ab, the day when the burning of the temple was remembered.

The Second Part

This section (3:9–4:4) is a poem on the theme "Where shall wisdom be found?" It is based largely on Job 28 but goes beyond it by equating wisdom with possession of the Law—that is, the Torah or Pentateuch (4:1-4). This point of view was characteristic of the later wisdom school (cf. Wisdom of Solomon 10). It would suggest a date not earlier than the second half of the first century B.C., but we cannot be very definite.

The Third Part

This poem of reassurance to the Jewish people (4:5–5:9) gives very little indication of date. The lamentation for captivity of Zion's children to a "nation from afar" (4:15) does not mention any specific event. It suggests a time during the first century A.D. before the disaster of 70.

The Final Book

The two poems were no doubt added to the first part sometime in the late first century A.D. At that time the mood of most Jews was not in tune with the final work, and it was not very influential among them. Among Christians, however, it came to be widely accepted. In many of the Septuagint manuscripts, it stands between Jeremiah and Lamentations. The passage 3:36-37 was taken to be a prophecy of the Incarnation, and many church fathers quote the book as scripture. The little book is especially valuable as a testimony to thought and piety among Jews of the Dispersion in the latter part of the first Christian century. Later the loss of Jerusalem and the rise of Christianity destroyed these older ways of thought and gave birth to the more regimented rabbinism of the Talmud.

I. THE PRAYER OF CONFESSION (1:1–3:8)

1:1-4. *Authorship and Date.* On **Baruch** cf. Jeremiah 36; 43:5-7; and 45:1-5. The **seventh day** of the **fifth** "month" probably should be read instead of **year**, for that was the day Nebuzaradan put the torch to the temple and to **Jerusalem** (II Kings 25:8). At that time, however, Baruch was in the city with Jeremiah, not **in Babylon**. The **river Sud** is unknown. This introduction is designed to give the little work an air of authenticity.

1:5-9. *Gifts for the Temple.* After the destruction in 586 worship of some kind was continued on the temple site (cf. Jeremiah 41:4-5). But we do not hear of any priesthood, and this **Jehoiakim** is unknown. Probably he is an invented detail, though the author may possibly be misdating the postexilic high priest Joiakim (Nehemiah 12:10). In verse 8 no doubt he is thinking of the **vessels** mentioned in Jeremiah 28:3, but Baruch would not have had access to them. **Sivan** is the Babylonian name for the third month, and so this would be nearly a year later. Perhaps the author has in mind II Chronicles 31:7.

1:10-14. *Prayer for the Ruler.* The mistake of calling **Belshazzar** the son of **Nebuchadnezzar** obviously comes from the story in Daniel 5. He was actually the son of Nabonidus (556-539). The purpose of this document now emerges: to encourage cooperation with the ruling authorities (see Introduction).

1:15-20. *Prayer of Confession.* The phraseology is biblical, but cf. especially Daniel 9:7, 10 (see Introduction).

2:1-10. *Warnings Realized.* The terrible **calamities** of which the prophets warned have come true. On verse 3 cf. Leviticus 26:29 and II Kings 6:25-30.

2:11-26. *Appeal for Mercy.* The argument of verses 17-18 is that the **dead** cannot praise God in **Hades**—that is, Sheol, the underworld home of the dead. But the living, however **feeble**, can; therefore may God let Israel continue to live. It is based on Isaiah 38:18-19 and should not be taken as evidence of the author's own belief concerning life after death. He is simply concerned to echo a biblical passage (see below on 3:1-8). With verses 21-23 cf. Jeremiah 25:10-11. Verse 24 refers to Jeremiah 8:1-2. The author shows great familiarity with Jeremiah.

2:27-35. *The Pattern of Compassion.* The author relies on the general teaching of the Old Testament that punishment is followed by restoration. He asks God that, now that punishment has taken place, forgiveness may follow. He writes of the period after 586 but is thinking of his own times. In referring to **Moses** he may have Deuteronomy 28 especially in mind.

3:1-8. *The End of Iniquity.* The prayer ends on a note of fine intensity. The author says that he and his peers have put away the sins of their **fathers**, and that their fathers, who sinned so grievously, are pleading on their behalf. This thought of life after death contradicts 2:17 but probably reflects more truly the author's own conviction.

No doubt he has Jeremiah 31:29 in mind. He accepts the idea of the solidarity of Israel and the nation's need to confess the sins of many generations. But he is beginning to suggest that Israel's sufferings are no longer justifiable in terms of punishment for its own sin. The picture of suffering righteous Israel—a teaching of later Judaism—is beginning to emerge. The prayer may well come from the first century A.D. (see Introduction).

II. A COMMENDATION OF WISDOM (3:9–4:4)

This is an excellent example of the work of the Hebrew wisdom tradition. It stands in line with Job 28, on which it is modeled; Proverbs 8; Ecclesiasticus 51:13-30; and the Wisdom of Solomon 7:1-30, especially 10:1-21.

3:9-14. *The Reason for Weakness.* Israel is wretched because it has **forsaken the fountain of wisdom.** On **Hades** see above on 2:11-26.

3:15-31. *The Way to Wisdom.* Wisdom will not be found with pleasure-loving **princes** (verses 15-19) or with lusty youth (verses 20-21) or in the traditional centers of sagacity (verses 22-23). **Canaan** here probably means Phoenicia. **Teman** was a city and district of Edom. **Merran** is probably a misspelling for Midian. **Sons of Hagar** means Ishmaelites (cf. Genesis 16:15). All were early neighbors of Israel who had a reputation for shrewdness.

Wisdom rests neither with the legendary **giants . . . of old** (cf. Genesis 6:1-6) nor in distant parts (cf. Deuteronomy 30:12-14). No one knows where wisdom abides (cf. Job 28:12-28).

3:32–4:4. *God's Gift to Israel.* God the Creator knows where wisdom is to be found and has given her to Israel—the wisdom which is the **book** containing the **law** (the Pentateuch, the first five books of the Bible). If Israel will observe the law it will not be wretched (cf. 4:10-12). Knowing **what is pleasing to God,** Israel will be **happy** indeed.

III. ENCOURAGEMENT FOR ISRAEL (4:5–5:9)

4:5-20. *Zion's Supplication.* The author reminds his fellow Jews that they are being punished for **sins**. But he exhorts them to be of good cheer, for God will **deliver** them. **Zion**, their mother, will herself plead for them.

4:21-29. *The Return of Joy.* Zion rejoices because she knows that God will soon intervene to restore her **children** from afar. She calls on her children, since they were headstrong in sin, to have a **tenfold zeal** in repentance.

4:30–5:9. *Jerusalem Exhorted.* Previously the city has been exhorting her children. Now the author calls on the city to recognize the coming salvation. She is to put off her widow's weeds, to **put on for ever the beauty of the glory from God**. Her children who have gone out **on foot** will come back **carried . . . as on a royal throne**. The **hills** will lie down and **valleys** will rise up. Trees will shade their walk. This little exhortation to hope is very dependent on Second Isaiah (Isaiah 35:1-2; 40:4; 49:22-23) and on the Psalms of Solomon (11:2-7) but nevertheless has a freshness of its own. The piety is akin to that of Luke 1–2.

THE LETTER OF JEREMIAH

Stanley Brice Frost

INTRODUCTION

This little book follows Lamentations in the earliest manuscripts of the Septuagint. In the Vulgate, as well as in many later Greek manuscripts, it was attached to Baruch and thus came to be numbered as chapter 6 of that book. The older English versions included it in Baruch. The Revised Standard Version and other modern translations recognize it as a separate work, though they retain the established numbering for convenience of reference.

The work is best described as the transcript of a hortatory address rather than a letter. It is a rambling, repetitious attack on idols and idol worship, said to be written by Jeremiah to Jews about to be taken as captives to Babylon. "Jeremiah" is an obvious pseudonym. But the descriptive details point strongly to the probability that "Babylon" means the actual city of Babylon—rather than Rome as it often does in later literature. The letter is an earnest appeal to Jews living in Mesopotamia not to succumb to the worship of the Babylonian deities.

It is likely that the author himself lived in Babylon or some other city of the region and had often witnessed what he here describes. He chose to associate his work with Jeremiah because Jeremiah 29:1-23 tells of a letter sent by Jeremiah to the captives in Babylon. Also, Jeremiah 10:1-16 expresses the sentiment on which he wanted to speak. No doubt it seemed to him very fitting that he should send out his letter in Jeremiah's name in the hope that it would exemplify the spirit and mind of the great prophet.

In 6:3 it is predicted that the captives will remain in Babylon "up to seven generations," rather than the seventy years of Jeremiah 25:11 and 29:10. This suggests that the author may thus be designating the interval from 586 (or 597) to his own day. If so, assuming the standard biblical generation of forty years, the date of writing is around 306 B.C. Though this is earlier than most other books of the Apocrypha, there is no evidence against a date late in the fourth century or early in the third. Some scholars, however, prefer to place it in the Maccabean period (see Introduction to I Maccabees).

The work is extant only in Greek and translations from the Greek. However, it was probably written in Hebrew—or in Aramaic, as a few scholars maintain. In some passages the translator into Greek has misunderstood the original text and as a result has produced nonsense. Sometimes retranslation into Hebrew reveals a probable cause for the error and makes possible reconstruction of the original (for example, see below on 6:59, 72).

The author has given his work a superficial appearance of structure. At intervals he repeats a summarizing statement or question to the effect that the idols "are not gods" (6:16, 23, 29*b*, 40*a*, 44*b*, 52, 56*b*, 65, 69) and on this basis the Revised Standard Version divides into paragraphs. These divisions do not mark units of thought, however. The ideas follow no logical order and are often repeated. The main arguments are that the idols are not gods because:

   (1) They cannot look after themselves, let alone anyone else (6:12-13, 22, 26-27, 55-56, etc.).

   (2) They and their worshipers are immoral and unclean (6:11, 28-29, 43).

   (3) They cannot play the saving role of a true god (6:34-38, 41, 53-54, 66).

(4) Not being obedient to the grand design of the universe, they have no place in its unity of purpose (6:60-64). This is by far the most original thought in the letter, but it is the least developed.

The little work displays the moral earnestness of Judaism around the fourth to third centuries B.C. It stands worthily in the tradition of Psalms 115; 135; Isaiah 44:9-20; and Jeremiah 10:1-16. The Apology of Aristides, a defense of Christianity addressed to the Emperor Hadrian around A.D. 130, reveals its influence. An attack on dying paganism by Julius Firmicus Maternus around A.D. 350 borrows extensively from it. Evidently the letter meant much to the Christian church in the pagan atmosphere of the Roman Empire.

COMMENTARY

6:4. The author no doubt often saw processions in which idols were **carried on men's shoulders** (cf. verse 26; Isaiah 46:1-2, 7; Jeremiah 10:5)—especially at the great New Year festival.

6:18. The comparison to **gates . . . shut on every side** on a political offender seems to refer to house arrest of a very strict kind—but it is a curious simile.

6:20. The idols, being made of wood with a thin plating of gold or silver, are attacked by insects along with the temple woodwork.

6:29-30. In ancient Hebrew thought a woman **in menstruation or at childbirth** was religiously "unclean" (cf. Leviticus 12; 15:19-30). The idea of her transmitting the uncleanness to **sacrifices** would be especially shocking to Jewish readers. Similarly, the fact that a woman should even **serve meals** to the image of a god would be quite offensive. Jews limited participation in religious rites to males and had a long tradition of opposition to cult prostitution.

6:41-43. The **Chaldeans**—that is, Babylonians—cannot see that their god **Bel** is in the same plight as the **dumb man** he is being asked to heal. If they could, they would forsake such impotent gods. Verse 43 evidently alludes to a custom whereby a woman had to surrender her virginity before marriage to any passer-by as a tribute to Ishtar. The Greek historian Herodotus described this custom as prevalent in the Babylon of his day (around 450 B.C.).

6:59. The idea of a **king who shows his courage** is a fine one. But a modest concept would be more in keeping with the rest of the verse. It has been suggested very plausibly that the original Hebrew was "better a stick in a man's hand." This fits better with **household utensil**—that it is better to be something lowly and useful than to be idle and useless.

6:60-63. Cf. Psalm 104:1-4. The author's thought is that anything which is not part of Yahweh's harmony of service is self-condemned.

6:70. This **scarecrow** image is borrowed directly from Jeremiah 10:5—but it is a telling illustration for the subject at hand.

6:72. The same Hebrew word meant both **linen** and "marble" (see the Revised Standard Version footnote). The translator into Greek apparently knew only one meaning—the wrong one for this context.

THE PRAYER OF AZARIAH
AND THE SONG OF THE
THREE YOUNG MEN

George A. F. Knight

Additions to the Book of Daniel

The two titles—the Prayer of Azariah and the Song of the
Three Young Men—now form together one book of the
Apocrypha. Along with Susanna and Bel and the Dragon they
comprise the three so-called principal Additions to the biblical
book of Daniel. These Additions are not found in the original
Hebrew and Aramaic of Daniel. Therefore they do not appear in
Protestant English translations. They are, however, included in
the Septuagint, which was the Bible of the early church.

These writings are an integral part of the Bible used by the
Roman Catholic Church. We may find them today in a
translation from Theodotion, a Jewish convert who sometime in
the second century A.D. produced what seems to be a free Greek
revision of the Septuagint on the basis of the Hebrew. The
Theodotion version of the Additions displaced the Septuagint
text in the early Christian centuries.

In the Greek versions Susanna forms an introduction to the

biblical book of Daniel. In Susanna (verse 45) Daniel is described as "a young lad." Appropriately, then, this story comes first. Then the double book, the Prayer of Azariah and the Song of the Three Young Men (or "Holy Children," King James Version) is found in Daniel 3, between verses 23 and 24. Bel and the Dragon, really two stories, occurs as a supplement to the book of Daniel. When Jerome made his important Latin translation of the Bible—the Vulgate—around A.D. 400, he drew attention to the fact that these stories did not occur in the Hebrew Bible. He indicated that Bel and Susanna at least were merely "fables."

Date and Composition

The Prayer and the Song both originated in the same period as the book of Daniel—around 165 B.C. The Prayer of Azariah was evidently composed independently of Daniel during the period when worship at the temple was impossible, owing to the Jewish war with Antiochus IV Epiphanes. The Song appears to have been written only a matter of months after Daniel, for we read in the Song that the faithful in Israel exulted at the restoration of worship at the temple. This historical incident is represented by the sentence that declares how God "has rescued us from Hades . . . from the midst of the fire he has delivered us" (verse 66). The Song was probably written originally in Hebrew.

The Song has been used in the liturgy of the Christian church throughout the centuries. Verses 35-65 appear as an alternate canticle in the regular morning prayer service of *The Book of Common Prayer*. They take their name—the *Benedicite*—from the opening word in Latin.

The Teachings

The great biblical themes of the sovereignty of God, the judgment of God upon the apostasy of God's own people, and of God's delight in showing abundant mercy are all in evidence in the Prayer. The Song is one of the greatest paeans of praise of the Almighty that anyone has ever penned.

I. THE PRAYER OF AZARIAH (Verses 1-22)

Azariah is the Hebrew name of Abednego (Daniel 1:6-7). He was one of the three young Jews whom Nebuchadrezzar thrust into the fiery furnace for refusing to worship the golden image. The Prayer purports to be what Azariah uttered in the flames. It is a blessing of God, not a thanksgiving. In the Old Testament a blessing was something potent and conveyed something from the speaker to the one blessed. The willingness of the Almighty to receive a blessing from a human being is a revelation of God's loving condescension.

Verses 3-8. In blessing him, Azariah thanks God also for God's **just** exercise of judgment. With the great prophets, he knows that God's judgment *is* God's saving love in action. He believes that such judgment on Israel is justified, as did the writer of the book of Lamentations when Jerusalem fell in 586 B.C. (Lamentations 1:5). In both cases the reason was the same. Israel had not obeyed God's commandments and so had not kept its side of the covenant (cf. Exodus 19:5).

Verses 9-22. The **unjust king** mentioned here is Antiochus IV Epiphanes (see Introduction to I Maccabees). He sacked Jerusalem and desecrated the temple in 168 B.C. Azariah pleads that while Israel has indeed broken its side of the covenant, God should not break the divine side: **deal with us in thy forbearance and in thy abundant mercy.** "Steadfast love" is the Revised Standard Version translation of the original Hebrew word behind "mercy" and is the word selected to represent the content of the covenant relationship. God should remember **Abraham,** a "friend" (Isaiah 41:8), and **Isaac,** a **servant,** and that **Israel** is God's **holy one.**

It is true that God has every right to break with a faithless people. Yet they are God's "holy nation" (Exodus 19:6) only because God is the Holy One. Thus for God's own **name sake** the Lord will not let them go. This tension in the heart of God is well expressed in Hosea 11:8-9. The steadfast love that Israel should show toward God can only reflect God's love for Israel.

Verse 13 refers to God's promise to Abraham (Genesis 15:5;

22:17). Without temple, without high priest, without sacrifices and offerings, Azariah prays as did Samuel that a **contrite heart** may be the true **sacrifice** that God will accept (cf. I Samuel 15:22). Verse 18 is a declaration of faith out of the depths. Such faith is possible only because Azariah knows of God's marvelous works in the past—the Exodus, the restoration from Exile, etc., by which God has been shown as the Lord, the only God. Therefore Azariah prays: **Let them [all] know that thou art the Lord, the only God, glorious over the whole world.**

This prayer comes out of "the midst of the fire" (verse 1). Its theological significance therefore rests in the fact that people have learned to praise God wholeheartedly only when they have met with adversity. Adversity is here represented as fire. Thus even in tribulation the faithful three young men are still "in" God, or God is still with them. No wonder they want to praise God.

II. The Song of the Three Young Men (Verses 23-68)

Verses 23-28. To give this great benediction a setting in the Maccabean Wars, verses 23-28 describe it as another hymn that all three young men—Shadrach, Meshach, and Abednego—sing in the burning fiery furnace. The fiery furnace represents the painful experiences the faithful had to undergo when they battled against the forces of Antiochus Epiphanes (cf. I Maccabees 1).

Verse 26. The prose introduction refers to the "son of the gods" of Daniel 3:25 as **the angel of the Lord.** In the Old Testament an angel could represent God and speak for God, as if God dwelt in the angel. The Septuagint frequently translates the Hebrew phrase "sons of God" as "angels."

Verse 31. From **blessed art thou in the temple of thy holy glory** we may conclude that this Song was written some years later than the Prayer. Perhaps it was composed for the rededication ceremonies when the temple was consecrated for use again.

Verses 32-68. The Song uses language that would come naturally to those who knew the accepted scriptures of their day. The refrain reminds one of that in Psalm 136. Much of the Song is similar to Psalm 104, a poem which amplifies and theologizes upon the story of creation in Genesis 1.

But it speaks also of the God who seeks intimate communion with people, the God **who sittest upon cherubim**—that is, whose mercy seat is between the cherubim that stretch their wings over the ark (cf. Exodus 25:20-22; I Samuel 4:4). Yet God is also the God who **lookest upon the deeps**, the "waters under the firmament" (Genesis 1:7). The phrase refers to the chaos out of which God brings forth order, salvation, and light.

Thereafter the Song becomes a summons to all creatures in heaven and earth, animate and inanimate, to **bless the Lord**. In Old Testament times to bless another was to convey something of one's own soul, to confer something which the other did not already possess. In God's case, however, that is not possible. God is all in all and so lacks nothing that human beings can give. Yet the biblical view, paradoxically, is that God seeks human love and blessing, as if in need of them.

The Song ends with the words, **for his mercy endures for ever,** like the refrain of Psalm 136. **Mercy** is understood to be the concept of steadfast love found in the Revised Standard Version.

THE BOOK OF SUSANNA

George A. F. Knight

INTRODUCTION

For the date and composition of Susanna see the Introduction to Prayer of Azariah and the Song of the Three Young Men.

A Moral and Didactic Tale

It is interesting to see to what extent the art of short-story writing was mastered in Israel. This little book is an example of the abiity of the Jewish mind to produce moral and didactic tales that are literary gems, a delight to read. The book belongs to the same general class of literature as the story of Joseph in Genesis, where we have a similar incident in reverse. Moreover, it demonstrates that God is always faithful and loyal even to individuals, just as God has been loyal to the chosen people as a whole ever since the days of Moses.

There are only a few characters in the story, and they present a vivid contrast to one another. The issues dealt with are vitally important. The stakes are life or death. We note the buildup of suspense. As in a good detective story we are led to ask: How will the author extricate his heroine from her plight?

That this book is a didactic *story* and not a historical incident is clear from its geographic setting. The setting is more likely that of Judea than that of Babylon. Just as some of the great Italian

Masters could naïvely paint biblical scenes with medieval Italian backgrounds, so this Babylonian story is firmly set in Judea.

The Teachings

Daniel was a legendary wise man who was well known for his judgments. In this book he comes to a judgment on the basis of divine inspiration and an understanding of human psychology, just as did Solomon of old (cf. I Kings 3:16-28). It is almost as though he knew the methods employed by a modern detective.

But the important point to remember is that, like the meaning of his name, "God is judge," Daniel's judgment is actually the righteous judgment of God. Thus this book emphasizes for the first century B.C. what must be said at all times—that there is an absolute will of God, which God has revealed and by which all people must live.

One aspect of this revealed will of God is that God hates adultery and passes judgment upon those who indulge in it. Adultery represents a fundamental disloyalty within the marriage covenant. True marriage ought to reflect that perfect loyalty and unshakable love which God has consistently shown to God's divine "spouse," Israel (cf. Isaiah 50:1; 54:5-8; Malachi 2:14-16). The climax of the story is found in verse 60: "Then all the assembly shouted loudly and blessed God, who saves those who hope in him."

As in the case of Bel and the Dragon, the text which the Revised Standard Version uses is the translation of Theodotion. This Jewish convert during the second century A.D. produced what seems to be a free revision of the Septuagint based on the Hebrew.

COMMENTARY

Verses 1-2. Perhaps **Joakim** is meant to represent the captured king of Judah, Jehoiachin. We read how he was taken to Babylon in II Kings 24. The behavior of his wife Susanna would then have a direct bearing on the messianic line.

"Susanna" is the Hebrew word for "lily." The phrase Israel "shall blossom as the lily" (Hosea 14:5) might suggest that all Israel was represented in this one woman, the mother of the royal line. Thus the manner in which she withstands temptation is all-important for the future of God's people.

Verses 2-3. When the author states that Susanna **feared the Lord**, he is using the nearest equivalent of the English "to be religious." To be **righteous** was not to be perfect but to seek to live by the **law of Moses**.

Verse 5. The Lord is the God of Israel. It is God who gives true insight to faithful judges. Only evil judgments, on the other hand, can come forth from **Babylon**.

Verses 9-12. People are deliberately free to turn **their eyes from looking to Heaven** and to play with lascivious thoughts. The two elders keep their desire for Susanna to themselves. It is something about which a man does not speak even to his best friend.

Verse 20. Thinking that **no one sees** them, the two elders approach Susanna. She would have destroyed her divinely blessed marriage with Joakim if she had succumbed to temptation.

Verse 23. Adultery is a sin against God. Leviticus 20:10 and Deuteronomy 22:22 both consider it therefore worthy of death.

Verse 34. The two elders lay **their hands upon her head** to point out the accused (cf. Leviticus 24:14).

Verses 42-43. Susanna is confident that God is in control of the powers of secrecy and darkness manifested in the two false witnesses. She knows that all she need do is trust in God.

Verses 44-46. Although **Daniel** left Jerusalem as a young man either in 597 or 586, here he is still a **young lad**. At this point it is important to remember that this story is not meant to be historical but to teach a great truth.

The meaning of Daniel's name, "God is judge," is the important element here. The manner in which Daniel discovers the truth is in line with Solomon's judgment between the two mothers (I Kings 3:16-28). There we read that "the wisdom of

God was in him, to render justice." Here, then, Daniel exercises judgment and conveys the justice of the living God.

Verse 56. The Canaanites did not possess the law of Moses, and so they were addicted to sexual perversion.

Verses 60-61. God does indeed save **those who hope in him**. Here God does so through Daniel, who takes his stand solely upon the Word of God.

Verse 62. The people execute the elders **as they had wickedly planned to do to their neighbor**. Deuteronomy 19:16-21 prescribes the treatment of a false witness. The execution of the two elders is also an example of the *lex talionis*, "an eye for an eye." It was to counter this attitude that Jesus said, "But I say to you, Love your enemies" (Matthew 5:44).

THE BOOK OF BEL
AND THE DRAGON

George A. F. Knight

INTRODUCTION

For the date and composition of the book see the Introduction to Prayer of Azariah and the Song of the Three Young Men.

Two Separate Stories

Like the Prayer and the Song, this book also is in two parts. In fact it is composed of two separate stories. In many ancient manuscripts the book occurs at the end of the Psalter. Its design is liturgical. It was meant from the beginning to be sung in worship. It has been used in Christian worship since the fourth century.

The book has survived in two principal forms, both in Greek. One is found in the manuscript of the Septuagint known as Codex Chisianus (87), and the other is the text of Theodotion (see Introduction to the Prayer and the Song). Modern English editions use a translation of Theodotion, since it became the accepted text in the early Christian centuries.

I. THE STORY OF BEL (Verses 1-22)

Bel was the chief god of the Babylonians. Originally known as Marduk, he was founder and "patron saint" of the city of Babylon. He was represented there by a colossal statue in a magnificent temple. He was believed to have an enormous appetite. His priests provided him daily with great quantities of delicious foods and wines. Xerxes I plundered and, according to the Greek historian Herodotus, destroyed this magnificent temple in 479 B.C.

In the troublous times of the Maccabean Wars this story, illustrating how the God of Israel is stronger than mighty Bel, would give heart to the Jews. At that time they were fighting against another Bel, or figure of evil, the Syrian king Antiochus Epiphanes. The story is told with a light touch, as if to bring a smile to the lips of hard-pressed Israel. And it is told interestingly, almost in the vein of a detective story.

The prophet now known as Second Isaiah had stressed the folly of worshiping idols when he was living in Babylon as an exile himself (Isaiah 44:9-20). He described also the statue of Bel as it was carried to its shrine in the great pilgrimage through the city during the autumn festival—how it was unable to save itself from falling when its carriers stumbled on the cobblestones of the street (Isaiah 46:1-2).

Verse 6. Now, in the next decade after Second Isaiah's description, King Cyrus, who had succeeded to the throne of Babylon, supposedly believed that Bel was a **living God**.

Verses 8-20. Daniel shows the king that the food left for Bel has not been consumed by the god but by the priests and their families. The trap he sets is another example of this man's wisdom. Note the cleverness of Daniel, who does not reveal the truth to the king until after the monarch has said, **You are great, O Bel; and with you there is no deceit, none at all**. The deceit was in the hearts of the priests. **Then Daniel laughed.** He had made his point.

Verse 22. This incident is not historical. Daniel did not destroy the **temple** of Bel. Yet the wholesale execution and the "poetic justice" are both in keeping with the spirit of an eastern didactic tale. For Maccabean times, the point of Cyrus' acknowledgment of Bel's defeat and of the power of the living God was that it was foolish to doubt the final victory of Israel's God.

II. THE STORY OF THE DRAGON (Verses 23-42)

The theme is again, Which God is the living God? The story would be on a level with one from the "Arabian Nights" were it not that it is told in order to press this theme. Dragons normally reject pitch and hair for supper. And it is only in the land of flying carpets that angels carry prophets seven hundred miles through the air by the hair of the head. So it is this primary theme that we must not miss. It is of timeless interest and value.

In the creation story of how God brought an ordered world out of the waters of chaos, the word for "deep" (Genesis 1:2) is taken from the name of a Babylonian goddess. She was a monster who personified the deeps of chaos. Those deeps remained under the earth, even though Yahweh conquered them in the initial struggle and is now in complete control over them.

Throughout Israel's history the monster of the deeps continued to be pictured, sometimes as a sea serpent and sometimes as a dragon. This monster is given various names in the Old Testament: Leviathan (Psalm 74:14; Isaiah 27:1), Rahab (Psalms 87:4; 89:10; Isaiah 51:9), or the Hebrew *tannin* (Psalm 74:13; Jeremiah 51:34). In Jeremiah 51:34 Babylon is the monster that swallows up Israel and thus takes the people of God into exile (cf. Jonah 2:1–3:3).

According to Israelite thought, one particular figure could represent the whole people or nation. Thus, if a nation behaved "monstrously," its king was regarded as a monster himself. In this way Pharaoh was the dragon of evil to Isaiah, even as the king of Babylon was to Jeremiah. Revelation 12:9 applies the figure of "the great dragon . . . that ancient serpent" to the devil, as the chief figurehead over the powers of evil.

Medieval morality plays usually dressed up King Herod, who massacred the infants in New Testament times, in a red costume and decked him out with a red beard. This was because dragons were thought to be red—as was the goddess of chaos, red with the blood of her enemies. They were in the habit of spitting flames of fire from their mouth. To this day Mephistopheles on the stage must wear a red costume. The Christian hero, St. George, has to slay a red dragon in the old legend, and then must rescue the fair maiden (the church, the bride of Christ) from its fiery mouth.

Verse 27. Here the story reaches its climax. When the dragon eats the hairy cakes that Daniel made, he bursts open. **See what you have been worshiping!** exclaims Daniel.

Verses 28-31. The king has become a Jew was, of course, what Israel hoped one day to hear. Some renegade Jews in Maccabean days had succumbed to the extreme pressure put upon them. They were joining their Gentile neighbors in acknowledging King Antiochus Epiphanes to be divine. The faithful in Israel, however, had withstood the forces of evil in the shape of the Syrian army, even to shedding of blood. Now they had to suffer the horrors of **the lions' den**.

Verses 29-32. Jewish pride in Daniel forces our storyteller to exaggerate. It is hardly likely that the courtiers would threaten their king with death or that he would give in to them when pressed. There is yet another exaggeration. In Daniel 6:18-23 the time spent in the lions' den is one night. Here he is not rescued until the seventh day (verse 40), and there are also seven lions.

Verses 33-39. Habakkuk is now introduced into the story. He is taken to Babylon in an unusual way (but cf. Ezekiel 8:3). He had lived in Jerusalem in days of great tension (about 600 B.C.) when the power of the Babylonians had threatened the utter destruction of Israel. His had been the cry: "Why, O Lord? Why do you allow your faithful people to suffer in this way?" In answer there had come a great word from God: "The righteous shall live by his faith" (Habakkuk 2:4*b*). It is this prophet—who long since had thus interpreted the place of faith in the presence of suffering—who now becomes the instrument of help and comfort to Daniel.

Verse 42. The punishment of Daniel's enemies is not to be understood as mere vindictiveness. It represents the just judgment of a just God. God's saving love for sinners, as revealed in Christ, was not yet fully understood.

THE PRAYER OF MANASSEH

Stanley Brice Frost

INTRODUCTION

Manasseh (687/86-643/42) was the most evil of all the kings of Judah. Indeed he was the chief cause for Yahweh's punishment of Israel through the Babylonian conquest, in the view of the Deuteronomic historian writing during the Exile (II Kings 21:1-16; 23:26-27; 24:3-4).

But with the passage of time his reputation came to be whitewashed. A later story told that after a period of wickedness he was taken as a prisoner to Assyria. There he repented of his evil ways, prayed for forgiveness, and was allowed by Yahweh to return home and inaugurate a reformation (II Chronicles 33:10-17). This amendment to history was designed to explain how such a wicked king could have had such a long and quiet reign.

In telling the story the Chronicler noted especially that Manasseh's prayer of penitence was preserved in two sources (II Chronicles 33:18-19). After these sources were no longer available, a Jew living probably in Alexandria, or elsewhere outside Palestine, undertook to compose a prayer such as Manasseh might have said at the time of his repentance. This occurred possibly early in the Maccabean period, though some scholars think in the first century B.C. or even later.

Perhaps the writer intended the prayer to be inserted in II Chronicles 33:13. But it never won a place in the text itself, though it came to be copied following II Chronicles in a number of Septuagint manuscripts. More often, however, it was included among a group of canticles and liturgical pieces—for example, the Magnificat and Benedictus—appended to the Psalms.

It is not possible to establish the original language, but probably it was Greek. If so, this would explain in part why it never found a place in II Chronicles. This book also, along with I and II Esdras, failed to win a place in the Old Testament canon of the Roman Catholic Church, which includes all the rest of the Apocrypha.

The structure of the prayer is clear: an invocation of God, with exposition of the divine nature (verses 1-7c); a confession of sin (verses 7d-13e); anticipatory praise (verses 13f-15). The little work is a fine testimony to Jewish piety in the last two centuries B.C. and is appropriately ranked with the poetry of Luke 1–2.

COMMENTARY

Verses 1-7c. Wrath and Mercy. The Creator is characterized by wrath and by mercy. The author is following closely Joel 2:12-13. There "repents of evil" means that God rescinds the divine judgments which bring suffering on men and women. Here **repentest over the evils of men** probably means that when people commit evil, God's attitude is ready to change if they will repent.

Verses 7d-13e. Confession of Sin. The mention of the sinlessness of the patriarchs suggests that this is a product of the late postexilic period, when the idea was widespread. **Setting up abominations** means "setting up idols." But here probably the thought is of erecting false gods in the mind and heart.

Depths of the earth is a traditional Old Testament expression for Sheol, the abode of all the dead regardless of their merit. In this Old Testament sense the line means merely "Do not make me die." At the presumed time of writing, however, the doctrine of reward or punishment in an afterlife was beginning to spread widely. Thus the author may be using traditional language to say: "Do not send me when I am dead to hell."

Verses 13f-15. *Coda of Praise.* In confident anticipation of forgiveness the penitent king lifts up his voice in praise. He joins the **host of heaven**—that is, the angelic army—in the universal song.

THE FIRST BOOK OF
THE MACCABEES

George A. F. Knight

INTRODUCTION

Nature and Contents

I Maccabees is a history book. It deals with a section of the period "between the Testaments." It is a sober and trustworthy account in chronological order of the "Maccabean Wars," the Jewish wars of resistance against the Syrian power from 175 to 135 B.C. Thus it includes the period during which the book of Daniel was written and circulated (see Introduction to Daniel).

In addition to the narratives of military campaigns, the book contains other significant material. Most interesting are six poems:

    1:24-28, a dirge for Judea
    1:36-40, a dirge for Jerusalem
    2:7-13, a lament over Jerusalem by Mattahias
    3:3-9, a song praising Judas
    3:45, another dirge for Jerusalem
    14:4-15, a song in praise of Simon

The author also quotes letters that are seemingly authentic—for example, 11:30-37, where King Demetrius writes to Jonathan.

In 14:18 we read that bronze tablets were used for letter writing by the Romans to Simon. Such a practice has been authenticated by the discovery among the Dead Sea Scrolls of two copper scrolls, originally parts of one roll. This copper scroll was put "in a conspicuous place in the precincts of the sanctuary" (14:48), while copies of it were deposited in the treasury.

The narrative of the bronze tablets inscribed to honor Simon (14:25-49) provides a reliable history of the period. The author, whose name we do not know, made use of every aid available in his search for accuracy. Possibly he paced over the ground where the battles he records had taken place. Possibly he figured out the movements of the contending armies as he stood on the spot. Almost certainly, if he lived too late to know what happened firsthand, he interrogated eyewitnesses and survivors. Thus he could furnish us with graphic pen sketches of those stirring events he records. He must have resided in Jerusalem in the calmer days after the wars were over, for he had access to the temple records and to written material probably preserved only there.

The book has come down to us in Greek. But that is certainly a translation from the original Hebrew text. The story of a war for the recovery of the sacred things of Yahweh would most likely be written in the sacred language. Moreover, examples of idiomatic Hebrew phrases occur translated literally into Greek. Yet as early as the end of the first Christian century Josephus, the Jewish historian, seems to have known only the Greek translation that we possess.

The style of writing is direct, factual, and informative. The story is grippingly told. The author is a true historian in that he does not obtrude his own personal views but seeks to tell his tale as factually as he is able. On the other hand, he follows the method used by ancient historians generally, of putting speeches of his own composition into the mouths of his characters. Again, he evidently exaggerates the numbers of warriors on both sides who go forth to battle, but this is a practice of ancient writers.

Date and Authorship

We have no sure knowledge as to when it was written. The author must have lived after the close of the period of which he writes (134 B.C.). In 13:30 he mentions a tomb which Simon built for Jonathan his brother and which "remains to this day." The burial took place in 142 B.C. The phrase "to this day" implies a fairly long memory of the event. The last verses of the book, however, are a more specific guide. The chronicles of John the high priest would be completed and so named only after his death. This took place in 104 B.C. This is probably then the earliest possible date for the writing of the book.

On the other hand, the author shows no effect of the arrival of the Romans in Palestine, which occurred in 63 B.C. We suppose therefore that he wrote before that time. It is more than likely, then, that he finished his book soon after 104, when the memory of the battles he records was still fresh in the minds of the older generation. But he may well have begun it a decade or so earlier.

The book is anonymous, like the history writing of the Old Testament. In his account of the Maccabean Wars the author shows that his sympathies lay with the Jewish warriors. Thus we may think of him as a loyal patriot. But beyond this we cannot be sure. By his day the pure fires of zeal for the law had died down in the royal line descended from Judas Maccabeus. Most of the country's leadership was split into parties, each of which believed that it represented the true Israel.

Our knowledge of the Qumran community, derived from the Dead Sea Scrolls, makes us certain that the author did not belong to the party represented by this group. As between the two major parties, the Sadducees and the Pharisees, there is too little evidence to assign him to either. This uncertainty is a compliment to his ability as a historian. That other good Jewish historian, Josephus, later on obviously makes full use of the material in I Maccabees, though he never acknowledges the fact.

Historical Background

Only a comparative handful of Israelites returned and rebuilt Jerusalem following King Cyrus' edict of 538 B.C.—which permitted all "displaced persons" in his realm to go home from Babylon if they wished. From that time on, the Jewish nation living in little Judea was only a small part—though still the "mother" element—of all Jewish people everywhere. The majority of them were now living in the "Diaspora" or as we would say, living abroad. Throughout the succeeding centuries Jews were to be found flourishing in Mesopotamia, Egypt, round the Mediterranean (as we learn from Acts and Paul's Epistles), and later even in Rome itself.

After Ezra had made his influence felt, the Jews in Jerusalem were always more "strict" and "orthodox" than those in the Diaspora. They had the advantage of possessing the temple. Their numbers were small, and they might well have lost their identity in the great sea of peoples around them had they not clung loyally to their peculiar customs.

In 334 B.C. Alexander the Great of Macedonia, or upper Greece, began his conquest of the East. Soon Palestine was absorbed into the great Greek empire. 1:1-4 summarizes this sweeping campaign and its outcome. It is alluded to also in Daniel 11:2-3 and probably in Zechariah 9:13.

At Alexander's death in 323 B.C. the vast empire split up into sections. Various generals seized power wherever they could. Ptolemy seized control in Egypt. Thus began the Ptolemaic dynasty, which ended only in 30 B.C. when Queen Cleopatra VII chose the wrong Roman on whom to exert her charms. Seleucus set up his throne at Antioch, north of Palestine. In 312 B.C. he established the rule of his dynasty over the area that today we call the Middle East. Little Judea lay immediately between those two new powers and became a prize that each sought to seize.

The books of Daniel and Esther reveal the eastern flavor of life that the Jews, being orientals themselves, could well appreciate. But the whole tone and atmosphere of the new Greek civilization was very different from the oriental way of life. By 300 B.C. the philosophical thought of Socrates and Plato was available in any of the centers of culture of the great empire. Soon also Aristotle's passionate interest in what we now call scientific analysis and the classification of phenomena was known to educated people everywhere.

The Greeks had a missionary zeal about their culture. They sought to propagate it from the Mediterranean to the Oxus and the Indus rivers. One means of doing so was to transplant Macedonian war veterans and give them land in one of the many new Greek settlements. There they would propagate what they fervently believed to be the highest form of civilization and culture the world had yet seen. Palestine had its share of these Greek cities, with their Greek names, language, culture, and religion.

We know next to nothing of what was happening in Judea in the third century B.C. During the years 323-198 the Jews were subject to the Ptolemies of Egypt and seem to have lived in comparative peace. They must have had ready access by land and sea to Egypt. By this time the Jewish population of the vast city of Alexandria was some two thirds of all the mixed peoples who lived and traded there.

Two intellectual movements of the century may be noted. First, in Jerusalem there must have been great activity in biblical studies. During this unknown century the prophetic material was evidently collected and edited. Also the later writings, such as those of the Chronicler (who gives us I and II Chronicles, Ezra, and Nehemiah) and the Psalter, were edited for public use. The ritual, daily and seasonal, at the temple, had now become highly elaborate.

A new class had come to the fore—those whom we call the sages, the "wise men" who have given us Job, Proverbs, and much of our intertestamental literature. Though their kind go back to the days of Solomon and Jeremiah (cf. Jeremiah 18:18), they flourished especially in the period leading to the Maccabean Wars. One whom we can name, Jesus son of Sirach (Ben-sirach), completed his important book Ecclesiasticus in 180 B.C. Yet all this theological and biblical ferment was evidently remote from the vast changes taking place in the life of the nations all around.

The second movement was very different. It was the intellectual awakening of Jews in the Diaspora, especially in Alexandria. They were reacting to the exciting new Greek culture and to a reverse movement in the area of propaganda. They were proud of their heritage, but they were aware that knowledge of it was hidden from the world in the strange Hebrew language. Therefore Jews in Alexandria took the initiative in having Jerusalem scholars help them translate the Old Testament into Greek. So the Septuagint gradually came into being.

The culmination of this missionary movement was the work of the great Jewish theologian and philosopher Philo, who was a contemporary of Jesus Christ. His importance lies in his successful efforts to expound the revelation of God to Israel in terms that the Greek mind of his day could appreciate.

Our concern, however, is with the Jews of Judea and Jerusalem. Following the lead of Ezra in the fourth century, they had sought to "put a fence around the Law." They had sought to keep themselves "unspotted from the world." The inevitable clash of ideologies had to come sooner or later, of course. It comes now in the period covered by I Maccabees. This clash is one of the main background issues of the book. It is more important to recognize its significance than it is to learn the details of the war which was its outcome.

By 198 B.C. the Seleucids had become the stronger kingdom, and Judea had fallen under its sway. This change of master made little difference at first to the Jews in Judea. But such are the ways of God that unless people meet with challenge and crisis from time to time their distinctive faith may fade away. It is of God's goodness, it seems, that troubles must be met and faced. The crisis came suddenly, but the faith of the Jewish people was equal to the occasion. Israel was roused, for the first time in centuries, to unprecedented heights of valor and faith.

Antiochus IV came to the Syrian (Seleucid) throne in 175 B.C. Daniel 11:21 calls him "a contemptible person." I Maccabees 1:10 refers to him as "a sinful root." II Maccabees 9:28 calls him a "murderer and blasphemer." He gave himself the special name of Epiphanes, which means "God made manifest." To the Jews that was a blasphemy. So once they had experienced the ferocity of his ways, they called him rather Epimanes, meaning "mad man."

The trouble began when a foolish group in Jerusalem revolted against him at the moment when the Romans had become a thorn in his flesh. So Antiochus took it out on the Jews, as he was unable to come to grips with the Romans. Within a matter of three days eighty thousand men, women, and children were brutally slain by his soldiers (II Maccabees 5:11-14). He himself stormed into the temple, plundered its riches, and tore down the curtain that hid the Holy of holies. He entered where no one except the high priest, and that but once a year, dared go (II Maccabees 5:15-16).

Then Antiochus sought to force the Jews of Jerusalem to do what they had resisted doing for a century and a half. He insisted that they adopt Greek culture. The plan was to do away with the distinctiveness of Judaism. All people in his dominion would think the same Greek thoughts. To accomplish this he enforced the cessation of Jewish worship.

There were three outward marks of worship which he forbade altogether: the reading of the Law—in accordance he ordered all scrolls to be destroyed, circumcision, and the observance of the sabbath. In the temple he ordered an altar set up on which were to be sacrificed swine—unclean beasts according to the Law (cf. Leviticus 11:7). Sacrifice was offered not to Yahweh, but to Olympian Zeus (1:41-63). Later generations remembered this act as "the abomination of desolation" (Mark 13:14; cf. Daniel 9:27, King James Version) or as "the desolating sacrilege" (Revised Standard Version).

At once resistance clustered round the family of one man. An old priest called Mattathias slew with his own hands the king's officer who had come to his village of Modein, between Jerusalem and Joppa, to enforce the royal decree. Then he killed a Jewish neighbor who was ready to collaborate with the rulers.

This little group immediately fled to the hills. Mattathias died almost at once, but his five famous sons then became the nucleus of resistance. The eldest, Judas, became the leader, and was given the name of Maccabee. The word probably means "hammer."

A guerrilla war was waged for three years. Finally the little army recaptured Jerusalem and rededicated the temple to the glory of Yahweh once again. This ceremony is remembered to the present day in the festival of Hanukkah, which falls about Christmastime. It is mentioned in John 10:22.

Unfortunately the recovery of Jerusalem did not mean freedom for all Jews. The war went on. Antiochus died the following year, but the struggle was carried on by his successors. When Judas was killed in battle, his brother Jonathan stepped into his shoes. But the nature of the struggle gradually altered. It became less a religious war and ever more nationalistic in intention. In fact it developed into a war for domination of Judea's immediate neighbors.

The first fine rapturous movement of the spirit in loyalty to Yahweh was thus eventually a thing of the past. By the period soon after the book ends the struggle developed into a sordid, mutually slaughterous strife, with murder and intrigue and the usual horrors of an eastern court. Yet in the year 142 B.C., as 13:41 puts it, for the first time for centuries "the yoke of the Gentiles was removed from Israel." Judea became a completely independent nation.

Though what follows is beyond the scope of I Maccabees, we may note that from 104 B.C. onward the little kingdom suffered desperately at the hands of a number of ferocious rulers. Finally it lost its independence in 63 B.C., for the last time, to the great new rising power of Rome.

Apocryphal Status

The historical reasons for rejecting I Maccabees as canonical scripture are no longer valid. The Jewish authorities were not willing to canonize a work which they thought was not originally written in the sacred language, Hebrew. At first the church accepted this Jewish criterion. Today, however, we are not so sure that the first draft of the book was not in Hebrew, and in this we follow the great scholar Jerome.

Again, the word "apocrypha," which in Greek means "hidden away," may have been chosen to describe certain books for one or both of two reasons:

(1) They were purposely "hidden" from the eyes of ordinary believers, on the ground that they contained esoteric lore understandable only to the initiated. There is nothing of such a nature in I Maccabees.

(2) They were deliberately "hidden" away because they were heretical in their teaching. This may be true of some books in the Apocrypha, but it could not be said of I Maccabees.

Message and Value

The heroes of I Maccabees were fighting for a faith which was revealed to them in God's action in their history. We, in our turn, benefit greatly as we read the book. We see how God was taking care of the chosen servant people throughout a turbulent period of their history and how believing men and women, motivated by the Word of God, could remain obedient to God even unto death.

We learn nothing new about God from I Maccabees. But we do learn how people can respond to the Word of God and give of themselves to the uttermost in response to God's initial act of love in entering into covenant communion with the chosen people. I Maccabees is not scripture, but it is evidence of how faith can grow directly out of scripture.

I. POLITICAL CHANGE AND A RELIGIOUS CRISIS (1:1-64)

A. HISTORICAL INTRODUCTION (1:1-9)

See Introduction above. In the fashion of the Chronicler (cf. II Chronicles 26:16), the author is concerned to show that Alexander the Great's pride is under the judgment of God. His dates are: born 356, became king 336, defeated the Persian power 333, died 323. He came from the **land of Kittim**, a word that the Dead Sea Scrolls also use for Greece, though some scholars believe that there the reference is to the Romans. The statement that Alexander **divided his kingdom among** his generals before his death is not historical. **The evils on the earth** which they caused refers to the endless wars between Egypt and Syria in which Judea became involved.

B. ANTIOCHUS IV EPIPHANES (1:10-15)

1:10. The author now leaps to the years immediately preceding the wars he wishes to chronicle. **Antiochus the king** is Antiochus III the Great (223-187 B.C.). His son Epiphanes is therefore Antiochus IV (175-164); he is the villain of the story to follow. The **one hundred thirty-seventh year of the kingdom of the Greeks** refers to the calendar of the Seleucids of Syria.

1:11-15. Verse 11 introduces us to the tension Judea now felt regarding the influence of Greek culture upon the ancient faith and customs of Israel. Certain **lawless men**—men acting against the law of Moses—sought to make a compromise with **the Gentiles round about** them. To begin with, this was a political **covenant**. One Jason raised an insurrection against his brother, Onias III, the high priest (II Maccabees 4:7-9). He secured the support of Antiochus, but part of the price was an agreement that he should open a gymnasium in Jerusalem.

Such an institution, for Greeks, was as innocent as a country club to us. The Greeks, however, were accustomed to practice their athletics naked. This custom was anathema to the good Jew. Those Jews who joined the "club" to show their repudiation of Judaism and declare their sophistication and up-to-dateness underwent an operation that **removed the marks of circumcision**. Thus they **abandoned the holy covenant**, of which circumcision was the external sign.

1:15. The statues of Greek gods looked down upon the social life of the gymnasium. Philosophers presented their speculative notions within its walls. The youth received cultural training in their own clubrooms—a training that was integrated with a pagan view of life. In fact, the gymnasium offered a total view of life that was completely incompatible with the revelation contained in the law of Moses. There could be no compromise between the two. It was a case of either-or.

From the Jewish point of view, therefore, when **they joined with the Gentiles** they **sold themselves to do evil.** Jason's act was therefore a declaration of war against Israel's God. The fate of the tiny state of Judea was now at stake within the vast sea of Greek culture that covered virtually the whole known world.

C. ANTIOCHUS' CONQUESTS; DESECRATION OF THE TEMPLE (1:16-28)

Once Antiochus had subdued Egypt and the Ptolemaic line, he naturally seized Judea. It had been a Ptolemaic province. For verses 20-24*a* see the Introduction. The use of Indian elephants in war must have been like tanks to a modern army. In times of peace, too, elephants had great prestige value. Some Seleucid coins proudly display this great animal.

Jerusalem fell an easy prey to Antiochus' soldiers. The **golden altar** is mentioned in Exodus 30:1-6; the **lampstand** in Exodus 25:31-39; **the table for the bread of the Presence** in Exodus 25:23-30. According to II Maccabees 5:21, the **hidden treasures** amounted to 1,800 talents, about 3½ million dollars. In verses 24*b*-28 the author introduces a dirge concerning the tragedy. Daniel 8:10 represents Antiochus as assaulting the very stars in an **arrogance** that reaches to heaven, like the king in Babylon in Isaiah 14:14:

> I will ascend above the heights of the clouds,
> I will make myself like the Most High.

D. THE SECOND DESTRUCTION OF THE CITY (1:29-40)

The **chief collector of tribute** gains access by trickery (cf. Daniel 8:25). II Maccabees 5:24 names him Apollonius. Verses

31-32 exaggerate somewhat in that Jews remained living in Jerusalem even after this terrible slaughter. **The city** or citadel **of David** was a strong fortification, the Acra, just west of the temple. **Lawless men**—that is, foreign troops—are stationed in the city, so again the author gives us a lament.

E. THE CALL FOR UNITY (1:41-64)

Antiochus orders the unification of all his subject peoples: **all should be one people, and . . . each should give up his customs** (see Introduction). The list of royal demands spelled death to Judaism—so it was death either way (verse 50). Yet once again the author shows his natural bias, for this process of Hellenization was not by decree but by force of political circumstances. But undoubtedly the best of the Jewish people recognized that a crisis had arrived and so went **into hiding.** God's people could do no other.

The impious acts of Antiochus culminate in the erection of a **desolating sacrilege upon the altar of burnt offering** in November or December of 167 (see Introduction and Daniel 11:31) and the erection of local pagan shrines in the villages of Judea. Any copies of the Torah they could find were torn up and burned. Anyone found possessing a copy was condemned to death. II Maccabees 5:22–7:42 should be read at this point, for it gives details of the persecution.

II. THE KING'S ORDER IS DEFIED; WAR RESULTS (2:1-70)

A. MATTATHIAS AND HIS SONS (2:1-14)

Modein was a village halfway between Joppa and Jerusalem. Mattathias was of a priestly family. Josephus calls his great-grandfather Hasamonaios. From that name the term Hasmoneans came to signify the dynasty of his descendants. Again the author writes a dirge and puts it in his hero's mouth.

B. The Outbreak of War (2:15-41)

2:15-26. The king's officers give Mattathias the chance to capitulate like the majority of the Jews. But the priest believes that the situation demands no compromise. He is a true zealot when he assassinates one of his own fellow villagers for succumbing to the royal decrees. Then he kills the king's officer too, and the die is cast. For the story of **Phinehas** and **Zimri** see Numbers 25:6-15.

2:27-41. Mattathias' action wins over many waverers. A group of them gather in the **wilderness** of Judea, southeast of Jerusalem, where John the Baptist later lived and where Jesus met with temptation. The area is wild and desolate, with only pockets of green where domestic animals can graze. But there are many caves to hide in.

As before, the authorities give them the opportunity to change their minds. By refusing to fight on the sabbath, the Jews do two things at once. They demonstrate their loyalty to the law of Moses, and they declare their opposition to a royal decree that would do away with the sabbath as a distinctive God-given day. So **a thousand** die there as martyrs to a cause they believe to be of God. But Mattathias and his friends recognize that such loyalty demonstrates a misplaced zeal (verse 41).

C. The Hasideans (2:42-70)

2:42-48. Now the struggle becomes clearly a religious war—always more ferocious than one for political or economic ends. The guerrilla fighters regard those Jews who do not join them as **sinners** and strike them down. Some flee to Gentile villages for safety.

The newcomers to the army in the hills are called **Hasideans**, meaning "loyal ones"—that is, loyal to the covenant made at Sinai (cf. 1:62-63; 2:34). The Hasideans were evidently a party that had formed earlier, less extreme than the group in the wilderness and more sincerely religious. They are mentioned cryptically in Daniel 11:33. They recognized the necessity of making common cause with the extremists even though they did not like them. Once the war was over, however, they parted company with the extremists and became the Pharisees, or "separate" ones.

2:49-64. Mattathias' dying speech again reads like the author's own production, yet such must have been the priest's thoughts and sentiments. Note that the author is acquainted with the book of Daniel (verses 59-60). The other biblical references are: **Abraham**, Genesis 22; **Joseph**, Genesis 41; **Phinehas**, Numbers 25:1-15; **Joshua**, Numbers 27:18-23; **Caleb**, Numbers 14; **David**, II Samuel 7; **Elijah**, II Kings 2:1-12.

The references to **Abraham** and **Joseph** reveal a theological trend of the period. The law of Moses is now more highly exalted than ever. It is looked upon as the eternal Word, and so in some sense must have been known to the patriarchs before it was revealed to Moses. It is "suprahistorical." Keeping it has become the means whereby Israel can achieve the favor of God and become worthy of God's promises. It is no longer, as with the psalmists, something one keeps gladly to show gratitude for God's mighty acts of redemption.

2:65-70. Finally the old man names his son **Judas** as his successor. The name **Maccabeus**, meaning "hammer," probably was a nickname he received later. **Simeon** (or Simon) was probably a less impulsive and wiser man, but Judas was the man of the hour. Then Mattathias dies in the year 166 B.C.

III. RESISTANCE UNDER JUDAS BEGINS (3:1-60)

A. AN ODE IN HONOR OF JUDAS (3:3-9)

The author probably wrote this poem himself. Note its vehemences. **He burned those who troubled his people. He destroyed the ungodly out of the land.** The Letter to the Hebrews, on the other hand, almost certainly refers to the amazing exploits of Judas and his men in chapter 11, especially verses 33-38. Judas is an example of those who recognize that it is impossible to be neutral in God's war. One is either for God or against God. War cannot be waged daintily. The fierce poem in Judges 5 begins this way: "That the leaders *took the lead* in Israel, that the people offered themselves willingly [for war], bless the Lord!" Judas did succeed in this way in gathering in **those who were perishing**. Redemption is a costly business.

B. JUDAS' INITIAL VICTORIES (3:10-26)

Apollonius was the meridarch, or military and civil governor, of Samaria and Judea. He is probably the "chief collector of tribute" mentioned in 1:29. So Judas wins the first round. **Seron**, a much more important officer than Apollonius, thinks it will be easy to crush the Jewish insurrectionists. Note in verse 15 where the author's sympathies lie; the enemy are **ungodly men**.

The **ascent of Beth-horon** is a pass that leads from Lydda on the coastal plain to Jerusalem. The road climbs steeply from the village of Lower Beth-horon to Upper Beth-horon. Judas was occupying the upper village. He thus had a tactical advantage. His little force had just to dash down the hill and sweep the larger army backwards. Thus he quickly routed them. This battle revealed Judas to be a clever strategist.

The Gentiles talked of the battles of Judas. It is not possible to know whether the sentiments Judas utters in his speech to his army (verses 18-22) were his or the author's. Probably they were the latter's. He is referring implicitly to the faith of Gideon (Judges 7) and to the manner in which God, not Gideon's army, won the victory at that time. **Heaven** is a substitute for "God."

C. THE FORCES OF EVIL RALLY (3:27-60)

3:27-37. Judas' victory caught the Syrian empire at a bad moment. Its eastern portion was in revolt, so Judea's rebellion was more than a thorn in Antiochus' flesh. The king's revenues were low because tribute from the east was at a trickle. Thus to give his soldiers **a year's pay** in advance just because he was suddenly panic-stricken at Judas' success was the mark of an unstable and insecure man. So too was his inhuman command to **Lysias** (verses 35-36). This then was to be nothing less than total war.

The boy **Antiochus** of whom Lysias was to be guardian was only seven years old at this time. He was later known as V Eupator. The **one hundred forty-seventh year** equals our 165 B.C. Antiochus was successful, by the way, in subduing the king of Armenia, the first of the **upper provinces** of verse 37.

3:38-41. Judas finally killed **Nicanor** in 161 (7:43). **Forty thousand** is a round number in Semitic expressions. Probably the army was one fourth that size. It encamps this time, not on a hill (verse 16), but **in the plain**.

3:42-53. The Jews see the struggle to come as a "holy war," for which the law has given them rules and regulations (Deuteronomy 20–21). For the **Nazirites** see Numbers 6. They could not fight unless released from their vows.

3:56-57. Verse 56 is based on Deuteronomy 20:5-8. It is reminiscent of Gideon's psychological preparation of those who were wholly committed to God's cause (cf. Judges 7:3-7). Judas does not now possess the advantage he had at Beth-horon.

IV. CONTINUED FIGHTING (4:1-61)

A. TWO FURTHER VICTORIES (4:1-25)

Renegade Jews **from the citadel** are evidently informers against **Judas**. But he has his sources of information too (verse 3). His greatest source of strength, however, is his faith in the God who saved the people from Pharaoh's chariots so long before. The Jews were fired by loyalty, faith, and trust both in God's covenant and in the rightness of their cause. The **foreigners**— mercenaries—were concerned only to earn their wages as soldiers. No wonder the latter were no match for the "covenanters." **Gazara** is Gezer, **Azotus** is Ashdod, and **Jamnia** is Jabneh. These are all on the Philistine-held coastal strip. **Idumea** at that time reached roughly to today's Negev.

Judas' second victory (verses 19-25) is again a psychological one. II Maccabees suggests (not necessarily correctly) that they ceased plundering because it was the eve of the sabbath. Psalms 118 and 136 both contain the line in verse 24.

B. A Year Later (4:26-35)

It is now October/November 164 B.C. **Beth-zur** protects Jerusalem from the south. Lysias must have marched from Antioch south down the coast to Philistia, turned east, then north. He was now in the land where **David** had led his soldiers and where **Saul** and **Jonathan** had fought against the Philistines.

Primitive peoples used to recite evil spells against an enemy. Judas relies upon God instead to **melt the boldness of their strength**. How different is his blessing of God from an old spell! Note how he historicizes his faith and sees the past as sacred history—to which he now belongs. Again, then, the faith and **boldness** of Judas' army sweep them to victory.

C. The Climax of the War (4:36-51)

The arrival in Jerusalem must have been a traumatic experience for the little army. They still have to fight their way into the **citadel**. **The defiled stones** are the altar to Zeus that Antiochus ordered built over the altar of burnt offerings (1:54). The loyalists have before them for guidance the decision of King Josiah in a similar case (II Kings 23:6).

The expectation of **a prophet** is interesting. It is based on the promise in Deuteronomy 18:18. In this period people now look for one like Moses who will sum up the work of all the prophets in himself (cf. John 1:21). The command about **unhewn stones** is in Exodus 20:25.

D. THE DEDICATION OF THE TEMPLE (4:52-61)

4:52-59. All preparations, copying the regulations to be found in Exodus, were completed on the eve of the great day. **The twenty-fifth day of . . . Chislev** is probably our December 14, 164 B.C., three years exactly after the desecration (cf. 1:59). **Dedication** in Hebrew is *hanukkah*. The celebration of Hanukkah, or the feast of lights, falls near the winter solstice, when the sun, the great light, begins to increase.

The loyalists are very conscious that it is God who has given them the victory. They praise God in a great eight-day act of worship (cf. II Chronicles 7:9). In John 10:22-23 we read: "It was the feast of the Dedication at Jerusalem; it was winter, and Jesus was walking in the temple."

4:60-61. Judas wisely realizes that he must consolidate his easy capture of Jerusalem. The Syrians will not rest content with his victory. But unfortunately, now that the "religious" war has been won, the Maccabeans make the continuing struggle a political and patriotic war. It is now the Jewish **people** as a whole (verse 61) who are at war with the Seleucid empire.

V. VICTORIES IN TRANSJORDAN AND GALILEE; DEFEAT AT JAMNIA (5:1-68)

A. THE WAR CONTINUES (5:1-54)

5:1-20. The author recalls the religious nature of the struggle by speaking of the Jews as **the descendants of Jacob** and the Idumeans as **the sons of Esau** (cf. Genesis 25:30; 36:1). **Akrabattene** in Idumea lay east of the Dead Sea—surely a long way for a sortie from Jerusalem. Some scholars identify it with a village between Judea and Samaria and so regard **in Idumea** to mean "with an Idumean population." **The sons of Baean** have not been identified (cf. II Maccabees 10:18-23).

Verses 6-8 show how Judas has now become like any local commander with a lust for conquest. But he becomes the hope of hard-pressed Jews in Transjordan (verse 9), who send him a letter asking his help. Then **Galilee** in the north sends a similar request. In Jerusalem a **great assembly** is held to discuss what measures should be taken. The decision is to set their fighting men in three groups. **Simon**, Judas' brother, is to take one battalion composed of three thousand men to fight in Galilee. Another brother, **Jonathan**, is to go with **Judas** and eight thousand men to Transjordan. The third battalion stays to defend Jerusalem.

5:21-54. Simon is successful. He rescues the Galilean Jews and brings them south—women, children, goods and all—to the "city-state" of **Judea**. Judas' army meets with some friendly Arabs, here called **Nabateans**. These people developed into a forceful empire in the next century. Their report is that the Jewish population have been taken as prisoners to a number of cities. In some cases they have fortified themselves, as in Dathema (cf. verse 9).

Judas' whirlwind campaign is entirely successful. Timothy's reasoning in verses 40-41 shows knowledge of human nature. Then Judas rescues the Jewish population and brings them over the Jordan and south to Judea. They hold a great service of thanksgiving, since the victories in both Galilee and Transjordan must have seemed miraculous. The Jewish armies now have been greatly strengthened.

B. The First Setback
(5:55-68)

In disobedience to Judas' express command (verse 19) **Joseph** and **Azariah** attack **Jamnia**. They are defeated. Their action may have arisen from jealousy of the highly successful Maccabean

family. Here is the beginning of dissension in the Jewish ranks
that was to continue for the next two centuries. But the author
evidently sees Judas in the light of Joshua of old, leading his
people, under God, to their promised land. Any divergence or
disobedience is thus a form of disloyalty. **Some priests** evidently
imagined that since they were fighting a "holy war," God would
protect them miraculously.

VI. DEATH OF ANTIOCHUS; PEACE OFFER ACCEPTED
(6:1-63)

A. GOD'S JUDGMENT UPON ANTIOCHUS (6:1-17)

The author relates the defeats of Antiochus in **Elymais in
Persia**, the biblical Elam, which was east of Susa. Like the
Deuteronomic editor of I and II Kings, he is concerned to show
the purposes of God working out in secular history (cf. I Kings
8:66; 14:7-10; II Kings 21:16).

Antiochus has to retreat to Babylon, a city of ill omen to the
Jews. He had refounded it himself as a military depot. Verse 11
reveals a curious sidelight on this harsh king's nature, as the
author sees it. The **flood** here is the old prophetic word for the
overwhelming of the wrath of God. We wonder to what extent
the author gives Antiochus a conscience he did not have. See
Daniel 4:34-37 for the suggestion that there was hope in God's
sight even for this cruel, pagan king.

B. THE BATTLE WITHIN JERUSALEM
(6:18-54)

6:18-47. We find it difficult to believe that an alien element of
Jews and others held out in the citadel, the Acra, even though
Judas had occupied all Jerusalem. The Acra actually dominated
the temple. These are now the enemy within, and they seek

help from the new ruler. The fierceness of this civil war is seen in verse 24.

Lysias and Eupator assemble a very large army, with thirty-two elephants that have already been in combat. As these beasts advanced with the brightly colored pillboxes on their backs, driven by their mahouts, they were surely an awesome sight. Yet the fortitude of one man, Judas' brother **Eleazar** (2:5), turned the tide of the battle. However, Judas' small army thought it wise to retreat.

6:48-54. It is interesting to note another aspect of Jewish loyalty to the Word of God. They kept the sabbatical year even in such extremity. The year ran from autumn to autumn and so included both sowing and harvesting. It meant they had **no food in storage** when the king's army besieged Jerusalem. Moreover, their numbers had been greatly swollen with the admission of refugees from Galilee and Transjordan.

C. THE LIFTING OF THE SIEGE (6:55-63)

6:55-59. Lysias refused to acknowledge the will of the dying Antiochus, who offered Philip the succession and bade him be the guardian of his nine-year-old son and bring him up to be king (verses 14-17); Lysias took on the task himself. **Philip** is now seeking to make himself sole ruler of the empire. Lysias obviously rationalizes the situation when he seeks an excuse to lift the siege. He must know well the food situation in Jerusalem.

6:60-63. The surrender terms are remarkable. The Jews receive all that they have been fighting for. They are permitted to remain the people of the covenant, follow the Law, practice circumcision and the sabbath, and keep distinct from Gentile culture (cf. 1:44-50). In return they evacuate the Acra. On marching in, Lysias realizes how strong it is. So, breaking the terms of the treaty, and for his own safety, he orders its wall torn down. II Maccabees 11:12-38 gives more information about this treaty. Philip fled to Egypt.

VII. FURTHER POLITICAL AND MILITARY DEVELOPMENTS
(7:1-50)

A. ANOTHER CLAIMANT FOR THE THRONE (7:1-20)

7:1-14. We are now one year later than the above events.
Demetrius is a third claimant for the Syrian throne. He
establishes himself by having his rivals murdered. The dissident
party among the Jews, led by **Alcimus**, goes over to him.
Bacchides is chosen **governor of the province Beyond the
River.** The name is from the old Persian point of view and
applies to the area between the Euphrates and Egypt. Thus
Bacchides has the same responsibility as Lysias before him.

Since Alcimus is truly of the Aaronic line of priests, the pious
in Jerusalem are ready to trust him. That **a group of scribes**, as
well as **the Hasideans**, are prepared to treat with him shows
their dissatisfaction with the leadership of Judas and the
Maccabeans. Internal schisms were to be the bane of Jewish
history from this time on. In fact the scribes already seem to be a
party in themselves.

7:15-20. Alcimus soon reveals that he is prepared to gain the
high priesthood by treachery and blood. Verse 17 is in part built
from Psalm 79. Bacchides even massacres those **who had
deserted to him.**

B. FURTHER TREACHERY (7:21-38)

The civil war worsens. It leads to a treacherous peace offer by
Nicanor, the royal emissary (II Maccabees 14:18-30 sees this
incident in another light, however). Nicanor now has control of
Jerusalem, and Judas is again in the hills. His absence leaves the
priests in Jerusalem in an uncertain position. **The elders of the
people** are mentioned now for the first time. They are the
governing body of senior citizens. Cf. verse 37 with I Kings 8:29,
where Solomon declares that God's "name" is to be encountered
in the temple, the representation of God's very being.

C. A RESOUNDING VICTORY (7:39-50)

Before the battle Judas reminds God of the earlier divine intervention, sending the **angel** of death when the **Assyrians** under Sennacherib were camped round the Holy City (II Kings 19:35). Now his army is much reduced in size from the great three-year guerrilla war. Yet not only does he kill Nicanor and so rout the enemy, he pursues them down to the plain. Many in the villages join him now that he is winning, and together they make it a total victory. But still they do not yet control Jerusalem (verse 47).

VIII. AN ALLIANCE WITH ROME (8:1-32)

8:1-16. How wondrous the stories of Roman arms must have sounded to Jewish ears—stories of unimaginably far-off countries like **Spain**, the land of **the Gauls**, and the other places at **the ends of the earth**. The Romans **were well-disposed toward all who made an alliance with them**. Even the Seleucids, whom Judas knew as *the* world power, had been defeated by Rome in 190 B.C. at Magnesia (verse 6). A later revolt had again been crushed (verses 9-10), though our author may be referring here to an event that took place fifteen years later.

The Roman policy of permitting kings to rule under them is noted by Judas (verse 13). The fact that Rome was ruled by an oligarchy with an annual change of chairmen, and not by a king, is a matter of profound interest (verses 15-16).

8:17-32. The journey to Rome was a great adventure for provincials like the Jews in their hill country. The reply they brought back from the Roman Senate was written on two bronze tablets (see Introduction) one of which was kept for the record in Rome. It outlines a bilateral treaty between the mighty Roman state and the few thousand Jewish insurgents in the hills of Palestine. But it turned Rome into the enemy of Syria (verse 32).

IX. JUDAS SLAIN; JONATHAN SUCCEEDS HIM;
WAR ENDS (9:1-73)

A. DAYS OF DECLINE (9:1-22)

For **Bacchides** see 7:8, and for **Alcimus** see 7:5. Verse 3 shows us we are now in May, 160 B.C. After the enemy show their strength, Judas' army loses faith, and many desert. Judas takes a courageous yet militarily wrong course. He will **die bravely** if his **time has come**. The resulting battle is long and fierce and seemingly indecisive. But Judas is killed in action. The lament for Judas is an echo of that uttered by David for Saul and Jonathan (II Samuel 1:19). Verse 22 reads like a quotation from the history writing in Kings (cf. I Kings 22:45). Judas was a great man, one of the military patriots and heroes of all time.

B. JONATHAN SUCCEEDS JUDAS (9:23-53)

9:23-34. Judas' death is the signal for many waverers to defect, urged to do so by a famine that follows the sabbatical year (6:53). All his days Judas was dogged by his troops' readiness to desert. The **doers of injustice** may be actual criminals and fugitives from justice who turned outlaws when the fate of Jerusalem was in the balance.

Things are now at their lowest—worse than they had been since the days of Malachi (cf. Zechariah 13:3-6). The little remnant of the once great fighting force selects Jonathan, Judas' brother, to be the new leader. All then flee to the wilderness of Judea (cf. 2:29). There cannot be many of them if they can all camp round one waterhole.

9:35-42. Their morale is dealt an even worse blow when they lose all their worldly goods and brother John is killed seeking the help of the Nabateans, their old allies (cf. 5:25). Blood revenge follows, and a wedding festival is turned into a mourning for the dead. The baggage is recovered, and they retreat to the jungle marshlands of the Jordan.

9:43-53. In the next battle Jonathan seems to have a natural advantage of terrain in that his flanks are protected by a loop of the river. Bacchides perhaps supposes the Jews will not fight on the sabbath. They escape from what has developed into a trap by swimming, but they must have lost their goods once more. Bacchides, still in full control of Judea, places strong fortifications wherever he wishes, to keep it in subjection.

C. The End of the War (9:54-73)

9:54-61. In May-June, 159, **Alcimus** gives the order to pull down the wall separating the inner from the outer court of the temple. Gentiles formerly could use the outer court only. Now they can mingle with the Jews and worship as equals. On the surface this seems a good idea. But for the faithful it meant the end of the special covenant relationship between Israel and its God which the prophets had upheld in their interpretation of the law of Moses. Second Isaiah saw the covenant with Israel as the means God intended for the redemption of the Gentiles (Isaiah 42:1; 49:6). This is very different from saying, "All religions are at base the same. Gentiles, with their peculiar and sometimes bestial notions of the divine, are welcome to worship the Holy One along with us."

The author evidently regards the creeping paralysis from which Alcimus suffers as a divine judgment. The obverse side of his painful death is a two-year respite for the land of Judea, with the patriots lying low in the hills.

9:62-73. But the tide turns at last. The Maccabees fortify a small fortress near Bethlehem to act as a challenge and bring the enemy out. **Jonathan** and his brother **Simon** divide their forces. They are able to harass **Bacchides'** army to the point that he decides to retire. Jonathan then seizes the psychological moment to suggest a treaty, to which Bacchides agrees. **Thus the sword ceased from Israel**—but only for five years. Yet that was enough time for the resistance movement to gain control of many of the villages, though not of the towns or garrisons.

X. RESULTANT POLITICAL MOVES (10:1-89)

A. THE MACCABEES RETURN "HOME" (10:1-14)

The author's interest in describing how and why **Demetrius** sought **Jonathan** as an ally centers in the good news that at last, after at least a decade, the resistance fighters have a chance to go "home" to Jerusalem. There Jonathan at once seems to take command. He rebuilds the fortifications of the city. Now **Alexander Epiphanes**, son of Antiochus IV Epiphanes, in his turn seeks alliance with this bold warrior.

B. JONATHAN BECOMES HIGH PRIEST; DEATH OF DEMETRIUS I (10:15-50)

But at Alexander's instigation a new situation arose. For the first time in Israel's history religious, political, and military authority was placed in the hands of one man. Thus there was no balance of power as in former centuries. Trouble would surely ensue. The high priest's vestments (verse 20) are described in Exodus 28.

Provided that **thirty thousand** Jews serve in Demetrius' forces (the three thousand of 11:44 is the more likely figure), the nation is to be completely free from all the oppression it has known. The king offers enormous concessions. He even proposes that *he* pay for the restoration of the temple and the walls of Jerusalem! The people of Jerusalem cannot believe such promises by Demetrius, whom they know as a treacherous man. Anyway, Alexander was the first to make them a good offer. It was as well that they accepted the latter offer, for Alexander soon defeated and killed Demetrius in battle.

C. ALEXANDER WEDS CLEOPATRA (10:51-66)

Ptolemais is the biblical Acco, just north of the present-day Haifa. **Ptolemy** is Ptolemy VI Philometor, who has now ruled in

Egypt for a generation. The very name Ptolemais shows the influence of Ptolemy along the coast of Syria. Cleopatra is not, of course, the woman made famous by Shakespeare; she lived a century later. Jonathan accepts the invitation to Ptolemais and arrives looking every inch their equal. He is rewarded by being clothed in royal purple and by seeing his personal enemies flee. Yet of course he is really a vassal of King Alexander.

D. JONATHAN CONSOLIDATES HIS RULE (10:67-89)

Demetrius, the son of Demetrius I, is trying to regain the throne of his father. Naturally he is angry that Jonathan did not accept his offer and so challenges him to battle. Jonathan accepts the challenge even though they are to meet on the plain, where there are no stones that can be thrown from rocky crags and no caves to hide in (verse 73). Jonathan first took **Joppa** (now Jaffa) on the coast, a valuable harbor for the Jews. Its capture also cut Apollonius' land route in two. **Azotus** is about twenty miles farther south.

The routed enemy sought sanctuary in **Beth-dagon**—the house of Dagon, the god of the Philistines since before the days of David (cf. Judges 16:23; I Samuel 5:2-5). But Jonathan turned the temple into an extermination furnace. Alexander was pleased at his successes and gave him the northern part of the land of the Philistines as a gift.

XI. CONTINUED STRUGGLES (11:1-74)

A. PTOLEMY PUSHES NORTH (11:1-19)

This incident is typical of the deceitful manner in which kings in the Near East pursued their selfish ends. So far as the Jews were affected, Jonathan seems to have acted in good faith. Ptolemy **put on the crown of Asia**—that is, of the Seleucid empire. One wonders what his daughter thought of her fate and with what zeal, if any, the warriors of both sides faced one another. The author informs us that both kings lost (verses 16-18). The only one to gain from the whole treacherous episode was Demetrius, the son of the man who had been the tireless enemy of Jonathan (10:67).

B. JONATHAN'S BARGAIN (11:20-37)

For Jonathan to besiege the Acra in Jerusalem was an act of rebellion. Young Demetrius II was then only sixteen years of age. Jonathan wins over the new king just as he won Alexander. The king puts the new agreement in writing, a copy of which is to be displayed in Jerusalem. The Acra and Beth-zur (6:49) were actually the only two remaining centers of Syrian authority left in Judea. Jonathan seems to have made the better bargain (cf. 10:29-45).

C. DEMETRIUS II (11:38-53)

The islands of the nations were Crete and others nearby (10:67). The Antiochus in verse 39 later becomes Antiochus VI. Jonathan gets his wish at last. The foreign troops in the Acra are dismissed. The city that rises against Demetrius (verse 45) is Antioch. Other authorities credit the king's Cretan mercenaries with most of the carnage. The Jewish mercenaries were probably regarded as heroes on returning home.

D. WARS AND RUMORS OF WARS (11:54-74)

The history of events here reads wearisomely. Troops change loyalties; kings offer bribes; cities are burnt; armies are routed. Jonathan comes out of it all a hero—but how many have died to make him so?

XII. FRIENDSHIP WITH ROME AND SPARTA; DECEIT OF TRYPHO (12:1-53)

A. ALLIANCE MAKING (12:1-23)

In chapter 8 we read of a Jewish committee visiting Rome. Hellenistic diplomacy required the renewal of a treaty if a change had taken place in the condition of one of the signatories, such as an accession, a death, etc. So Jonathan reaffirms his treaty with Rome. If we look over the events recounted in chapters 9–11, we see how little this treaty had meant to the Jews. Any treaty with Sparta, then, would mean even less. **Arius I** was king of Sparta 309-265 B.C. **Onias I** was high priest 323-300. So the treaty is intended to belong between 309 and 300. Its historicity is doubtful.

But the reply is even more so. It is impossible to imagine any kind of Greek claiming to be descended from Abraham. Possibly the author really believed these letters were sent. Possibly they were sent, but it was all a kind of diplomatic game of polite nothings. Possibly the author supposed that letters genuinely interchanged nearly two centuries before belonged to the period he was describing.

B. CAPTURE OF JONATHAN BY TREACHERY (12:24-53)

12:24-38. The wearisome war with the Seleucids continues. When the enemy slips from his grasp, Jonathan turns his wrath on a hapless Arab clan. For recent events in **Joppa** see 10:75 and 11:6. The walls of Jerusalem had already been rebuilt by Jonathan (cf. 10:10). The barrier around the fortress is a new thing (verses 35-36).

12:39-53. Jonathan now has to be ready to fight on a second front (verses 39-40). Instead, **Trypho** makes an ally of him. But Trypho is as deceitful as was expected of a Near Eastern king. Jonathan is betrayed and taken prisoner by Trypho. His men get home safely by keeping their heads. **The Great Plain** is the Esdraelon in southwestern Galilee.

XIII. THE RISE OF SIMON (13:1-53)

A. SIMON THE NEW LEADER (13:1-30)

13:1-11. Simon is the last remaining member of the Maccabean family. He is now fifty years old, older than Jonathan. He has already shown both wisdom and valor. Thus he becomes the inevitable choice as leader. His first speech is both powerful and courageous, and is effective.

13:12-27. Trypho tries the usual deceit to win his ends. **The money that Jonathan your brother owed** is a polite circumlocution for "ransom." Simon would have been blamed whether he paid up or not. Trypho, as was to be expected, broke his word and began an expedition against Jerusalem from the south. It was not the snow that stopped him but the fact that Simon's army was always on higher ground than his (cf. 3:24).

Trypho has his prisoner, Jonathan, murdered. Jonathan was not as great a man as his brothers, yet he held the rule for eighteen years. He was susceptible to the flattery of kings. He changed sides several times if he could thereby gain an advantage. He did not endear himself to his people.

13:28-30. Simon must have prepared the seventh pyramid for himself. It is interesting that Simon used both oriental and Hellenic motifs together on the columns (verse 29). Eusebius tells us that part of this great mausoleum was still standing in his day, the fourth century A.D.

B. SIMON CONSOLIDATES (13:31-53)

13:31-42. General Trypho of the Seleucid army was not of royal blood. The fact that he could keep control for four years of a section of the empire shows how weak the empire had become.

He also murdered the teenage successor to the throne. Trypho then becomes the common enemy of Simon and Demetrius. He brings them together, not as allies, for Simon is still a vassal, but in a pact of nonaggression. The Jews now no longer must pay tribute to Antioch, but their young men are to do military service there. But the Jews are delighted to imagine that they are independent of the Seleucids at last (verses 41-42). This was now the year 142 B.C.

13:42-53. Gazara was the Old Testament "Gezer." It was an important place in the Shephelah, the lowlands bordering on Philistia. Simon shows that he is both a good general and a religious zealot. He brings this city under the rule of the law of Moses.

Simon's final triumph was the surrender of the citadel in Jerusalem. He shows unusual clemency in just dismissing the foreign soldiers who surrendered. This took place about the end of May, 141 B.C. The **great enemy** in verse 51 was the Acra itself, towering over the temple and the city for many years. With its capitulation Jewish independence had really begun. Simon recognizes his advancing years. Like a wise ruler, he decides to educate his son, John Hyrcanus, to take over the rule eventually.

XIV. SIMON IS LAUDED (14:1-49)

A. IN PRAISE OF SIMON (14:1-23)

After a very condensed note on Seleucid affairs, the author sings the praise of this Maccabee who was perhaps the greatest of all the brothers. The picture of each person sitting **under his vine and his fig tree** is to be found in I Kings 4:25, Micah 4:4, and Zechariah 3:10. The general picture of peace and quiet is an amalgam of Old Testament texts, especially Zechariah 8:4-23. We saw in 12:1 how the custom of the day was to renew a treaty if a change took place in the dynasty (verse 18). These letters again may be the author's invention. Or he may have accepted in good faith doubtful information about them.

B. SIMON CONFIRMED AS COMMANDER, ETHNARCH, AND HIGH PRIEST (14:24-49)

The Jews may have borrowed the idea of honoring Simon with an inscribed bronze tablet from the Greeks, who were in the habit of thus honoring individual "benefactors" (cf. Luke 22:25). The proclamation was made about mid-September in the year 140 B.C.—the third year of Simon's high priesthood. The footnote in the Revised Standard Version notes the difficulty of the word **Asaramel**. For **sons of Joarib** see 2:1. The proclamation covers the ground described in the previous chapters. Its nature and tone reveal why the book is called I Maccabees and not merely "A History of the Jews in Seleucid Times." For the arising of a **trustworthy prophet**, see 4:46 and 9:27. Finally they give Simon copies of this "testimonial" to pass down to his descendants.

XV. WAR BEGINS AGAIN (15:1-41)

A. THE BACKGROUND OF SELEUCID INTRIGUE (15:1-14)

This **Antiochus** was the brother of Demetrius II. He had been living in Pamphylia. He takes the title of Euergetes, or Benefactor. When he hears the news of his brother Demetrius' capture (14:3), he determines to try his luck. His letter reads too smoothly to be acceptable. He could not have said **certain pestilent men**—this represents a Jewish editing of the original. Dor lies near the later town of Caesarea. The nearer Antiochus draws to Judea, the more possibility there will be of trouble for Simon.

B. LETTER FROM ROME; WAR RENEWED (15:15-41)

The letter from Rome may be misdated here. But at least it shows how significant little Judea had become in the eyes of the world powers. Annoyance at Rome's favor to Simon, however, weighs more with young Antiochus (perhaps about 21 years old now) than Simon's gift of two thousand trained soldiers. He breaks with Simon and rescinds the letter quoted in verses 2-9. Then he picks a quarrel (verse 28). The year is now 138. The sum of one thousand talents was not an unusual tribute in such circumstances. Simon gives a dignified reply to **Athenobius**, Antiochus' emissary, and offers a hundred talents for the sake of peace. But the Seleucid king **was greatly angered**. And so the weary war begins again.

XVI. CLOSING DEEDS (16:1-24)

A. SIMON'S OLDER SONS: JUDAS AND JOHN (16:1-3)

Simon had sent his son to Gazara to learn the art of commanding troops (13:53). Before he brings his book to a conclusion, the author introduces us to Simon's sons, to let us know who ruled Judea after Simon's death. So then we meet John, Judas, and Mattathias, called after his grandfather. Simon does not need to boast to them of the exploits of his father and brothers. All he need do is tell the tale. This family truly belongs among the great heroes of all times. Simon is the last of the brothers left alive. He is now some sixty years of age, yet he is conscious that the purposes of God transcend the generations (verse 3).

B. THE EXPLOITS OF JOHN HYRCANUS (16:4-24)

Both the book and the life of Simon are drawing to a close. Now we read about the skill and loyalty of young John and of his great victory over the Seleucid general. A new chapter of violence and intrigue is opening with the murder of Simon and of John's two brothers. In 15:31 the young Seleucid king Antiochus VII threatens, "Otherwise we will come and conquer you." Other writers in later years take up the tale.

Antiochus was in fact sympathetic to Ptolemy's **report** (verse 18). In the year 134 he did in fact invade Judea and besiege Jerusalem for a year. John at last capitulated, only because his people were starving. Antiochus VII broke down the walls of the city and exacted tribute once again.

But John Hyrcanus was able to regain the independence of the Jewish nation when, five years later, the Seleucid king was killed in battle. Thereafter they remained a free and independent but quarreling people of many parties. Finally Judea was swallowed up in the Roman Empire sixty-five years later.

THE SECOND BOOK OF THE MACCABEES

Robert C. Dentan

INTRODUCTION

II Maccabees is not the sequel to I Maccabees. It is an account of the same historical crisis told from a different point of view and with a different selection of events. I Maccabees is written in a sober Hebraic style and relates the story in relatively straightforward fashion. II Maccabees exhibits the typical flamboyant, emotional Greek style of the Hellenistic period. It shows a predominant concern for religious edification, with great emphasis on the spectacular, the miraculous, and even the gruesome.

I Maccabees is interested in the rise of the Hasmonean house, which continued to rule the independent Judean state that grew out of the Maccabean revolt. It describes the careers of four of its heroes—Mattathias, Judas, Jonathan, and Simon. II Maccabees has only one hero—Judas Maccabeus. It ignores completely the role of his father, Mattathias, in starting the revolt. In order to preserve the heroic image of Judas it ends the story with his victory over Nicanor, ignoring his final defeat and death (cf. I Maccabees 9:5-18).

II Maccabees

II Maccabees seems to reflect the viewpoint of the Hasideans (Hebrew *hasidim*, usually translated "saints" or "faithful" in the Old Testament). This was the party among the Jews most deeply devoted to the Mosaic law. It was probably the spiritual ancestor of such later sects as the Pharisees and the Essenes. For a time the Hasideans were ardent followers of Judas (14:6; I Maccabees 2:42). But because their attitude was basically religious rather than political, they ceased to support him and his successors when they felt religious freedom had been secured (I Maccabees 7:13-14).

Authorship and Composition
The author of the book as we now have it is known simply as the "epitomist," since his book is professedly a "condensation" (Greek *epitome*, 2:28) of a five-volume work by a certain Jason of Cyrene (2:23). Cyrene is located on the northern coast of Africa. Nothing further is known of Jason.

Occasionally the epitomist seems merely to have summarized the original. More often he appears to have abridged Jason's narrative by including only those incidents that furthered his own purpose and omitting those that did not. Some scholars believe that his concluding formulas in 3:40; 7:42; 10:9; 13:26b; and 15:37a mark the respective conclusions of Jason's original five volumes. The epitomist may have added certain passages from some other source—the martyr stories, for example. The two letters at the beginning (1:1–2:18) probably have been prefaced by a later hand.

Date and Place of Composition
The epitomist's concluding remark that "from that time the city has been in the possession of the Hebrews" (15:37) places his work before the Roman conquest in 63 B.C. Probably it is to be dated early in the first century B.C., with Jason's five volumes late in the second century. However, there are no precise indications by which the times can be determined. The two prefatory letters were presumably written in Hebrew or Aramaic. The rest of the book was obviously composed in

Greek—probably in Alexandria, though Antioch has also been suggested.

Contents

After two letters purporting to be from the Jews in Jerusalem to those in Egypt, urging them to keep the feast of Hanukkah, the epitomist introduces his work (2:19-32). Chapter 3 tells of an unsuccessful attempt to plunder the temple treasury in the time of Seleucus IV Philopator (187-175). Chapter 4 describes the unseemly rivalry for the high priesthood following the accession of Antiochus IV Epiphanes (175-163). Chapter 5 begins the story of Epiphanes' persecution of the Jews (167-164). The rest of the book is concerned with Jewish resistance, under the leadership of Judas Maccabeus, to the repressive policies of the Syrian kings. Chapters 6–7 are an interlude on Jewish martyrs. The narrative reaches its first climax with the death of Epiphanes (chapter 9) and the rededication of the temple (10:1-9). Then follows the account of the Jews' continued resistance to the policies of Epiphanes' successors, Antiochus V Eupator (163-162) and Demetrius I (162-150). This reaches a second climax in the story of Nicanor's defeat (10:10–15:36). The book concludes with an epilogue by the epitomist (15:37-39). Chapters 5–15 roughly parallel I Maccabees 1–7.

Religious Interest

II Maccabees marks an important stage in the development of religious thought in Judaism. It is especially notable for its emphasis on the ideas of physical resurrection (7:9, 11, 14; 14:46), prayer for the dead (12:43-45), and the intercession of saints (15:12, 14). It also presents vivid pictures of the intervention of angels in human affairs (3:25-26; 5:2-3; 10:29-30; 11:6-8). Later these ideas were characteristically associated with the Pharisees (cf. Acts 23:8). The figure of the martyr, which was shortly to play so important a role in Christendom, first appears in this book (chapters 6–7; 14:37-46), as does the doctrine of creation out of nothing (7:28).

I. PREFATORY LETTERS (1:1–2:18)

1:1-9. *A Letter to Egyptian Jews.* The purpose of this letter is to urge the Jews in Egypt to follow the example of those in Judea in observing the **feast** commemorating the rededication of the temple by Judas Maccabeus (see below on 10:1-9). The Jerusalem Jews wrote a previous letter in 143 during the reign of **Demetrius II** (145-139/38; cf. I Maccabees 10:67–15:22). This told of the persecutions by the Seleucid kings, here said to have been occasioned by the revolt of **Jason** (cf. 5:5-7). But now in 124 (verse 9) all that is past. They can ask others to join with them in keeping the temple feast. The authenticity of both this and the following letter is open to considerable question.

1:10–2:18. *Another Letter to Egyptian Jews.* This letter purports to have been written earlier by **Judas**—presumably Maccabeus—and other officials in Jerusalem to **Aristobulus**. This man is identified by the Christian writers Clement and Eusebius as a famous Alexandrian Jewish philosopher. The occasion is the death of the persecutor **Antiochus** (1:11-17) and the consequent opportunity to **celebrate the purification of the temple** (1:18).

Thus the letter apparently is to be understood as written while the temple is being restored (cf. I Maccabees 4:42-51). The Egyptian Jews are urged to join in the feast that is to climax the process (1:18; 2:16; cf. 10:6-7). Past occasions of God's protection of the temple and its appurtenances (1:19–2:15)—largely legendary—are cited to reinforce the request.

This apparent order of events has Antiochus' death preceding the purification of the temple. It agrees with that in 9:1–10:9 (see comment on 9:1-29). According to I Maccabees, however, the temple was rededicated in December 164 (I Maccabees 4:52) and Antiochus died in 163 (I Maccabees 6:16). Historically the latter sequence is the more probable. Possibly, therefore, the letter should be understood as referring, not to the purification itself, but to the commemoration of its first anniversary in 163.

1:11-17. This story of Antiochus' death is inconsistent with the accounts in chapter 9 and I Maccabees 6:8-16. It may be the result of confusion of Antiochus IV Epiphanes with his father Antiochus III, who was indeed killed while attempting to plunder a Persian temple.

1:18-36. The festival (see below on 10:1-9) is said to be associated also with a **feast of the fire** commemorating the rebuilding of the temple and rekindling of the sacrificial fire by **Nehemiah**. Historically Nehemiah had nothing to do with the rebuilding of the temple. It had been standing for over seventy years when he arrived in Jerusalem. The story of the miraculous hidden fire is pure legend. **Persia** is an error for Babylonia. Nothing certain is known of the origin and meaning of the word **nephthar**.

2:1-8a. The mention of the hidden fire leads the author to recount a legend unknown to the Old Testament. It tells how **Jeremiah** instructed the Jewish exiles to take some of the altar fire with them to Babylonia. It also tells, irrelevantly, that he hid **the tent and the ark**, as well as **the altar of incense**, in a **cave** on Mt. Sinai.

2:8b-12. The author reminds his readers that **Moses** once called down sacrificial fire from heaven (cf. Leviticus 9:23-24). So did **Solomon** at the original dedication of the temple (cf. II Chronicles 7:1; not in I Kings 8:62-64). Solomon's **eight days** of celebration (cf. II Chronicles 7:8-9) are treated as precedent for the eight-day observance of this feast (cf. 10:6).

2:13-15. The author has wished to establish in some way a parallel between Judas' rededication of the temple and Nehemiah's supposed rekindling of the altar fire. Here he also attempts to find a parallel in the story that both of them **collected** sacred **books**. Nothing is known elsewhere of their connection with this kind of activity.

2:16-18. The letter ends with another appeal to keep the feast.

II. THE EPITOMIST'S PREFACE (2:19-32)

2:19-32. The epitomist (see Introduction) announces his theme (verses 19-22). He discusses both his source and his manner of writing (verses 23-32; see Introduction).

III. The Failure of Heliodorus (3:1-40)

This is called the **episode of Heliodorus and the protection of the treasury** (verse 40). It illustrates one of the main themes of the book—that God can protect the sanctuary from those who attempt to profane it. When the officer of the heathen king tries to appropriate the funds of the temple, he is driven off by angelic forces.

3:1-14a. Jerusalem is enjoying **peace** under the pious rule of the **high priest Onias** III. Even **Seleucus** IV Philopator (187-175) is supporting the temple. Then a certain temple official, **Simon**, quarrels with Onias. He goes to **Apollonius**, governor of the province of **Coelesyria**, which included Palestine and Transjordan, and reports that vast sums of money can be found in the temple treasury. Seleucus instructs his chief minister, Heliodorus, to confiscate the temple funds. Much of these funds do not belong to the temple but have been deposited there by private citizens for safekeeping.

3:14b-30. Heliodorus' demands cause passionate prayers for deliverance to be uttered throughout the city. When he arrives at the treasury he is attacked by an angel on horseback, who is accompanied by two other angels. Heliodorus is reduced to terrified impotence.

3:31-40. Heliodorus' life is saved by the intercession of Onias. He then offers a **sacrifice** to Israel's God and reports his failure to the king. On the concluding formula, **This was the outcome of the episode**, see the Introduction.

IV. Rivalry for the High Priesthood (4:1-50)

4:1-6. Onias goes to Antioch to defend himself before the king against Simon's slanders.

4:7-22. *Jason's Hellenizing Policy.* Before Onias could reach the court, Seleucus was assassinated by Heliodorus, who intended to seize power for himself. He was frustrated by the proclamation of Seleucus' brother, **Antiochus IV**, as king. His title **Epiphanes**, meaning "(god) manifest," expresses the common oriental belief in the divinity of kings.

Onias' brother, **Jason**, purchases the high priesthood for a large sum. He proceeds to introduce Greek customs into Jerusalem, especially those connected with athletic contests. The choice of a Greek name, Jason, in place of his correct Hebrew name, Joshua, indicates his sympathies. If successful his policy would have led to the complete abandonment of Judaism (cf. I Maccabees 1:14-15). The gravity of the situation is seen in the enthusiastic response activities of the priests (verses 14-15) and the sending of contributions to the worship of Hercules (verses 18-20).

4:23-50. The High Priesthood of Menelaus. According to the Jewish historian Josephus (late first century A.D.) Menelaus was not the **brother of . . . Simon** but another brother of Onias and Jason. When Menelaus succeeds in **outbidding** Jason for the high priesthood, Jason has to flee into exile in the neighboring country of **Ammon**.

4:30-38. The murder of **Onias** is presumably the event referred to in Daniel 9:26, "An anointed one shall be cut off." Possibly this means only his deposition. Some scholars believe that this story of his death is either erroneous or fictitious. They believe that it was this Onias who went to Egypt and founded the famous temple at Leontopolis frequently mentioned by Josephus.

4:39-50. Menelaus' brother and deputy, **Lysimachus**, provokes a riot in Jerusalem. As a result Menelaus is brought to trial. He gains acquittal by bribing **Ptolemy**, an intimate of the king (cf. 6:8; 8:8; 10:12-13).

V. The Revolt and Victories of Judas Maccabeus (5:1–15:36)

A. The Background of the Revolt (5:1-27)

5:1-26. Antiochus' Attack on Jerusalem. Jason takes advantage of a **rumor** that Antiochus has died while invading Egypt in 169. He attacks Jerusalem in an attempt to regain his former position. Though he is repulsed, Antiochus assumes that all

Judea is aflame and returns from Egypt to attack Jerusalem. He massacres a large part of the population. Led by the traitor Menelaus, he plunders the temple.

5:17-20. It is explained that Antiochus succeeded, where Heliodorus had failed, only because of the sins of the people. It is uncertain whether this explanation comes from Jason of Cyrene or from the epitomist (cf. 6:12-17).

5:21-26. The word translated **captain of the Mysians** is uncertain and may mean "detestable leader." Thus **Apollonius** may be the provincial governor (cf. 3:5; 4:4, 21) and perhaps the general later killed in an early battle of the revolt (I Maccabees 3:10-12). The massacre on the **sabbath** is evidently that described in I Maccabees 1:29-32 as occurring two years after Antiochus' attack—that is, in 167.

5:27. *Introduction of the Hero.* Abruptly there is a note that **Judas** and some companions escaped the slaughter and fled to the **mountains**. The nickname **Maccabeus** seems to be derived from the Aramaic word for "hammer." But it is uncertain whether it refers to a physical peculiarity ("hammer-headed") or to vigorous leadership ("the hammerer").

It is striking that the whole story of the revolt begun by his father, Mattathias is omitted (cf. I Maccabees 2). The omission, which is certainly deliberate, is probably due to the Hasidic and Pharisaic sympathies of the epitomist (see Introduction). In order not to glorify the Hasmonean dynasty he mentions Judas' brothers Jonathan and Simon only in passing (8:22; 14:17). He says nothing of their subsequent roles as high priests and chief leaders of the nation—the theme of the last half of I Maccabees. Even Mattathias is not mentioned, presumably because he began the Maccabean dynasty. Judas, the hero of the Hasideans (cf. 14:6), is the epitomist's only hero also. The account of Judas' activities is continued in chapter 8.

B. INTERLUDE: THE MARTYR STORIES (6:1–7:42)

6:1-11. *Antiochus' Forced Hellenization.* Antiochus now formally prohibits practice of the Jewish religion. He tries to compel the Jews to accept paganism. The temple of Israel's God in Jerusalem is converted into a temple of **Zeus**—as is the Samaritan temple on Mount **Gerizim**. Sexual debauchery, characteristic of certain forms of paganism, is practiced in the temple. Illegal sacrifices—no doubt including pigs, which were especially abhorrent to the Jews—are offered. Jews are forced to participate in the worship of **Dionysus** (Bacchus) and to adopt the Greek manner of life under threat of death. Horrible examples are made of some who persisted in the practice of circumcision or the observance of the sabbath. On **Ptolemy** see above on 4:39-50. On **Philip** cf. 5:22.

6:12-17. *The Epitomist's Comment.* Anxious to justify the power, wisdom, and love of his God, the epitomist—as is clear from the style (cf. 2:19-32)—explains these dreadful events. They were permitted in order to **discipline** the people of Israel and prevent them from falling into grievous sins. Other nations, who do not enjoy the Lord's favor, are allowed to continue in sin until the end. Doom comes without warning. Thus Israel's sufferings are a sign of God's special concern for them, not of God's impotence or neglect.

6:18-31. *The Aged Eleazar's Martyrdom.* Refusing to eat pork, or even pretend to do so, the ninety-year-old Eleazar goes heroically to torture and death.

7:1-42. *Martyrdom of a Mother and Seven Sons.* Confronted with the same temptation as Eleazar, the first of seven brothers refuses to **transgress the laws of our fathers**—laws similar to those of Deuteronomy 14:3-21. He is therefore subjected to hideous tortures, personally supervised **by the king**, which are recounted in graphic detail. The quotation from the **song** of **Moses** (verse 6) is from Deuteronomy 32:36.

7:7-14. After the death of the first brother, the second is treated in similar fashion. He announces his belief in an **everlasting renewal of life** (cf. verses 11, 14, 23, 29, 36)—obviously the source of his courage. The third brother makes clear that this involves belief in resurrection of the physical body, not merely immortality of the soul. As he stretches out **his hands** he expresses his **hope to get them back**

again. The fourth brother completes the statement of doctrine by announcing that **there will be no resurrection** for the wicked.

The book of Daniel, which arose out of the troubles of the Maccabean revolt, affirms in contrast the resurrection of both righteous and wicked (Daniel 12:2). The doctrine of resurrection appears elsewhere in the Old Testament only in Isaiah 26:19, where the text is uncertain. The emphasis on it here is therefore the more striking. It probably justifies our seeing in the book evidence of a Pharisaic point of view—especially when it also has so many stories to tell about the intervention of angels (see Introduction).

7:15-42. Both the fifth and the sixth brothers threaten the king with divine punishment. Finally the **mother**, who has witnessed the death of six sons, shows her mettle by urging the seventh and youngest to be no less courageous. She affirms her own belief in the resurrection. The creator of all things **did not make them out of things that existed** and is therefore able to recreate all things, including human life (verses 28-29). This is the earliest statement of the doctrine of creation out of nothing. After a final, climactic denunciation of the king's wickedness, the seventh young man dies, as does his mother also. The epitomist then concludes the interlude, perhaps indicating the end of Jason's second volume (see Introduction).

C. THE BEGINNING OF THE REVOLT (8:1–10:9)

8:1-36. *Judas' First Victory Over Nicanor.* The story interrupted after 5:27 is now resumed. Judas gathers an army and begins guerrilla warfare against the enemy. **Philip**, the governor at Jerusalem (cf. 5:22; 6:11), reports Judas' successes to **Ptolemy**, who is now the provincial governor (see above on 4:39-50; 5:21-26). Ptolemy dispatches an army under **Nicanor** and **Gorgias** to suppress the revolt (cf. I Maccabees 3:38–4:25, where Gorgias rather than Nicanor is the principal commander).

8:12-23. Before joining battle Judas exhorts his troops to fight with the power of God. On the **time of Sennacherib** cf. II Kings 18:13–19:37. The **battle with the Galatians** is otherwise unknown. Two of Judas' **brothers**, **Jonathan** (cf. I Maccabees 9:28–12:53) and **Simon** (cf. I Maccabees 13:1–16:16), later succeeded him as leaders of the nation. Both became high priests (see above on 5:27).

8:24-36. Nicanor's army is put to flight. I Maccabees says the reason the Jewish fighters stopped pursuing the enemy was the presence of another army close by (I Maccabees 4:16-18). This account, with its typical concern for piety, says it was in order to observe the **sabbath**. Additional victories are won in battles with **Timothy** (cf. I Maccabees 5:37-44) and **Bacchides** (cf. I Maccabees 7:8-20). Nicanor goes back in disgrace to Antioch. He will return to Judea to meet defeat a second time, and to die, in chapters 14–15 (see below on 14:11-14).

9:1-29. *The Death of Antiochus Epiphanes.* This chapter contains one of the major chronological problems of the book. It places the death of Antiochus before the rededication of the temple (10:1-8; see above on 1:10–2:18), whereas the sequence in I Maccabees is the reverse (I Maccabees 4:36-59; 6:8-16). Scholars differ as to which is correct, but probability is on the side of I Maccabees. It has been suggested that chapter 9 originally followed 10:1-8 (cf. 10:9) and was transposed by the editor who added 1:10–2:18. But this theory would solve only one of the chronological problems (see below on 11:1-15).

9:1-17. While on a campaign in Persia (cf. I Maccabees 3:31-37) Antiochus Epiphanes is defeated in an attempt to **rob the temples** (cf. 1:13-16; I Maccabees 6:1-4). On his way back west to vent his wrath on the Jews he is stricken with a loathsome disease and suffers a fall from his chariot. He repents and vows to free Jerusalem. He will repay **many times over** the plunder he has taken from the temple, as well as **become a Jew** himself. The style of this section is highly emotional and rhetorical. The details are not to be taken as serious history (cf. I Maccabees 6:8-16).

9:18-27. Antiochus Epiphanes writes a letter to the Jews commending his **son Antiochus** as his successor. This document is very moderate in tone when contrasted with the rest of the chapter. It may well reflect an authentic communication from the king to his partisans in Jerusalem.

9:28-29. The king dies and his body is brought back to Antioch by **Philip**—probably not the Philip mentioned previously (5:22; 6:11; 8:8). The report of Philip's flight to **Egypt** raises another chronological problem—whether it occurred before or after his seizure of the government in Antioch (13:23). According to I Maccabees, Antiochus Epiphanes earlier appointed Lysias (see below on 10:10-38) regent and guardian of his son (I Maccabees 3:32-37). On his deathbed he gave the same assignment to Philip (I Maccabees 6:14-15). Thus on his return with the army from Persia, Philip claimed the regency while Lysias and the new young king were in Judea fighting Judas. Lysias hastily came to terms with Judas and returned to Antioch to overthrow Philip (I Maccabees 6:55-63). Josephus adds that Lysias had Philip executed, but he may simply have assumed this.

10:1-9. *The Purification of the Temple.* Judas and his forces seize the temple and the city—though not its citadel (cf. I Maccabees 4:41; 6:18-27). The worship of the God of Israel is restored. They purify the sanctuary from the pollutions of paganism in a ceremony which I Maccabees (4:36, 59) calls a "dedication" (Hebrew *hanukkah*). This occurs **on the twenty-fifth day of . . . Chislev** (November-December), exactly **two years** after the heathen profaned it. I Maccabees gives the year dates 167 and 164, indicating an interval of three years (I Maccabees 1:54; 4:52). The eight-day celebration resembles the **feast of booths** (cf. 1:9, 18) because the guerrillas were not able to observe that feast properly three months earlier when they were still fighting in the hills. They order that this occasion be celebrated every year at the same time. This event marks the climax of this part of the book. The second climax is reached in 15:36 with the establishment of Nicanor's Day. The epitomist's concluding formula (verse 9) may mark the end of Jason of Cyrene's third volume (see Introduction).

D. CONTINUING WARFARE (10:10–13:26)

10:10-38. *Beginning of Eupator's Reign.* Epiphanes' son **Antiochus Eupator** was a mere child at his accession. **Lysias** is his guardian and regent (see above on 9:28-29). Lysias also becomes **governor of Coelesyria** (see above on 3:1-14*a*) following the suicide of **Ptolemy . . . Macron**, whose policy in that office is now said to have been pro-Jewish (contrast 8:8-9).

10:14-23. Probably material omitted by the epitomist made clear that **Gorgias became governor**, not of Coelesyria, but of Idumea, to the south of Judea (cf. 12:32). The **Idumeans** were descendants of the Old Testament Edomites, who moved into southern Palestine during the Exile. With their allies, hellenizing Jews **banished from Jerusalem**, they pursue the war against Judas' forces and are severely defeated.

10:24-38. Judas has defeated **Timothy** on a previous occasion (8:30-32). When Timothy invades Judea he is soundly thrashed a second time, with the aid of angelic forces. The story of Judas' capture of **Gazara**—the Old Testament Gezer—is evidently erroneous. Actually it was taken by his brother Simon more than twenty years later (I Maccabees 13:43-48). This fits the tendency of this book to increase the honor of Judas at the expense of the rest of his family (see above on 5:27). The story of Timothy's death shows the epitomist's carelessness in the use of his sources. Timothy reappears, quite alive, in 12:2.

11:1-15. *The Defeat of Lysias.* This account is out of order. In I Maccabees 4:26-35 this battle with Lysias takes place during the lifetime of Antiochus Epiphanes. The victory makes possible the rededication of the temple. At **Beth-zur**, about fifteen miles south of Jerusalem, Judas meets the army of Lysias. Again with angelic help, he puts it to flight. Lysias makes peace with the Jews.

11:16-38. *Four Letters Concerning the Peace.* Scholars disagree as to the authenticity of these letters. However, there is nothing in their style and tone to forbid the assumption that they are genuine. They are dated before the purification of the temple—the first probably in November 165, the last two in

April 164. In the letter of **Lysias to . . . the Jews** he promises his help in return for their cooperation. **Antiochus** Eupator in a letter to **Lysias** approves the restoration of the **temple** to the Jews and freedom to practice their religion.

In his letter **to the senate of the Jews** the king permits them to return peacefully to their homes in the countryside. Though the hellenizing policy of **Menelaus** (4:23-50; 5:15, 23) has been defeated and he himself is in exile, Antiochus still recognizes him as high priest and leader of the nation.

The final letter, from the **Romans,** is evidence of the growing power of Rome in the Near East. A hundred years later it would result in the incorporation of Judea into the Roman Empire. Here the Romans ask merely for consultation on the terms of the peace agreement.

12:1-45. *Judas' Wars with Neighboring Peoples.* At least a temporary peace has now been established with the central government. But it is still necessary to deal with some of the local **governors** and with neighbors who are old enemies of the Jewish nation.

12:3-9. Judas attacks **Joppa** (modern Jaffa), a seaport about thirty-five miles northwest of Jerusalem. He then turns on **Jamnia** (modern Yabneh), near the coast about twelve miles south of Joppa. In both cities the local Gentile authorities wipe out the helpless Jewish minorities.

12:10-31. The account of an attack by Arab nomads in verses 10-12 can hardly be the sequel to the battles at Joppa and Jamnia. It belongs most naturally with the campaign east of the Jordan described in the following section (verses 13-31). The name of the place to which **a mile from there** refers in verse 10 must have been somehow lost. Presumably it was some site in the Nabatean country of southern Transjordan. This passage is apparently another version of the events recounted in I Maccabees 5:24-53.

Caspin is probably the Caspho of I Maccabees 5:26, 36. **Charax** is unknown. The **Toubiani** are no doubt the Jews of the "land of Tob" (I Maccabees 5:13), a city and region in northern Transjordan. **Charnaim** and **Ephron** were also cities in northern

419

Transjordan. **Atargatis** was a Syrian goddess. **Scythopolis** is the Old Testament Beth-shan on the western side of the Jordan south of the Sea of Galilee.

Having made a swinging movement through Transjordan from south to north, Judas and his troops now complete the circle by turning south from Scythopolis toward Jerusalem. On the **feast of weeks**, Greek **Pentecost**, cf. Deuteronomy 16:9-12.

12:32-45. Again there is a battle with **Gorgias, the governor of Idumea** (see above on 10:14-23). **Marisa**, the Old Testament Mareshah, was evidently included in Idumea, whereas **Adullam** was in Judea. The relation of verses 36-37 to the context has been obscured by the epitomist's clumsy abridgment. The discovery of pagan cult objects on the bodies of the Jewish soldiers both explains their deaths, according to the orthodox philosophy (verse 40), and leads Judas to provide expiatory sacrifices for them (verses 43-45). Verse 44 has, historically, been the most important prooftext for the practice of praying for the dead.

13:1-26. *The Second Invasion by Lysias.* With many variations in detail, this chapter tells the same story as I Maccabees 6:18-63. In verses 19-26 the epitomist has reduced his story to an outline. These verses provide evidence of his claim that the book is an abbreviation of a much larger work (2:26-31).

13:3-8. For selfish reasons **Menelaus** (see above on 11:16-38) urges **Antiochus**—that is, Lysias—to invade Judea. It may be that the account of his death in verses 4-8 has been dislocated by the epitomist and should follow verse 23. **Beroea** is the modern Aleppo in northern Syria.

13:9-22. When they hear of the invading army, Judas and his people engage in prayer. They advance to meet it as it moves south along the coastal plain. **Modein**, where the Maccabean revolt began (I Maccabees 2:1, 15-28), lies in the foothills northwest of Jerusalem. According to I Maccabees 6:43-46 it was Eleazar, Judas' brother, who **stabbed the leading elephant** and was crushed to death beneath it. The scene shifts southeast to

Beth-zur (see above on 11:1-15) in the mountains, where Eupator and Lysias are defeated.

13:23-26. The account in I Maccabees 6:55-63 makes clear that the seizure of the government in Antioch by **Philip** (see above on 9:28-29) not merely made possible the renewal of peace between the boy king and his Jewish subjects but saved Judas and his forces from a disastrous defeat. The area **from Ptolemais** (Old Testament Acco) north of Mount Carmel **to Gerar** in the Philistine country to the south means the whole of Palestine. The epitomist's concluding formula in verse 26*b* may mark the end of Jason of Cyrene's fourth volume (see Introduction).

E. VICTORY OVER NICANOR (14:1–15:36)

This account parallels I Maccabees 7. It provides the second and concluding great climax of the book (see above on 10:1-9).

14:1-2. *Demetrius' Seizure of the Throne.* On the death of **Seleucus** IV in 175 his son Demetrius would have become king instead of Seleucus' brother Antiochus Epiphanes if he had not been a hostage in Rome. He now escapes from Rome, revolts against his young cousin Antiochus Eupator, and executes both him and Lysias (cf. I Maccabees 7:1-4). **Three years later** is apparently an error. Most data indicate that Eupator reigned less than two years (163-162). **Tripolis** is north of Beirut in modern Lebanon.

14:3-11. *Treachery of Alcimus.* Possibly the epitomist omitted some record of Alcimus' former service as high priest. I Maccabees 7:5 says, with great probability, only that he "wanted to be high priest." On the **Hasideans** see the Introduction. Alcimus convinces Demetrius that peace is impossible **as long as Judas lives.**

14:11-36. *Appointment of Nicanor.* Josephus states that Nicanor was one of the group who escaped from Rome with Demetrius. If he was the same man who fought Judas earlier (8:9-36), he presumably went to Rome sometime after his ignominious defeat with the hope of recouping his fortunes by helping Demetrius gain the crown. On the other hand the reference to Nicanor's having commanded the **elephants** may indicate that Jason of Cyrene included him in Lysias' army (cf. 11:4; 13:2). With **immediately** in verse 12 contrast I Maccabees 7:8-25.

14:15-25. After an initial skirmish at **Dessau** (the place is unknown) Nicanor endeavors to make friends with Judas. I Maccabees 7:27-30 expresses a more cynical view of Nicanor's motives: he was planning treachery.

14:26-36. By raising suspicions of Nicanor's loyalty Alcimus succeeds in thwarting his efforts toward securing a peaceful settlement. When Judas escapes, Nicanor threatens to destroy and desecrate the temple if Judas is not surrendered to him. The priests call for divine help.

14:37-46. *The Martyrdom of Razis.* This story of persecution and suicide is told with even more gruesome details than those of chapters 6–7. Suicide is rare in the Old Testament and among Jews in general. Thus the account is given a special pathos.

15:1-36. *Nicanor's Defeat and Death.* Both sides now prepare for battle. Instead of putting Judas' army vaguely **in the region of Samaria** I Maccabees 7:40 says he was encamped at Adasa, about ten miles northwest of Jerusalem. Some Jewish conscripts in Nicanor's army attempt, unsuccessfully, to dissuade him from fighting on the **sabbath**.

15:6-16. Judas encourages his troops by general exhortation and by **relating a dream** in which **Onias**, the martyred high priest (cf. chapter 3; 4:33-34), and **Jeremiah, the prophet**, appeared to him. The vision of Onias and Jeremiah provides evidence for belief in the intercession of saints at this period (cf. Tobit 12:12, 15). In view of verses 1-5 the vision seems intended to give God's approval for resisting Nicanor's attack on the sabbath, but this is not clear in the present text. Possibly the epitomist was unwilling to admit that Judas fought a battle on the sabbath (cf. 8:26-27; contrast I Maccabees 2:41). Thus he omitted this element from his source. Verse 9 shows that **the law and the prophets** had been canonized by the date of writing, but apparently not the Writings, the third division of the Old Testament canon.

15:17-36. The battle is won by the Jews as an answer to their prayers. Afterward they cut off Nicanor's **head and arm** and cut out his **tongue**. However, they can hardly have hung his head from the **citadel**, which was not at that time in their possession (see above on 10:1-9). The annual celebration of these events is decreed to take place on the **day before Mordecai's day**—that is, Purim (cf. Esther 9:20-22, 26). **Adar** is February-March.

VI. THE EPITOMIST'S EPILOGUE (15:37-39)

Cf. 2:19-32. In the sense that the religious freedom of its citizens is no longer threatened the city is now firmly **in the possession of the Hebrews**. But the garrison of the citadel would not be removed for twenty years (cf. I Maccabees 13:49-52). The epitomist's concluding formula (see Introduction) appears for the last time in verse 37*a*.

FOR FURTHER STUDY

THE BOOK OF HOSEA

W. R. Harper, *Amos and Hosea*, 1905. S. L. Brown, *Hosea*, 1932. H. W. Robinson, *The Cross of Hosea*, 1949. Norman Snaith, *Mercy and Sacrifice*, 1953. John Mauchline in *Interpreter's Bible*, 1956. Gunnar Osborn, *Yahweh and Baal*, 1956. G. A. F. Knight, *Hosea*, 1960. J. D. Smart in *Interpreter's Dictionary of the Bible*, 1962. J. M. Ward, *Hosea: A Theological Commentary*, 1966, and in *Interpreter's Dictionary of the Bible Supplement*, 1976.

THE BOOK OF JOEL

J. A. Brewer, *The Book of Joel*, 1911. H. C. Lanchester, *Joel and Amos*, 1915. G. W. Wade, *The Books of the Prophets Micah, Obadiah, Joel and Jonah*, 1925. G. A. Smith, *The Book of the Twelve Prophets*, Volume I, rev. ed., 1928. A. S. Kapelrud, *Joel Studies*, 1948; an attempt to connect the book with a preexilic enthronement festival. J. A. Thompson in *Interpreter's Bible*, 1956. Jacob M. Myers, *Hosea, Joel, Amos, Obadiah, Jonah*, 1959. William Neil in *Interpreter's Dictionary of the Bible*, 1962.

THE BOOK OF AMOS

W. R. Harper, *Amos and Hosea*, 1910. J. M. P. Smith, *Amos, Hosea and Micah*, 1914. N. H. Snaith, *The Book of Amos*, Parts I-II, 1945-46. R. S. Cripps, *Amos*, 2nd ed., 1955. H. E. W. Fosbroke in *Interpreter's Bible*, 1956. A. S. Kapelrud, *Central Ideas in Amos*, 1956. J. D. W. Watts, *Vision and Prophecy in Amos*, 1958. J. D. Smart in *Interpreter's Dictionary of the Bible*, 1962. R. L. Honeycutt, *Amos and His Message*, 1963. J. M. Ward in *Interpreter's Dictionary of the Bible Supplement*, 1976.

THE BOOK OF OBADIAH

J. A. Bewer, *The Book of Obadiah*, 1911. H. C. Lanchester, *Obadiah and Jonah*, 1915. G. W. Wade, *The Books of the Prophets Micah,*

Obadiah, Joel and Jonah, 1925. G. A. Smith, *The Book of the Twelve Prophets*, Volume I, rev. ed., 1928. Nelson Glueck, *The Other Side of the Jordan*, 1940. S. Bullough, *Obadiah, Micah, Zephaniah, Haggai, and Zechariah*, 1953. J. A. Thompson in *Interpreter's Bible*, 1956. Jacob M. Myers, *Hosea, Joel, Amos, Obadiah, Jonah*, 1959. James Muilenburg in *Interpreter's Dictionary of the Bible*, 1962.

THE BOOK OF JONAH

J. A. Brewer, *The Book of Jonah*, 1912. H. C. Lanchester, *Obadiah and Jonah*, 1915. G. W. Wade, *The Books of the Prophets Micah, Obadiah, Joel and Jonah*, 1925. G. A. Smith, *The Book of the Twelve Prophets*, rev. ed. 1928. G. A. F. Knight, *Ruth and Jonah*, 1950. André Parrot, *Nineveh and the Old Testament*, 1955. James D. Smart in *Interpreters Bible*, 1956. William Neil in *Interpreter's Dictionary of the Bible*, 1962. G. M. Landes in *Interpreter's Dictionary of the Bible Supplement*, 1976.

THE BOOK OF MICAH

J. M. P. Smith, *Micah, etc.*, 1911; a standard scholarly work which, except for certain details from recent research, has not been superseded. S. Goldman in *The Twelve Prophets*, ed. A. Cohen, 1948; includes parallel Hebrew and English texts. R. E. Wolf in *Interpreter's Bible*, 1956. John Bright, *A History of Israel*, 1959, pp. 252-87; lucid and comprehensive on the historical background of Micah and his period. John Marsh, *Amos and Micah*, 1959. Bruce Vawter, *The Conscience of Israel*, 1961, pp. 130-61. E. A. Leslie in *Interpreter's Dictionary of the Bible*, 1962. Samuel Sandmel, *The Hebrew Scriptures*, 1963, pp. 98-103. J. M. Ward in *Interpreter's Dictionary of the Bible Supplement*, 1976.

THE BOOK OF NAHUM

Alfred Haldar, *Studies in the Book of Nahum*, 1947. André Parrot, *Nineveh and the Old Testament*, 1956.

THE BOOK OF HABAKKUK

W. F. Albright, "The Psalm of Habakkuk" in H. H. Rowley, ed., *Studies in Old Testament Prophecy*, 1950.

THE BOOK OF ZEPHANIAH

G. A. Smith, *The Book of the Twelve Prophets*, Volume 2, revised edition, 1928.

THE BOOK OF HAGGAI

G. A. Smith, *The Book of the Twelve Prophets*, Volume II, rev. ed., 1928. Raymond Calkins, *The Modern Message of the Minor Prophets*, 1947.

THE BOOK OF ZECHARIAH

G. A. Smith, *The Book of the Twelve Prophets*, rev. ed., 1928. Raymond Calkins, *The Modern Message of the Minor Prophets*, 1947. N. H. Snaith, *The Jews from Cyrus to Herod*, 1956. D. W. Thomas in *Interpreter's Bible*, 1956. H. H. Rowley, *The Relevance of the Apocalyptic*, rev. ed., 1964.

THE BOOK OF MALACHI

J. M. P. Smith, *Malachi*, 1912. L. E. Browne, *Early Judaism*, 1920. G. A. Smith, *The Book of the Twelve Prophets*, rev. ed., 1928. Raymond Calkins, *The Modern Message of the Minor Prophets*, 1947. R. C. Dentan in *Interpreter's Bible*, 1956. N. H. Snaith, *The Jews from Cyrus to Herod*, 1956. William Neil in *Interpreter's Dictionary of the Bible*, 1962.

THE FIRST BOOK OF ESDRAS

S. A. Cook, in R. H. Charles, ed., *The Apocrypha and Pseudepigrapha of the Old Testament*, 1913. Nigel Turner in *Interpreter's Dictionary of the Bible*, 1962.

THE SECOND BOOK OF ESDRAS

G. H. Box, *The Ezra Apocalypse*, 1912; "IV Ezra," in R. H. Charles, ed., *The Apocrypha and Pseudepigrapha of the Old Testament*, 1913, II, 542-624. W. O. E. Oesterley, *II Esdras*, 1933. Nigel Turner, "Esdras, Books of," in *Interpreter's Dictionary of the Bible*, 1962.

THE BOOK OF TOBIT

D. C. Simpson in R. H. Charles, ed., *The Apocrypha and Pseudepigrapha of the Old Testament*, 1913; a translation of the longer Sinaiticus text with introduction and commentary. W. O. E. Oesterley, *An Introduction to the Books of the Apocrypha*, 1935. R. H. Pfeiffer, *History of New Testament Times, with an Introduction to the Apocrypha*, 1958; a translation of the longer Sinaiticus text with introduction and commentary. Allen Wikgren in *Interpreter's Dictionary of the Bible*, 1962.

THE BOOK OF JUDITH

A. E. Cowley in R. H. Charles, ed., *The Apocrypha and Pseudepigrapha of the Old Testament*, 1913. R. H Pfeiffer, *History of New Testament Times, with an Introduction to the Apocrypha.*, 1949, pp. 285-303. Paul Winter in *Interpreter's Dictionary of the Bible*, 1962.

ADDITIONS TO THE BOOK OF ESTHER

J. A. F. Gregg in R. H. Charles, ed., *The Apocrypha and Pseudepigrapha of the Old Testament*, 1913, I, 665-84. R. H. Pfeiffer, *History of New Testament Times, with an Introduction to the Apocrypha*, 1949, pp. 304-12. E. W. Saunders in *Interpreter's Dictionary of the Bible*, 1962.

THE WISDOM OF SOLOMON

J. A. F. Gregg, *The Wisdom of Solomon*, 1909. B. M. Metzger, *An Introduction to the Apocrypha*, 1957, pp. 65-76. J. Reider, *The Book of*

Wisdom, 1957. M. Hadas in *Interpreter's Dictionary of the Bible*, 1962. J. Geyer, *The Wisdom of Solomon*, 1963.

ECCLESIASTICUS

G. H. Box and W. O. E. Oesterley, in R. H. Charles, ed., *The Apocrypha and Pseudepigrapha of the Old Testament*, volume I, 1913. W. O. E. Oesterley, *The Wisdom of Jesus the Son of Sirach, or Ecclesiasticus*, 1912. R. H. Pfeiffer, *History of New Testament Times with an Introduction to the Apocrypha*, 1949, pp. 352-408. B. M. Metzger, *An Introduction to the Apocrypha*, 1957, pp. 77-88. T. A. Burkill, in *Interpreter's Dictionary of the Bible*, 1962. P. W. Skehan in *Interpreter's Dictionary of the Bible Supplement*, 1976.

BARUCH

B. M. Metzger, *An Introduction to the Apocrypha*, 1957. Sydney Tedesche in *Interpreter's Dictionary of the Bible*, 1962.

THE LETTER OF JEREMIAH

C. J. Ball in R. H. Charles, ed., *The Apocrypha and Pseudepigrapha of the Old Testament*, 1913. B. M. Metzger, *An Introduction to the Apocrypha*, 1957. Sidney Tedesche in *Interpreter's Dictionary of the Bible*, 1962.

THE PRAYER OF AZARIAH AND THE SONG OF THE THREE YOUNG MEN

R. H. Pfeiffer, *History of New Testament Times with an Introduction to the Apocrypha*, 1949. R. C. Dentan, *The Apocrypha: Bridge of the Testaments*, 1954. F. V. Filson, *Which Books Belong in the Bible?* 1957. B. M. Metzger, *An Introduction to the Apocrypha*, 1957.

THE BOOK OF SUSANNA

R. H. Pfeiffer, *History of New Testament Times with an Introduction to the Apocrypha*, 1949. R. C. Dentan, *The Apocrypha: Bridge of the*

Testaments, 1954. F. V. Filson, *Which Books Belong in the Bible?* 1957. B. M. Metzger, *An Introduction to the Apocrypha*, 1957.

THE PRAYER OF MANASSEH

H. E. Ryle, in R. H. Charles, ed., *The Apocrypha and Pseudepigrapha of the Old Testament*, 1913. L. H. Brockington, *A Critical Introduction to the Apocrypha*, 1961. Allen Wikgren in *Interpreter's Dictionary of the Bible*, 1962.

THE FIRST BOOK OF THE MACCABEES

R. H. Charles, *The Apocrypha and Pseudepigrapha of the Old Testament in English*, 1913; Tedesche and Zeitlin, *The First Book of Maccabees*, 1950; J. C. Dancy, *A Commentary on I Maccabees*, 1954; F. V. Filson, *Which Books Belong in the Bible?* 1957; B. M. Metzger, *An Introduction to the Apocrypha*, 1957; L. H. Brockington, *A Critical Introduction to the Apocrypha*, 1961.

THE SECOND BOOK OF THE MACCABEES

James Moffatt in R. H. Charles, ed., *The Apocrypha and Pseudepigrapha of the Old Testament*, 1913. C. C. Torrey, *The Apocryphal Literature*, 1945. R. H. Pfeiffer, *History of New Testament Times with Introduction to the Apocrypha*, 1949. S. Tedesche and S. Zeitlin, *The Second Book of Maccabees*, 1954. H. M. Orlinsky and W. H. Brownlee in *Interpreter's Dictionary of the Bible*, 1962.

ABBREVIATIONS AND EXPLANATIONS

ABBREVIATIONS

D — Deuteronomic; Deuteronomist source

E — Elohist source
Ecclus. — Ecclesiasticus
ed. — edited by, edition, editor
e.g. — *exempli gratia* (for example)
ERV — English Revised Version
esp. — especially

H — Holiness Code

J — Yahwist source
JPSV — Jewish Publication Society Version

L — Lukan source
LXX — Septuagint, the earliest Greek translation of the Old Testament and Apocrypha (250 B.C. and after)

M — Matthean source
Macc. — Maccabees
MS — manuscript

N — north, northern
NEB — New English Bible

P — Priestly source
p. — page
Pet. — Peter
Phil. — Philippian, Philippians
Philem. — Philemon
Prov. — Proverbs
Pss. Sol. — Psalms of Solomon
pt. — part (of a literary work)

Q — "Sayings" source

rev. — revised
RSV — Revised Standard Version

S — south, southern

trans. — translated by, translation, translator

viz. — *videlicet* (namely)
Vulg. — Vulgate, the accepted Latin version, mostly translated A.D. 383-405 by Jerome

W — west, western
Wisd. Sol. — Wisdom of Solomon

QUOTATIONS AND REFERENCES

In the direct commentary words and phrases quoted from the RSV of the passage under discussion are printed in boldface type, without quotation marks, to facilitate linking the comments to the exact points of the biblical text. If a quotation from the passage under discussion is not in boldface type, it is to be recognized as an alternate translation, either that of another version if so designated (see abbreviations of versions above) or the commentator's own rendering. On the other hand, quotations from other parts of the Bible in direct commentary, as well as all biblical quotations in the introductions, are to be understood as from the RSV unless otherwise identified.

A passage of the biblical text is identified by book, chapter number, and verse number or numbers, the chapter and verse numbers being separated by a colon (cf. Genesis 1:1). Clauses within a verse may be designated by the letters *a, b, c,* etc. following the verse number (e.g. Genesis 1:2*b*). In poetical text each line as printed in the RSV—not counting runovers necessitated by narrow columns—is accorded a letter. If the book is not named, the book under discussion is to be understood; similarly the chapter number appearing in the boldface reference at the beginning of the paragraph, or in a preceding centered head, is to be understood if no chapter is specified.

A suggestion to note another part of the biblical text is usually introduced by the abbreviation "cf." and specifies the exact verses. To be distinguished from this is a suggestion to consult a comment in this volume, which is introduced by "see above on," "see below on," or "see comment on," and which identifies the boldface reference at the head of the paragraph where the comment is to be found or, in the absence of a boldface reference, the reference in a preceding centered head. The suggestion "see Introduction" refers to the introduction of the book under discussion unless another book is named.

The Near East in the time of the Assyrian Empire

- - - Approximate extent of Assyrian domination in the latter part of the 8th century.

Later, under Esarhaddon (681–669), Assyria conquered Egypt.

0   100   200   300 Miles
0   100   200   300 Kilometers

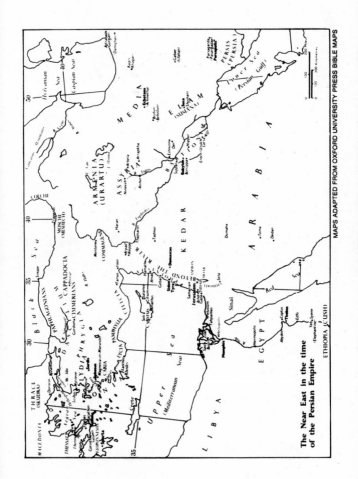

The Near East in the time
of the Persian Empire

ETHIOPIA (CUSH)

MAPS ADAPTED FROM OXFORD UNIVERSITY PRESS BIBLE MAPS